INSIDE SOFTIMAGE 3D

ANTHONY ROSSANO

IMAGERY CREATED BY DAVID CHOI

COVER ART BY BRYAN BALLINGER

New Riders

201 WEST 103RD STREET, INDIANAPOLIS INDIANA 46290

INSIDE SOFTIMAGE 3D

WARNING AND DISCLAIMER

EXECUTIVE EDITOR
Alicia Buckley

DEVELOPMENT EDITOR
Linda Laflamme

PROJECT EDITOR
Kevin Laseau

COPY EDITOR
Michael Brumitt

INDEXERS
Bruce Clingaman
Kelly Talbot

TECHNICAL EDITOR
David Choi

SOFTWARE DEVELOPMENT SPECIALIST
Adam Swetnam

PRODUCTION
Carol Bowers
Mona Brown
Ayanna Lacey
Gene Redding

COVER DESIGNER
Nathan Clement

BOOK DESIGNER
Louisa Klucznik

Contents at a Glance

TRADEMARKS

TABLE OF CONTENTS

PART III: ANIMATION & RENDERING

ABOUT THE AUTHOR

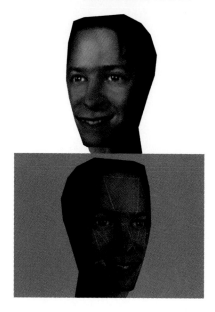

Anthony Rossano joined the computer revolution in 1981 when he was introduced to personal computers at the tender age of 13. At 19, while still an undergraduate at the University of Washington, he signed up for a tour of duty in the Microsoft Corporation's Macintosh Technical Support department.

In 1988, Anthony deserted his post at Microsoft to start a computer consulting firm with four of his buddies. That firm evolved into Mesmer, Inc., where Anthony is now the chief executive officer.

After receiving his Bachelor of Arts degree in psychology from the University of Washington, Anthony combined his love of how the human mind works with his passion for high technology. As a producer at Mesmer, he headed up a team that produced interactive media content and products for Microsoft, Delta, Sierra Online, Softimage, Edmark, and many other clients.

Technically proficient in a wide range of authoring, animation, and 3D modeling programs for the Macintosh and Silicon Graphics Workstation, Anthony's expertise lies in Softimage 3D|Extreme, Alias|Wavefront Explore, PowerAnimator, and Composer. He is a level 2 certified Softimage instructor and has been teaching and using the tool in production since 1994.

In 1995, Mesmer, Inc., became a Softimage authorized training center serving the professional film, television, and games markets and now has locations in both Seattle and San Francisco. Anthony can be reached at anthor@mesmer.com and visited in cyberspace at www.mesmer.com.

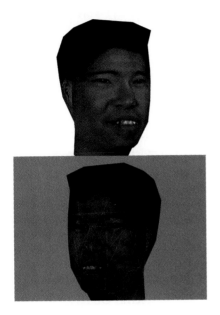

David Choi has always been and will be an artist in any form: actor, singer, painter, designer, animator. Born in Seoul, Korea, he was raised in Seattle where he currently resides with his wife and son.

Having been a child of television and movies, David found a perfect fit in 3D animation. After trying acting, where his moment of fame was sitting behind Tom Skerrit in the movie "Singles," and working in 2D graphics, he discovered 3D animation.

David has gone through the Softimage Training program at Mesmer Animation Lab. He is now working at Microsoft where he has been for the last two years as a 3D artist on such titles as *Microsoft CART Precision Racing* and *Microsoft Combat Flight Simulation WWII European Series.*

David is currently under way on *Microsoft Flight Simulation 2000* and an independent animated short.

He can be reached at dchoi@nwlink.com.

This book is dedicated to my beautiful and talented bride to be, Annesa Hartman.

—Anthony Rossano

ACKNOWLEDGMENTS

This book is the culmination of six months of frantic writing and research, made possible by the kind and generous support of a great many people.

My fiancee, Annesa Hartman, not only listened sympathetically to me as I whimpered in the face of each daunting chapter, she provided timely Softimage technical support and donated several images to the book. David Choi worked ceaselessly to prepare the thousand or so figures used throughout the book, scrutinizing the text for errors of fact, laboring long into the night and on weekends to keep up with his awesome pace. Without David's Herculean effort the book might never have been completed.

Bryan Ballinger produced the fabulous art for the cover of the book and allowed me to reprint many of his works as chapter-opening graphics.

I wish to express my profound thanks to Alicia Buckley, executive editor at New Riders Publishing, who for some reason provided me the opportunity to write this book and then kept my nose to the grindstone until I finished it. Laura Frey, development editor at New Riders, deserves my thanks for keeping track of so many missing pieces. I gratefully thank Linda Laflamme, development editor at New Riders Publishing, who was, through the medium of MS Word revision notes, my constant companion in the editing process, and put up with a lot of my snottiness besides.

I am also indebted to Colette Crawford, Annesa Hartman, Karen Zinker, Matt Ontiveros, and the rest of the staff at Mesmer Animation Labs for picking up my slack at work while I stayed home to write. Without you I couldn't have taken up this wonderful challenge.

I wish to gratefully thank those in the CGI industry who contributed their thoughts, words, and images to this book. I thank Josh and Tim Greenberg at Lume, Michael Carp of Lunarfish, Betsy De Fries and Jerry Van De Beek of Little Fluffy Clouds, Joshua Staub of Cyan, Nick Philip of H2O, Thomas Schelesny of Tippett Studios, Jessica Forys and Eric Ingerson of LucasArts. You folks are the best! Your work is my inspiration.

I want to acknowledge the vision, the dedication and the hard work put in over the last 11 years by the engineers at Silicon Graphics. Your technology leadership, your innovation, and your products made my career possible. I want to thank the engineers at Softimage for crafting a brilliant software package, and I want to thank the Softimage training team, Mauricio Bussab and Pierre Tousignant, for letting me into the club and nurturing my skills.

Finally, my most heartfelt appreciation goes out to my tireless writing partner, Agnes, my Apple PowerBook 160.

—Anthony Rossano

Macmillan Computer Publishing would like to acknowledge all of the long hours, sleepless nights, worked weekends, gray hairs, headaches and backaches, and endless dedication that went into creating this masterpiece.

Special thanks go to: Anthony Rossano for taking on the daunting challenge of writing this book and being entirely devoted to the project. Inside Softimage 3D is a true masterpiece—your work is fantastic and you should be very proud. Your commitment to bringing the best to the industry at the sacrifice of a personal life is truly amazing. Will life go on without us breathing down your neck? Here's your new to-do list: have a beer, get married, go on your honeymoon, relax, and have a life again!

David Choi for being the master of the artwork and technical accuracy. Your contributions to the book are invaluable! We deeply appreciate your commitment to the project and thank you for putting your all into it.

The MCP graphics team, Alicia Buckley, Linda Laflamme, Laura Frey, Julie MacLean, Michelle Newcomb, Brice Gosnell, Kevin Laseau, Michael Brumitt, Kelly Talbot, Carol Bowers, Mona Brown, Ayanna Lacey, and Gene Redding for sorting out all the pieces, bending the rules, and being 100% committed to quality.

TELL US WHAT YOU THINK!

As the reader of this book, you are our most important critic and commentator. We value your opinion and want to know what we're doing right, what we could do better, what areas you'd like to see us publish in, and any other words of wisdom you're willing to pass our way.

As the Executive Editor for the 3D graphics and animation team at Macmillan Computer Publishing, I welcome your comments. You can fax, email, or write me directly to let me know what you did or didn't like about this book—as well as what we can do to make our books stronger.

Please note that I cannot help you with technical problems related to the topic of this book, and that due to the high volume of mail I receive, I might not be able to reply to every message.

When you write, please be sure to include this book's title and author as well as your name and phone or fax number. I will carefully review your comments and share them with the author and editors who worked on the book.

Fax: [317-817-7070]

Email: graphics@mcp.com

Mail: Executive Editor

3D Graphics and Animation
Macmillan Computer Publishing
201 West 103rd Street
Indianapolis, IN 46290 USA

© 1997 Cyan, Inc.

INTRODUCTION

Over the last 11 years the field of computer animation has grown from the flights of fancy of computer science researchers into a dynamic and vibrant entertainment industry.

3D computer graphics have found their way into TV commercials and video games and have breathed new life into the film industry by enabling new productions of tried and true insect, dinosaur, and disaster epics.

3D animation has in fact become a component of the worldwide rush to the digitization of all media. Entire new categories of workers are emerging called Digital Content Specialists, and new businesses rise to greatness almost overnight providing the digital content demanded by consumers of media and technology.

There is no evidence to suggest that the trend toward the digitization of the world will slow anytime soon, or indeed ever.

In this short history of digital media and computer animation, the name Softimage is a standout.

Softimage, Inc., founded in Montreal, Canada, in 1986 by Daniel Langlois, has been pioneering 3D animation technology since the company's inception, inventing Inverse Kinematics, motion capture technology, and much more.

Today, Softimage, Inc., is the leading developer of high-end software for visual content production. Softimage's mission is to bring the widest possible array of tools for 2D, 3D, video, and film production to the broadest possible professional audience. Work created and edited with Softimage tools dominates the entertainment market, with particular strongholds in film and interactive games. Softimage products currently run on hardware from a wide range of manufacturers and on two operating systems, Microsoft Windows NT and Silicon Graphics IRIX.

Along the way, Softimage creative tools became popular in the best and brightest media, film effects, and games companies. Current customers include Blue Sky Productions, BUF Compagnie, CBS Television, Digital Domain, Electronic Arts, Inc., Psygnosis, Fox Animation Studios, Industrial Light & Magic, Lucas Arts, NBC, Nintendo, Mainframe Entertainment, Pacific Data Images, R/Greenberg Associates, Sega Enterprises, Tippett Studios, Viacom New Media, and Cyan, Inc.

Softimage, Inc., has gathered an impressive array of awards over the last decade, including awards from *Computer Graphics World, Digital Video Magazine, PC Graphics and Video, 3D Design, PC Magazine, Multimedia World, Post Magazine*, the Imagina Conference, the Canadian Genie Awards, Prix Ars Electronica, the Academy Awards, and the Emmy Awards.

In June of 1994, Softimage, Inc., was acquired by Microsoft Corp. of Redmond, Washington. Softimage had been locked in a desperate and expensive battle for the high-end market with Wavefront Technologies of Santa Barbara, California, and Alias Research of Toronto. These three companies were each selling a small quantity of expensive, high-end software tools with similar feature sets, each running primarily on UNIX-based systems from 3D workstation manufacturer Silicon Graphics of

Mountain View, California. The research and development resources required to stay ahead of the competition were an increasing burden, while the market for the tools remained small. Microsoft brought Softimage, Inc., an entirely new market, the Windows NT platform. In return, Softimage introduced Microsoft to the technology used in digital content creation, and to the huge markets thriving in the world entertainment industry. Approximately 16 months later, the first Windows NT version of Softimage 3D, version 3.0 NT, was released for NT machines with Intel, Alpha, and MIPS microprocessors.

Immediately following the acquisition of Softimage as a wholly owned subsidiary of Microsoft Corp, Silicon Graphics, Inc., (SGI) acquired both Wavefront Technologies and Alias Research, merging both their operations and product lines.

How to Use This Book

This book has been designed to be appropriate both for complete newcomers to the world of computer animation and for those who have already created animations with Softimage 3D|Extreme or other 3D products. Those who complete the book will become productive animators, capable of planning a scene, building models, arranging elements, applying materials and textures, lighting, animating, and rendering the finished work out to disk.

Readers starting from scratch should read this book from the beginning and work towards the end, taking time to perform the many tutorials included within these pages, and to experiment on their own.

The book will also be useful to users who have been with Softimage 3D for several years, and who are interested in exploring more of Softimage's features than they currently use on a day to day basis. For these more advanced Softimage users, I recommend that this book be used as a reference volume, where cogent explanations of technology and the direct application of techniques are organized by topic for easy research and discovery.

Required Skills

A reader of this book will not need previous animation experience to get the most out of it. Experience in other 2D graphics software, such as Macromedia FreeHand, Adobe PhotoShop, After Effects, or Premiere is always a good idea, however. The reader should have access to a computer and Softimage 3D for purposes of practice and exploration.

Readers who want to further their education in Softimage 3D and make themselves maximally marketable in today's digital workplace should explore the use of the command line utilities that come with Softimage 3D and should gain a working understanding of the UNIX networking functions that surround us daily and facilitate the work of animation.

SCOPE

This book is intended to be a thorough overview of the features and functionality of Microsoft Softimage 3D|Extreme. Topics covered in great detail will include modeling tools and techniques, animation with paths and transformations, shape animation, spline, patch, and lattice deformation, material and texture attributes, rendering technology, and mental ray. Because of the tremendous size, depth, and complexity of the Softimage 3D|Extreme program and associated tools, a student of animation in Softimage 3D will of course have more to study.

A discussion of some advanced features, such as Extreme Effects, Motion Capture, Compositing with Softimage, Command line scripts, and the Particle program, will remain outside the scope of this book.

LEARNING METHODOLOGY

Over the many years I have spent teaching computer application software and animation to my students at the Mesmer Animation Labs, I have developed my own theories to describe the necessary components of successful learning. I have distilled those theories into a learning methodology and applied it to this book.

To remain engaged, the user must immediately begin to use the tool and get the positive feedback of having personally accomplished tasks. The goal of all computer animation is the render, so this book leads the user to a basic render as soon as possible. Within a few short chapters, the reader will complete a simple camera animation through Stonehenge.

For each section of the book, the following pattern will be applied.

An opening lecture format explanation will describe what the tool is, what it means, how it got there and why it's important.

A tutorial section will explain how to use the tool in a basic step-by-step manner to actually accomplish the task that it was designed for. I have striven at all costs to find and use real world tutorials whenever possible, so the tools are connected to actual application and not just demonstrated on a cube or sphere.

The topics are taught in a sensible order. That means that the user begins by learning the basic fundamentals that underlie all other tools, then the workflow and organization of the product, and finally explores the features of the product in order of ascending complexity and difficulty.

In this way beginners aren't overwhelmed with things they don't yet understand, and the book becomes more and more valuable to them as they progress through it. More advanced users can use the latter portion of the book as a reference to the productive use of complex tools.

The book also contains side panels of interviews with professional users explaining how they use the product, what they think is the most important feature, and how the Softimage 3D software changes their lives and their art. These professional perspectives on the 3D industry are extraordinarily valuable and informative.

Finally, I have reprinted with permission some of the finest work ever done with Softimage 3D, by the most talented artists and animators on the planet. Their work serves as an inspiration and a guide, providing visual confirmation of all that is possible in this amazing software.

WHAT TO DO NEXT

This is the first and, at press time, the only book ever entirely dedicated to the fundamental understanding of Softimage 3D|Extreme, the cornerstone product in the Softimage suite of creative tools. My hope is that this book will bring many people closer to an understanding of 3D animation in general, and Softimage 3D in particular. My hope is that the mix of theories, techniques, and tutorials found within these pages serves to enlighten, inform, and educate each and every reader.

But for serious 3D animators and digital content creators, this book will only be the first step in a lifetime of learning. For many, the next step will be to seek personal instruction in advanced topics. Softimage maintains a network of Authorized Training Centers, including Mesmer Animation Labs, throughout the world to provide intensive training classes at a professional level. Search for more information about publicly available training classes and private corporate training sessions at www.mesmer.com and at www.softimage.com.

Finally, there is simply no substitute for experience. Seekers of the 3D truths should immediately gain access to the Softimage 3D|Extreme software and the hardware to run it on, so that they might continue their learning process through the act of creation.

Anthony Rossano, 1998

TOURING SOFTIMAGE

Shot from within the room with the elevator partially penetrating the water. ©1997 Cyan, Inc.

CHAPTER 1

EXPLORING THE SOFTIMAGE INTERFACE

Welcome to Softimage 3D\Extreme! At this point in a book about an animation product, it is customary for the author to talk up the software, using such adjectives as powerful, awesome, new, and flexible. This is usually an attempt to justify the reader's investment in the book and in the software. Other software products have built cult followings by repeating such a mantra of adjectives over and over. Softimage 3D\Extreme simply doesn't require that sort of breast-beating. Softimage 3D\Extreme is the de facto standard for animation in the entertainment industry and has been for many years.

Instead of wallowing in the traditional praise of the software, take a look at the topics covered in this chapter:

- Starting Softimage 3D|Extreme
- The Softimage 3D interface
- Using the menu cells
- Understanding Cartesian space
- The five modules of Softimage 3D
- Customizing the interface
- Custom hot keys
- Learning the terminology

STARTING SOFTIMAGE

Because Softimage 3D|Extreme is available for two separate platforms with different operating systems, some differences in how it is used are unavoidable. On the whole, however, Softimage 3D|Extreme is remarkably similar on machines running the Microsoft Windows NT and Silicon Graphics IRIX operating systems. One of the few differences is how the program can be started.

IRIX STARTUP

On IRIX, you have two options. If your Softimage 3D|Extreme account has been properly set up, you see a menu named Softimage in the Toolchest and within it the names of the Softimage tools you have installed (see Figure 1.1). Clicking one with your mouse launches that product.

The second, better method is to create a UNIX shell window. Use the Toolchest and select the menu item Desktop→Open Unix Shell. In the shell window, type the word **soft** and press return. This command executes the Softimage 3D|Extreme program and launches the graphical user interface onto your monitor. Using a shell window to run Softimage 3D|Extreme has two main advantages:

- You can see any error output that Softimage might write to the shell window, helping you to debug problems.
- You can always minimize Softimage 3D|Extreme and terminate the application in the shell window if things go wrong and the program hangs up during an operation.

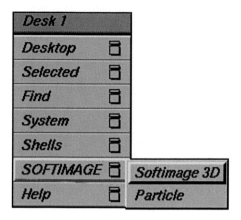

FIGURE 1.1   *The Softimage menu in the Toolchest lists the installed Softimage tools.*

WINDOWS NT STARTUP

On Windows NT, find the program group created when Softimage 3D|Extreme was installed and double-click the 3D icon. You can otherwise run the DOS shell also found in that program group. Then type the command soft into the shell and press the Enter key.

STARTUP SIMILARITIES

On both platforms you can run Softimage 3D|Extreme on the command line with special options. In your shell, enter the command soft -h to see these. You can also run multiple copies of Softimage 3D|Extreme on a single machine, but this is rarely useful and wastes precious machine resources.

Once the graphical Softimage 3D|Extreme interface has come up, you can discover which release version you have by clicking the left mouse button on the Softimage|3D logo in the top-left corner of the screen (see Figure 1.2). The dialog box that comes up reveals the machine type, OS, and which version of Softimage 3D|Extreme you have installed. For this book, I've chosen to use version 3.7.02.001 running under IRIX 6.3 on a Silicon Graphics O2 with 128MB of RAM.

SYSTEM REQUIREMENTS

No matter which operating system you use, make sure your system meets the machine requirements for running Softimage 3D|Extreme. Your machine must be able to drive a monitor at a resolution of no less than 1280 × 1024 pixels. If your machine can't run a monitor at that resolution, you will be missing parts of the

Softimage 3D|Extreme interface, and you won't even know it. Your graphics hardware should also support 24-bit color at 1280 × 1024 resolution. Anything less and you are missing the point of Softimage, which is photorealism.

FIGURE 1.2   *The System Information dialog displays the vital statistics of Softimage and your system.*

You also need a three-button mouse, which is standard on SGI machines but not so common on NT machines. Almost all Softimage 3D|Extreme commands require the middle mouse button, so if you don't have one you won't get very far. And don't try to slide by with a middle mouse wheel or some other mini-button. Bad equipment just slows you down.

SOFTIMAGE INTERFACE ORGANIZATION

The Softimage 3D|Extreme interface is organized in a simple, yet elegant and efficient manner (see Figure 1.3). The goal of the Softimage 3D|Extreme workspace is to enable you to work with the greatest efficiency possible, organizing your tasks into a series of steps that flow easily from one to the next in an orderly process. This concept is called *workflow,* and it is one of the greatest advantages that Softimage 3D|Extreme has over the large and growing field of competitors.

When working in Softimage 3D|Extreme, you very rarely find your view of the scene obscured by layers of floating tool palettes and option boxes. Almost all Softimage 3D|Extreme commands cascade in unobtrusive hierarchical menu boxes and then go away. Most commands are organized so they can be applied to multiple objects in the scene at once or in series. The major functions of the software are divided into *modules,* organized by their role in the workflow process (see Figure 1.4).

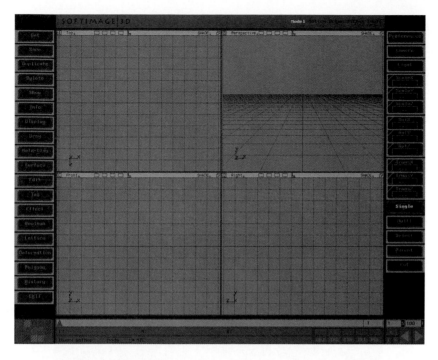

FIGURE 1.3   *Softimage's main interface.*

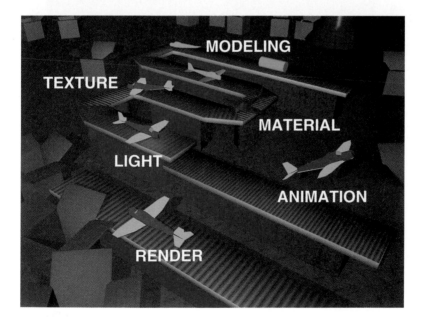

FIGURE 1.4   *An airplane's progress through a typical workflow process.*

THE MODULES

Along the top of the screen is a colored bar, with the Softimage|3D logo at the left side and a series of Module buttons on the right side (see Figure 1.5). Each module introduces new menu buttons to the stacks on the right and left sides.

FIGURE 1.5   *Softimage's five main modules.*

THE VIEW WINDOWS

In the middle, the screen area is divided into four squares, showing four different views into the 3D space that Softimage creates for you. These are the Top, Front, Right, and Perspective views (see Figure 1.6). We'll come back to them a little later in this chapter.

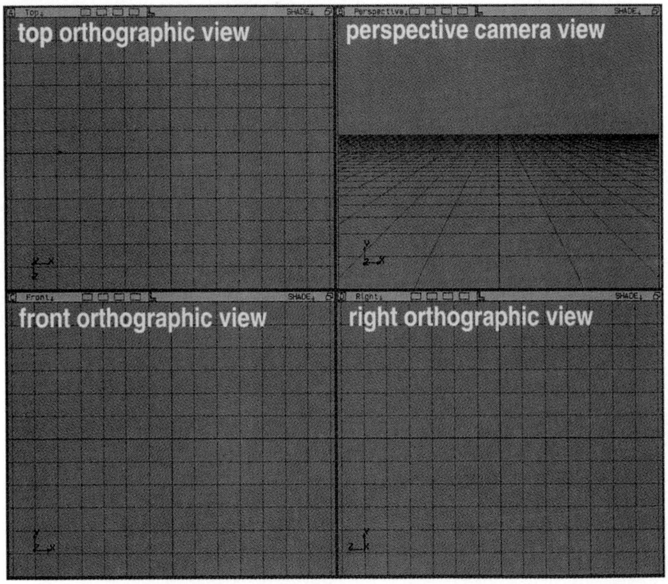

![The four View windows showing top orthographic view, perspective camera view, front orthographic view, and right orthographic view]

FIGURE 1.6   *The four View windows.*

THE COLOR BOX, TIME SLIDER, AND STATUS BAR

At the bottom of the screen is a small Color Box available at all times to assist in color coding your models. It is activated by clicking the gray bar on the left side and selecting a color from the 12 available. With a color active, you can pick objects in your scene to change the color of the wireframe that appears onscreen.

At the bottom of the screen are the Time Slider and the Status Bar (see Figure 1.7). The *Time Slider* allows you to move through the frames in your animation by dragging the gray triangle left and right, or by entering in a frame number in its direct entry box. The *Status Bar* gives you feedback about which command is currently active and what each one of the three mouse buttons does within that command.

FIGURE 1.7   *The Color Box (at left), Time Slider (middle), and Status Bar (right).*

THE MENUS

All commands are located in rows of vertically stacked buttons, called *menu cells*, that run down the left and right edges of the screen. On the left edge are the menu cells that typically correspond to commands and functions. The top seven menu cells—*Get, Save, Duplicate, Delete, Show, Info,* and *Display*—are consistent throughout all the modules, except for the *Tools* module (see Figure 1.8).

Even though these menu cells stay in place throughout the workflow, some of the menu commands come and go in different modules as it makes sense for them to be there. The remaining cells along the left side are different within each module, except for the bottom one, EXIT, which is how you leave the Softimage 3D|Extreme program. You use the menu cells on the left side to load and save scenes, draw splines, make surfaces, apply colors and textures, paint objects, and to perform almost all other functions.

The menu cells on the right side of the screen are generally persistent throughout all the modules, except the Tools module. These menu cells contain functions that are not specific to one part of the workflow but are generally useful throughout the Softimage 3D|Extreme interface. These menu cells include commands for manipulating *preferences,* the *camera, lights,* and for performing *transformations* on objects. The three transformations are: *scale, rotation,* and *translation.* Scale means to change the relative size of an object, rotation means to change its relative orientation, and translation means to move it through 3D space.

The right stack of menu cells also contains the selection tools and the tools for creating hierarchies.

FIGURE 1.8
The left-edge menu cells.

USING THE MENU CELLS

Let's try out a menu cell to explore how it is used. Place your mouse over the Draw menu cell and click with the *left* mouse button. A list of all the Draw options cascades down to the right of the Draw menu cell. This list is a *hierarchical popup menu*. Notice that your mouse cursor disappears while in the hierarchical popup menu. You can do nothing else until you choose a menu command or exit the popup menu. As you move your mouse up and down, a different menu item is highlighted (reversed out of the menu). You can also move up and down through the menu with the Up and Down arrow keys.

At the bottom of the list is always the EXIT POPUP menu item, which puts the cell away. Try it out by going back to the Draw menu cell and clicking with the left mouse button to show the menu popup. Now click with the *right* mouse button. The right mouse button also exits the menu popup without making a selection. The Escape key on your keyboard also does the same thing.

Back in the Draw menu popup, look at the menu items. One, the Curve menu item, has a small black triangle next to it (see Figure 1.9). Others have a small plus sign (+) after their names. The plus signs indicate that these are custom effects, which are basically plug-ins for Softimage 3D|Extreme that other people have written. The triangle indicates that other menu commands are stacked beneath it in another hierarchical popup menu. Choose the *Draw→Curve* menu cell to see the new menu items. To recur one level in the hierarchy (go back to the previous menu), use the EXIT POPUP menu cell at the bottom of the menu popup. To exit the menus altogether, use the right mouse button.

Go through the Draw→Curve menu and choose Draw→Curve→ Cardinal. This command creates a Cardinal curve from the points that you place on the screen with your mouse. Now cast your gaze down to the bottom of the screen and observe the contents of the Status Bar.

The Status Bar is a critical tool within Softimage 3D|Extreme and will help you immensely if you look at it once in a while. It displays the current functionality of each mouse button and often a hint about what you need to do next to complete the command.

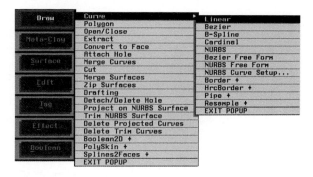

FIGURE 1.9   *A sample menu popup expanded.*

In this case, the Status Bar tells you that your left mouse button will add a point to the end of the line segment, your middle mouse button will add a point between existing points in the line, and your right mouse button will add points before the first point in the line segment. Try these different mouse functions out by clicking and dragging in the front window to draw a sunflower with the Draw→Curve→ Cardinal curve. Watch the Status Bar to see what it's telling you while you work.

The only mouse button we haven't used on the menu cells yet is the middle mouse button. It has a very powerful use, which is that it recalls the last command you chose and executes it again. In our case, the middle button allows us to create a new Cardinal spline. Try it out by clicking with the middle mouse button on the Draw menu cell. You'll note that nothing appears to happen: no menus cascade, but the command has been re-executed, and you can now draw a separate Cardinal line segment. Try drawing your sunflower with each of its petals as a separate Cardinal curve (see Figure 1.10).

CARTESIAN SPACE AND THE VIEW WINDOWS

Softimage 3D|Extreme sets up a virtual 3D world for you that is almost infinitely big but completely empty. This 3D space is organized according to the *Cartesian coordinate system.* This means that any point in the Softimage virtual world can be located precisely with three values: the point's location along the X axis, the point's location along the Y axis, and the point's location along the Z axis.

Each of these three axes—X, Y, and Z—is an invisible straight line (a vector) stretching infinitely far in both directions. Each axis (X, Y, and Z) runs at a right angle (90 degrees) to each of the other axes. In other words, each axis is perpendicular to the other two axes (see Figure 1.11).

FIGURE 1.10   *A sunflower composed of Cardinal curves.*

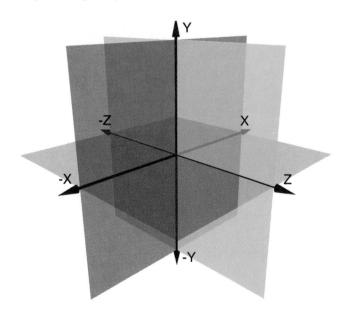

FIGURE 1.11   *The X, Y, and Z axes.*

If you are sitting in front of your computer looking in Softimage 3D|Extreme's Front View window, the X axis is usually visualized as running from left to right, directly in front of you, like a horizon line. The Y axis is the "up" axis and is usually visualized as running from the bottom to the top of your screen. The Z axis is invisible to you because you are looking at the exact end of the line, running in and through your screen.

Each of these axes runs through a point in the exact center of the virtual 3D world called the global origin. All of the axes meet as they pass through it. As they proceed on through the global origin, they extend in both the positive and negative directions.

Every point along an axis has a value, expressed in *Softimage units*. Softimage units are arbitrary, imaginary units and don't correspond to any real-world unit of measure. They could be inches, centimeters, miles, or light years. You may consider them to be whatever unit is most convenient for a specific job. For instance, if you were animating microbes, the Softimage unit might be a micron. If you are modeling a building, the units might be decimal feet.

Because every position on the individual axes can be measured, you can define a point in space by choosing one point on each axis (see Figure 1.12). Any point in space can then be located in a Cartesian coordinate system by specifying the values of the three axes, as in X=-7, Y=41, Z=30 or, in short hand, (-7,41,30).

Softimage 3D|Extreme has the job of converting the 3D virtual space I just described into a 2D virtual space that it can draw on a flat computer monitor for you to see and work with. The program does this by projecting each point in the virtual 3D space onto a 2D plane (called the *projection plane*) and drawing it to a View window (see Figure 1.13).

Each of Softimage 3D|Extreme's View windows can display the projection plane from a different perspective, called the view plane. By default, the windows use the Top, Front, Right, and Perspective view planes. Each view plane comes with a small icon showing you the orientation of the three axes in that view, so you can orient yourself in 3D space. Because each plane is really only a two-dimensional construct, it can show you only two out of the total three axes in the 3D space. The Top view shows the X and Z axes, which make up the XZ plane, the Front view shows the XY plane, and the Right view shows the ZY plane. Each of these views is orthographic, which means that all parallel lines are projected to the screen as actually parallel. In this way, you see a view that acts as a flat view port into the 3D world.

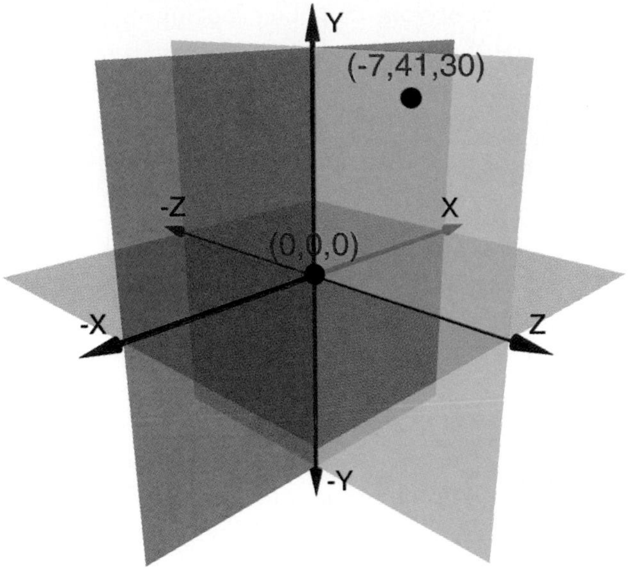

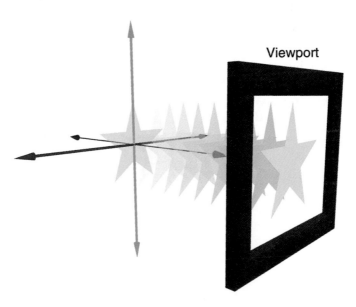

FIGURE 1.12 *The global origin at the axes' intersection and a point defined by the values on each axis.*

FIGURE 1.13 *Softimage uses a projection plane to convert 3D space into a 2D display.*

The last window is the Perspective View window. In Softimage 3D|Extreme, the Perspective View window is the camera window. This is the view that your camera sees when you render your animation. In this window, you can define a custom View plane, which doesn't have to stay parallel to two of the major axes although it's still a 2D View plane. In other words, you can move the camera freely throughout the 3D virtual space and look at the scene from any angle, not just the top, front, and right sides. This View window is not orthographic, but *perspective*, which means that Softimage performs *perspective-correction projection* when it draws the 2D view plane. In this way, Softimage can show you a 2D simulation of 3D space that provides you with a simulation of depth: parallel lines converge into the distance and objects seem to grow smaller as they move farther away. The severity of these effects changes depending on the width of the camera view angle used, so that you can easily simulate a fish-eye lens or a telephoto lens.

EXPLORE THE VIEW WINDOWS

To try out the controls for the different views, go to the Get menu cell at the top left of the screen and choose Get→Text. Enter your name in the Text box and choose the Century Gothic typeface. Leave the Model Generation radio button set to Faces (see Figure 1.14). Click the Ok button with your mouse or press the Enter key until the Text dialog box closes. This creates a hierarchy of the letters in your name and draws it to the screen. Because the letters are

> **NOTE**
>
> An Orthographic View window, located in the View Style menu box, allows a 3D view of your scene. It will be discussed later in this chapter.

bigger than the viewports, we can't see much but part of the first letter. That's okay—we'll use this opportunity to learn how to control the View windows.

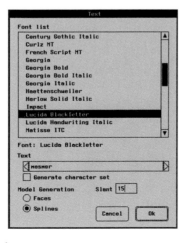

FIGURE 1.14   *The Text dialog box.*

MOVING AROUND WITH THE SUPRA KEYS

To move around in the Top, Front, and Right View windows, position your mouse anywhere inside of one View window, hold down the Z key on your keyboard and the left mouse button, and drag your mouse around. The Z key is called the Zoom supra key. *Supra keys* are keyboard shortcuts essential to working with Softimage 3D|Extreme.

Now try using the Z supra key with the middle mouse button. This zooms into the View window. Try the Right mouse button to zoom out of the View window. Now hold down the Z supra key and look at the Status Bar at the bottom of the screen. The Status Bar shows you the result of the supra key for each of the three mouse buttons.

If you use the Z supra key to zoom in and out of the Perspective window, you aren't just scaling the view, you're increasing or decreasing the width of the camera lens, which affects how distorted your Perspective view gets. It is a good idea to use the P supra key instead of the Z supra key in the Perspective window wherever possible. The P supra key is the Dolly supra key, which actually moves the camera back and forth to see more or less instead of changing the view angle of the camera. Try it out in the Perspective window.

The P supra key has another feature that is common to many functions in Softimage 3D|Extreme. When you hold down P, each of the mouse buttons does the same thing but in varying amounts. For instance, the left mouse button dollies slowly, the middle button dollies at a medium rate, and the right mouse button dollies rapidly. This way you can get the exact amount of control you need for big moves or for small precise ones.

Another crucial supra key that works in the Perspective window is the Orbit (O) supra key. The Orbit supra key allows you to change the view plane of the camera by orbiting it around the camera interest (the point in space where the camera is aimed). Try it out in the Perspective window (it doesn't work in the Top, Front, or Right views). The Orbit key allows you to see your work from any angle. As you orbit your name, watch how Softimage 3D|Extreme uses perspective correction to make the part that's farther away seem smaller (see Figure 1.15). This effect is the basis of simulating a 3D space with a 2D image plane.

Some other supra keys are useful to know as well. The F supra key frames the selected element, showing you the entire element in the active View window. This is often faster than zooming around until you can see the whole object. The A supra key frames all of the objects in the scene. You may also zoom into a rectangular selection onscreen by simultaneously holding down the Shift key and the Z supra key and dragging a rectangle onscreen with your left mouse button. Doing the same with your right mouse button zooms out of a rectangular section area of the screen. Take a few moments to try these supra keys.

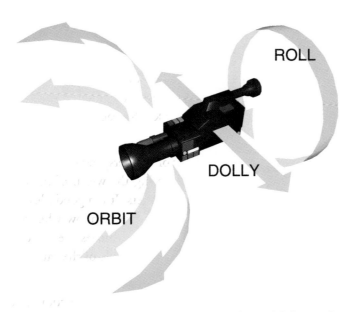

FIGURE 1.15   *The Orbit supra key moves the camera's view plane, while leaving the camera interest where it started.*

MENU EQUIVALENTS

For those of you who have to know where the equivalents of these supra key functions are in the interface, look in the top-right corner in the Camera menu cell. You'll find Camera→Frame Selection, Camera→Frame All, Camera→Rect Zoom, Camera→Zoom, Camera→Orbit, and Camera→Dolly. Two more Camera functions don't have supra keys, Camera→Tracking and Camera→Roll. Tracking moves the camera and interest simultaneously, as if you just picked it up and dragged the whole thing to another location. Roll revolves the camera around an axis that runs through the lens, critical for banking turns and tilted shots like those popular in the old *Batman* TV series. Choose these from the Camera menu cell and look at the Status Bar to see how they are used (see Figure 1.16).

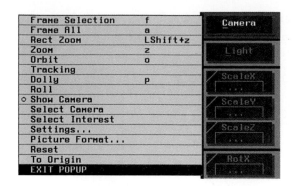

FIGURE 1.16 *The Camera menu cell.*

REARRANGING THE VIEW WINDOWS

You can customize the view that you see while working with Softimage 3D|Extreme. Although you can never have more than four View windows onscreen at any one time, you can have fewer. You can arrange the windows as well by changing their orientation, the plane they show, and their relative sizes.

First, note that the views are all marked with a letter to designate them, A, B, C, and D. You can make any one window the selected window by clicking that letter with your mouse. Although this is rarely necessary, it has some uses that we will discuss in the rendering section.

RESIZING THE VIEWS

On the opposite corner from the letter is a small Resize box (see Figure 1.17). Clicking a View window Resize box with the left mouse button expands the window to fill the entire screen, removing the other windows from view. Clicking the Resize box again with any mouse button causes the window to regain its former size. Clicking the Resize box with the middle mouse button causes that window to grow vertically, replacing the window above or below it, but leaving the other windows to the side. Clicking again with the middle mouse button causes it to regain its former size. Clicking the Resize box with the right mouse button causes the window to grow horizontally, displacing the window to the side but leaving the windows above or below. Try these options to find a view layout that you like.

If all four View windows are visible, you can hold down the W supra key, causing a small gray box to appear at the center of the screen where all the views come together. You can click and drag this window marker to resize the windows to an arbitrary size. You can then also reduce the number of windows with the Resize box.

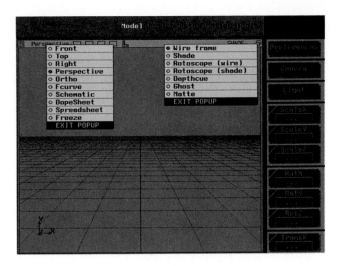

FIGURE 1.17   *Click a View window's Resize box to expand the window to full screen.*

CHOOSING DIFFERENT VIEWS

You may also change the working view plane for the different View windows. Right next to the View window's letter is the name of the view (Top, Right, Front, or Perspective) and a small arrow pointing down. The arrow indicates that there are menu options below the text. Click directly on the text to see the Views popup menu appear. Here you can change the window's view plane to any other view (from Top to Front, for example). The Ortho view option acts like a Perspective view without perspective correction, allowing you to orbit in a 3D view.

The popup menu offers some other options as well. The F-curves view, the Schematic view, the DopeSheet, and the Spreadsheet are discussed later in this book. The last item in the menu is Freeze, which allows you to lock a window so that Softimage 3D|Extreme does not bother to update the display, saving redraw time in complex scenes.

SAVING VIEWS YOU LIKE

At the top of each View window is a group of four empty boxes. These are the Saved View boxes and you can choose to save a specific combination of zoom, pan, orbit, and dolly moves here for later retrieval. A good time to use these is when you are working on several areas of a scene and you want to be able to jump back and forth between different saved camera positions to check your work.

To use these features, simply get a view you want to save using the O, Z, or P supra keys and then click an empty Saved View box with your middle mouse button. The box fills in black to indicate that it now contains a saved view. Try setting a different view in the same View window and saving it as well. To recall a saved view, click the filled square with your left mouse button. Softimage restores the View window to the state it was in when you saved the view.

VIEW LAYOUT OPTIONS

Immediately to the right of the Saved View boxes is a small icon that looks like a ruler bent into the shape of an L. This is the Layout dialog box and it allows you to set a number of different options that relate to the contents of the View window (see Figure 1.18). Here you can:

- set an *editing grid*, so that points and objects that you place snap to even numbered units

- decide to show or hide the visible grid that represents the view plane of that View window

- show rulers down the left and bottom edges to assist you in measuring distances

- turn on a *turntable* that allows you to "spin" a 2D view plane around one axis

- turn on, in the Perspective view, *field guides*, which indicate the title safe, action safe, and viewable areas of the frame when output to television. (More on these in Chapter 6, "The Model Shop—All About Modeling.")

Try these different options out now to get the hang of them.

Three more important features of Softimage 3D|Extreme are located in this dialog: the Clipping Plane, the Magnet, and Fast Playback. The Clipping Plane determines how far from the camera a point in space may be before the view simply decides not to show it. The advantage of setting the near and far clipping planes is that you can eliminate points from the display that might confuse you while editing.

While working on a human face, for instance, you could set the Clipping Plane to cut off the back of the head so you don't accidentally manipulate any of those points while adjusting the nose. The Magnet is a simple way to make sure that points you draw snap exactly to existing points on another object, so that the edge between the two is perfectly seamless. Fast Playback assists in viewing your animations in real time by loading all the frames of a sequence into memory before playing them back in the View window.

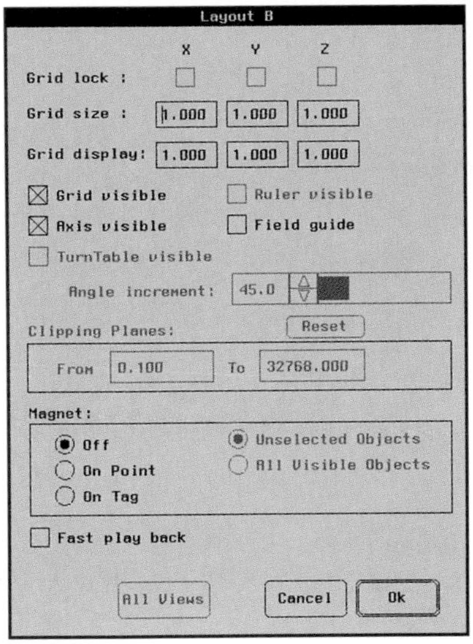

FIGURE 1.18   *The Layout dialog.*

THE DIFFERENT VIEW STYLES

On the right side of each View window, the final menu, which was shown in Figure 1.17, is the control for the view display style. Softimage 3D|Extreme can show you the contents of the View windows in a variety of styles: Wirefame, Shade, Rotoscoped (Wire), Rotoscoped (Shaded), Depthcue, Ghost, and Matte. The first option, Wireframe, is the view that you have used up to this point. If you still have your name up onscreen, great. If not, please recreate it by going to the Get→Text dialog box and entering your name, choosing a font, and clicking the Ok button.

Toggle through the display options and orbit around your name in the Perspective window to get an idea of how they look (see Figure 1.19).

> **NOTE**
>
> The View Display menu is a toggle. If you choose Shade, it shows Wireframe. If you choose Wireframe, it shows Shade. In other words, it doesn't represent what the current display type is, but rather what the type will be if you click it with the middle mouse button. You can change the toggle options by choosing a different style with the left mouse button.

SHADED VIEW

Shaded view uses the OpenGL graphics hardware in your workstation to tessellate the Wireframe representation into a number of triangles and shades them according to the number, color, and position of the lights in the scene (see Figure 1.20). (If you haven't created a light in your scene, Softimage 3D|Extreme creates one for you as a default light that goes away automatically when you create your own.)

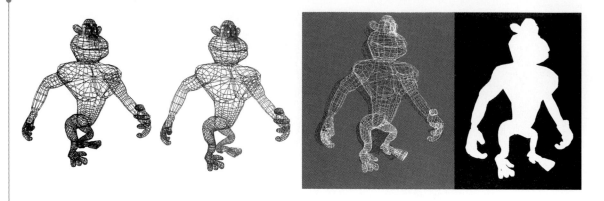

FIGURE 1.19   *Julian the Gorilla models various display options (from left): Wireframe, Shade, Rotoscope (wire), Rotoscope (shade), Ghost, Matte.*

FIGURE 1.20   *Julian in Shaded mode.*

The Shaded view can give you a better visual representation of where things are in your scene and what they will look like in the final render, but it can be quite slow if the complexity of the scene exceeds the capabilities of your OpenGL hardware. You can set a number of useful parameters for the Shaded view. They can be accessed from the Setup menu, which appears to the left of the View Display menu (see Figure 1.21).

FIGURE 1.21 *The Shade View Setup dialog.*

If your OpenGL Hardware supports hardware texture mapping, you can check the Setup menu's top box, labeled Enable Hardware Texture. This activates the options in the group below it. By selecting one from each group of radio buttons, you can decide whether Softimage 3D|Extreme shades and textures only the currently selected model or all models onscreen, whether it obeys texture repeat patterns, and whether it obeys the alpha channel blending options for textures. I recommend leaving these controls at the default settings.

The second group of radio buttons determines how Softimage 3D|Extreme displays the local and global materials for all objects. Leave it at the default setting for best results.

The last group of buttons has a few important uses. The Display Optimization options are the controls you will use most often in this dialog box. By default, if you have the View Display set to Shade and you edit an object or you orbit, pan, and zoom in the View window, the display snaps out of Shaded view and into Wireframe while you work. It snaps back to Shaded view when you stop editing the view.

If you want the view to *stay* in Shaded view all the time, even when editing, you can set the Display Optimization to Shade. This removes textures while editing but leaves the display in Shade mode. If you set the Display Optimization to None, the view stays in the Shaded view *with* textures while you edit. Users with machines that don't have sufficient texture memory will find this unbearable and curse the hardware vendor who sold them the equipment. I recommend Shade Display Optimization remain at Wireframe while working, unless you have a very small scene.

The Surface Precision number entry box is another way to optimize the shaded display. It determines how accurately patch surfaces are tessellated into triangles for display. A setting of zero uses the parameterization of the actual patch object to tessellate for display. A setting of one reduces the tessellation to the lowest possible number of triangles, thus speeding up the shaded display. Higher numbers result in smoother shaded surfaces that take longer to display.

The Show Icons option is a newcomer to Softimage 3D|Extreme and is extremely useful. It really is a hybrid between the Wireframe *and* Shaded views, allowing you the benefits of the Wireframe view, such as the capability to see points and lines with the advantages of the Shaded view, such as back culling of polygons and more solid-looking objects. Turn it on and try it out.

Antialiasing results in a smoother shaded display, but don't turn it on unless your 3D visualization supercomputer supports OpenGL hardware antialiasing (which is very rare) or your display slows to a crawl.

Show Garbage Matte is another new option that shows a video-ready alpha channel matte of your scene. This option is useful for creating virtual sets and again requires some special video hardware to use.

When you have selected the options you desire for the Shaded mode, click the Ok button to accept the changes.

Rotoscope View Mode

The Rotoscope view mode is a tool that allows you to bring in a sequence of frames as a background image and then see the images behind your work in Softimage. This rotoscoping technique is often used in film work where real-life film content ("practicals") is integrated with computer graphic imagery (CGI).

For example, if you as an animator are adding an animated character to a scene in which a group of computer-generated characters sit down for dinner in a real-life restaurant, you could shoot film of the table in the restaurant, with waiters wandering by and real people dining in the background. The film would be developed, scanned into a computer, and provided to you as digital frames. You could then bring these background plates into Softimage so that you can verify the correct placement of the computer-graphic characters you are animating.

The two Rotoscope views offer the capability to view your scene over the background in either Wireframe or Shaded mode (see Figure 1.22). Softimage now allows you to import background frames as a numbered sequence of PIC images, an SGI movie file, a QuickTime movie file, or a Windows AVI movie file. You determine how many frames Softimage 3D|Extreme should read into memory (or "cache" into memory), which in turn determines how much memory is used to store the frames while you work.

Depthcue View Mode

Depthcue is a system that fades the scene into the distance, giving you a simple way to tell which elements are behind which other elements in the scene (see Figure 1.23). Softimage automatically calibrates the amount of fading to fit the extent of your scene. To change the colors that Softimage uses or to change the fading scale, click the Setup menu icon.

Ghost View

The Ghost view offers you a way to see the frames that come before and after the animation's current frame superimposed on the existing frame and displayed in a different color (see Figure 1.24). This is an important tool for evaluating the motion in a scene, as an animator can tell how much a character moves over a period of frames, and what the character's shape is at each frame.

> **NOTE**
>
> Back culling is a display process in which Softimage 3D determines which polygons in the scene are facing toward the View window by looking at the angle between the View window and the normal of that polygon. If the angle exceeds 180 degrees, the polygon must be facing away from the view, so Softimage doesn't bother to draw it to the screen. Back culling can be used in the final render as well, but if you have open surfaces or surfaces with bad normal orientations, you may see strange results that look like holes in objects or objects turned inside out.
>
> A related method is Z-Buffering, which examines the Z-depth of each polygon to determine if one polygon occludes another from view. Occluded (hidden) polygons are not drawn to the screen.

You can also set up Ghost view to display all keyframes that have been set for the objects in a scene. Ghost mimics the use of *onionskins* in traditional animation, which lets an animator see through a translucent piece of drawing paper to the previously drawn frame, so the next key shape can be drawn consistently from the last. This tool is a tremendous boon to character animators.

FIGURE 1.22   *The Shaded (top) and Wireframe (bottom) Rotoscope views enable you to see your model in front of a sequence of frames.*

FIGURE 1.23   *Julian in Depthcue view.*

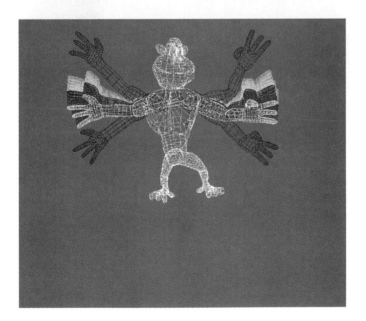

FIGURE 1.24   *Using different colors, Ghost view shows all the keyframes for a scene.*

MATTE VIEW

Matte view outputs a matte channel of the current frame (see Figure 1.25). This means that areas of the screen that are not filled with an object turn black and areas where there is an object are colored in solid white. This is an approximation of the alpha channel that Softimage renders with each frame and can also be used (with appropriate real-time video hardware) to perform real-time keying of Shaded mode scenes with a separate video background. This technology is most usefully found in virtual sets and in some live TV shows that feature animated characters.

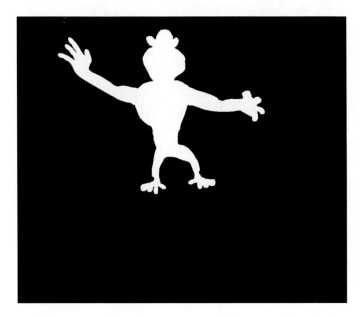

FIGURE 1.25   *Matte view shows a scene's objects in white and all other areas in black.*

WORKFLOW

Proper *workflow* gives form to the process of animation. It creates a process with an achievable result. Workflow defines the most efficient manner of producing the result required. If you create a single object, animate it, apply color, model it some more, add more color, create another object, and then follow the same meandering path again, it will be very difficult for you to complete your work. Segmenting the various duties of animation into workflow steps allows you to move through the process more efficiently in an assembly line fashion. Softimage 3D|Extreme assists you when you work like this by automating some of the functions for you. If you create all of your objects first and then animate them, you will find that Softimage's menu cells are arranged to help you by reducing the number of steps in each of the workflow processes.

Another method used by Softimage to enhance your workflow is the concept of *modes*. When you choose a menu command that might possibly be executed many times in a row, Softimage executes the command on the first object you specified, and *stays* in that command mode until you hit the Esc key or choose another menu command. This makes it easy for you to group your tasks into processes and apply a command to many objects in a sequence.

If you have completed modeling a large number of objects individually and now need to group them into hierarchies, for example, the Parent command stays in the Parent mode as long as you need it, allowing you to construct many elaborate hierarchies without choosing the Parent command again. When you are done with a command, make a habit of pressing the Esc key to put the command away, which avoids unintentional use of that tool the next time you click an object. Not all tools in Softimage work like this, just the ones that can be executed without calling up a dialog box. The active modes are displayed in the Mode box in the lower-right corner of the interface. (See Figure 1.26.)

FIGURE 1.26   *The Mode box highlights the currently active modes.*

Another workflow tool is the *Multi* mode. In the Multi mode, you can select a group of objects that might not be in the same hierarchy and apply commands to all of them at once. Again, this does not work with all commands in Softimage, but it's useful in quite a few. It is also a good idea to change Multi mode back to *Single* mode when you are done with it to avoid unexpected, unintended results.

If you pay attention to workflow within Softimage, you will be a more successful, productive animator.

THE FIVE MODULES OF SOFTIMAGE

Softimage 3D|Extreme has five different *modules* that correspond to different phases of the workflow process that you use to create animation. Each of the modules replaces some of the menu cells on the left and right menu columns, while leaving other menu cells that are applicable in all modules. The modules are listed along the top right corner of the screen: Model, Motion, Actor, Matter, and Tools. You can enter these modules either by clicking the text labels in the top-right corner, or by pressing the supra keys that represent them: F1 for Model, F2 for Motion, F3 for Actor, F4 for Matter, and F5 for Tools.

The first four modules (Model, Motion, Actor, and Matter) are the core components of the Softimage workflow. The last, Tools, is useful occasionally when importing images, converting files, looking at your work, and sending your finished frames to a disk recorder or film recorder for finished output. The first four modules share most of the menu cells on the right menu column and the top seven menu cells of the left menu column. Tools replaces them all completely, sharing only the Exit menu cell. Rather than detailing each of the functions in these modules here, we'll generalize about their use, and then go through the functions together in context as we work through this book.

MODEL

You start your workflow in the Model module, where you construct all your scene elements. Model's tools enable you to create objects from primitive shapes, draw curves, and develop surfaces from those curves.

MOTION

You then move to animate some parts of your scene, using the animation tools found in the Motion module. The Motion module allows you to set animation keyframes for objects, assign objects to paths, and see and edit the resulting animation onscreen. After you have refined your animation using the F-curve tools, you move to the next module, Actor.

ACTOR

The Actor module contains the special Softimage tools for setting up virtual actors, assigning inverse kinematic skeletons, assigning skin, adjusting skeletal deformations, and weighting the skin to the IK skeletons. Actor also contains the controls for physical-based animation—Dynamics, Collisions, and Qstretch—which is an automatic squash-and-stretch feature.

MATTER

When your modeling, animation, and acting is complete, you move to the fourth module: Matter. In the Matter module, you assign color and material values to the objects in your scene, determining how they will look in the final render. At any time in the first four modules, you can create lights and adjust their effect on the scene. The Matter module is also where you perform the last step in the workflow process, rendering.

TOOLS

Tools contains a variety of utility programs for viewing, editing, and exporting your work. You may view individual images, sequences of images, and linetests. You may bring in images created in other programs as image maps or import objects created in other programs as geometry. You can composite sequences of images together, reduce colors in sequences of images for reduced color games systems, and move your finished work to video disk recorders and film recorders.

CUSTOMIZING THE INTERFACE

Softimage 3D|Extreme's interface is not easy to customize. What few options are available can be found in the Preferences menu in the upper-right corner of the screen.

Zoom On Cursor directs the zoom mechanism to focus in on the location of your mouse cursor when you use the Z supra key.

The Mouse Preference dialog box controls mouse speed and behavior within Softimage. Here you may set options for where the mouse returns after dialog boxes appear, for the size of the cursor, and for how fast the mouse pointer moves across the screen when you move the physical mouse on your desktop mousepad.

The Desktop Colors dialog box gives you the capability to choose your favorite colors for the elements of the dismally monochromatic Softimage operating system. You may save these files so that you can reload your favorite settings at a later date.

The Auto-save feature does just what it sounds like: it saves your scene at specified intervals. Although this sounds very useful, allowing you to revert to an earlier version if you screw up your scene beyond repair, it works at odds with another of Softimage's features. By default, Softimage keeps five revisions of your scene. If you use Auto-save, all the revisions are likely to be different from one another by only a few minutes—not much help, especially if you've spent half the time staring at the mess you made. Without the Auto-save feature, Softimage keeps your last five manual saves (as long as you don't change the scene's name), so you could revert the version from the end of your previous day's work session, for example, if you get hopelessly messed up.

The Preferences→Animation menu cell allows you to set some useful and interesting options, including having Softimage automatically assign keyframes any time you scale, rotate, or translate an object, and the feedback option of having elements flash into a different color on frames where they have a keyed value. I suggest that you leave these options at the defaults until you are familiar with how Softimage normally does things.

In general, Softimage remembers most of the setup options you choose on a scene-by-scene basis, including the render options, screen layouts, and saved views. These tidbits of information, and others of value, are stored in the SETUP_SOFT directory of your scene database. The file located there named setup is *not* loaded by default for a new scene, so don't bother trying to save your default settings there.

CUSTOMIZING SUPRA KEYS

The supra keys are defined in the Keyboard Setup file and can be edited to include custom keyboard shortcuts with the Preferences→Keyboard Setup→Learn command. To add a favorite function that ought to have a supra key but doesn't, such as Delete→Delete All, just choose the Learn command and then select the menu cell for which you want to create a supra key. That function is not executed, but a keyboard layout appears that you can use to select the supra key, or combination of keys, that you want assigned as a shortcut. When you click the Ok button, Softimage creates the supra key. Press the Esc key to exit from the Learn mode.

You can add more than one command to the same supra key to create a simple sort of *macro* functionality. If you assign a feature on top of another feature, it is executed after the previous function. (A great practical joke is to assign the Parent function to the Spacebar supra key while your best friend is at lunch.)

Unfortunately, Softimage does not automatically save your keyboard setups with your scenes and has no simple mechanism for making them a default. To add them at startup, run soft in the shell window with the -s option and specify the path and name of a saved keyboard file.

Softimage 3D|Extreme has a new way to execute commands that is a blatant rip-off of the very functional Marking Menus in Alias|Wavefront PowerAnimator. In Softimage, the new tool is called Radial Menus, and its primary goal seems to be to maintain parity with the Alias|Wavefront tool. It is rarely, if ever, used.

LEARNING THE TERMINOLOGY

Before you can get started using the tools in Softimage 3D|Extreme to make models and scenes, you'll need to learn the body of terminology used throughout this book and the Softimage 3D|Extreme product. Most of these terms are used in ways that are standard to the 3D animation world, but some are not. If you take the time to understand the terminology now, even when it becomes technical, you will have an easier time using Softimage to create good work.

POINTS AND LINES

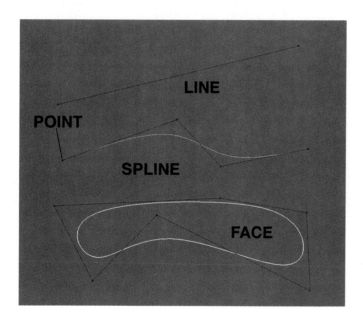

FIGURE 1.27   *The basic building blocks in 3D modeling.*

Almost everything in Softimage is constructed by placing points in 3D space (see Figure 1.27). A point is simply a zero-dimensional location in 3D space, usually given by the X, Y, and Z coordinate system. Two points connected together can define a straight line. If something is linear, it is composed of straight line segments, each with a point at either end. Each linear segment is a one-dimensional object, because a straight line lays in only one dimensional plane. In fact, a straight line is the definition of one-dimensional. If two segments are joined together, they become a two-dimensional object, because they now occupy a space defined by two axes. A two-dimensional plane is easiest thought of as a square floating in space, where one of the line segments is one edge, and the perpendicular edge is the other line segment. If three segments are joined together so that each segment is perpendicular to the other two, then they become a three-dimensional object (see Figure 1.28).

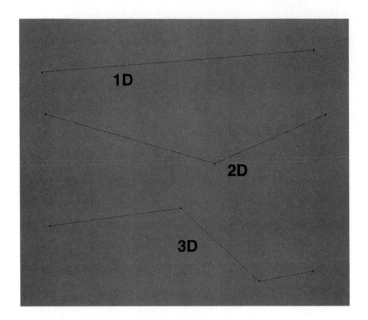

FIGURE 1.28   *A visual definition of 1D, 2D, and 3D objects.*

SPLINES

A *spline* is a line shape that is defined by two or more points. A synonym for spline is *curve*. Softimage uses both terms interchangeably. There can be *linear curves*, even though the names seem to be exclusive of one another. Softimage uses five different kinds of curves: *Linear, Bezier, B-Spline, Cardinal, and Non-Uniform, Rational B-spline (NURBS)* (see Figure 1.29). Each has a slightly different mathematical structure and different features.

All curves are actually composed of a number of *segments*, although you as the user perceive an unbroken curve. The segments are joined together at invisible intersections called *knots*. The knots may or may not lie at the same place as the Control points that you see when you create a curve. Being composed of a series of knots makes a curve piecewise. The mathematical formula that describes each line segment between knots can be of varying complexity. A *first-order* curve has a linear equation, a quadratic equation is used for *second-order* curves, and a cubic equation is used for *third-order* curves. NURBS may be of any order up to 23.

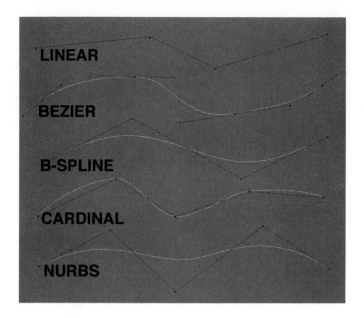

FIGURE 1.29   *The various types of curves, or splines.*

The order of the curve segment defines how smoothly it transitions into a neighboring segment. In a linear curve the segments share a knot and a point, but they are not tangent to each other at that knot. Two segments that are not tangent to each other seem to break into a sharp angle at the point at which they intersect. Tangent curves transition smoothly from one to the next, so that without the Control points showing, you wouldn't know where one ends and the next begins.

A higher order curve maintains positional and tangential continuity as it travels from one segment to another. This creates very smooth curves that seem to be one unbroken filament.

CARDINAL CURVES

Cardinal curves are first order curves, and the curve itself travels directly through the points you place to create it. This type of curve is useful for path animations as the object travels directly through the points you set. Try it out by entering the Model module and choosing Draw→Curve→Cardinal. Now add points to the segment by clicking with your left mouse button in a View window. A minimum of three points is required to place a Cardinal curve.

BEZIER CURVES

NOTE

For the curious or mathematically minded, here is a question: How does Softimage determine and maintain the tangency of the start and the end of the curve? In other words, what determines where the curve is aiming at the end of the segment? Answer: Softimage actually has to place two more invisible points called phantom keys, one before the first point in the curve, and one after the last point in the curve. You can show these by unchecking the Phantom Key option in the Info Selection dialog box.

Bezier curves are the curves that you are most likely to have used before. In addition to its points defining the start and end of each segment, the Bezier curve has two handles that determine the tangency at each point. The curve travels directly through each of the edit points. Macintosh and PC drawing programs most often use Bezier curves, I'm told, because Adobe Postscript is based on Bezier curves, so that's what Macintosh and PC programmers were familiar with. I find them difficult to work with, but they are the most useful curves for creating and editing arcs because you can control the rounding of the arc with the tangency handles. An example of such an arc is the path followed by a ball bouncing down stairs. Try out the Bezier curve from the Draw→Curve→Bezier menu.

B-SPLINES

The B-spline is a curve that does not go through the edit points used to create it. Each line segment is influenced equally by the three points (and two phantom keys) that make it up and performs a best fit line that finds a way between the points in a smooth and fluid manner. B-splines are very easy to control and very useful in Softimage.

NURBS CURVES

Of all the curve types, the NURBS (Non-Uniform, Rational B-Spline) is the most complex, and the most useful. Its curve segments can be of various orders and of different *parameterization*, which is to say that the knots connecting the segments can be spaced in different ways. The NURBS, being a variant of the B-spline, also finds a best fit through the Control points, but four Control points (and *no* phantom keys) are required to create a minimum segment.

The NURBS curve has several benefits. The points can be unequally weighted, so that one point attracts the curve more closely than the others. This is what makes the curve *rational*. This allows for the creation of corners in an otherwise smooth curve. It may also be trimmed to any length, because the knots defining the ends of segments can be placed at any point along the curve. Other curve types can only be trimmed at a Control point.

CLOSED SPLINES

If a spline is closed, that means that the end of the last segment of the curve is co-located with the start of the first segment, creating an unbroken path. By themselves, splines are invisible, since the line segment is two-dimensional at any one point. Splines do not show up in the render.

FACES

A *face* is a closed spline that has been filled in, so that the spline is now visible in the renderer. Faces behave very much like polygons, with the exception that their sides do not have to be composed of linear segments. Softimage tessellates faces down into triangular polygons called *tris* for display and rendering.

CENTERS

Each object is located in *Cartesian space*. The coordinates of the object are given by the position of the object center relative to the global center (also called the *origin*). This means that every object in Softimage has an object center, called a *local center*. The local center not only defines the position of the object in space, it determines the rotation of the object and the relative scale of the object. You can move the location of the local center relative to the rest of the object.

The local center is the point from which the object scales, so if the local center of a ruler is in the geometric center of the ruler, it grows equally outward from the middle when you scale it. If you move the center to the bottom of the ruler and scale it, the ruler grows up from the bottom edge.

> **NOTE**
>
> For you techies, point locations and vertex locations are actually offsets from the local center, making the hierarchy of transformation in 3D space possible.

Similarly, the object rotates around the local center. Put another way, the local center is the axis of rotation for that object. To make a door object swing open appropriately, you would need to move the local center to the hinge edge of the door. Then the door rotates around the edge of the door instead of the middle.

This local center is fundamental to the behavior of every object in the Softimage 3D creative environment.

POLYGONS

The *polygon* is another basic building block in the Softimage object system. A polygon is a shape defined by three or more points called *vertices* (plural), arranged in space. Each *vertex* (singular) is connected to two neighboring vertices with straight line segments called *edges* (see Figure 1.30). This method of linking points in space by *edges* creates the geometric shapes called *polygons*.

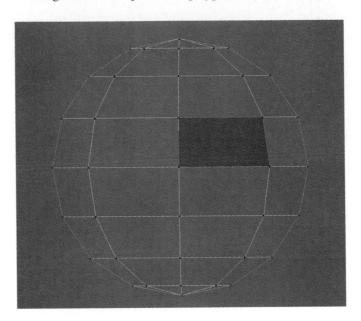

FIGURE 1.30   *A polygonal element of an object.*

There are several kinds of polygons. The most basic polygon has only three sides and is called a trigon, or triangle. The next size up from a triangle is a square, also called a quad, which has four vertices and four sides. From there on up, polygons are called ngons (pronounced "engons") or n-sided polygons (see Figure 1.31).

POLYGON MESHES

An object can be composed of a single polygon or a group of polygons. An object composed of many polygons is called a polygonal mesh (see Figure 1.32). (Wags call this a polygonal mess.) A polygon mesh object is composed of one or more polygons that may or may not share vertices and edges. Because each vertex contains a value for the X position, the Y position, and the Z position, polygon datasets can be quite large.

One way Softimage keeps the size manageable is to allow adjacent polygons to share vertices. If two polygons share two or more vertices, they also share an edge between those vertices. Polygons like this remain connected at the edge like Siamese twins connected at the hip: move one polygon and the other has to stretch to stay joined at the edge. Polygons that share edges can be broken up so that they no longer share edges.

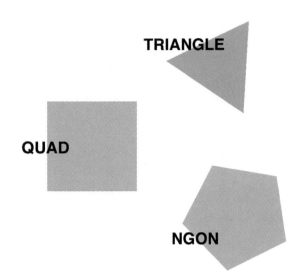

FIGURE 1.31   *Types of polygons.*

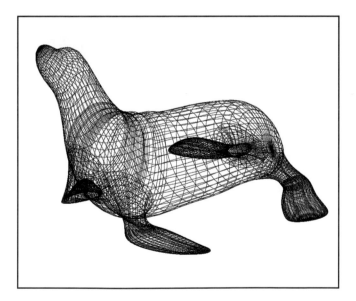

FIGURE 1.32   *A complex polygonal mesh.*

NORMALS

Each polygon has another important component called the *normal*. The normal is a vector line segment emanating from the vertex of the polygon that indicates which way the polygon is facing—that is to say, which side of the polygon is the front side and which is the back (see Figure 1.33).

FIGURE 1.33   *A polygonal mesh with normals visible.*

Softimage uses this information in several important ways. First, it determines at render time which polygon's front sides are facing the camera and renders only those polygons to save render time. Second, it prevents you from drawing polygons that share edges but have inverted normal orientations, which would lead to models with severe geometry problems, like holes in the surface. Third, Softimage uses the normal during the render to smooth the shading on edges between polygons, helping to reduce the typical jagged, faceted look of polygonal models.

The normals can be shown or hidden in Softimage. When shown, they look like thin, blue hairs sprouting from the surface of your polygon models.

PATCHES

The most complex object building block in Softimage is the *patch* (see Figure 1.34). The patch can be thought of as a network of spline curves, with the intersections between the curves connected by a web of geometry called a *surface*.

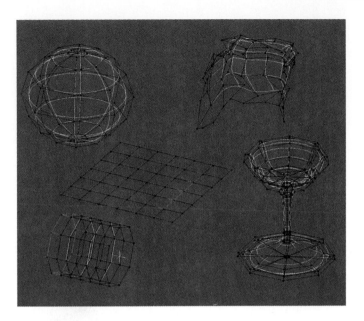

FIGURE 1.34   *Sample objects composed of patches.*

The edges of a patch are often called the *boundary curves* because they define the boundaries of the patch. One boundary runs in the U direction and one boundary runs in the V direction (see Figure 1.35). When the patch is more or less rectangular, the boundary curves look like they are the edges, but when the patch looks more like a sphere, the boundary curves look more like the poles of a planet (see Figure 1.36).

Because of the planet analogy, it is also useful to think of the UV system as being similar to the latitude and longitude system on our Earth, where the V direction is latitude and the U direction is longitude. Each location in UV space exactly describes a location on the patch surface, just as every longitude and latitude combination describes a unique location on the Earth. This precise capability to locate positions in the UV parameter space is one of the main advantages that patches have over polygon objects.

Patches can, like splines, be closed or open. In an open patch, the two U edges, or the two V edges, are connected. A patch with one edge (or parameter) closed looks like an unbroken ribbon. A patch with both parameters closed looks like a solid object where the U and V parameters stretch completely around in an unbroken surface.

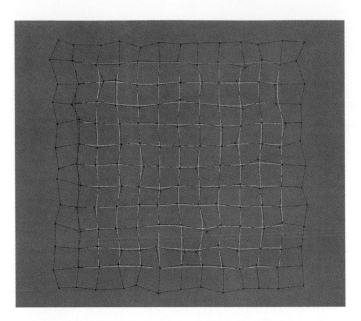

FIGURE 1.35   *A patch with U and V boundary curves highlighted.*

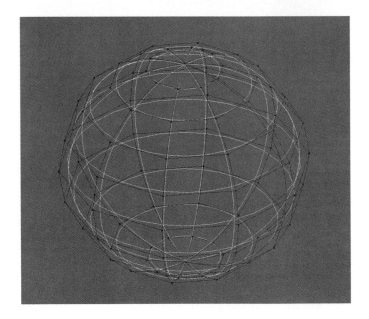

FIGURE 1.36   *On a sphere, boundary curves look like the planet's poles.*

APPROXIMATION AND TESSELLATION

Because Softimage renders only triangles, a patch is really only an approximation of a surface made of triangles. How closely the polygonal surface approximates the mathematical precision of the patch determines how smooth and accurate the final surface is. The process of approximating the surface by breaking it down into a number of triangles is called *tessellation*.

As a general rule, the more triangles that are used to approximate the patch, the better it looks. The degree of approximation used to tessellate the patch down into triangles at render time can be controlled precisely in Softimage by setting the Step parameter (in the Info→Selection→Render Setup dialog box or if you use the mental ray renderer, by allowing the mental ray to choose the proper Step for you). The Step is the number of times each UV patch section is divided into smaller sections before it is finally divided into two triangles (see Figure 1.37). This capability to easily trade off between surface smoothness and the number of triangles is another key advantage of using patches over polygons in your modeling tasks.

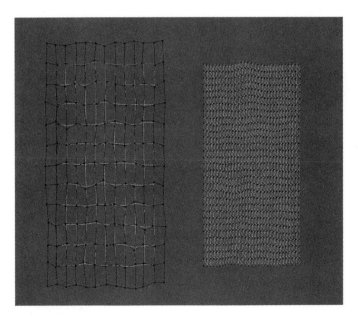

FIGURE 1.37   *The same patch with different Step settings.*

NURBS PATCHES

NURBS patches are a special kind of patch composed of NURBS (Non-Uniform Rational B-Splines) curves. Just like NURBS curves, NURBS patches have some advantages that normal patches do not. Because the knot of a NURBS curve can be located at any point along its length, a NURBS curve can be trimmed to any length. Similarly, a NURBS patch can be trimmed to any shape by *projecting* another NURBS curve onto the first surface, in the same way that you trim a cookie out of a sheet of dough with a cookie cutter. The trim curve can just be projected onto the surface for later use, it can define a hole in the surface, or it can become the outer boundary of the surface, causing everything outside the curve to go away.

Because of the more flexible parameterization of NURBS patches, it is also possible to connect two separate NURBS patches into one contiguous surface by *merging* the two original surfaces. Another method of achieving a similar result is to create a third surface that blends evenly between two original surfaces to create a joint between them, much like using putty to fill in the crack between sections of drywall in building a house.

Points on NURBS patches can also be weighted, just like points on NURBS curves, so that NURBS surfaces can have combinations of smooth curves and sharp angles.

NURBS currently represent the most sophisticated way of creating complex surface geometry in surface modelers, such as Softimage. Although using NURBS is more complex than using regular patches or polygons, the additional features and flexibility of NURBS make them the only way to go for many types of surfaces, including organic shapes and complex precision surfaces.

CONCLUSION

That was a lot of technical jargon and terminology for one chapter! Some of it may have seemed quite dry, but rest assured that it'll come in handy all throughout your career as an animator. You should now have a pretty clear understanding of:

- Starting and moving around in Softimage 3D|Extreme on IRIX or Windows NT.
- The Softimage 3D interface organization, the menu cells, and the five modules of Softimage 3D.
- How Cartesian space works and what the X, Y, and Z axes mean in Softimage 3D.
- Customizing the interface and using the supra keys as keyboard shortcuts.
- 3D surface geometry and objects, including polygons, splines, patch surfaces, and NURBS.

Image courtesy of David Choi and Microsoft.

CHAPTER 2

GETTING STARTED — MOVING IN SPACE

In this chapter, we'll dive right into Softimage, using some simple scenes to demonstrate some complex tools, including transformations, the Softimage hierarchy, and the Schematic view. By the end of this chapter, you'll know how to set up a scene, create basic animation, and play those frames back to check your work.

Specifically, this chapter will cover:

- Starting a new scene
- Saving your work
- Using text
- Using primitive objects
- Scaling, rotating, and translating objects in space
- Using the hierarchy and the Schematic view
- Manipulating the local and global centers

MAKING THE SCENE

In Softimage, everything you work on at one time is called a *scene*. The scene encompasses the models, the animation, the lights, and the textures—in fact, it includes everything. When you get ready to quit for the day or want to move on to another task, you save the scene you are working on. When you get a scene, you load work that has already been done into your workstation's RAM.

Softimage scenes are quite a bit different from how most animation programs save their information, however, and are a lot more flexible. Most PC and Macintosh animation programs bind all the saved work, including models, animation, lights, and so on into one file when you save your work. This method is simple to grasp, but inefficient and inflexible. Softimage saves each model, each material, each light, and each animation path into different, smaller files, and organizes all these thousands of files in a directory structure called a *database*. This means that Softimage can save only those parts of a scene that changed or load just one light from another scene, or it uses animation you made for another project.

The file that ties all these parts together is called the *scene file*, located in the SCENE folder in the database. In the form of a simple text file, the scene file simply contains the names of all the other files that contain the information in the scene. Use your favorite text editor to take a look at one.

Another useful trick is that when you load a scene on top of an already loaded scene, the first scene doesn't close; it is merged with the new scene. This makes it easy to work on small parts and then bring them all together.

SAVE SCENE

When you launch Softimage, you are presented with a blank scene. Nothing you do is saved until you use the Save→Scene command (found at the top-left corner of the screen) to pick a name for the scene and write it to your hard drive. Save→Scene writes out all the information in the scene that has changed in the current session and saves the scene file with a consecutive version number, such as Scene.1-0.dsc, followed by Scene.2-0.dsc, then Scene.3-0.dsc, and so on.

By default, Softimage saves all your work for the last *five* revisions of the scene. This means that you can always give up on a scene and go back to an earlier version by choosing the Delete→All command and loading the same scene with a previous version number.

The Save menu's Scene dialog box also has commands that allow you to save just the selected models and any selected elements you wish (see Figure 2.1).

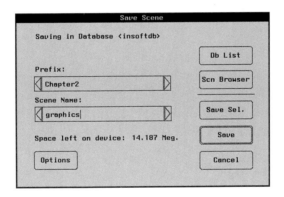

FIGURE 2.1   *The Save Scene dialog box.*

THE GET MENU

The Get menu is the only way to load premade shapes, completed scenes, text, PostScript files, and other files into your scene (see Figure 2.2). The Get menu also contains the dialog boxes that allow you to create new databases, and to manage what scene information is stored in your current database. Let's start with the simple stuff first.

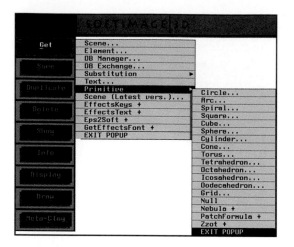

FIGURE 2.2   *The Get menus.*

GET SCENE

As you can probably guess, the Get→Scene command brings up a dialog box that lets you browse your file system and any connected networks for Softimage databases. When you encounter a Softimage database, the file browser automatically sends you to the SCENES chapter of the database. The SCENES chapter is just a directory on your hard drive named SCENES, which is within the directory named after the database. Scene files have the file suffix .dsc.

Because the scene file is really just a bunch of links to many other files that make up the entire scene, deleting the scene file manually from your computer does not remove the rest of the scene. It will make it impossible to find all the files that belonged to that scene, however, so never try to clean up your database manually by deleting files. Always use the DB Manager.

GET ELEMENT

Because Softimage stores every single thing in its own file, you can always retrieve any single item with the Get→Element command. Like the light you created last week? Bring it in to your current scene with the Get→Element command. Using it is simple: Select the command from the Get menu and browse the Load dialog box that appears until you find what you want. Click the Load button to bring it in. Here is a list of all the elements that you can load separately (as of this writing):

Animation	Materials	Softimage Setups
Cameras	Material Shaders	Shadow Shaders
Camera Shaders	Models	Shapes
Clusters	Output Shaders	Spreadsheet Setups
Environment	Palettes	Struct KeysShaders
Expressions	Pictures	2D Textures and Shaders
Lattices	Rendered Pictures	3D Textures and Shaders
Lights	Scenes	Volume Shaders
Light Shaders	Flocking Setups	Waves

GET DB MANAGER

Go to the Get→DB Manager menu (see Figure 2.3) to start new databases (for a new client or a new project), delete old databases after they are no longer needed, set the default working database, link and unlink other databases into your active database list, and delete scenes and elements within a database.

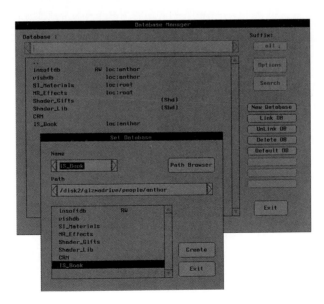

FIGURE 2.3 *The Database Manager dialog box.*

To create a new database, click the New Database button and name the database. The path you choose will be the location on your hard drive or network where the database is physically located. You must have read and write permissions to the directory you chose or the operation will fail.

The DB Manager reads a file stored at the current user account's working directory. Called the DatabaseDir.rsrc, the file contains the name and location of the active databases and looks like this:

```
DATABASE AnthoLabdb
PATH /usr/people/soft37/AnthoLabdb
DATABASE Mesmerdb
PATH /usr/people/soft37/Mesmerdb
DATABASE SI_Materials
PATH /disk2/soft37/databases/SI_Materials
```

The database listed first (AnthoLabdb in this case) is the default working database and, unless you specify otherwise, all files read and written will be from and in this database. To make a database the default, select it in the DB Manager and click the Default DB button.

NOTE

The Default DB button is perilously close to the Delete DB button, and they look awfully similar. Many animators have accidentally deleted all their crucial work by clicking the wrong button and then not paying attention to the dialog box asking them to confirm the deletion. Usually this happens late at night, after 1:00 or 2:00 a.m. Be very careful because when a database is deleted, it is gone for good.

To remove a database from this list without deleting it from the hard drive, use the UnLink DB command. To add a database to this list, either locate the database in the DB Browser and use the Link DB button, or just click into the database in the browser and it will be automatically added to the active DB list.

You can also use the DB Manager to manage the scenes you have inside your database. If you enter the SCENES chapter, the buttons in the DB Manager change names and allow you to view the scene, see the contents of the scene file (it is just a text file), lock the scene, share the scene with others in the workgroup, and delete the scene.

The last button, Delete, is the most important, because it is the *only* way to clean up your database and free up room on your hard drive without risk to your scenes. Using the Delete button on a scene file doesn't just remove the scene file, it first reads the scene file contents and compares them to every other scene saved in that database. If the contents of the scene aren't used elsewhere, the objects are removed and deleted from their locations in the database directory structure. That way only items that aren't needed somewhere else get cleaned out.

GET→DBEXCHANGE

The Database Exchange Management dialog box has a simple purpose: to move scenes and elements between different databases (see Figure 2.4). There are two file browsers, one on the left and one on the right. You may select chapters within a database on the left side and choose a destination on the right. Clicking the Move button moves the selected scenes or elements to the destination, removing them from the source. Copy makes a copy in the destination, leaving the source untouched. You may use this tool to safely rename elements, as well.

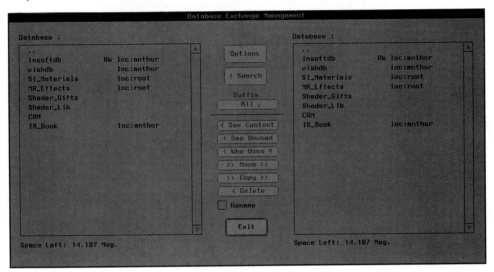

FIGURE 2.4 *The Database Exchange dialog box.*

GET TEXT

The easiest way to bring type into Softimage is to use the Get→Text command. Softimage ships with a number of typefaces that have been converted for use in Softimage (see Figure 2.5). You simply type the text you want into the dialog box, select the typeface you want from the scrolling list box, and click the Ok button. The other controls allow you to add a slant to each letter (faking italics) and to determine whether the letters are created as splines (invisible to the renderer, but useful for extrusion) or faces (visible to the renderer, but flat).

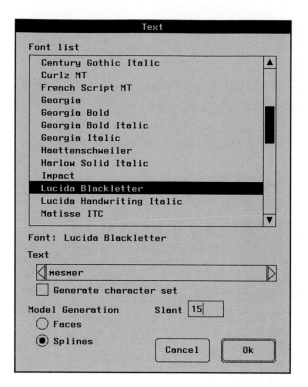

FIGURE 2.5   *Text comes into Softimage 3D via the Get → Text command.*

GET PRIMITIVES

Softimage includes a variety of premade primitive shapes that are useful in basic modeling (see Figure 2.6) and are accessed on the Get→Primitives menu. These primitives include both splines and surface shapes. The primitive surfaces are all polygonal, except for the sphere and grid surfaces, which have a dialog box that allows you to choose between polygon-, patch-, and NURBS-based surfaces. The spline primitives, circle, arc, and spiral, each have a dialog box that you may use to set the spline type and other parameters.

The Sphere, Torus, Cylinder, and Cone menu items call up an additional dialog box that allows you to choose how the surface is subdivided in U and V. (See Figure 2.7.) Increasing the subdivisions makes the objects appear more smooth when they are rendered. The Patch Objects dialog also gives you the option of determining the curve type used to create the object, between linear, Bezier, Cardinal, B-spline, or NURBS. If you choose NURBS, you can determine the degree of the NURBS curve—linear, quadratic, or cubic.

FIGURE 2.6   *The generic primitives, both splines and surfaces. When you look at the Get→Primitives menu, you'll notice some commands at the bottom of the menu are marked with a plus symbol (+). These are custom effects: Nebula (a simple particle generator), PatchFormula (creates a mathematically defined surface), and Zzot (a lightning generator).*

Starting with a primitive shape and then cutting, transforming, or deforming that shape into something else is the most basic form of modeling, and it's a quick way to get things done. Experiment with the primitives in the Get→Primitives menu to see what's there.

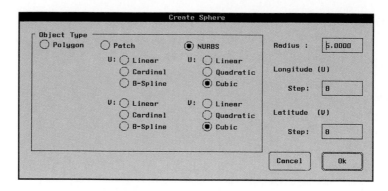

FIGURE 2.7   *The Create Sphere dialog has options for different kinds of spherical surface objects.*

GET→EPS2SOFT

With the Get→Eps2Soft command, Softimage directly imports EPS (Encapsulated PostScript) files, including Adobe Illustrator and Macromedia Freehand files. This is a great boon to designers who have art in these programs. EPS files can be imported and used as a construction curve anywhere you would use a spline drawn directly in Softimage. Rather than redrawing client logos or complex type treatments, use this tool. EPS curves are imported as Bezier splines but may be converted to any spline you want with the Effect→Convert command in the Model module.

STARTING OVER

When you want to get rid of everything onscreen without saving changes, or if you simply want to load a fresh scene to work on, use the Delete→All command to clear the scene. This command removes all objects from use, but they remain in your workstation's RAM. Loafing there, they clog your available memory and slow down your future work. To clear the undo stack as well, choose the History→Dispose command, which wipes them away and frees up the memory that they used for other models.

CHOOSING OBJECTS: SELECTING VERSUS PICKING

Most commands in Softimage operate on the currently selected object or objects. They follow this pattern: You select the object and click a menu cell to perform the command. Other commands, however, operate in the opposite order: You click a menu cell to activate the command, then pick an object and execute the command.

The difference lies between selecting and picking. Selecting means to make the object active in the scene, where it is drawn in a white wireframe to show that it is selected, and remains selected until it is deselected. Picking means to simply point at an object with your mouse and click the left mouse button.

To select items, hold down the Spacebar, point at the item onscreen, and click the left mouse button. The object should highlight and stay highlighted. You may also draw a marquee around an object (or just a part of an object) to select it, in the same manner, by holding the Spacebar down and clicking and dragging with the left mouse button. Selecting is, by default, a toggle command. If you select an object that is unselected, it becomes highlighted. If you select an object that is already selected, it becomes unselected. Experiment with this on a set of primitive objects. When you use these methods, you can select only a single object.

MULTI MODE VERSUS SINGLE MODE

Some commands can be applied to many objects at once; therefore it's possible to select a group of objects. There are, in fact, two separate ways with different uses. The simple method is to click the Multi menu cell in the lower-right corner of the interface (see Figure 2.8). Now you can select more than one object and apply a command like a transformation to them. Be warned, however, that most Softimage commands *don't work* in Multi mode. In fact, it's a good idea to stay in Single mode while working and use Multi mode for specific effects only. The approved method of selecting multiple objects for commands is to use a hierarchy, discussed a little later in this chapter.

FIGURE 2.8   *The Multi mode and Single mode menu cells.*

TIP

Historically, Softimage 3D|Extreme has had memory leaks that could sink the Titanic. That means some tools never free up the memory they use after they are no longer needed, causing Softimage's memory consumption to grow over time as you work. After a few days of solid use (and that happens a lot in production work), Softimage becomes slow and unresponsive, or finally just runs out of memory and crashes. The most guilty tools are usually the custom effects and plug-ins, which are sometimes written without the kind of testing and maintenance that they ought to have had.

It's a good idea to exit the program at least once a day, which gives IRIX or NT a chance to reclaim all the wasted memory for productive use. Then when you run Softimage again, it is more responsive.

For those of you running IRIX (my favorite operating system), another good idea is to keep vswap turned off. Vswap is imaginary memory space that gets used after the OS runs out of real RAM and out of swap space on the hard drive. When code or data gets written to virtual swap space it goes away to data heaven, and Softimage will probably crash. As root, execute the command

```
chkconfig
```

to see if vswap is turned on, then use

```
chkconfig vswap off
```

to turn it off. Changes take place after a reboot.

Transformations: Scale, Rotation, Translation

The three basic operations for all objects are the transformations: scale, rotation, and translation. Each of these functions can be performed relative to one axis, two axes, or three axes at a time. For instance, you can rotate an airplane-shaped object around the X, Y, or Z axes. Rotating all three at the same time causes an object to tumble.

Scale means to expand the size of the object, either uniformly along one or two axes, or in such a way that the internal volume of the object keeps the same squashing and stretching. When you scale an object in all axes at the same time, the object grows or shrinks while retaining its proportions. If you scale in only one axis, however, it grows or shrinks along that axis.

Translate means to move an object. You may of course choose to move an object in one, two, or three dimensions at a time.

Because these three methods of transformation are so common in modeling and animation, the Transformation menu cells along the right side of the interface remain persistent throughout the first four modules of Softimage—Model, Motion, Actor, and Matter. You can use these menu cells in several ways. (See Figure 2.9.)

Clicking with your mouse on the white area that borders a group of menu cells for one transformation (for example, ScaleX, ScaleY, and ScaleZ) causes that transformation to become active for all three axes. To transform the object, drag with any of the three mouse buttons: The left mouse button operates on the X axis, the middle mouse button on the Y axis, and the right mouse button on the Z axis.

To scale a cube into a rectangular tabletop, for example, you could click in the white area around the scale cells. Then you would drag the middle mouse button up to make the cube shorter and the left mouse button to make the tabletop longer in the X dimension. To scale the tabletop uniformly, hold down all three mouse buttons and drag. (See Figure 2.10.)

Figure 2.9

The transformation cells for use on all axes at once.

To operate in only one axis, you may click in the black area that contains the title of the menu cell you want. For instance, to scale in X only, click the word "ScaleX." In this case, each of the three mouse buttons does the same thing, but at a different rate: The left mouse button goes slowly, the middle mouse button goes more rapidly, and the right performs the action the fastest. By using each mouse button, you can get exactly the level of control that you need. Look to the status area at the bottom of the screen to see a description of each mouse button's function within the menu cell. (See Figure 2.11.)

If you click directly in the area of a Transformation menu cell where the decimal number reads out, you can enter a value directly into that box. Clicking with the left button allows you to edit the existing value, while clicking there with the middle mouse button selects the value in the box so that when you enter a number you completely replace the current value. Hitting the Enter key or selecting another cell causes the change to take place.

Finally, if you click into the triangular tab at the top left corner of each cell, you can directly enter numbers into a text dialog for all three axes of that transformation and choose whether the values you enter are to be absolute or added to the current values (see Figure 2.12).

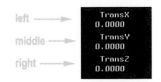

FIGURE 2.10

The Transformation menu cell for use on only one axis at a time.

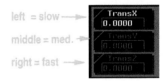

FIGURE 2.11

The three mouse buttons provide various levels of control for the transformations.

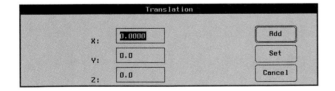

FIGURE 2.12   *Setting transformations numerically on all axes at the same time.*

TUTORIAL: STONEHENGE

Let's try all this out by constructing a simple scene that simulates the collection of obelisks found at Stonehenge in Wiltshire, England.

FIGURE 2.13   *The completed Stonehenge scene.*

We'll use only primitive cubes of varying sizes and proportions. The power of Softimage is that you can do in a few minutes what teams of druids took many years to complete. Then when you learn about lights, you can place a sun where it would be during the winter solstice and see what pattern the stones make. Of course, it was their idea first and creativity counts for a lot in this world whether you're a druid or an animator.

TIP

I like to use the numeric keypad. Click the Numlock key to activate it so you can use it. After you enter a number into a box, hit the Enter key to advance to the next editable box in that dialog. After the last box, the Enter key will operate the Ok button for you, saving some time.

1. Lay the Ground Plane.

Start by building a ground plane with a simple grid object. Use the Get→Primitive→Grid command to bring up the Grid dialog box. Choose to make the grid out of a patch made from B-splines in both the X and Z axes. Leave the Cell Size at 1 but increase the Cell Count in both X and Z to 15. Click Ok to create the grid.

The grid isn't large enough to cover the area in front of us in the scene, so we'll need to enlarge it. Click the triangle tab next to the ScaleX menu cell and enter 3 into the value for X, Y, and Z. Click the Add button, which has the effect of tripling the size of the grid in each axis. Of course, because the grid is flat and has no dimension in the Y axis, we could have left that box blank.

Now the grid stretches to the horizon, but it's awfully flat looking. Let's bump it up in a random rolling fashion by using a randomize command on the grid. Choose Effect→Randomize (with the grid still selected), change the Size Y multiplier to 0.1, and click the Ok button. The Randomize effect will randomly move the location of each Control point in the grid a little, creating a rolling hillside. Look at it in Shaded view. (See Figure 2.14.)

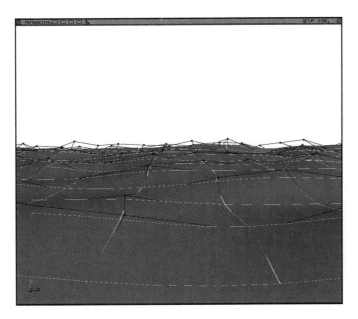

FIGURE 2.14   *The randomized ground plane.*

2. **Make the First Post.**

Before we start making posts and lintels, let's mark out the plan for the area so we know where things go. Look at the overhead view, the Top view (the XZ plane), hold down the A supra key, and click with your mouse somewhere in that view to frame all objects. Now create a primitive circle with the Get→Primitive→Circle command. In the Circle dialog box, leave the parameterization at Linear, but change the Radius to 10, and press the Ok button. We'll use this circle as a guide when we place the stones, but since it was created in the XY plane and we want it in the XZ plane, we'll have to rotate it first. With the circle selected, click directly into the numeric area of the RotX menu cell with your middle mouse button and enter the value 90, which means 90 degrees. Press the Enter key to execute the command. In the top view you should now see the circle.

Make the first post by using the Get→Primitive→Cube command with a length of 10 (the default length) and scale the resulting cube with the Scale menu cells to be about 0.15 in X, 0.5 in Y, and 0.1 in Z. These values are relative to the original size of the object, not to Softimage units, so you could read the above as 15% of the original size in X (1.5 Softimage units), 50% original size in Y, and 10% original size in Z.

TIP

The easiest way to translate objects is to drag them around in a View window with the left mouse button. This is called drag mode and is enabled by selecting the DRG button in the mode box in the lower-right corner of the screen.

Place the post on the circle and flush with the ground plane with the Translation menu cells. I recommend clicking in the small white border area to the right of the individual cells, which activates them all so you can translate in each direction. Then in DRG mode, click with your mouse in the Top view to drag the post to the circle. Use the Front view to adjust the position in Y. Duplicate the post by using the Duplicate→Immediate command, or by holding the D supra key and clicking the first post. The new post will be in the same place, so you won't see any change, but if you translate it to the side, you will now see two posts. (See Figure 2.15.)

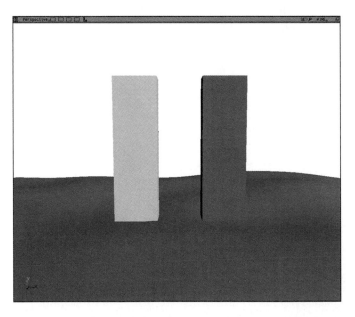

FIGURE 2.15   *Two posts made from primitive cubes.*

3. Rough Up the Posts for Realism.

The posts are supposed to be rough-hewn granite blocks. Let's make our posts a little more natural in shape.

First, if you can't see the vertices, check the Show menu cell to make sure that Show→Point is enabled. If it isn't, turn it on.

Then move a few of the corner vertices in order to make the shape less regular. In any window, click a vertex with the M supra key held down and drag with your mouse.

That's better, but no matter what you do, the post still has only six sides and looks pretty geometric. To add more detail, use the Effect→Subdivision command, which adds more vertices to the object for us to play with. We mainly want subdivisions in the vertical, Y axis, so set the parameters in the Subdivision dialog to 1 for X, 4 for Y, and 1 for Z, and click the Ok button.

Now use the Effect→Randomize command again to rough up the vertices. Try values of 0.1 for X, 0 for Y, and 0.1 for Z. If you want more displacement, use the command again until you are satisfied.

Edit the other post in a similar manner but with different values so it looks different.

Place the posts side by side, about four Softimage units apart (you may look at the grid for simple distances and placement). (See Figure 2.16.)

FIGURE 2.16 *The roughened posts.*

4. Build a Lintel.

Build the lintel, the flat, broad piece of stone that caps the two posts, the same way with a primitive cube. This time, set the Length of the cube to 1, which means that the cube sides will be 1 Softimage unit long and therefore easy to measure and multiply for scale.

Now scale the cube with the Scale menu cells or click on the triangluar tab to use Add in the Scale dialog. Make the cube 5 units in X, 1 unit in Y, and 1.5 units in Z. Use the Translate and Rotate menu cells to place it roughly on top of and resting on the two posts. You may rough it up as well by dragging points and randomizing the surface.

5. Make the Other Doorways.

Copy the stones you've built and place them in groups to match the layout of Stonehenge in Figure 2.17, or if you wish, construct your own mystical portals and lay them out as your spirit dictates. Because we haven't yet discussed how to group objects, you will have to scale and rotate the giant stone blocks one at a time. You may, however, duplicate and move the blocks in a group by using Multi mode to select more than one item. (See Figure 2.17.)

FIGURE 2.17   *Grouped blocks make up the Stonehenge gateways.*

6. Examine Your Work.

Place your camera wherever you wish in the scene by using the O, P, and Z supra keys within the Perspective window.

View your work in Shaded mode by selecting Shade from the View Style drop menu at the top of the Perspective view.

You are done! Save your scene with Save→Scene. The Stonehenge exercise helps you pull together a scene into a cohesive, visible work of art. Seeing the collection of shapes come together into a scene is the most rewarding part of the animation process (outside of visiting your personal banker).

HIERARCHIES AND THE SCHEMATIC VIEW

As you can see in the Stonehenge tutorial, even a simple scene can grow to have quite a few objects in it. As you work in Softimage, the scenes you create will be more and more complex. Simply finding the object you want in the scene can be difficult, and without organization, your scenes will become unruly.

It would also be nice to arrange objects into a group, so that, for instance, you could move, rotate, and scale both a stone portal's posts and lintel together. Softimage has tools to solve both of these problems and understanding them is critical in using Softimage 3D|Extreme well.

HIERARCHIES

In Softimage, objects can belong to a *hierarchy*. One object can have many other objects that belong to it and are therefore part of the same hierarchy. One object is the *parent object*, and those that belong to it are called *child objects*. Each of the children can themselves be the parent of another object, and so on, indefinitely. All of these parents and children combine into an entire hierarchy, called a *tree*.

The very first object, the top object, of the tree is called the *root*. That root splits off into individual *branches* and those branches may have other branches below them. Each object in the tree is called a *node*, although a better term is leaf (sometimes, the last node in a tree is called a *leaf node*). (See Figure 2.18.)

FIGURE 2.18   *A graphical illustration of a hierarchy.*

THE SCHEMATIC VIEW

You can view the hierarchical organization graphically by converting a View window to show the Schematic view. To do this, click the View drop menu at the top-left of a window (the bottom-right window is the traditional choice) and select Schematic from the option list.

The Schematic view now shows each of the objects in your scene as individual small boxes with a name in them. Objects are black, lights are red, materials are blue, and textures are dark blue. You can select these objects in the Schematic view in the usual manner, with the Spacebar. You can also translate them around the Schematic view as you wish, which is helpful for organization. (See Figure 2.19.)

SETTING UP HIERARCHIES

To make your own hierarchy, use the Parent command in the Model module. When Parent is active, you may use the mouse buttons for different effects. When you have one object selected and use the *left* mouse button to pick an object, the *selected* item becomes the *parent* of the picked item. When you use the *middle* mouse button, quite the opposite happens: the *picked* item becomes the *parent* of the selected item.

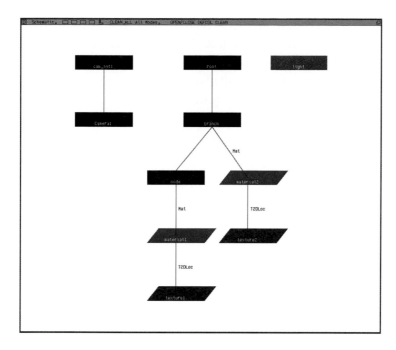

FIGURE 2.19   *Hierarchies of objects are shown by the dark lines that connect objects.*

In this way you can create hierarchies in either direction: from the child you can select the parent (middle mouse button) and from the parent you can select many children (the left mouse button).

The right mouse button (and the Esc key) ends the command. It is always a good idea to end the Parent command when done to avoid accidental parenting. When you wish for a parent to orphan a child, remove the child from the hierarchy by selecting the poor thing and choosing the Cut command.

Here is the important part, so *read this twice:* When you select an object with the Spacebar and the *left* mouse button, you are selecting a node, which is a single object. To select a branch of a tree, (a parent and all its children) you use the Spacebar and the *middle* mouse button. To select the entire tree (all connected parents and all their children) use the *right* mouse button and the Spacebar. This may not seem so important now, but remember this next time you want to know how to select, transform, or operate another command on multiple objects at once.

TRANSFORMATIONS ON A HIERARCHY

Back in the Stonehenge tutorial, you may have noticed that if you selected multiple objects (with the Multi command) and then scaled or rotated them, each object was transformed relative to its own local center. For instance, if you selected two posts and a lintel and tried to rotate them in Y so that you could align them with the circle, each part would spin on its own, losing contact with the other pieces. Similarly, if you wanted to scale a portal smaller, using the Multi method simply makes all the parts smaller, and then you have to reassemble the pieces. That's not too hard when the model is made of three cubes, but for more complex models it would be unforgivable. There is a better way.

When objects are in a hierarchy, they can be transformed relative to their parent's local center, instead of their own. If the hierarchy has several levels to it, each level can be a different local center for the transformations. That means that if the portal is in a hierarchy, for example, with the lintel as the parent of both posts, selecting the whole hierarchy with the right mouse button and the Spacebar would allow you to move, scale, and rotate the portal as you wish. Its parts would always remain in the correct proportions and orientation. In addition, most animation can be performed on hierarchies, at the node, branch, and tree levels. This is a concept of *great* importance in Softimage, because without it you could never build and animate anything with more than one piece.

To firm up the concept with some practical use, try the following tutorial.

TUTORIAL: THE PLANETS

Our solar system is a great example of a hierarchical system. The top level is the universe, and within the universe lies our galaxy, the Milky Way. Within our galaxy lies our solar system, within the solar system lies our planet. Our planet has one child, the moon.

At each level in this hierarchy, the children move relative to the parent. In some hard to fathom way, we are all moving relative to the planet, the sun, the galaxy, and the universe. We will build just the solar system in this tutorial, our sun and the nine planets, with moons. (See Figure 2.20.)

1. **The Sun.**

   Use the Get→Primitive command to get a primitive sphere, made of polygons with a radius of 10 Softimage units and the default number of steps, then name it "sun" by using the Info→Selection dialog box. Leave the sun in the global center.

2. **The Planets.**

   Create nine more spheres of varying sizes between 0.5 Softimage units in radius and 5 units in radius. Place them in varying locations in the Top view, spread about the center, and the sun. In order of distance from the sun, name them Mercury, Venus, Earth, Mars, Jupiter, Saturn, Uranus, Neptune, and Pluto (see Figure 2.21).

FIGURE 2.20   *The completed, rendered Planets scene.*

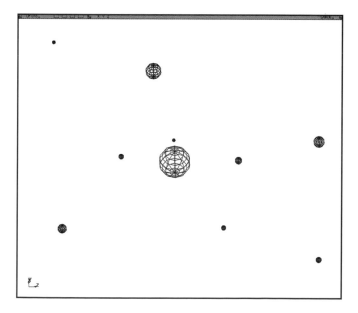

FIGURE 2.21   *The wireframe sun and planets.*

3. The Moons.

To jazz it up a little, add in a moon for the Earth. Create a new sphere with a radius of 0.1 units and move it to the approximate location of the Earth. Then select the Earth and zoom in with the Z supra key until it fills about a third of the front view window. Move the moon to a position outside of the Earth, where it could be orbiting.

Make few moons for Jupiter and a ring made of a flattened primitive torus for Saturn.

4. Create the Hierarchy.

Change one of your View windows to be the Schematic view. See that each planet and moon is a separate object, unconnected with the rest. (See Figure 2.22.)

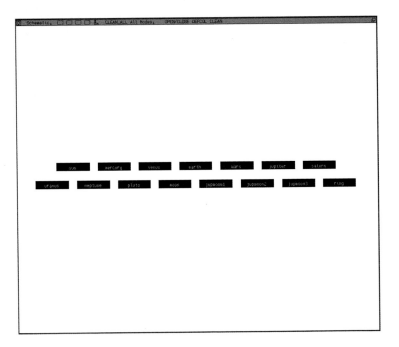

FIGURE 2.22   *The unconnected Schematic view of the planets.*

Now comes the fun part. Select the Sun and click the Parent menu cell. Pick (not select, but pick, which means no Spacebar) each planet in turn.

Look at the Schematic view as you do this and see how the Sun is now the top of a hierarchy that connects all the planets together.

When all the planets are in the hierarchy, it's time to parent the moons and rings. *Select* (not pick) the Earth, and with the Parent menu cell still selected, pick the moon. Look at the Schematic view.

Select Jupiter and parent in the moons that belong to it. Do the same for the Saturn and its rings (see Figure 2.23).

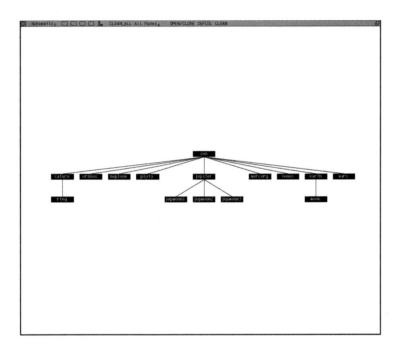

FIGURE 2.23   *The planets connected into a hierarchy.*

5. Check It Out.

In the Perspective view, use the A supra key to view all. Now select just the Earth with the Spacebar and the left mouse button, which is the Select Node mouse button. Just the Earth becomes selected.

What if you want to select the Earth and the Moon? Select the Earth again with the Spacebar and the middle mouse button, which is the Select Branch button. Now the Earth *and* the Moon are selected.

What if you want the whole solar system? Select the Earth again with the right mouse button, which is the Select Tree button, and the whole solar system is selected.

With the solar system selected, use the RotY menu cell to see that everything now revolves around the top of the selected hierarchy, in this case the Sun.

Try translating the whole tree to see that it stays together. Try scaling the whole thing uniformly (using all three mouse buttons or the UNI mode) to see that the solar system retains its proportions within the hierarchy.

Neat, huh? One last secret: The selection buttons are a toggle system. That means that after you have selected something as a tree, to unselect it you *have* to use the same mouse button and the Spacebar again.

The hierarchy is a very powerful organizational and animation tool. Understanding how to pick parts of the hierarchy with the left, middle, and right mouse buttons is a crucial Softimage skill.

ORGANIZING THE SCHEMATIC VIEW

The Schematic view window is a pretty important window in Softimage and can quickly get cluttered. Feel free to move the items in the Schematic window around as much as you like, just as you would move objects around the scene, with the translate menu cells. It's even a good idea to lay out the items in some sort of order that makes sense to you in relation to the model you are building.

For example, if you are building a model of a '57 Chevy, you could organize the schematic so the car body is in the center and tires are placed off to each side, one front and one rear. That way you can easily choose whichever tire you want to work on, without struggling to find it in the scene.

There are also automatic commands to clean up and organize the Schematic view, located in the menu bar at the top of the Schematic View window.

The Layout icon, shaped like an L in the title bar, brings up a dialog (see Figure 2.24) with many options for you to explore. The options I find most useful are the Fit to Window Ratio button, which organizes objects in a rectangular area; the Compact Empty Areas check box, which keeps objects from migrating out in the Schematic window until its a mile wide; and the Draw Parallel Links box, which uses horizontal and vertical lines to connect objects in hierarchies instead of diagonal lines. Try them out.

With the dialog box closed, The CLEAN_ALL command in the menu bar moves all the objects in the scene to a default organization, which is good if your organization is a mess, but bad if you have things laid out just as you want them.

DEFCOL applies default coloring to an object, an option that is enabled by default.

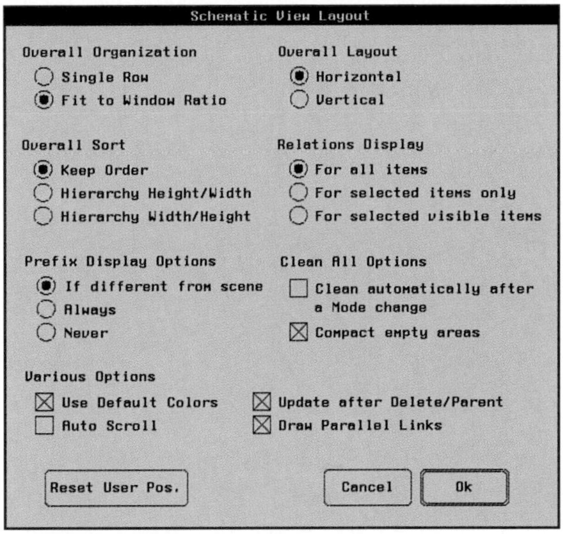

FIGURE 2.24   *The Schematic View Layout dialog box.*

Open/Close allows you to collapse hierarchies that take up a lot of space in the window, simplifying your scene view. With Open/Close activated, the middle mouse button collapses and the left mouse button expands. If the object you clicked is not a branch node, the left mouse button brings up the Info Selection dialog, useful for naming your objects.

In recent versions of Softimage you can accomplish all these things without the Open/Close command, by simply double-clicking a hierarchy or object with the same buttons. (See Figure 2.25.)

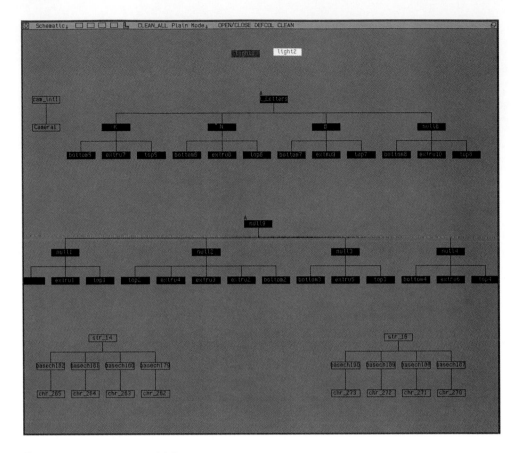

FIGURE 2.25   *An organized Schematic view.*

MOVING THE OBJECT LOCAL CENTER

Because objects scale, rotate, and translate from the local center of an object, moving the local center offers a lot of interesting opportunities. At the simplest level, moving the local center allows you to define where the axis of rotation is for each object.

Moving the center is simple: Click the CTR mode box in the lower-left corner to enter the center mode. The local center becomes visible now, as a small red, green, and blue set of axes. Now all the transformations apply to the local center of the selected object, not the vertices of that object.

TUTORIAL: THE PLANETS, ROUND 2

Recall the Planets scene to try out moving local centers. (See Figure 2.26.)

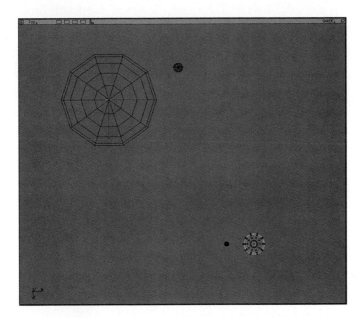

FIGURE 2.26 *The Earth with its local center moved to the center of the Sun.*

1. **The Sun.**

   When you scale the Sun, it seems to grow from the center. That's because the local center of the object is in the geometric center of the Sun. If the center is outside the sun, things would happen differently.

   Try this out by moving the local center away from the sun with the CTR mode button activated and then, back in OBJ mode, scaling the Sun. The Sun should deform oddly, seeming to expand and contract away from the local center.

   To put the center back, set the scale of the Sun back to 1,1,1 with the triangular Scale tabs and then use the Effect→Freeze→Transformations. This useful effect moves the center back to the global center (not the center of the object, the center of the universe) and resets any rotation or scaling that has been performed on the center. Now the Sun should scale normally, from a local center in the middle of its volume.

2. **The Earth.**

Currently, the Earth cannot orbit the Sun independently. If the local center of the Earth is in the center of the Sun, however, the Earth (and child moon) could revolve around the Sun in a natural manner.

Select the Earth, and move the local center into the global center, which happens to be the center of the Sun, by either manually translating the local center in CTR mode, or by using the Effect→Freeze→Transformations command. Now, back in OBJ mode, select the Earth as a branch (middle mouse button, which selects the moon as well) and use the RotY menu cell. Now the Earth orbits its local center, which is attached to the Sun. Since the Sun is the parent of the Earth, when we select the Sun as a tree (right mouse button) and move it out of the global center, the relationship with the Earth remains as it should, and the Earth still orbits the Sun.

3. **The Moon.**

Move the local center of the moon to the center of the Earth, and see how the moon now orbits the Earth, which can orbit the Sun, which can orbit about itself. Softimage hierarchies make this possible by keeping the transformations of each node relative to the branch above it.

The hierarchy of objects keeps your scenes organized and also allows the manipulation and animation of complex, inter-related systems like our galaxy. Good scene management with named objects and organized schematic views keeps your work moving forward.

CONCLUSION

In Chapter 2, you were introduced to some of the basic concepts involved in using the software to make new animation scenes. These fundamental commands form the backbone of your creative work.

Specifically, you learned how to:

- Create, save, and delete your scenes.
- Move scenes around and manage scene components with DB Manager and DB Exchange.

- Create models built from primitive objects and text.

- Move objects around in space and arrange them as needed.

- Organize complex sets of objects into a hierarchy and manipulate the whole hierarchy as one object.

© Bryan Ballinger 1998

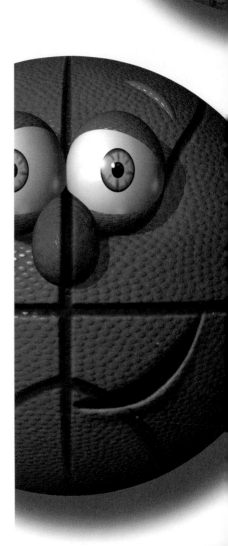

CHAPTER 3

PRODUCING YOUR FIRST SOFTIMAGE ANIMATION

Now that you know how to create simple shapes, lay them out with transformations, group them into hierarchies, and organize your scenes, it's time for you to take the last steps toward producing your first complete animation. You're ready to tackle the basics of lighting, camera work, and rendering. In this chapter, you learn how lighting works within Softimage, what you can do with the virtual camera, and which renderer to choose to use for your animations.

This chapter covers:

- Lighting terminology
- Basic color theory
- Different types of lights
- The Softimage Lighting dialog box
- Camera fundamentals
- How rendering works
- Different renderers in Softimage 3D|Extreme
- Trading off time versus quality

LIGHTING BASICS

When you have a scene layed out just the way you want it, the next step is often to design the lighting that you want. Just as in film and on the stage, lighting in Softimage makes all the difference. Good lighting makes a scene come alive, and bad lighting makes it look flat and disinteresting, or worse. Designing good lighting isn't any tougher than setting up bad lighting; it just requires three prerequisites:

- Understanding the technical aspects
- Understanding basic color theory
- Making a lighting plan

The technical aspects of lighting for the movies or the stage are a lot more demanding than they are for Softimage. In Softimage, you don't have to know your volts, watts, and amps, you never repair electrical cords, and you never heft huge, hot light racks. But you will need to know some physics, so you can describe what you want from Softimage. In this chapter, you learn about a few kinds of light emitters and to look at how light works in the natural surroundings in which you find yourself every day.

Basic understanding of color theory is what separates an artist from a technician. Understanding how colors mix, which colors look good together, and which colors to use for specific tasks helps you make better color choices than just taking a random stab at the color picker. In this chapter, we'll discuss just the rudiments of color: some different color spaces, the spectrum, and color mixing.

After you know how to pick colors, the last step is to spend some time thinking about what you want the lighting in your scene to look like. Everyone can make a lighting plan, but few people do! A friend of mine is fond of saying "When you fail to plan, you plan to fail," and that is certainly true in lighting. Simply thinking about what you want before you do it leads to better results: actually diagramming your lighting plan is what separates the amateurs from the experts. A lighting plan can be simple: just make sure that you have an outline of how to provide illumination for the areas of the scene to which you want to draw attention, while leaving the unimportant areas dim.

My theory is "obscure, don't illuminate," which means that I spend just as much time draping the stuff I don't want seen in a veil of darkness as I do focusing light on a shot's center of attention. Remember, patterns of light and darkness add detail and interest to a scene. In general, hang lights to shine on all the important elements, then adjust their intensities to reach the balance you want in the scene.

LIGHT AND COLOR

The best way to understand how to choose and mix colors is to examine the *hue, saturation,* and *value* (HSV) color system. (See Figure 3.1.) One good way to visualize the contribution of hue, saturation, and value is to imagine a bucket filled with white paint that you need to mix to a specified shade to cover a wall.

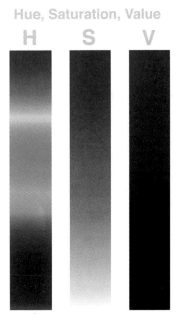

FIGURE 3.1   *The Hue, Saturation, and Value scales.*

Before you get your paint stirrer out, a little physics: What we perceive as the color of light is the wavelength of the light that is bouncing off of the items we are looking at and is recorded by our optic array. The wavelengths of light in the visual spectrum range from red at the low end to violet at the high end. This is often called the *ROY G. BIV* color scale, which is a useful mnemonic for red, orange, yellow, green, blue, indigo, violet. The colors at the lower end of the spectrum are called the *warm* colors, whereas the high end colors are called the *cool* colors. The more accurate term for the colors in the spectrum is *hue*. The first step in mixing your paint is to pick the hue (the pigment) you want from the spectrum. (See Figure 3.2.)

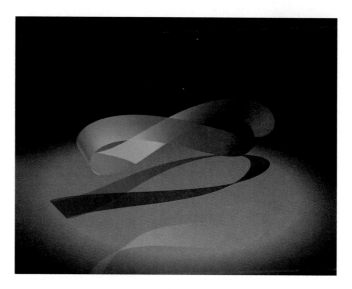

FIGURE 3.2   *Hue: The ROY G. BIV spectrum.*

NOTE

In Softimage lighting, changing the value of the light is the only way to turn the intensity of the light up and down. Lights may even have a negative value, causing them to suck light out of a scene, like a black hole.

Saturation is the proportion of hue (pigment) to white in the light. As the saturation goes down, the color approaches white. As the saturation goes up, the color of the light (and the paint) becomes more vibrant and intense. In the paint analogy, the saturation is how much pigment you add to the white paint. The more you add, the more colorful the paint becomes. (See Figure 3.3.)

Value is technically how much light is absorbed versus emitted by the color applied to a surface. As the value decreases, the color gets darker and darker, finally becoming black. In the paint analogy, it's like adding a black pigment to deepen the color, turning bright purple paint to eggplant. (See Figure 3.4.)

FIGURE 3.3   *Saturation: More saturated and less saturated colors of the same hue.*

FIGURE 3.4   *Value: The same hue and saturation with different values.*

The most common system for mixing colors in a computer is the RGB (red, green, blue) system. By mixing these primary colors in the right proportions, it's possible to make almost any shade. But it's not easy. In fact, using RGB to pick colors is like running a marathon while carrying a bowling ball. For instance, you can't pick colors by spectrum. And, if you do finally get a hue that you like, there is no way to keep the hue constant while you saturate or desaturate, or make the color brighter or dimmer. The best thing to do is never use the RGB system and immediately convert to using the HSV system. You can always switch in Softimage by clicking the RGB button in the Create Light dialog until it says HSV.

DIFFUSE, AMBIENT, SPECULAR LIGHT

Now let's talk about the different components of lighting on objects. When you hold a white plastic ball up in front of a light, it displays the effects of *diffuse* lighting, *ambient* lighting, and *specular* highlighting. (See Figure 3.5.)

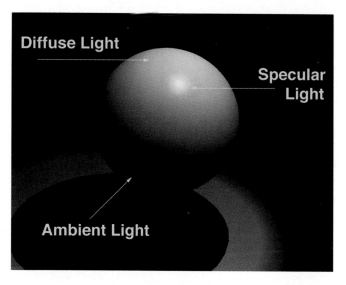

FIGURE 3.5　*Diffuse, ambient, and specular light.*

Diffuse lighting is the lighting caused by direct illumination of a light shining directly on the surface. The diffuse light is the color of the light, bouncing off the surface and coming to your eyes. The diffuse color you perceive is actually the color of the light mixed with the color of the surface it bounced off. If the plastic ball is white, you can assume that the color of light you see on the ball is, in fact, the color of the light. If the ball is pink, the light would look pinker than it actually is. Diffuse light is the most important component of lighting in the scene because it shows the coloration and texture of the objects in that scene.

Ambient lighting is the light that reveals the back, unlit side of an object. In real life, ambient light starts out from the direct sources of illumination and then bounces many times off the objects in the environment until it comes in very small amounts from all directions. It tends to be mixed in color and not very powerful. It's the kind of light that you see under the couch or behind the refrigerator. Because there is no such thing as indirect illumination in raytracing (the radiosity algorithm does not provide it), you need to add a little ambiance to make the scene look real. Unfortunately, Softimage by default adds about 30% gray ambient light to the scene and to each material, which makes objects look dull and lifeless. The ambient component can be turned down in Atmosphere→Ambient and on each material when you define its color. On your plastic ball, the ambient light is on the dark side of the object. The final ambience on an object is affected by both settings.

Specular light is the highlight that you see on shiny surfaces. It is a slightly diffuse reflection from the light source (or light sources) in the room. Very smooth shiny objects have a very small, precise specular dot, whereas rougher matte colored objects have a broader, more spread out specular smear. Metals, being both reflective and often rough, tend to have very broad and very bright specular highlights called *blooms*. The specular highlight is also a visual cue showing you the number and direction of the light sources.

SHADOWS

In real life, every light casts shadows. But in Softimage, you can choose whether each light casts shadows. (See Figure 3.6.) If you decide a light needs shadows, you can choose from two different methods of creating them.

FIGURE 3.6   *This car was rendered without shadows.*

The most accurate method is to *raytrace* the shadows, which means that the raytracing rendering algorithm will be used on all objects that are hit by the light. Raytracing is a somewhat slower rendering algorithm than scanline shading, so raytraced shadows come at a cost of additional rendering time. Raytraced shadows, however, are more accurate. (See Figure 3.7.)

FIGURE 3.7 *The hard shadow edges show that this car was rendered with raytraced shadows.*

The other option is to use a *depth map* to fake the shadows. (See Figure 3.8.) Softimage automatically creates a depth map, which is similar to a texture map, for each light with depth-mapped shadows. The depth map tells Softimage how far away objects are from the light, so it can make a choice about which objects shadow which other objects. This method is inaccurate, however, and is limited by the resolution of the shadow map that you choose.

HARD SHADOWS VERSUS DIFFUSE SHADOWS

Shadows in real life don't have hard edges. But in CGI imagery, we most often see perfect shadows with very sharp edges delineating them. That looks unnatural and keeps us from good lighting. In the computer, the source of illumination is one single, infinitely small point in space from which all illumination proceeds. That means that when the raytracing algorithm draws a line between the light point and the edge of the object, that shadow edge is going to be very consistent and accurate.

FIGURE 3.8   *The softer shadow edge shows that the image was rendered with depth-mapped shadows.*

In real life, light doesn't come from such a point source. Every light bulb that we use is coated on the inside with a white powder that diffuses the light so that rays come from all over the surface of the bulb. Overhead lights often have large plastic diffuser screens, and fluorescent lights emit from a very large surface area. In these cases, because light comes from many different locations, there is no hard edge to the object shadow, and it looks more natural. There are two ways to get this effect in Softimage, by using Soft Shadows or mental ray Area lights. Mental ray Area lights simulate more accurate soft shadows and better diffuse lighting at the expense of additional rendering time (more on these later).

THE UMBRA AND PENUMBRA

In real life, if there is one light in the room, and you hold an object in the way of the light, it casts a shadow that is very dark. The *umbra* (in Softimage) is the area of the image that is in the shadow. In Softimage, you can adjust the amount of umbra. The *penumbra* is the area between the umbra and the nonshadowed areas where the light and dark blend together. (See Figure 3.9.) When you choose Soft Shadows you can also have a penumbra, and change the softness and value of that penumbra.

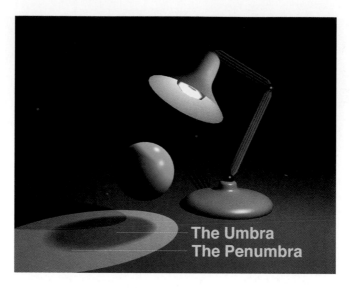

The Umbra
The Penumbra

FIGURE 3.9   *The umbra and penumbra.*

LIGHT FALLOFF AND INTENSITY

If you think back to your basic physics class in high school, you will probably remember that light can be thought of as a wave that is emitted from a point in space and that propagates outward in all directions.

Light has a certain amount of light energy that it generates each instant (a *lumen*), and as each wave of light expands, that quantity of light energy is distributed over a larger and larger area. As it is spread over a greater area, the *intensity* of the light energy on any object in the wave's path decreases. This is called *falloff* (see Figure 3.10), and we know that it's true because a flashlight works better on near objects than on far objects.

The way that light falls off from a point source is simply exponential, so in real life the intensity of the light at a given distance away from the source is given by 1 divided by the radius squared. (Softimage doesn't seem to be accurate to real life falloffs, however.) All right you say, but who cares? Doesn't Softimage do this for me when I use the light?

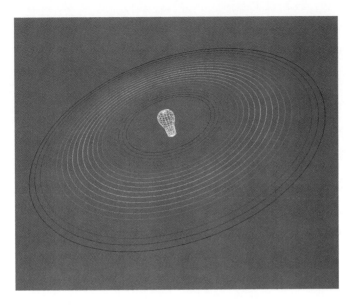

FIGURE 3.10   *Falloff means less light energy farther from the bulb.*

Well, sort of, but unless you understand the technical part you'll never be able to control your lights, because Softimage doesn't have a command for the intensity of your lights, just for the *falloff*. In Softimage, by default, all lights have a start and end falloff of 10,000 Softimage units, which means that the light will be infinitely bright until it suddenly becomes completely dark, thereby defying the laws of physics. (See Figure 3.11.)

To give your lights a natural falloff, you have to change the settings for Start Falloff (the distance at which the light begins to get dimmer) and the End Falloff (the point at which your light no longer adds any light to the scene). One more thing about the falloff and light intensity: Because the intensity falls off exponentially, your light gets dim fast! Most of the light peters out in the first third of the falloff, and objects in the last half of the falloff range get just about no light. So if you place a light and you can't see the effect, check the falloff with this in mind.

THE LIGHTS MENU

In Softimage, all the commands for creating, editing, and using lights can be found in the Lights menu cell. Choosing Lights→Define or Lights→Edit brings up the same dialog box, which is shown in Figure 3.12.

FIGURE 3.11   *Light falls off fast!*

Lights in Softimage 3D|Extreme may be of four basic types: Point, Spot, Infinite, and Sun. Each one behaves a little differently, so it's useful to understand those differences before you choose one to work with.

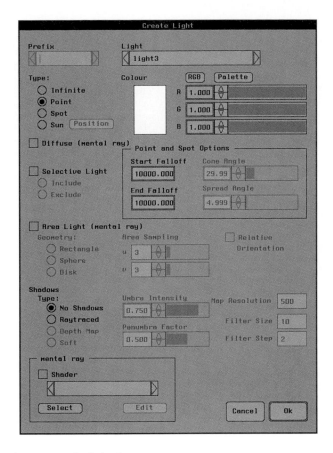

FIGURE 3.12   *The Create Light dialog box.*

POINT LIGHTS

The *Point* light is the most commonly used, simulating a bare light bulb hanging in an empty space. The Softimage icon that represents the Point light looks, in fact, like a light bulb. (See Figure 3.13.) Rays of light are emitted from a Point light equally in all directions, so the rays are nonparallel and converge at the location of the light. The falloff determines the radius around the light that it affects. Objects closer to the light are illuminated more brightly, objects farther from the light are more dim. Point lights may have shadows, but only raytraced shadows. If you plan to use the mental ray as your renderer, you might choose the Area Light option with the Point light.

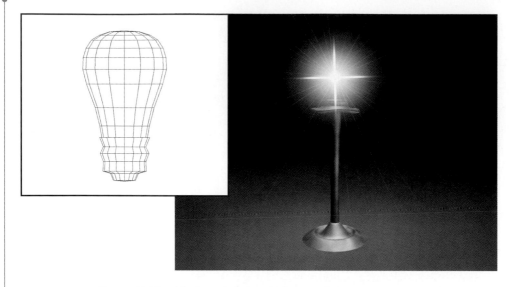

FIGURE 3.13   *The Point light icon and a Point light in action.*

You can translate around a Point light to any position in the scene, but you can't rotate or scale it. The color, falloff, and position of the light may be animated by setting keys within the Lights dialog box.

SPOT LIGHTS

Spot lights are directional lights, with all rays emanating from a single point in a cone that you define. (See Figure 3.14.) If the cone is not visible, you can show it with the Show→Cone menu command. The cone is measured in degrees from dead center with the Cone Angle slider. The edge of the cone can have a soft transition from light to dark, and you can set the width of the transition in degrees from the cone edge with the Spread slider. The direction of the cone is determined by the *light interest*, which is a null object that acts as a target for the light. The falloff of the light can be manipulated, and the cone will show the ending falloff distance. The interest and the light itself can be moved and rotated, but not scaled.

You can set the Cone Angle directly in the Light→Define or Light→Edit dialog box, next to the Falloff controls. The softness of the edge between the cone of light and the outer darkness can be modified with the Spread Angle, creating a softer transition around the Spot light area.

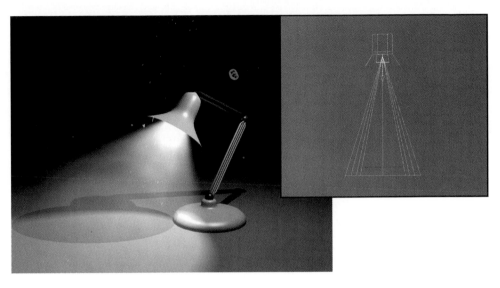

FIGURE 3.14   *The Spot light icon and a Spot light in action.*

A Spot light can have shadows, either depth mapped or raytraced. If they are depth mapped, a Spot light may have soft shadows (accomplished by blurring the edge of the shadow map). If the shadows are raytraced and you plan to render with the mental ray, you may use the Area Light (mental ray) option with a Spot light.

The light color, falloff, cone and spread angle, light and interest location, and rotation can all be animated by setting keys within the Create dialog box.

INFINITE LIGHTS

Infinite lights are lights that imitate a very bright, very distant light source. (See Figure 3.15.) All rays are parallel, so shadows will have a very hard edge. An Infinite light can be translated around, and the icon will show a vector drawn to the global center. The direction of the vector will be the direction of the rays. Infinite lights are great for sunlight or starlight. Infinite light will reach all objects in the scene equally and does not have a falloff. Infinite lights can have shadows. The color and position of the Infinite light may be animated.

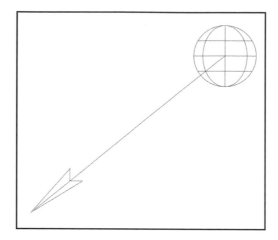

FIGURE 3.15 *The Infinite light icon.*

SUN LIGHTS

Sun lights are special forms of the Infinite light that can be created and placed by latitude and longitude in the imaginary Softimage space, and by time in the real world. (See Figure 3.16.) For instance, you may set a Sun light to show you the lighting angle at 12:01 PM in Paris, France on January 11, 1988. That location and time may be changed and keyframed to animate along a realistic path. Sun lights may have ray-traced shadows but not falloff.

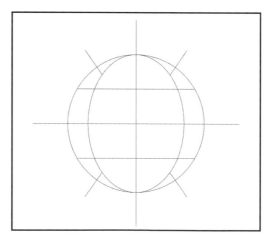

FIGURE 3.16 *The Sun light icon.*

TUTORIAL: LIGHTING UP STONEHENGE

In this tutorial, you use each of the types of lights to illuminate the Stonehenge scene, giving you a feeling for using each of them.

1. Using Point Lights.

Use the Get command to retrieve the Stonehenge scene that you made in Chapter 2, "Getting Started—Moving in Space." If you want, you may use the premade scene, named Stonehenge, in the content database on the CD-ROM. Point lights are good for two primary types of lighting: fill lights and natural light sources, such as fires and light bulbs. Use the Light→Define menu command to call up the Lights dialog box, and choose the Point light type. Set the Start Falloff value to 0 and the End Falloff to 50 Softimage units, making a Point light that will illuminate all objects within a sphere of 50 Softimage units in radius. Click the color model selector button (RGB) until it is set to the HSV model, and then get a color for the light that is a warm yellow hue, with a Value of 0.15 and a very low Saturation, like 0.125, and a Value of 0.75. This means that the light will be mostly white, with a little bit of yellow mixed in, and the light will be at 50% intensity. Turn on the Raytraced Shadows option. (See Figure 3.17.)

FIGURE 3.17 *A single point light within the circle, with raytraced shadows.*

Place the light about 8 Softimage units off the ground plane in the middle of the portals. Switch to the Matter mode, and use the Preview→All command to see a rendered preview of the scene. Note how all the shadows fall away from the center of the circle of portals, and how the portals pick up some of the color of the light.

Now go back to edit the light by selecting it and using the Light→Edit menu cell. Change the Value parameter of the color to 1, which turns the light up to 100% intensity. Render another preview to see the difference.

Finally, edit the light again and change the hue to a cool blue, with an intensity of 40% (Value parameter at 0.40), increase the Saturation to about 0.2, and set a Start Falloff of 100 and an End Falloff of 200. Translate the light to be 4 units in Y from the ground plane, and 40 units in negative X so that the light is off to the side of the Stonehenge circle. Preview the scene again. This light will now be your fill light and will add dimension to the scene.

If you haven't already, set the Atmosphere Ambiance down to very nearly black, instead of the default gray. (See Figure 3.18.)

FIGURE 3.18   *The same scene, with less ambient light and stronger shadows.*

2. Using Spot Lights.

Use the Light→Define menu to get a new light. In the Create dialog box, choose the Spot light type. Choose a color that you like, and set the Cone Angle to 45 degrees and the Spread to 10 degrees. Leave the shadows off for this light, name it PortalSpot1, and close the dialog box. (See Figure 3.19.)

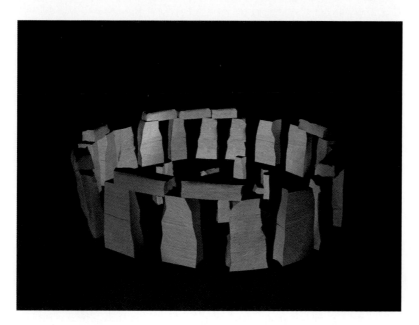

FIGURE 3.19 *Two Spot lights shining on the portals.*

Now change one of your View windows to be the Schematic view, and locate the light you just made at the right end of the Schematic layout. The light will be colored orange and be composed of two objects: the light itself and the interest. Select the light and translate it to a position of 15 units in front of a portal, on the ground plane. Now select the interest, and translate it to a point above and beyond the portal, so that the Spot shines up on the portal. Render a preview to see how that looks. You can aim the Spot light at any of the other portals by simply moving the interest to the point where you want the Spot light aimed.

Make another identical Spot light by selecting the one you just made and duplicating it with the Duplicate→Selection menu cell. Place this light in front of another portal and aim it so that it lights the portal from the bottom up.

FIGURE 3.20   *An infinite moonlight.*

3. Using Infinite Lights.

Create a new light, this time an Infinite light. (See Figure 3.20.)

Name it Moon and give it a purple hue with very little saturation (so the color is more white than purple) and a Value of about 0.8. Use raytraced shadows, and set the Umbra to 0, which means that the area in the shadow of the moonbeams will be completely obscured, unless another light shines on that area. Close the dialog box, and translate the moon above the scene and a little to one side so that the moon casts shadows away from the portals. (See Figure 3.21.)

Render a preview. You should now have a nice dark night scene, with Spot lights illuminating a few portals and moonlight illuminating everything with a cold glow.

4. Using Sun Lights.

It's time for the sun to come up. Create another light, this time a Sun light, with a yellowish hue and a Value of 1.5. (You have to enter that by hand because the slider goes up only to 1.) Use raytraced shadows with an Umbra of 0.5. Use the Positions button to bring up the placement dialog box, and choose the appropriate latitude and longitude for south England where Stonehenge is located. Try a latitude of 50 degrees 20 minutes and a longitude of 3 degrees. Set the time to noon on the winter solstice, December 22nd. (See Figure 3.22.)

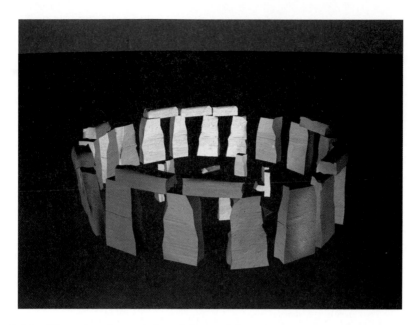

FIGURE 3.21   *The circle with moonlight and the Spot lights.*

FIGURE 3.22   *Sunlight overpowers all the other dramatic lights.*

Render another preview, and note how the much more intense Sun has overpowered the effects of the other lights. The other lights, however, are still there and because the color difference between the warm sun and the cool moon and fill lights is complimentary, the effect maximizes the dimensionality of the scene and emphasizes the shadows. Save the scene you have, because we'll come back to it later and finish it off with a camera path animation.

THE CAMERA

When the lighting is to your liking, you're ready to set up the virtual camera (see Figure 3.23), determining the point of view to be rendered. The Perspective View window shows you what the camera sees in your virtual space. Unlike a real camera's, the virtual camera's motion is not limited by any physical hardware or construction: You can place the camera anywhere you want to get a shot. But just because you *can* do anything with the camera doesn't mean you *should*. Relying on traditional cinematography, knowing when to move the camera and when to keep it still, and breaking your animation into discrete shots instead of continuous camera flythroughs will make your work look more professional.

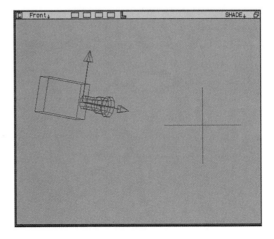

FIGURE 3.23 *The Camera icon and the Schematic representation.*

BASIC CAMERA MOVEMENT

You can move the camera in several ways. As mentioned in Chapter 1, "Exploring the Softimage Interface," when you use the O, P, and Z supra keys in the Perspective window, you are actually moving the camera around in space and changing the zoom angle of the lens. Usually, you simply see the results of these moves, not the camera's location. By default, the camera is hidden in your scene. You can show it with the Camera→Show Camera command. When the camera is shown on screen, you can select it just like any other object, and translate it and the camera interest through space to get the shot you want. Similar to a light interest, the camera interest is a null object that acts as a target for the camera. Because the camera always looks at the interest, the first step in framing a shot is to place the interest where you want to look.

THE CAMERA VIEW CONE

A tremendously helpful tool for placing the camera is the *camera view cone*, which is a rectangular projection from the camera that shows what will be in the field of view. (See Figure 3.24.) Toggle this on and off with the Show→Cone command. When it is on and the camera is selected, you will see the cone in the all views except Perspective. If you want to see the camera cone even when it is not selected, use the Show→Cones (Unselected) command.

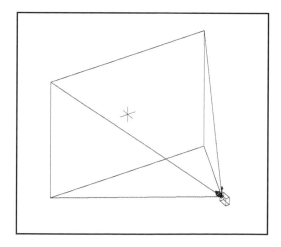

FIGURE 3.24 *The camera view cone shows where the camera looks and how far the camera can see.*

*Coca-Cola Factory. Client: The Coca-Cola Company. Ad Agency: Edge Creative.
Digital Animation: Little Fluffy Clouds. ©1997 the Coca-Cola Co.*

Betsy de Fries and Jerry van de Beek, Founders

Little Fluffy Clouds was founded in May of 1996 by English designer/producer Betsy de Fries and Dutch animation director, Jerry van de Beek. Little Fluffy Clouds (www.littlefluffyclouds.com) specializes in 3D animation and design, enhancing traditional cel animation by harmoniously integrating traditional styles with the best that digital design has to offer.

In a short time the studio's work has received much recognition. "Coca-Cola Pictogram" received a 1997 Gold Creativity 27 award. "Mainstay Up...Down... Up...," received a 1997 Bronze Clio and a London International Advertising Award for Best Animation of 1997. Both spots were featured in the 1997 SIGGRAPH Computer Animation Festival. "Coca-Cola Factory" garnered a best direction award at the 1998 Pasedena World Animation Festival.

Anthony: Lets talk about "Coca-Cola Factory," and your animation technique, the rubber hose style. Is that is typical of your style, or did the client bring it?

Jerry: George Evelyn, the director, for (Colossal) Pictures, came up with the idea for the story, using the rubber hose style. To quote him, "In rubber hose everything you see is a character."

George always wanted to do something in 3D. He came to us with an idea for a Coke commercial based around a factory with funky machines, not like a regular factory, but one where everything had a face and a personality and where everything was alive. In this style of animation everything is bouncing, usually to a syncopated rhythm. With a 3D animation package, like Softimage, you have the freedom to easily bend and stretch all kinds of objects, even a machine and a factory. It's also a faster way

Anthony: Do you think there is a freedom to working on this type of deadline?

Jerry: I like it a lot. I don't like long deadlines. People start looking at every little detail and the life of the project goes down the drain. On a short project, like this one, you make the decisions as you work, going by your intuition— and if you are an artist, your intuition is creative.

to animate. The production timeline for the first Coke Factory was 12 weeks—including developing new techniques, writing an in-house program, DIANA, to integrate the 2D cel animation with the digital, digital ink and paint, compositing, post, music, and colorization—in short everything!

A flow chart showing the process of creating Coca-Cola Factory. Client: The Coca-Cola Company. Ad Agency: Edge Creative. Digital Animation: Little Fluffy Clouds.

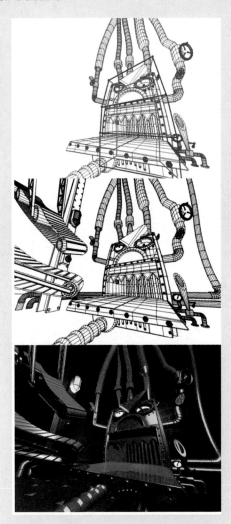

Different stages of the modeling process show the evolution of the machines and the lattices that animate them. Client: The Coca-Cola Company. Ad Agency: Edge Creative. Digital Animation: Little Fluffy Clouds. ©1997 The Coca-Cola Co.

The modeled frames are converted and output as guides for 2D cel animators to draw the characters over. Client: The Coca-Cola Company. Ad Agency: Edge Creative. Digital Animation: Little Fluffy Clouds. © 1997 The Coca-Cola Co.

Anthony: Only lately have I been trying to read about color. Your work strikes me as having very rich and beautiful color.

Jerry: Yeah, what we do is think about the style, what kind of look we are trying to achieve. Using 2D drawings, 3D animation, and compositing effects we nail down that style. Using colors: primary colors, saturated or not, complex shadows or simple shadows, like the little puddle shadows that we used in "Coca-Cola Factory" or ray-traced reflections as opposed to non-ray-traced reflection maps, and so on.

Betsy: You want to make sure that the colors balance each other out. It's a definite art, being a colorist.

Jerry: Normally you would use one color for the diffuse color, black for the ambient color, and white for the highlight color. Using black, the saturation falls off, getting dirtier and dirtier as the color changes to the ambient color of the object. But if you don't use black as the ambient—for example using a non-pure red on a yellow material, as the ambient color—you will get a nicer falloff on a longer 24-bit range. The reason for this is that you stay in the 24-bit color range which gives you the maximum amount of steps to go from your diffuse color to your ambient color. Were you to use black as an ambient color you would go from a 24-bit color to an 8-bit color, which lessens your falloff range. This also happens if you use pure red, pure green, or pure blue. Those three together form the 24-bit color. Individually they are only 8 bits deep.

So, my tip is to be careful in your use of primary colors and gray-scale and try to use the full color range for your highlight, ambient, and diffuse colors. Playing with ambient color and highlight color is very useful to create a warm or a cooler image. Having your diffuse color falloff to a blue towards the highlight and ambient is good for a rainy day scene. Having it falloff to a yellow or an orange will create a warmer scene for a sunny day. A lot of times we use a different highlight color, making it cooler, and sometimes we do change the color of the light. When each shot is different you can change the lighting for each shot to make it look good.

Anthony: What's your take on creativity and working with a partner?

Betsy: The magic in the collaboration is in the mix of abilities and a well-rounded knowledge. That's what produces creativity.

A completed 3D rendered frame with 2D cel animation composited on top. Client: The Coca-Cola Company. Ad Agency: Edge Creative. Digital Animation: Little Fluffy Clouds. ©1997 The Coca-Cola Co.

Jerry: Betsy is a walking directory of art and history. She knows everything! A lot of times the initial idea comes from Betsy. We go to museums together to look at art; we wander around and talk about concepts. Our foundation is not only based on knowing the software packages. As an animator you want to work with someone that has a wide range of knowledge in art, and you want to learn as much about art and culture yourself. It gives you more options in creativity.

Anthony: You've certainly achieved a remarkable level of acclaim in your first two years. Where do you plan to take your studio?

Betsy: As a company, we formed to do creative work together—and to take more holidays. We didn't want to have a large company, although I think some of those initial goals changed by what happened to us.

What we thought would take us maybe three years has really only taken us about a year: setting up, reaching certain goals, creating an identity, establishing ourselves, and remaining solvent. We are way ahead of where we thought we would be. But there is that danger that we could run before we really know how to walk. It's a fine line. Everybody says, "Don't get big. You'll spend all your time managing. You'll have to change to accommodate all the growth." It does seem that if you have a lot of people you pretty much have to take anything and everything that comes along to keep the studio going. I think we were pretty determined not to take on infomercials and non-creative productions. We really want our hand in the creativity. Eventually that creativity will lead to expansion and hopefully we will have built a solid foundation to be able to take that growth in our stride.

114

115

© 1997 The Coca-Cola Co.

© 1997 The Coca-Cola Co.

Avoiding Camera Distortion

A common problem for rookies in Softimage is that after they work with the camera supra keys, the Perspective view becomes terribly distorted and generally frightful. This usually happens when users zoom out as far as possible using the Z supra key in an attempt to see as much as possible of the scene. The extreme zooming creates a 180-degree fisheye perspective view that distorts elements in view. (See Figure 3.25.) The solution is to leave the zoom at a reasonable 45 degrees, and use the P supra key to dolly in and out instead. When the camera view becomes too confused for you to deal with, use the Camera→Reset to restore the camera to a default zoom and position.

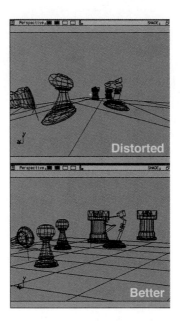

Figure 3.25   *A distorted view caused by a super wide angle and the same view with a better zoom angle.*

Other Camera Commands

Three more commands round out the Camera menu cell: Roll, Settings, and Picture Format. You'll need them to fine-tune your camera's movement, focus, and aspect ratio, respectively.

The Camera→Roll command allows you to set the roll of the camera, as if the camera were on a pivot running down the axis it looks along. The roll is useful for first person views from a plane, boat, submarine, and so on, where the view needs to rotate.

The Camera→Settings command calls up the Camera Settings dialog box (see Figure 3.26) with a great many complex-looking controls in it, but only two are commonly useful: the Custom-Angle, which sets the precise field of view and has the same effect as the Z supra key with the middle and left mouse buttons; and the Depth of Field controls.

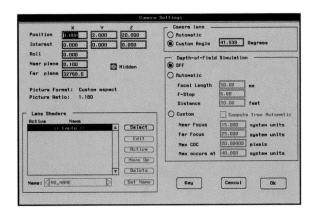

FIGURE 3.26   *The Camera Settings dialog controls the camera view angle, and near and far view planes.*

The Camera→Picture Format command brings up the very important Picture Format dialog box (see Figure 3.27), where you set the *aspect ratio* of the view for your camera. Aspect ratio is the ratio between the width and the height of the image you plan to render. Different output formats have different requirements. Television, which conforms to the NTSC standard in the U.S., uses an aspect ratio of 1.333, which means that the image is slightly wider than it is tall. Film ratio is much wider than it is tall. Choose the aspect ratio that meets the specs of your output. If you don't know what to pick, use NTSC.

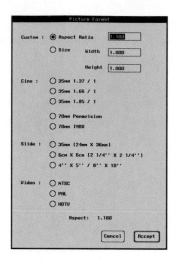

FIGURE 3.27   *The Picture Format dialog controls the aspect ratio of the camera view.*

TUTORIAL: SET THE CAMERA FOR STONEHENGE

Finally, it's time to learn a simple method of animation: camera movement. At the most basic level, animation is just the change in something over time. Here in the Stonehenge scene, you will change the position of the camera over time, to create a simple fly through of the space. To do this, you affix the camera to a spline called a *path*. The camera follows the path, while remaining pointed at the camera interest.

1. Draw the Camera Path.

The first step is to draw the path that the camera will take, using a Cardinal spline. Switch back to the Model module, and maximize the Top view so that it fills the screen. Zoom out with the Z supra key until you can see the entire Stonehenge and some of the surrounding terrain.

Choose the Draw→Curve→Cardinal command to activate the spline drawing tool, and start the spline at the edge of the screen, away from the circle of stones, by clicking the left mouse button there. Place the next point halfway to the stones, but closer to one side so the camera doesn't simply head for the middle of the circle. Place another between two portals, followed by another between two portals on the opposite side of the circle, and then a last point further outside the circle. (See Figure 3.28.) This will be the path the camera takes in your animation.

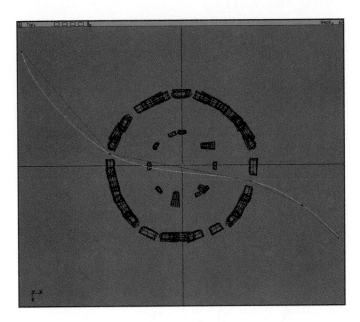

FIGURE 3.28   *Draw a path in the Top view for the camera to follow.*

Now minimize the Top View window back to its original position, so you can see all the views. The spline should still be selected. Because you drew it in the Top view, the XZ plane, it has no Y value, and so lies in the ground plane. Use the TransY menu cell to raise the curve to a height somewhere in the middle of the portals.

2. **Place the Interest.**

   To see the icons that represent the camera and the camera interest, use Camera→Show Camera command. Then select the camera interest, either in the Perspective view (it's the cross-shaped object in the dead center of the Perspective view) or in the Schematic view. Remember, the camera will be looking at the interest at all times. Place the interest in the approxiamted center of the circle, at a height midway up the stone pillars.

3. **Affix the Camera to the Path.**

   Connect the camera to the path you drew. First, select the camera, in one of the Orthographic views, in the Schematic, or with the Camera→Select Camera command. Now switch to the Motion module by pressing the F2 key and choosing the command Path→Pick Path. Click with your left mouse button on the camera path you created to complete the command. A dialog box will pop up asking you for the path timing. The *path timing* is the frame at which the camera will start along the path, and the frame at which it will complete its course along the path. Click the dialog box's Ok button to accept the default range of frames. The camera should now jump to the beginning of the path. (See Figure 3.29.)

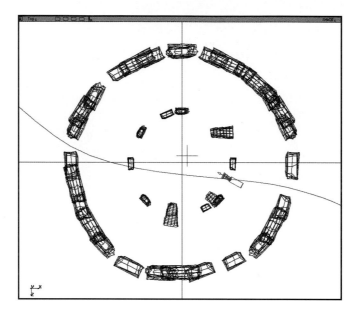

FIGURE 3.29   *The camera now travels along the path and remains focused on the camera interest.*

Click on the play forward triangle in the Time Slider to view the results of your work in the Perspective view.

If, after viewing the animation, you want to change the path taken by the camera, simply use the M supra key (the Move Point command) and click on points that make up the curve to drag the points to other locations. The curve will redraw, and the camera will automatically follow the new path. If you want another interest location, just select the interest and translate it, or draw a path for it as well and use the Path→Pick Path command to set it in motion. When you are satisfied with your work, save the scene.

RENDERING YOUR SCENE

Rendering your scene is the last step in the creative process, and it's the most satisfying because it's the least work. (See Figure 3.30.) Rendering is the process where the computer actually performs the calculations necessary and creates all the final frames of your work. Rendering can be very quick or very time-consuming, depending on a number of factors that include the complexity of your scene, the quality parameters chosen, the size of the image desired, the number of frames needed, and the rendering engine used. In either case, the computer does the hard work, while you get a cup of coffee or go snowboarding for the day.

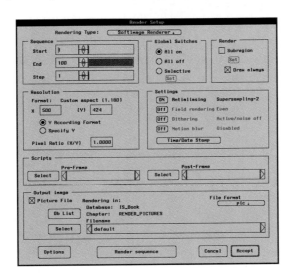

FIGURE 3.30   *The Render Setup dialog in the Matter module.*

HOW RENDERING WORKS

The basic method of rendering works very much like a pinhole camera operating in reverse. Starting at the top-left corner of the frame, Softimage shoots a ray from each pixel through the center of the imaginary camera lens and into the scene. There Softimage follows the ray as it travels through space, until it strikes an object. When the ray strikes an object, Softimage looks at the material color applied to the object, looks at the texture color at that spot on the object, and checks to see what lights shine on the object and how far away the lights are. Using that information, Softimage decides what color the object should be at that precise spot, returns the ray to the pixel from which it was cast, and colors the pixel in with the color of the object that the ray hit.

Sometimes a ray shoots into the scene and doesn't hit anything before reaching the end of the camera far plane. This means there was nothing to see at that point. Softimage uses the background color (usually black) for the pixel that created the ray and records a black pixel in the alpha channel of the image so that other images can be composited into the background.

After all the pixels have had rays cast from them and been colored in, the image is complete. When the frame is done, the finished image is written to disk in the REN-DER_PICTURES subdirectory of the active database, or wherever else you specified that it should go. The files are named with the name you chose, followed by a period and the frame number, followed by a period and the pic file extension that tells other programs what file format it is. An example of a rendered frame filename is stonehenge.2.pic.

To Raytrace or Not to Raytrace

There are complications, of course. If a ray strikes an object that is reflective, the ray has to accumulate some color from that object and then bounce off to strike another object. The Ray Traced Depth, which you specify in the Render Setup dialog's Options dialog (see Figure 3.31), determines how many bounces a ray will follow before it gives up and dies. (See Figure 3.32.) When a ray hits a transparent object, it picks up some color info and then passes through along its original path to hit another object. If the transparent object is refractive, the ray is bent slightly, according to the index of refraction, as it passes through each surface of the object. (See Figure 3.33.) When an object is transparent, refractive, reflective, or lit by a light with a raytraced shadow, Softimage uses the raytracing algorithm for the ray being cast. Otherwise, Softimage uses the faster scanline algorithm. The capability to use different algorithms for different pixels in the same image is an advantage of the Softimage renderer, and part of the reason that the Softimage renderer is so fast.

Antialiasing Means Quality

Because a finished frame is made up of a finite number of small pixels, it's possible for the image to look jagged when complete. We perceive these jaggies (called *aliasing*) when the contrast between neighboring pixels is very high, and especially when the border between areas of high contrast is slightly diagonal on the rendered frame. Called *antialiasing*, the solution is to reduce the contrast between pixels as much as possible, so that pixels blend smoothly into one another. (See Figure 3.34.) Softimage's antialiasing controls are found in the Render dialog's Antialiasing dialog.

Antialiasing becomes particularly noticeable and unpleasant when your work reaches videotape because of technical aspects in how the image is scanned to the TV monitor in separate passes called fields. Good antialiasing is another thing that separates the amateurs from the professionals. Unfortunately, good antialiasing costs more rendering time.

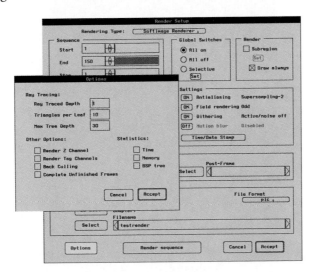

FIGURE 3.31   *Set the Ray Traced Depth for your render in the Options dialog of the Render Setup dialog.*

Normally, rays are cast at the center of each pixel. That means that when adjacent pixels are sampled, the colors in each can be quite different because each ray hits a different part of the scene. To smooth the color values of adjacent pixels accurately, the renderer would need to cast rays at the corners of the pixel as well as the center, and then average the color values it came up with. That, in fact, is how antialiasing works. Setting Antialiasing to 0 casts one ray per pixel, in the center. Setting Antialiasing to 1 casts a 2×2 grid of four rays, more or less at the corners of each pixel, but randomly placed with a jitter quotient to avoid moiré artifacts. Antialiasing of 2 casts a grid of 3×3, or nine rays per pixel, now including the centers of the neighboring pixels in the calculations. So as the Antialiasing value increases, the number of sample rays required increases exponentially.

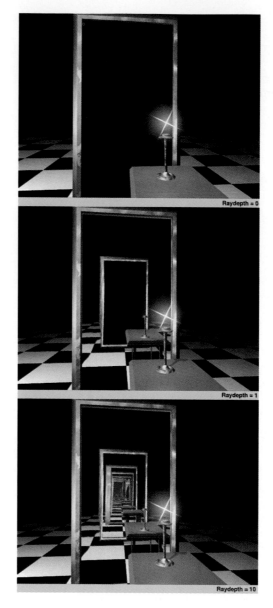

FIGURE 3.32   *The mirrors show the effects of increasing the Ray Traced Depth.*

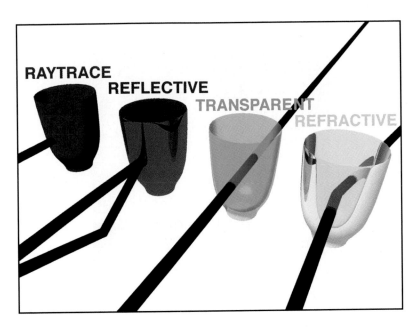

FIGURE 3.33 *Rays bouncing, penetrating, and bending through materials.*

AVAILABLE RENDERING ENGINES

When you're ready to render, you use the Matter module's Render menu cell to open the Render dialog box. A little exploring reveals that the dialog box's Rendering Types drop-down menu contains a number of options. Each of these is a different *rendering engine*, which is a program written to take the information in your scene and convert it into a visual image. Each of the rendering engines takes a different approach and uses a different set of programming techniques called *algorithms* to color in each pixel. Some of the methods result in a more realistic-looking image than others. Usually the better-looking images require more computations per pixel, so when you choose a renderer, you make a choice between quality and time. Some rendering engines enable you to make choices that affect the rendering speed and quality.

NOTE

A little math illustrates why a nice looking render takes so long. Say the image is 640 × 480 pixels in size, or 307,680 pixels. Set Antialiasing to 1 and you cast 1,230,720 rays. At 2 steps of Antialiasing, you cast 2,769,120. At 3 (a reasonable setting for print or video), you get 4,922,880 rays, or 16 times as many as you started with.

FIGURE 3.34   *Three levels of antialiasing on the same image.*

THE OPENGL RENDERER

Generally speaking, rendering an image without shadows, reflections, refractions, or volumetric effects is the fastest method. This technique is called a *scanline renderer*, and all it really considers is the color of an object, the color of the light shining on the object, and the distance and angle between the object and the light. Images rendered this way are great for preview but they lack realism. The OpenGL hardware renderer is an example of this.

THE SOFTIMAGE RENDERER

If you want more realism, the next step up is the Softimage internal renderer, which supports shadows, transparency, reflection, and refraction. The Softimage renderer probably takes longer than the OpenGL renderer, but its results look nicer. The Softimage renderer gains speed by using the scanline approach when it can, and a raytracing algorithm only for objects that require it. The Softimage renderer treats shadows and reflections very quickly, but transparency is slower, and refraction is really slow.

THE MENTAL RAY RENDERER

The mental ray is a stand alone high-quality renderer that comes with only the Extreme version of Softimage 3D. The mental ray is shader based, uses both scanline and raytracing algorithms, and can also render volumetric effects. The mental ray is an extremely flexible rendering tool (see Figure 3.35), and arguably the most powerful renderer available to the public (the other contender being Pixar's RenderMan). The mental ray is a very attractive renderer as well, producing good depth of color and effective bump mapping.

The mental ray can mix a number of different algorithms to make an image. Pictures created with the mental ray tend to look better than those made with the Softimage renderer, but the mental ray often takes more time per image. The mental ray can run in an entirely scanline mode, which allows use of shadows (depth mapped, not raytraced), reflection maps (not raytraced reflections), and transparency, but not refraction. This mode, enabled by turning off the Trace and Shadow check boxes in the mental ray render options, makes the mental ray a very fast renderer, and retains sufficient quality for professional use.

If you choose to use the raytracing algorithm with the mental ray, you may also use volumetric rendering by choosing a volume shader for such effects as volumic lights, smoke, fog, lightning, and so on. This volumic technique requires a great deal of computation, and is the slowest effect you can use.

The mental ray is also a technologically advanced piece of code, supporting distributed rendering on very large computers, including shared memory and massively parallel supercomputers.

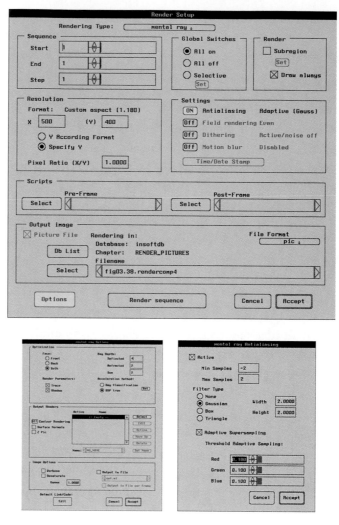

FIGURE 3.35   *The mental ray rendering dialogs.*

In the near future, the mental ray will become the primary renderer for Softimage, so it's high time to get used to it. You use the mental ray by selecting it from the drop box at the top of the Render dialog box.

RENDERERS COMPARED

To get an idea of the different rendering styles and the trade-offs they offer between quality and time, take a look at the rendered images in Figure 3.36 and Table 3.1, which shows the times they took to render.

Renderer: Depthcue   Time: 2 Seconds

Renderer: OpenGL   Time: 5 Seconds

Renderer: Softimage   Time: 33 Seconds

Renderer: mental ray   Time: 5 minutes, 23 Seconds

FIGURE 3.36   *The same image produced by four different renderers.*

TABLE 3.1   TABLE OF COMPARABLE RENDER TIMES

RENDERER	*TIME*
Depthcue	2 seconds
OpenGL	5 seconds
Softimage	33 seconds
Mental ray	5 minutes, 23 seconds

TUTORIAL: RENDERING STONEHENGE

You're ready to try the final stage of the Stonehenge project: rendering. This really is the easy part. Load your most recent Stonehenge scene, and play it back in with the Time Slider to make sure that the animation is ready to go. When you are assured that the camera path is as you like it, you will render the finished scene to a series of files on disk.

1. **Set Up the Render.**

    Now switch to the Matter module (F4 on your keyboard), and choose the Render menu cell. The Render dialog box appears.

    First, look to the top of the dialog box, and click into the Rendering type drop-down menu. All the available renderers are listed here. The full-quality renderers are the Softimage renderer and the mental ray. Choose the Softimage renderer.

    Now note the start and end frames. This sets the range of frames rendered out. Using the Step value, you can render every other frame, every third frame, or any increment, thereby saving time while sampling your work.

    To the right of the Resolution controls are the Settings controls. The Antialiasing button shows the current antialiasing settings. To change them, click the On toggle box, and make your choices. The Bartlett method should be avoided, as it generates more samples than necessary and impacts rendering time tremendously. The Adaptive method first checks adjacent pixels to determine if they are more different than the Div Threshold you specify, and only then casts more rays. Choose a Max Filter of 2.

    The Global Switches allow you to turn off some rendering features, such as reflections, refractions, and shadows, to save time. Leave the Global Switches all on.

2. Set the Options.

Below the Frame Sequence sliders is the Output Resolution box. You may enter a resolution in X and then press the Tab key to use the current aspect ratio to calculate the Y resolution, or you can click the Specify Y radio button and enter a different value by hand. For this project, set the resolution to 300 × 200, which is a good size for a preview because it won't take so long to render.

Leave the other render options alone for now, and enter the name "stonehenge" for your animation in the Filename Edit box. If you have correctly set your own database to be the default database, its name will appear above the filename. If it isn't there, use the DBList button to navigate your filesystem and find your database to save the rendered images into.

3. Start Your (Rendering) Engines.

When you are done, you may click on the Render Sequence button to start the render process. Congratulations, the machine is now doing all the work for you! If you choose the Accept button instead of Render Sequenced, all the changes you made would be saved and the dialog box would be dismissed. All the rendering setup is saved with the scene so you don't have to do this every time you render a frame.

In a moment, a black window obscures the screen, and you see the render begin to draw your scene, frame by frame! Each frame is saved as it is completed, so that power interruptions or system crashes won't cost you all your work. It is, however, a very good idea to save your scene before rendering.

4. View Your Work.

When the rendering is complete, your scene reappears, and all the frames have been saved into the RENDER_PIC-TURES subdirectory of your database. To see them played back, switch to the Tools module and choose the FlipBook command. In the FlipBook dialog box, browse until you find the first frame in the sequence named Stonehenge.

In the FlipBook, you may set the Frame Range you want to see, as well as the Frame Rate, and a Multiplier that will enlarge your rendered frames during playback. The default settings should be appropriate for you, so click the Ok

> **NOTE**
>
> You may see all your frames compiled into icons by clicking on the Options button and choosing Show As Icons. Seeing images of all your frames makes finding a specific one easier but can be slow if the RENDER_PICTURES directory has thousands of frames in it.

button and the frames will load into memory. When loading is complete, click the L (loop) button in the Time Slider and then the forward playback triangle to see your frames played back.

That's it! You are done with your first complete, modeled, animated, lit, and rendered animation in Softimage 3D|Extreme.

WHAT TO DO WHILE YOU RENDER

For many people (myself included) the actual process of rendering images is oddly compelling. What did you do while the Stonehenge tutorial rendered? A natural tendency is to eagerly await your render, checking in on the progress every few minutes to see if the effect you desired is coming through. The gratification that comes from seeing the work unfold is immense—and very addicting. I've sat and watched—immobile—entranced, for hours as each line is drawn across the screen.

This is not good.

Being an animator is hard enough on your health and human relationships without spending what little free time you have staring at a growing image for hours or days. Rendering is a special time when, for once, your intervention is simply not required for the deal to go down. Learn the habit of leaving the machine for the duration of the render, and use that time to go eat, work out, see movies, visit with friends, engage in relationships with others of your species, or just sleep.

Here's how you do it:

1. Get a stopwatch or clock with a second hand and keep it near your workstation.

2. Work on your scene and delay rendering until the end of each phase of workflow. For example, build all the models, place them in the scene without any materials, textures, or lights, and then test render. Next, apply materials and textures to everything, and then when done, test render.

   Unnecessary previewing is part of the pathology I'm describing here. Every time you wait a few minutes to see part of the scene that you know isn't done yet you are delaying your eventual completion.

3. When you think you are ready to see the whole thing in glorious color, you really aren't. Things are *never* right the first time, or the second, or probably the

third time you render. So, when you are ready to check your work, always do a fast, small, low-quality render; use OpenGL or the Softimage renderer without any shadows, reflections, or refractions, just so you can see your work and make edits quickly. Start the low-quality render, and time the first five frames with your stopwatch. Divide the time to completion by five to get the render time per frame, and multiply by the total number of frames for the whole render to get an idea of how long it will take.

If you are over a minute per frame, that's too long for a preview at an early stage. Set the size, quality, antialiasing, and other options lower to get under a minute per frame.

4. Leave. Go away from the machine until the time you estimate your test render will be done. You may have noticed, while at user group meetings, trade shows, or other places where animators congregate, that a great many of them look unhealthy or simply ungroomed. That's because they spend all their waking hours hunched over a workstation. (I myself find it hard to make time for a haircut.) If you use the time during renders to get outside, go to the gym, or just hang out, you'll be a happier person and a better animator.

5. For final renders that may take days or weeks to complete, start the render and then point out to your boss that you're just twiddling your thumbs until the render finishes. Hang around her office and bug her until she tells you to go home.

BAD DEFAULT SETTINGS RUIN YOUR WORK

In the real world, if you use your hand and a flashlight to cast a shadow on the floor in a dark room, the resulting negative image of your hand will be very black in a very light circle. The reason is that the area in shadow has almost no light in it because the object that's casting the shadow is occluding the only light source in the room.

In Softimage, if you put a single light in the scene, turn on raytracing, then create a shadow with an object and render the scene, you can see plenty of the floor in the shadow. In fact, the shadow will barely be visible! What's going on? It's the work of two more default settings in Softimage designed to keep the amateurs from doing any good work. (See Figure 3.37.)

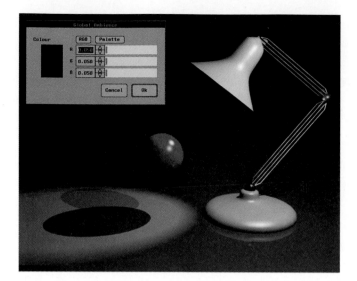

FIGURE 3.37   *The Global Ambience dialog and the difference it makes in a scene.*

The first problem is that there seems to be a lot of gray light being added to the scene in areas where there is no direct illumination. This is called *pure ambient light*, and it's garbage light that's just wandering around in the scene making everything look bad. It can be disabled in the Atmosphere→Ambiance menu cell, which shows you that Softimage by default adds 30% gray light to all ambient pixels during the render. Imagine Van Gogh adding a 30% gray wash to all his paintings after they were done, and you'll see why this is a bad idea. Turn all the values to 0, or near 0, and look at your scene again. It should look much more dramatic, but the shadow is still a little thin.

That's the fault of the second bad default setting, the Umbra setting in the Light Edit dialog box. By default, it is set to 0.75, which means that the shadow will have 75% of the same light as the nonshadowed areas. In real life, unless the object is translucent, objects cast 0% shadows, so turn the Umbra setting down to 0.1 or so and try it again. Now you'll get a good thick shadow. (See Figure 3.38.)

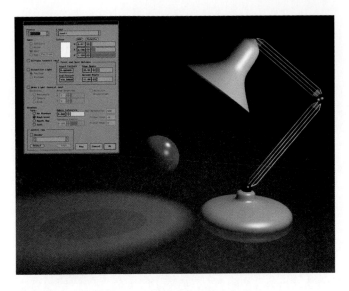

FIGURE 3.38   *The difference the Umbra setting makes in deep shadows.*

CONCLUSION

In this chapter, you finally got to see some exciting and beautiful images of your work come out of the rendering engines within Softimage 3D|Extreme. You learned quite a bit about lights, the camera, and playing back your rendered frames.

You should now be able to:

- Arrange lights in your scenes.
- Pick colors for the lights based on the visible spectrum.
- Determine the different shadow casting options you want your lights to have.
- Set up Falloff, Cone Angle, and other parameters.
- Move your camera into position for a render.
- Choose a rendering engine and set some of the quality parameters.

Image courtesy of Lume, Inc. © 1998 Lume, Inc.

CHAPTER 4

ADVANCED INTERFACE CONCEPTS

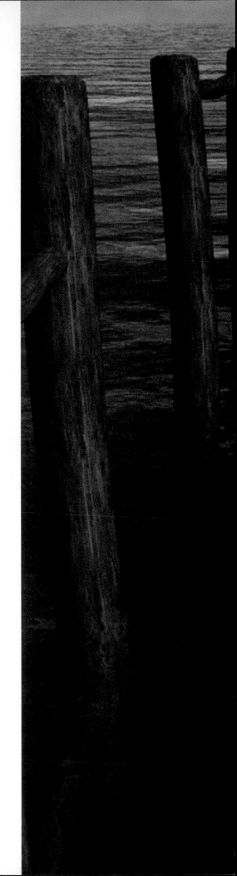

Now that you have a grasp on the basic Softimage tools needed to create a scene, you're ready to learn a few more of the interface tools that make your life easier. Some, like the Mode box, enable a whole universe of different features. Some, like the Display and Show menus, help you choose what to look at as you work in your scene. All in all, this chapter presents some difficult concepts, but when you understand them you'll get along better with Softimage 3D\Extreme.

Specifically, we will examine:

- The Object, Center, Tag, Polygon, and Texture modes
- The XYZ, Uniform, and Constant Volume scale modes
- The Local, Global, Reference, and Drag translation modes
- Null objects and how they are used
- Showing and hiding objects

THE BASIC MODE BOX: OBJ, TAG, CTR, TXT, AND POL

The Mode box is the small box in the lower-right corner of the interface that contains 10 square buttons (see Figure 4.1). The Mode box's buttons modify the behavior of the transformation menu cells. Depending on which of the Mode buttons is active, the Translate, Rotate, and Scale commands operate on different parts of the object and work relative to different axes.

FIGURE 4.1   *The Mode box.*

The top row of buttons in the Mode box tells us what will be affected by the Transformation commands.

OBJ MODE

In OBJ (Object) mode, whole objects can be translated, rotated, and scaled. (See Figure 4.2.) OBJ is the most common mode; you've already encountered it. You used it to move, scale, and rotate objects for the Stonehenge scene in Chapter 2, "Getting Started—Moving in Space." When in OBJ mode, the Transformation keys work on all the vertices of the current object equally.

CTR MODE

When CTR (Center) mode is selected, the Transformation keys operate only on the local center of an object. (See Figure 4.3.) The object vertices remain located in space where they were before the transformation. Moving the center of an object allows you to change the axis of rotation and determine where the object scales from and where the object's position in space will be measured from.

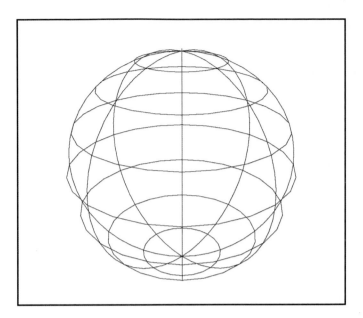

FIGURE 4.2   *The whole object is transformed in OBJ mode.*

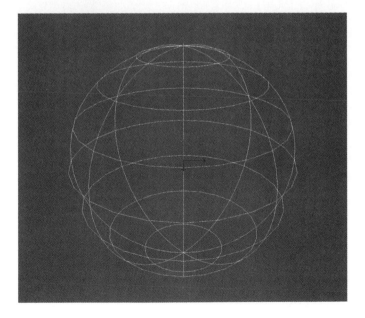

FIGURE 4.3   *The object center is transformed in CTR mode.*

TAG Mode

When in TAG mode, only tagged groups of polygons on the selected object are affected by the transformation. (See Figure 4.4.) This means that in addition to performing vertex-level manipulation, you can choose groups of vertices to transform all at the same time. You tag the vertices with the TAG→Rect command, which allows you to draw a rectangle around points to select and deselect them.

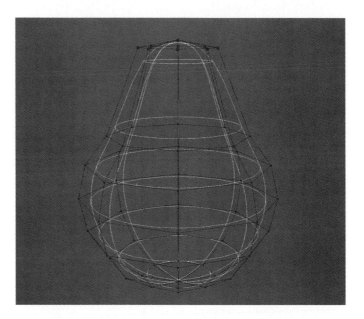

FIGURE 4.4 *Only the tagged points on the objects are transformed in TAG mode.*

Tagging is so commonly used in Softimage that there is a supra key for it, T. Whenever you hold down the T supra key, you can select and deselect points to add to the current tagged group for that object. (See Figure 4.5.) Then after the points are tagged, click in the TAG mode box to direct the Transformation menu cells to work on that tagged group only.

You can try this out by tagging points on a sphere with the T supra key and then translating them to make a pear. Check the Status Bar when you have the T supra key held down to see how the three mouse buttons operate differently.

POL Mode

POL (Polygon) mode is very similar to TAG mode in that when Softimage 3D|Extreme is in POL mode the transformations apply only to selected polygons. (See Figure 4.6.) This is a very useful mode for game developers and others interested in precisely controlling the location and construction of each individual polygon in an object. POL mode also enables a variety of Softimage tools that apply only to polygons, including Polygon Extrude and Polygon Duplicate.

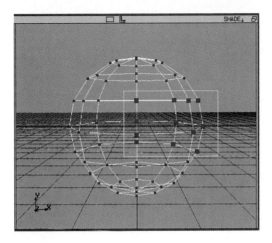

FIGURE 4.5   *Use the T supra key to tag points by dragging a marquee around them.*

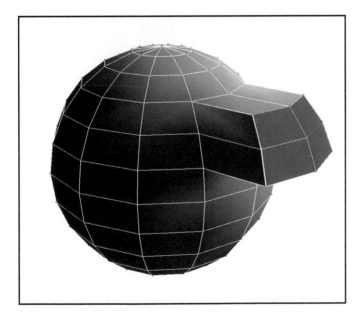

FIGURE 4.6   *Only selected polygons on the object are transformed in POL mode.*

Polygons may be selected (only on a Polygon mesh object, of course) with the Polygon→Select by Rectangle command (supra key Y) and the Polygon→Select by Raycasting command (supra key G).

Select by Raycasting is the most useful, because it allows you to point at an object with the mouse and select those polygons that lie beneath your mouse pointer. Raycast selects only those polygons facing you (as determined by the normal), so if you point at a sphere with the G key held down, only the polygons on one side of the sphere are selected. The Select by Rectangle method does not pay attention to normal orientation, but instead selects those polygons that lie entirely within the marquee that you draw. When you use it in conjunction with raycasting, you have different tools for different circumstances. Polygon modeling will be covered in detail in Chapter 7, "Polygon Modeling."

TXT MODE

When TXT (Texture) mode is active, it applies all the Transformation cells to the 2D texture currently active on the selected object. (See Figure 4.7.) Obviously, if the object has no texture, this mode is of little use. On Polygon objects, the method of projection for the texture is represented onscreen in red lines: Planar projections, such as XY, look like a box; cylindrical projections look like a cylinder; and spherical projections look like a ball.

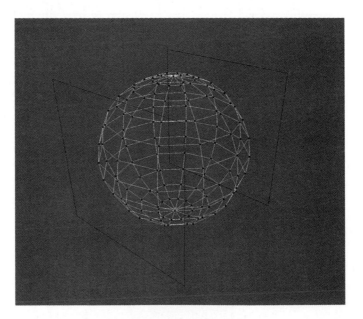

FIGURE 4.7   *Textures on the selected object are transformed in TXT mode.*

Scale reduces or expands the area covered by the projection, Rotate revolves the axis of the projection, and Translate moves the center of the projection to a different spot on the surface. For patches with UV Projection, the texture coordinates appear directly on the patch and can be scaled and translated as a decal map to any size and location on the surface.

SCALE MODES: XYZ, UNI, AND VOL

When you have one or more of the Scale menu cells activated, you are in the Scale mode, and a few new options appear in the lower row of the Mode box. (See Figure 4.8.) These options, XYZ, UNI, and VOL, help you scale objects in different ways.

FIGURE 4.8 *The Scale mode options.*

XYZ MODE

The XYZ mode is the typical, and default, setting. When XYZ mode is active, each of the three mouse buttons scales along a different axis. The left mouse button scales in X, the middle in Y, and the left in Z.

UNI MODE

UNI is the uniform scaling mode. When you are sizing objects after modeling them and want them to scale up evenly in each axis, one way to do it is to simply hold down each of the three mouse buttons at the same time while you drag. The problem with this method is that you may not get each mouse button depressed at exactly the same instant, which causes the model to become distorted slightly as it scales up.

If you activate all the Scale menu cells by clicking in the light colored area to their right, click in the UNI mode box, and then drag your mouse, you are assured that the model will scale uniformly. As an added bonus, the left mouse button causes the object to grow slowly, the middle mouse button causes the object to grow at a medium rate, and the right mouse button makes the object grow most rapidly.

VOL MODE

If at all possible, VOL mode keeps the internal volume of the selected object constant while you scale it. This means that Softimage calculates the internal volume of all shapes as they are built (you can check the volume with the Info→Selection command).

VOL mode is very useful in cartoon animation, where cartoon characters follow the rule of conservation of space, meaning that if a character squashes down, becoming shorter, he must also get fatter. This concept is the basis of squash and stretch animation and the VOL mode in Softimage takes care of it for you. If you scale down in X, the object scales up in Y and Z proportionately.

TRANSLATION MODES: LCL, GLB, REF, AND DRG

The Translation modes are extremely useful at all phases of the animation process because they change the way your mouse movement translates into the object movement. Sometimes you just want to be able to drag the object freely around the screen, sometimes you want the object to move relative to the global center, and sometimes you want the object to move relative to its own center or another object. The Translation modes make this easy. (See Figure 4.9.)

FIGURE 4.9   *The Translation mode options.*

LCL MODE

In LCL (Translate Local) mode, the selected object moves relative to its own axes. (See Figure 4.10.) For instance, let's say you modeled a chair on a stage and rotated the chair at an angle to the crowd in front. Now you want to animate the chair moving directly back as the character gets up and shoves the chair with his legs. You could use the LCL mode with the right mouse button. This causes the chair to move backwards, no matter which way it is facing on the stage.

Backwards, forwards, left, right, up, and down are all human terms for moving relative to our own local axes in Z, X, and Y, respectively. Think about it: If I'm on an airplane (and I am as I write this), I know the plane is moving forward, but I don't know what my compass heading is. The plane is moving relative to its own local axes. Some transformations (along a path, spline deformation, and UV patch placement) rely on the concept of local mode.

FIGURE 4.10 *Moving in LCL mode means being relative to your own local axes.*

GBL MODE

In GBL (Translate Global mode), the selected object moves relative to the ever-present, immovable, immutable global axes. The left mouse button translates in global X, the middle in global Y, and the right in global Z. This is useful if you become lost in space, because the global axes are always consistent, so you always know what the object will do.

REF MODE

Although arcane, REF (Reference) mode is useful. It allows you to move a selected object relative to the local axes of another object. Using the airplane example, if I want to get up and move down the aisle, I move relative to the local axes of the airplane, which is itself traveling through space. I could even turn sideways, so my local Z axis is directed to the windows of the plane, and move along the aisle perfectly straight in reference to the plane's local Z axis. In modeling, the REF mode is useful for placing detail on a model precisely even when the model is not square with the global axis, like a train traveling along a curvy track.

DRG MODE

DRG (Drag) mode is the default mode and the mode you will most often use. When you are in DRG mode and you translate an object with all the Trans menu cells active, the object can move freely in whichever plane your mouse is in when you start clicking and dragging with the left mouse button. So, if you have a character that needs to be placed along a ground plane, selecting the object and dragging in the Top view with the left mouse button moves the object freely in the XZ plane. Dragging in the Front view moves the object in the XY plane, and dragging in the right or left views moves the object freely in the XZ plane.

Dragging in the Perspective view moves the selected object in an arbitrary plane, but this is not recommended because you will often move the object in ways you do not intend. If you drag in DRG mode and use the middle, you can constrain the translation of the object to left-right movement in whichever plane you click. Using the right mouse button constrains movement to up and down.

ROTATION MODES: LCL, GBL, ADD, REF, AND PLN

The Rotation modes make it possible to rotate objects in different ways for different modeling needs. Some are easier in certain circumstances. By default, objects can rotate continuously and the angle of rotation just continues to increase.

For instance, as a car tire revolves it might go from a rotation in X of 30 degrees to a rotation in X of 30,000 degrees. Of course, because the object is in the same orientation each 360 degrees, this might be redundant. If you want to see the object rotation in a manner where it never exceeds the range from −180 to 180 degrees, uncheck the default setting of Preferences→Continuous Rotation.

Softimage offers five Rotation modes: LCL, GBL, ADD, REF, and PLN.

- LCL is the Local Rotation mode. The object revolves around its local axis.

- GBL is the Global mode. The object (or its tagged points) revolves around the global axis at 0,0,0.

- ADD (Additive) mode is the most commonly used mode and the default. In ADD mode, the object revolves around the local X axis and the parent Z axis.

- REF (Reference) mode gives you the choice of another object to define the rotation axes.

- PLN (Plane) mode revolves an object around the local axis corresponding to the axis perpendicular to the plane of the current view.

NULL OBJECTS

In the Get→Primitive menu cell, you find a command that seems a little obscure at first. Called Get→Primitive→Null, it brings a special kind of object into being. A *null* is an object that has no geometry at all—no lines, no points, no polygons, no surface at all. It is an object that consists of only a local center.

The tremendous utility of the null comes from the fact that when objects are linked in a hierarchy, each parent node adds transformations to all the child nodes. This means that a null object can be used as a parent in a hierarchy when you just wish all the children objects to be linked together at the same level. The whole null grouping can then be scaled, translated, or rotated together by selecting the top of the hierarchy as a branch. That null can also be animated and the animation on the null cascades down into the child nodes connected to it.

Nulls are also a critical part of Inverse Kinematic skeletons in Softimage and they can help out tremendously in constraint-based animations.

A null can also be thought of as a spacer between a parent and a child, adding another degree of freedom between the two. For instance, when importing motion data into Softimage, it most often comes in as a hierarchy of nulls, in the shape and proportions of the person that generated the motion. If the motion actor is a six-foot-tall modern dancer, however, and the creature you wish to apply it to is a three-foot potbellied dwarf, you could use a null in between each Motion null and the Character null, scaling the intermediate nulls into the right shape for the dwarf.

TUTORIAL: THE PLANETS, REDUX

The solar system we built in Chapter 2 was actually a very simplistic model and didn't fully take advantage of the effects of nulls in the hierarchy, moved object centers, and the Mode options. In this tutorial, we'll explore how these features can be used to build a more flexible, accurate solar system (see Figure 4.11).

FIGURE 4.11 *The rendered solar system.*

1. The Sun.

Get a primitive sphere of about 10 units, and leave it in the global center. Make the local center visible with Show→Centre so you can see the local axis with the small red, green, and blue vectors.

In this system we want the sun to be able to rotate independently of the planets (if need be), so we must create a null object to be the parent of both the Sun and the planets. Use Get→Primitive→Null to get a null and name it "solarsystem" by double-clicking it in the Schematic view. Make it the parent of the Sun with the Parent command and remember to use the Esc key (or the right mouse button) to end the Parent mode and avoid creating unwanted children. Now the entire solar system can be transformed by selecting the node named solarsystem as a tree, or just the Sun can be transformed by selecting it as a node (see Figure 4.12).

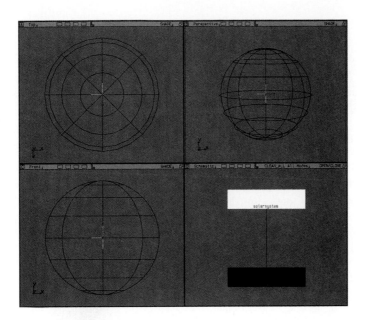

Figure 4.12 *The Sun, with a parent null object.*

2. **The Earth.**

The Earth has some behavior that is much more complicated than it seems at first. The Earth does orbit the Sun (once every 365.26 days), but it also revolves around its own axis, the poles. These poles aren't aligned with the axis of rotation around the Sun, so we'll need a null between the solarsystem node and the Earth, making it possible for the Earth to revolve around two Y axes simultaneously, one in the center of the planet and one in the center of the Sun.

Create a primitive sphere and translate it away from the Sun a good distance to simulate the orbital distance of the Earth from the Sun. Now use the RotX menu cell to rotate the Earth so that the north and south poles are not exactly aligned with the global axes. Try about 20 degrees. This brings different parts of the Earth into more direct sunlight at different parts of the Earth orbit.

Create a null for the Earth to orbit around and leave it at the global center, which is also the center of the Sun. Make it the parent of the Earth and name it "earthpivot."

Now experiment by selecting just the Earth as a node (Spacebar and the left mouse button) and rotating it around the Y axis. It should stay where it is and spin around the poles. Now select the earthpivot as a branch (Spacebar and the middle mouse button) and rotate around Y. The Earth should now swing in a circle around the null in the center of the Sun.

Finally, make the earthpivot null a child of the solarsystem null.

3. **The Moon.**

The Moon orbits the Earth but with a small twist. The Moon always remains oriented around its poles so that the same side of the Moon faces the Earth at all times. Get another sphere and scale it smaller than the Earth. Place it away from the Earth enough to simulate the orbital distance of the Moon. Now switch to the CTR mode, translate the Moon's local center to the exact center of the Earth, and switch back to OBJ mode. Try rotating the Moon around Y. It should orbit the Earth in such a way that one face always remains directed to the Earth. Complete this step by making the Moon a child of the Earth, so that when you rotate the Earth around the Sun, the Moon goes with it (see Figure 4.13).

FIGURE 4.13 *The Moon, with its center in the middle of the Earth.*

4. **Complete and test.**

You should now have a complete hierarchy descending from the solarsystem to the Sun and the Earth, and from the Earth to the Moon. (See Figure 4.14.)

Experiment with this system by selecting different parts as a node, branch, or tree and rotating them. You may also select the entire hierarchy as a tree and translate the solar system through the galaxy.

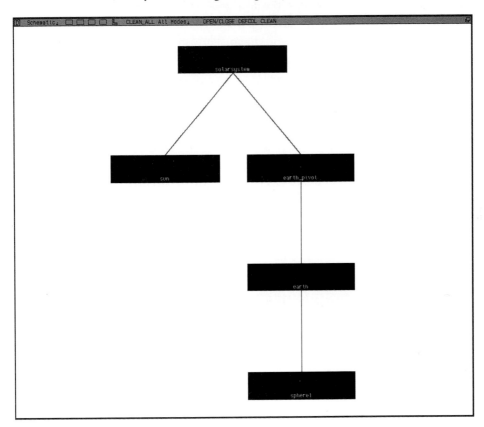

FIGURE 4.14 *The solar system hierarchy for the Sun, Earth, and Moon.*

Add in the other planets at your leisure, either with a pivot null above them providing the axis of rotation around the Sun or by simply freezing the translation of the planet, which causes the local center of the planet to leap to the global center.

The capability to group objects with nulls gives you more than one center per object. That means more than one axis of rotation as well, enabling complex animated motion, such as that necessary for the planets to move realistically. The Planets exercise is just the beginning of what you can do with null hierarchies.

SHOWING AND HIDING

Softimage can easily handle scenes with thousands of objects, millions of polygons, and infinitely complex hierarchies. But just because the software can handle it doesn't mean you can. In fact, as the scene gets more and more complicated, just looking at all the stuff begins to slow you down. Locating what you want in the scene can be challenging when all you see is a massive tangle of black lines. Each line, point, curve, vertex, and link also needs to be redrawn in each window with every change you make. Eventually your workstation will begin to slow down between redraws and your frustration will grow as you wait for the screen to redraw or for the command to take effect.

One solution to these problems is to hide those items you no longer wish to see. Softimage doesn't have a system of layers for organizing objects in the way that some other 3D and CAD packages do. Instead each object in the scene can be turned into a bounding box, ghosted into dotted lines, or hidden altogether. Hidden objects don't show up in the render either, and you can animate the visibility of each object as well.

SHOWING AND HIDING OBJECT INFO

As you know, each object in a scene is made up of points, lines, centers, nulls, and normals. In addition to this basic information, Softimage can show you graphical representations of other effects, such as links between objects, lattices, tags, and edge flags. All this can be shown or hidden with the Show menu cell. (See Figure 4.15.)

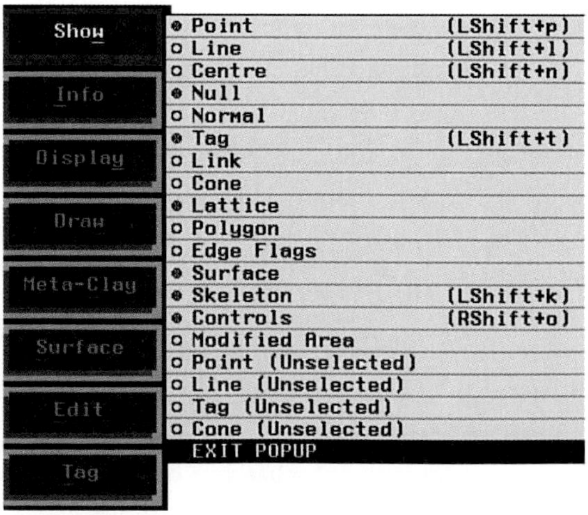

FIGURE 4.15   *The Show menu cell toggles.*

Each of the 16 Show commands is a toggle, so you can see whether it is currently enabled, and then turn it on or off (see Figure 4.16).

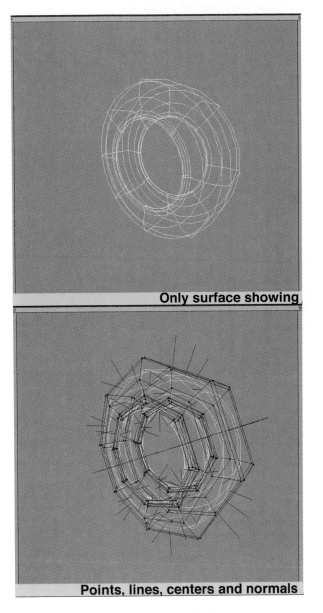

FIGURE 4.16   *The same object with Show options on and off.*

- Show→Point shows or hides the Control points that make up a patch surface, or if the object is a Polygonal mesh, it shows the vertices.

- Show→Line toggles the Control lines drawn between Control points and is different than the curves that show the actual surface of the object.

- Show→Center toggles the visibility of the local centers of the selected?

- Show→Null toggles the visibility of the null parent of the selected hierarchy.

- Show→Normal toggles the thin blue lines (the normals) that are vectors demonstrating which side of the patch or polygon is the front side. (Effect→Inverse swaps the orientation of all the normals on an object.)

- Show→Tag shows or hides the group of tagged points that is currently selected on an object.

- Show→Link draws a graphical representation of the hierarchy in the View windows, not just in the Schematic view. In other words, parent objects are connected to the child objects with small white lines.

- Show→Cone toggles the cone of visibility for the camera and Spot lights. The cone demonstrates where the Spot light shines or the camera looks.

- Show→Lattice toggles the lattice on the object, if the object has one.

- Show→Polygon toggles the visibility of the selected polygons, which are drawn in a pink shade.

- Show→Edge Flags draws the edges of a surface in a different color, so you know where they are on complex surfaces. On Polygonal surfaces, the edge flags show the shared and unshared edges. For patches, the edges show the starting U and V directions and edges.

- Show→Surface shows the curve networks that make up a patch surface.

- Show→Skeleton toggles the visibility of all the IK skeletons in the scene.

- Show→Controls shows or hides Control icons, such as Dynamics icons.

- Show→Modified Area shows the portion of the model being modified by an effect.

- Show→Point, Line, Tag, Cone (Unselected) show the points, lines, tags, and cones even if they are currently unselected.

SHOWING AND HIDING ENTIRE OBJECTS

What if you want an entire object or an entire hierarchy of objects to simply disappear? The Display→Hide→Toggle commands cause the entire selected object or hierarchy of objects to disappear and reappear in the scene. Objects that are hidden are indeed invisible to the renderer and show up in the Schematic view as outlined (not solid) objects. Because invisible objects do not have to be redrawn every time the screen display is updated, hiding objects makes your workstation more responsive as well. The hidden objects are still in the scene, and if you save the scene, they are saved along with everything else (see Figure 4.17).

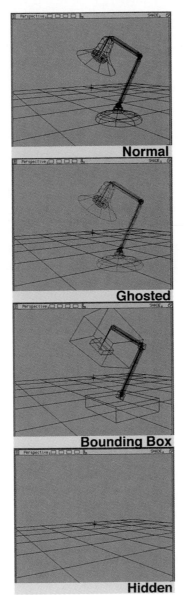

FIGURE 4.17 *The same object in normal representation, ghosted, in bounding box representation, and hidden.*

Viewing Objects as Bounding Boxes

The Display→Bounding Box menu also works to simplify the objects in a scene. When you use the Display→Bounding Box command on a selected object or hierarchy of objects, each object is replaced with a rectangular box that is scaled to the same size as the outer extents of the object. These *bounding boxes* act as visual reminders of objects and positions, but because the geometry of a box is so simple, they redraw faster and are less confusing to look at than the originals. The Softimage renderer renders them as boxes, colored to match the material of the objects they represent, but the mental ray replaces them with the original objects at render time.

Ghosting Objects

The Display→Ghost menu has a similar complement of commands for toggling objects. When ghosted, an object is represented in less detail, without Control points, and with dashed lines for the edges. Ghosted objects may also not be selected in the regular View windows (fact check), but they must be chosen in the Schematic View window. Like Display→Hide and Display→Bounding Box, it is a toggle function, so operating the command again on the same selected object restores it. Unlike Show/Hide, bounding boxes and ghosted objects cannot be animated.

Showing and Hiding the Camera

The camera and the camera interest may be hidden or shown, just like objects. The command to toggle the camera visibility is located in the Camera menu and called Camera→Show Camera. The camera is hidden by default but still works exactly the same whether hidden or shown.

Conclusion

In this chapter, you learned more about the special modes in Softimage that limit functions and commands to special types of objects. You worked with nulls and learned how to keep your scene clutter free by hiding those parts you don't need to see. You now know:

- How to manipulate objects, centers of objects, polygons, tagged groups of points, and textures.
- How to scale on all axes independently, to scale on all axes together, and to scale while keeping the object volume constant for squash and stretch animation.

- About null objects and some of their uses.

- How to show or hide points, lines, centers, cones, and whole hierarchies of objects.

From the film Starship Troopers. *Property of TriStar Pictures ©1997, courtesy of Tippett Studio.*

INTERPOLATION

So what happens to a value inbetween the keyframes you set at two different points in time? Softimage *interpolates* between the keyframes you set so that the value smoothly transitions from one value to the next. Softimage fills in the blanks for you so that you don't have to be explicit about the value being changed at each and every frame in the animation.

By default, Softimage 3D|Extreme uses *spline interpolation* so that the rate of change in the value is lowest near each keyframe. This is called *ease in/ease out.* In practice, it causes a value to accelerate from a stop to a constant rate of change, then decelerate back to no rate of change at the next keyframe, like a car speeding away from a signal and then stopping at the next light (see Figure 5.3).

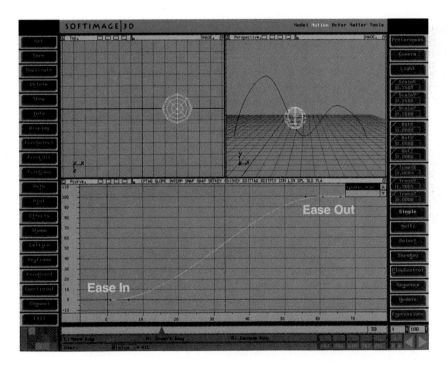

FIGURE 5.3 *Softimage uses spline interpolation to ease in and ease out of keyframes.*

TIME

In Softimage, all time is represented by frames. How long is a frame? However long you want it to be. By themselves, frames do not have any special relation to real-world units of time measurement; they are relative to the speed at which they are played back.

In the United States, television plays back at 30 frames per second. In Europe, it plays at 25 frames per second. Motion pictures play at 24 frames per second. Some traditional animation is played (or "run") as slow as 12 or 15 frames per second (so the animators don't have to draw quite so many frames by hand). You need to decide before you start animating how you will be planning to view your animation. Often, that determines how the Softimage frames translate into real units of time.

A side effect you need to think about is that running your finished animation at different speeds has the effect of slowing down or speeding up the action in them. This means that the timing that looked perfect when you were previewing your animation onscreen might not look so hot on video or on film. Make sure you preview your work and perfect the timing at the same frame rate as you will use for your final output.

TUTORIAL: THE WATCH

To examine how keyframing and interpolation work, let's build a watch similar to the one in Figure 5.4.

FIGURE 5.4   *The rendered watch scene.*

1. **Begin the Watch Body.**

   Enter the Model mode to begin making the watch components. Build the body of the watch by creating a primitive sphere with the Get→Primitive→Sphere menu cell. Make it five Softimage units in radius and choose to create a sphere made out of cubic NURBS. Leave all the other parameters at the default settings.

2. **Refine the Shape.**

   Scale the sphere in the Z axis by clicking in the direct entry portion of the ScaleZ menu cell with your middle mouse button and typing in 0.25 followed by the Enter key. This gives you a flattened watch body with a rounded edge (see Figure 5.5).

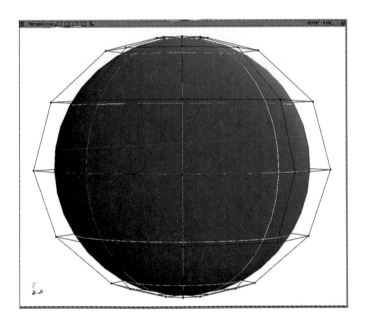

FIGURE 5.5 *Scale the sphere to flatten the watch body.*

3. **Create the Watch's Front Piece.**

   Next you need to create a front piece for the pocket watch by duplicating the original watch body sphere and cutting it along the middle of the NURBS parameter that runs around the rim of the watch. Use the Draw→Cut menu cell and then pick the curve that you want to become the new edge. When the NURBS Surface Cut dialog appears, click the Cut button to cleave one of the NURBS parameters of the watch. Immediately click the Cut button again to cleave the other side of the watch (see Figure 5.6).

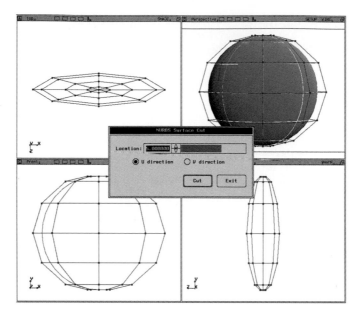

FIGURE 5.6 *Use the NURBS Surface Cut dialog to separate the watch cover from the watch body.*

Softimage leaves both halves in existence, so find the back half and delete it with the Delete→Selection menu cell.

Select the new watch front cover and translate it forward in the positive Z axis about 0.1 Softimage units so that when the watch is closed there is a space between the case of the watch and the closed front cover.

You want the watch open, so you need to move the local center so that the front cover hinges in the right place. To do this, go into CTR mode (lower-right mode box), and then translate the local center in the X axis to the left edge of the front cover. Change back to OBJ mode and then rotate the front cover manually using the RotY menu cell until the pocket watch is open (see Figure 5.7).

4. **Add the Ring.**

   Add a watch fob with a primitive torus and two cylinders from the Get→Primitive menu (see Figure 5.8).

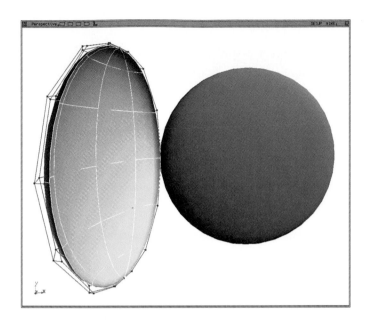

FIGURE 5.7 *Open the pocket watch using RotY.*

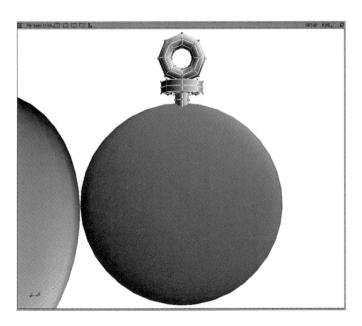

FIGURE 5.8 *A primitive torus is the basis for the top ring.*

5. **Draw the Minute Hand.**

In the Front view, use a B-spline curve to draw the outline of a minute hand with Draw→Curve→Bspline. Start at the point of the hand and work your way around to the other side. When you reach the point again, close the curve with the Draw→Open/Close command (see Figure 5.9). The curve must be closed before you can convert it to a face and, therefore, make it visible to the renderer. Convert the hand shape to a face with the Draw→Convert to Face command. Look at it in Shaded mode and adjust the position of the points until they are to your liking. (If no points show on the curve, turn them on with Show→Points.)

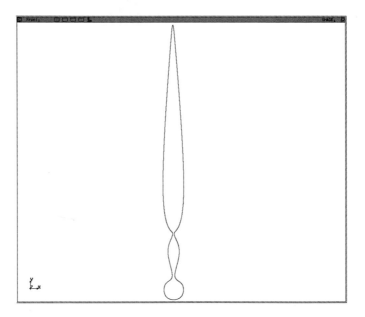

FIGURE 5.9 *Use a B-spline curve to draw the minute hand.*

6. **Adjust the Hand's Local Center.**

Move the local center of the minute hand to the bottom of the shape by changing to CTR mode and using the TransX menu cell. Now all transformations to the minute hand take place relative to the bottom of the object, which helps you rotate and scale the hand to suit your taste.

7. **Position the Hand.**

Switch back to OBJ mode and move the hand in the Z axis until it is in front of the watch face. Use the Top view to see what is happening while you translate the hand in Z space. In the Front view, make sure the watch hand is positioned with the center in the middle of the watch face, which should be at the global center (0,0,0).

Here you can also scale the minute hand to fit the size of the watch by using the Scale menu cells. Use the Uniform Scale mode (UNI) to avoid distorting the hand you make.

Try rotating the watch hand about its local center by choosing the RotZ menu cell, checking to make sure you are in the LCL mode, and then dragging back and forth. The minute hand should swing around the middle of the watch face in a satisfying fashion.

The intrepid among you may wish to duplicate the hand (try the D supra key rather than the Duplicate menu cell) and scale it down to form the hour hand (see Figure 5.10).

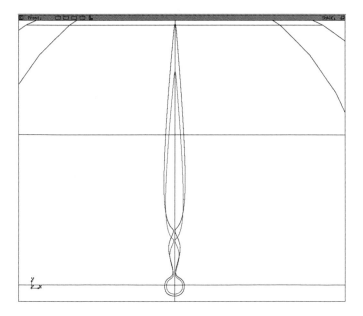

FIGURE 5.10 *Duplicate and scale the minute hand to create the hour hand.*

8. Set the Keyframes.

At last, with the model built, we are ready to animate it by setting some keyframes. Because all the animation commands

---

TIP

Two techniques can help you draw an attractive minute hand here.

The first technique is to turn on Grid Lock so you can precisely place points on a grid. Do this by clicking the Layout icon in the Front view. Turn on Grid Lock and set an appropriate grid size, such as 0.2 Softimage units. Now it will be easier for you to precisely position points where you want them.

The second technique is to draw the first half of the curve, positioned so that it lies with the first and last points exactly on the Y axis. Use the Symmetry custom effect, located in the Model module in Effect→Symmetry. You can choose which plane of symmetry to use when mirroring the curve. If you drew the curve in the Front view (the XY plane), however, you will want to mirror your curve around the YZ plane to create a perfectly inverted copy. Now you can join the two curves with the Draw→Merge Curves command, which attaches the end of the first curve to the start of the second. Use the Draw→ Open/Close command to close up the resulting spline and convert it to a face with Draw→ Convert to Face. Hide the construction elements you used to make it by selecting them and choosing the Hide→Toggle Selected Items command.

are located in the Motion module, go there now by clicking the word Motion in the top-right corner of the interface, or press the F2 key.

The correct order to use when setting keyframes is always to set the time, then set the value to be animated, and then save a keyframe. Set a beginning keyframe for the minute hand by following this simple process: First move the Time Slider to frame 1. Next select the minute hand and rotate it to aim directly up in the 12 o'clock position. This should be 0 degrees in Z. Finally go to the SaveKey menu cell and choose SaveKey→Object→Rotation→Z. Now repeat the process for the remaining keyframes.

TIP

Because each menu cell remembers which command was last chosen from it, you can save time by recalling the last command executed from a menu cell by clicking it with the middle mouse button. This is an example of how Softimage can organize your workflow to make you more efficient as an animator.

Move the Time Slider to frame 30. Select the minute hand and set the rotation in Z to negative 180 degrees. Save a keyframe for the object's rotation in Z with SaveKey→Object→Rotation→Z.

Now move to frame 60 and set another keyframe for the minute hand at negative 360 degrees rotation in Z, back at 12 o'clock.

If you created an hour hand, set two keyframes for it, one at frame 1 pointing to the 3 o'clock position, and one at frame 60 pointing at the 4 o'clock position.

9. Play Your Animation.

If you look at the right end of the Time Slider, you see two triangles, one pointing left and the other pointing right. These are the Play Forward and Play Reverse controls. Click them to examine how your watch animates.

So why, if you set only three keyframes for the hands of your watch, do they change orientation in every frame between the keys? That is the secret to 3D computer animation: the software looks at your keyframes and decides how you want the value to change during the in-between frames. Interpolation is the genie in the software that does so much of the work for you (see Figure 5.11).

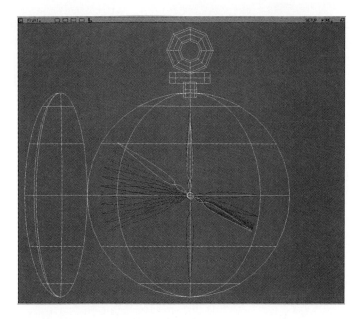

FIGURE 5.11 *Interpolation at work.*

PLAYING YOUR ANIMATION

Of course, the first thing you'll want to do after you animate an object by setting keyframes is see how that object moves and changes over time. Seeing your animation on the computer screen is not only the big payoff for the animator, it's what the client pays for. And the only way to make sure that the animation you get is the animation you wanted is to check, check, and recheck the playback. You can play your animation in a number of ways, but they all start with an understanding of the Time Slider and how frames in Softimage relate to real time.

THE TIME SLIDER AND BASIC PLAYBACK

The Time Slider at the bottom of the screen is not only a way to set the current frame. It is a way to view your animation. As you drag the Time Slider back and forth along the Timeline, the animation plays in all the active view windows. Softimage can draw your scene very quickly in the Wireframe mode, so "scrubbing" the Time Slider, dragging it along the Timeline, is often a good way to get a feel for how your animation will look.

If you want to see the scene play by itself, you can simply click one of the triangles at the right side of the Time Slider. As mentioned in the watch tutorial, these are the Play Forward and Play Reverse controls, and they attempt to play your animation as smoothly as possible (see Figure 5.12). With very light scenes, this may play too fast. You can modify the Play Forward and Play Reverse buttons with other options for more control.

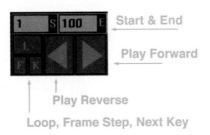

FIGURE 5.12   *The Playback controller.*

Next to the playback triangles are three more toggle buttons marked by single letters: L, F, and K. L is the Loop button. Toggle it on and click the Play Reverse button to loop your watch animation in reverse. F is the frame-by-frame playback toggle. With it activated, the forward and reverse buttons move through the animation one frame at a time. This makes it easy to step slowly through an animation or to advance only one frame while setting precise keyframes. Finally, the K toggle causes playback to jump from keyframe to keyframe.

The PlayControl dialog box in the Motion module gives you some additional control over how Softimage plays your animations. If you activate the Keep Timing option, Softimage strives to maintain the frame rate you specify, neither faster nor slower. Setting PlayControl's Frame Delay option to 0 also helps your playback.

IMPROVE THE PLAYBACK RATE

As your scenes become more and more complex, it will not be possible for Softimage to play each frame back at a constant rate of 30 frames per second. There are a couple of things you can do, however, to help the playback maintain an appropriate speed.

First you can reduce the number of View windows that are refreshed each frame by using the Freeze option in the View mode of each view you don't need. The fewer Views that have to be refreshed, the more computational power your system can spend on drawing your animation in the View you care about, and the faster it plays.

Second, in the Perspective view, call up the Layout dialog box (click the L-shaped icon in the center of the top title bar) and set the option for Fast Playback. Then set the Playback controller to loop (the L button in the Time Slider) and click the Play Forward triangle. The Fast Playback option goes through all the frames in the animation and stores each image in a playback cache. Then it loops back again, this time using the precalculated images it stored on the first time through. It plays the Wireframe mode in white instead of black to indicate that Fast Playback is in use. To cause the animation sequence to recalculate (after you've made changes, for instance) press the R key on frame 1 and repeat the Play Forward command to recalculate and store all the frames. This method takes the same amount of time on the first pass through the animation, but it plays subsequent loops more smoothly.

SHADED MODE PLAYBACK

If you need more of a feel for your objects than Wireframe mode provides, Softimage can also play your animation in Shaded View mode. This mode uses OpenGL to shade all the surfaces in your scene, and OpenGL in turn uses a combination of your workstation's graphics hardware and CPU to do the work.

Be warned: Drawing a scene in Shaded mode requires a great deal more computational power than the simple Wireframe mode, however. It may not work very well on scenes that are large in polygon count. Setting the Patch Precision to 1 in the Shade View Setup dialog box helps with patch-based objects. Hiding unnecessary objects (Display→Hide→Toggle Selected Objects) and ghosting others (Display→Ghost→Toggle Selected Objects) also helps speed Shaded view playback.

The truth of the matter is that Shaded mode playback is not useful in very many cases because scenes of any interest usually far exceed the real-time playback capability of today's computers. Don't get fooled by hardware vendors who try to convince you to buy expensive, suped-up OpenGL cards. They aren't worth the cash.

LINETESTS

Seeing a real-time playback of the animation in your scene is *critical* to good animation during the feedback loop portion of your workflow. If you don't watch it at the speed your consumers will, you can't possibly know what it will look like when they see it. And if you don't know what it will look like, it probably will look bad. The solution is to use non-real-time methods of drawing frames, and real-time methods of playing them back.

Softimage includes a method that mimics the traditional pencil test, also called a motion test, designed to give you the feedback you need to evaluate your work quickly and make edits. It's called the *linetest* and can be rendered quite rapidly in either *Hidden Line Faceted* style or in *Hidden Line Smoothed* style. The Hidden Line Smoothed style looks remarkably like a pen and ink tracing of the objects in your scene. The Hidden Line Faceted style adds a faceted look to the smoothed version. The best part of linetests is that they can almost always be played back in real time, using the Linetest player in the Tools module.

To do a linetest, simply go to the Matter module and choose the Render command. When the Render Setup dialog comes up, choose the range of frames you want and set a name for the completed linetest (see Figure 5.13). Then choose either Hidden Line option (Faceted or Smoothed) from the Rendering Type dropbox and click the Render Sequence button. Softimage draws the rendered frames in the Perspective view and writes them to disk in the RENDER_PICTURES subdirectory of the active database, with the usual numbering scheme and a .lin extension.

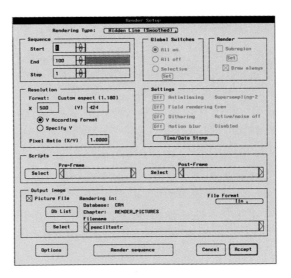

FIGURE 5.13 *The Render Setup dialog configured for a linetest.*

To play them back, enter the Tools module and click the Line→Show Sequence menu cell. The Show Line Sequence dialog (see Figure 5.14) allows you to choose the frames to play back, the size to play them at (linetests are resolution independent, so go for it), and the frame rate to run at. Some other less useful options, such as background color, are also available. When you click the OK button, Softimage loads the frames into memory and plays them at the speed you indicate.

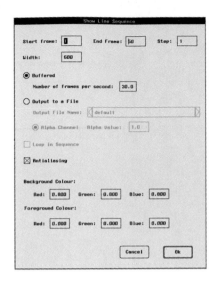

FIGURE 5.14   *The Show Line Sequence dialog.*

I can't say enough about how important it is to check your animation timing with linetests as you work. Until you see it at 30 frames per second (for TV), you'll have no idea if your timing looks realistic or amateurish. Remember, no one can get it perfect the first time; what makes professional work look like it's worth money is the review and revision process.

RENDERING PREVIEWS WITH OPENGL

If your computer has OpenGL hardware acceleration, Softimage can use that hardware to render frames very quickly. OpenGL-rendered previews are Phong-shaded only, but they use multiple light sources. That means that this method shows color, texture, and lights on surfaces, but it won't show transparency, refraction, or reflection. The process is the same as viewing frames in Shaded view, but each frame rendered is then saved to disk for later playback.

To create an OpenGL rendered sequence, enter the Render dialog in the Matter module, set up your render start and end frames, and give the sequence a name. Then change the Rendering Type drop menu to the GL Hardware Renderer option. When you click the Render button, Softimage creates rendered frames in the range you specified and stores them in the RENDER_PICTURES subdirectory of the default write database with a .pic filename extension. To view the frames, enter the Tools module and click the FlipBook menu cell. The FlipBook dialog box is the most generally useful tool for viewing your rendered work. In the FlipBook, choose any frame of the sequence you want to view from the scrolling list box (see Figure 5.15).

TIP

In the Options sub-dialog, you can choose to view sequences of frames as a single icon in the browser window. This can be a good idea if you don't have too many frames in your REN-DER_PICTURES subdirectory. If you have, however, 20 sequences of 500 frames each, you'll wait for a long time while the browser window collects the 10,000 frames into icons.

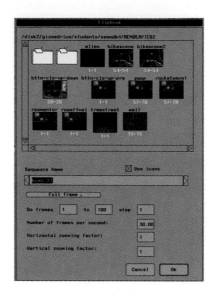

FIGURE 5.15   *You can play animation in the FlipBook.*

You can set the start and end frames and a step factor if you do not wish to see every frame or did not render every frame. You can also set a scale factor that increases the size of the image played back, but as you blow up frames they look chunkier (more pixelated). When you click the OK button, Softimage reads the sequence of frames you chose from the disk and stores it in memory. When all the images are cached in RAM, the program displays the first to a window. To play the FlipBook, click the Loop button (L) and then the Play Forward triangle on the Time Slider. To halt the playback, press all three mouse buttons simultaneously, and the FlipBook player stops.

Because the entire sequence must be loaded into RAM for smooth playback, it is very possible to select a sequence that won't play smoothly because it's too big for the available free memory in your workstation.

In general, the OpenGL renderer isn't all that useful because the Softimage renderer is a lot higher quality and can run almost as fast if set up correctly.

TRANSLATION: PATH VERSUS EXPLICIT

Now that you understand everything there is to know about playing back your animations, let's get back to creating some. The most basic animatable parameters are the transformations: Scale, Rotate, and Translate.

To animate the scale of an object, use the SaveKey→Object→Scale→All command to save the object scale in all axes at the current frame. If only one keyframe is set, the object simply remains that size during the animation. When two or more scale keyframes are set, the object smoothly interpolates between them. You can also choose to animate the scale of the object in only one axis at a time by setting a keyframe with SaveKey→Object→Scale→X (or Y or Z). This level of control gives you complete authority over your objects.

Animating the rotation of an object works exactly the same way: Just select the object, move to the point in time where you want the keyframe by dragging the Time Slider, and set a keyframe for the rotational axis you want with SaveKey→Object→Rotation. Again you can save the rotation in all axes, or just in a specific axis.

While scale and rotation have only one method for keyframing their values, translation is a bit more complicated. There are three different translation methods for animating the motion of an object through 3D space. The first is ordinary *path translation*. If you save a keyframe for a car model as it rolls through space using SaveKey→Object→Translation, you are using path translation. The results are easy to see because if you move to a different point in time and set another keyframe for the car in a different location, Softimage automatically adds a spline path to your scene indicating the path taken by the car. As you move the Time Slider, move the car, and save another keyframe, the path grows. If you play back the animation, the car follows the path (see Figure 5.16).

One of the great advantages to path translation is that you can control the timing, or how far along the object is at any point in time, independently of the path it travels along.

You can even edit the position of the motion path's Control points using the M supra key, and the animation of the sphere is automatically updated to reflect the new path. This makes moving objects through space very simple, but it doesn't allow you to control the translation in each axis separately. The next kind of translation, *explicit translation*, does allow this level of control.

NOTE

As the size in pixels that you choose to render images at increases, so does the size in kilobytes required to store and see the image. A 640×480 pixel image requires about 921K of RAM to display (uncompressed), which you can safely round up to 1MB. If you want to view 100 frames with the FlipBook, you'll require 100MB of free RAM—that's in addition to the RAM used by the operating system, the soft executable, and other running programs.

If you don't have enough free memory, your computer may cache the frames back to disk in virtual memory, defeating the purpose of having them in RAM and causing jerky playback with skipped frames. If you don't have enough free RAM or virtual memory, Softimage 3D|Extreme gives you an error message saying there was insufficient RAM to play back the FlipBook.

If you have almost enough free RAM, consider quitting Softimage and using the command line executable also named flipbook (no upper case), which takes the arguments of the filename without number and extension, the start frame, the end frame, the step, and the frame rate desired. For instance, typing

```
flipbook mydb/RENDER_
PICTURES/explosion 1 100
1 30
```

into a shell window shows frames 1-100 of files named explosion, at 30 frames per second.

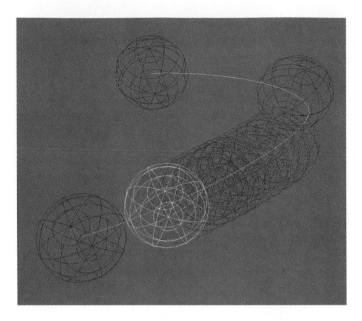

FIGURE 5.16 *Path translation: the white spline curve indicates the balls path between keyframes.*

The SaveKey→Explicit Translation menu cell allows you to save individual keyframes for an object's location in X, Y, or Z space, or in all three at the same time. This means that the motion in one axis can be animated without affecting the motion in the other axes. Using explicit translation does not create a motion path but rather "hard-codes" the object location relative to the global axis.

NOTE

The statement about explicit translation hard-coding an object's location is accurate, but not complete. Explicit translation really saves the position of the object relative to its immediate parent in the hierarchy, if it has one, and to the global center if it does not. This has powerful implications for layering animations and controlling animation within hierarchies.

The third and least used type of translation is the *trajectory*. A trajectory is somewhat like a cross between an explicit translation and a path translation. When an object with explicit translation has the translation converted to a trajectory, with either the Path→Convert to Trajectory or Plot→Trajectory command, a spline path is created with a keyframe set *at every frame*. This means that the timing between keyframes is no longer editable separately from the motion through space. Trajectories completely lack function curves, however, unlike either of the other two options.

To illuminate the differences between these methods of animating translation, cast your gaze on the following tutorial, "Shootin' Hoops."

TUTORIAL: SHOOTIN' HOOPS

Open the Shootin_Hoops scene from the courseware database, or just create a simple scene like the one in Figure 5.17, with a simple basketball court, a basketball hoop, and three basketballs placed around the three-point line. The object of the tutorial is to animate the balls as if they were thrown against the backboard, bouncing off the rim, and maybe going through the basket on the way to the floor.

FIGURE 5.17 *The basketball court.*

1. **Translate the First Ball.**

   Choose the first ball, the one on the right side of the court. Start with your Time Slider at frame 1 and translate the ball to standing height. Save a keyframe for it as explicit translation, with SaveKey→Object→Explicit Translation→All.

2. **Set Another Keyframe.**

   Move forward 15 frames and position the ball halfway through its arc, at the highest point it can reach and halfway to the basket. Save another keyframe by using your middle mouse button on the SaveKey menu cell (see Figure 5.18).

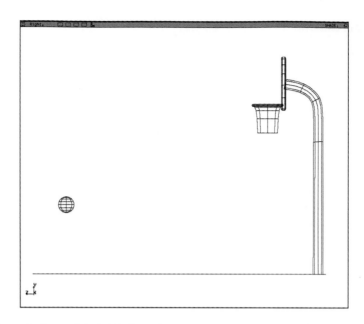

FIGURE 5.18 *A keyframe of the ball halfway through its arc.*

3. Finish the Ball's Animation.

Move to frame 30 and keyframe the ball at the backboard. Three frames later, keyframe the ball on the rim. Set a few more keyframes as you wish for the ball to fall to the floor and bounce to a quick stop. In the Info→Selection dialog box, name the ball Explicit_Ball. If you need to edit the motion of the ball, you have to move to the keyframe you want to change, translate the ball in space, and save a new keyframe over the old one (see Figure 5.19).

4. Set the Middle Ball's Path.

Move back to frame 1, select the middle ball, and repeat the process described in steps 1 through 3. This time, however, make the basket and use path translation (SaveKey→Object→Translation) instead of explicit translation. See how a path describing the basketball's arc is drawn through space and into the basket as you set the keyframes. This method is easier for you to edit because if you don't like the path taken by the ball, you can simply move the Control points on the path with the M supra key.

Name this second ball by opening the Schematic View window and double-clicking the ball (it should still be the selected object). This method brings up the same dialog as the Info→Selection menu cell. Name the ball Path_Translation_Ball.

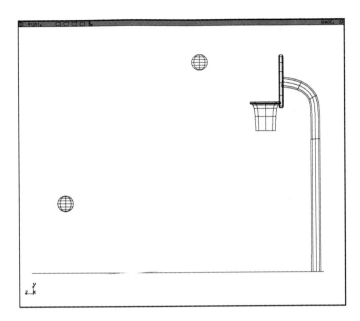

FIGURE 5.19   *Set more keyframes for the ball.*

5. **Use a Trajectory for the Last Ball.**

Repeat the process for the last ball using the Explicit Translation method. Name the ball Convert_To_Trajectory_Ball.

Now go to the Path menu in the Motion module, and choose the command Path→Convert to Trajectory. Select the motion path that appears for the ball to display the trajectory data. See how a keyframe is placed at every frame? The trajectory method locks in the timing along with the spatial location so that it cannot easily be changed. Trajectory is most often useful for plotting data, like acceleration or deformation data, and then storing it for later use.

6. **Save It.**

Save your scene as Shootin_Hoops2.

Play your scene back a few times. Pay attention to how the different balls move and how easy (or difficult) it is to edit the paths taken on the way to the hoop. Note that you can edit the path taken by the path and explicit balls, but you can't so easily change the timing to make the behavior look more realistic. You'll learn how to adjust the timing when you investigate function curves (F-curves).

FUNCTION CURVES: INFINITE CONTROL

Keyframing is only a beginning in Softimage. To define how a value changes over time, Softimage generates an equation based on the value of the keyframes you set and at what frame you set them. With this equation, Softimage can determine what a value should be at *any* point in time, not just the points you set explicitly. The equation is a *spline* and can be seen visually as a graph with the value being changed on the vertical axis and time in frames running along the horizontal axis. The official name in Softimage for this graph is a *Function Curve*, or *F-curve* for short (see Figure 5.20).

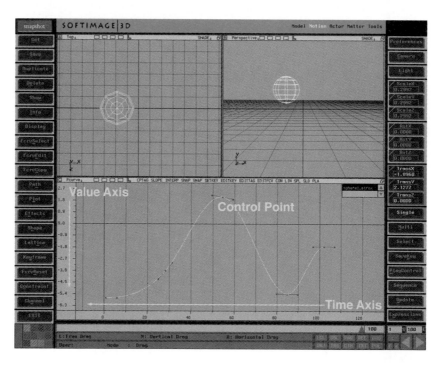

FIGURE 5.20   *An F-curve.*

The F-curve isn't just to help you visualize animation, however. The F-curve is a potent way to create and edit animation. Each object in your scene can have a separate F-curve for each animatable parameter, creating hundreds and hundreds of F-curves for you to work with.

Keyframes appear as points on the F-curve spline. Using the F-curve, you can:

- Add keyframes
- Delete keyframes

- Move keyframes
- Tag groups of keyframes and edit them
- Translate and scale the whole F-curve
- Copy and paste F-curve segments and whole F-curves

All these functions (and many more) are found in either the F-curve window or the F-curve menu cells in the Motion module.

Let's look at a simple example to get started. The tire in Figure 5.21 was animated to bounce along the floor using Explicit Translation. The F-curve window below the ball shows the three F-curves for Explicit Translation, TransX, TransY, and TransZ. The vertical axis of the F-curve shows the value of the parameters in Softimage units. The horizontal axis shows the time proceeding from left to right. Each F-curve tells us exactly where, in that axis, the object is at each and every frame in the animation.

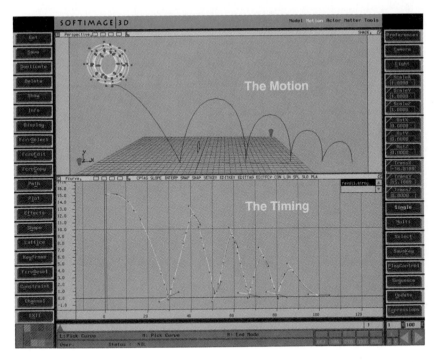

FIGURE 5.21   *The animation (above) and the F-curve (below). Notice the F-curve axes: The horizontal axis is for time and the vertical axis is for parameter values.*

Create your own bouncing ball by translating a sphere through space and setting keyframes for explicit translation with SaveKey→Object→Explicit Translation→All, so you can follow along, trying out some of the F-curve options. Display the F-curves for your ball by selecting it and choosing F-curve Select→Object→Explicit Translation→All.

Figure 5.22 shows a fairly typical F-curve. As the F-curve moves through time, it changes slope as it goes through the Control points you created by setting keyframes. By default, Softimage uses a Bezier spline for the curve, which means that the control handles of the Bezier modify the slope (the tangency of the curve) at every point along the curve. Technically speaking, the slope of the curve at any one point is the rate of change in the parameter being animated—think of this as "how fast it's going." The change in that slope over time (say, from the first point to the second point) is called acceleration, which is easy to think about as "how the animation is speeding up or slowing down."

Also by default, Softimage eases in from the first point and eases out to the last point. Using these Bezier curves avoids jerky-looking animation, because the values accelerate and decelerate at the start and the finish.

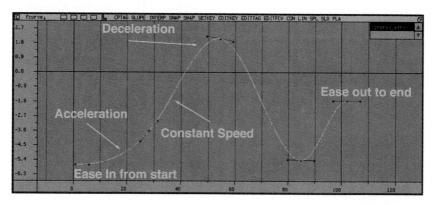

FIGURE 5.22 *F-curve terminology.*

EDITING ANIMATION WITH F-CURVES

If you wish to edit your bouncing ball's behavior, say, to make it bounce higher, you do not have to re-keyframe the new motion. You can simply edit the location of points in an F-curve with the M key, just as you would edit any curve! By holding the M key and dragging a point on the F-curve with the mouse, you can change the value of the animated parameter and move the point to a different frame in time.

Try editing the points' location by dragging the top points of the TransY F-curve higher in the F-curve window and playing back your animation (see Figure 5.23). You can also click the Bezier handles to adjust the curve tangency, which changes how the ball accelerates in and out of points.

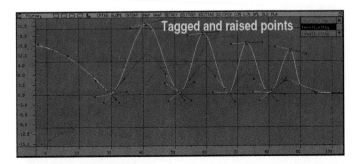

FIGURE 5.23 *F-curve tangency.*

So how do you know, if the window contains more than one F-curve, which F-curve is which? In the top-left corner of the F-curve window is a small scrolling box containing the abbreviations for the F-curves you have chosen to look at (see Figure 5.24). This is a big help if you are viewing multiple function curves in the same F-curve window and can't figure out which is which. Just pick an F-curve name in that small scrolling list box to select a curve to edit.

> **TIP**
>
> If you don't want to play a preview to see your changes, you can move the Time Slider to a frame affected by the F-curve point you plan to move, move the point, and then press R to refresh the scene. This instantly updates the scene at the frame you are on.

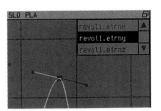

FIGURE 5.24 *The F-curve list.*

TAGGED GROUPS OF POINTS

You can also tag groups of points on the F-curve and move them all at once with the translation menu cells. Try it out by tagging all the highest points on the TransY F-curve, entering the TAG mode, and translating them up in Y twice as high as they were and slightly to the left (later in time). During playback, your ball should now bounce twice as high and hang a little longer before crashing to earth.

BRYAN BALLINGER

Tusky. Copyright Bryan Ballinger, 1996.

Bryan Ballinger

Softimage Animator

Kid Ballinger Productions

ATR: Bryan, tell the readers a bit about yourself.

Bryan: I'm a freelance illustrator doing mostly 3D illustration for print. My company's name is Kid Ballinger Productions. I'm also going to start working at Big Idea Productions, who do the Veggie Tales series of videos and books.

I graduated from the Columbus College of Art and Design in 1990 with a degree in illustration. I worked at Microsoft for 5 years as an illustration lead on many different multimedia productions, including Encarta, Explorapedia, Ants, and so on. When Microsoft acquired Softimage, I started using Softimage. Previously, I'd used Infini-D and Electric Image for 3D work.

ATR: What interests you most as an artist?

Bryan: Telling a story in an image is what I find a ton of fun doing. Especially if it's humorous. My two all time favorite artists are Etienne Delessert and Johnny Hart. Delessert is an amazing traditional illustrator. He did a children's book called *Ashes, Ashes,* which is my favorite kid's book. Johnny Hart is the cartoonist who does the strip B.C. Both have influenced my work a great deal.

ATR: What were the other skills you had before you met Softimage 3D|Extreme?

Bryan: Sculpting helped a lot. I'd done 3D illustration with clay and sculpy before working in Softimage. My background in illustration has helped a lot with designing scenes. I also took three years of color concept in college, which has been very valuable.

Toys. Copyright Microsoft, 1996.

ATR: Would you characterize your work as art, technique, skill, elbowgrease, or something entirely different?

Bryan: I have nowhere near the technical expertise of many Softimage users, but since I specialize in art for children, I treat Softimage as just another illustration tool. I've been doing children's art for about 10 years, so I tend to emphasize the art side over the techy, but both are important.

When I'm doing a job, I always start by sketching in my sketchbook first. After I've got the composition where I want it, then I jump into Soft. If I'm working on something that I haven't quite figured out how I'm going to build, I'll usually put on some ambient music, but if I'm just cranking something out I put on some heavier stuff. I spend most of my time in the model and material areas. Since most of my work is for print I don't spend as much time in Motion, but I do work in Actor a lot for posing of characters.

Eggs. Copyright Bryan Ballinger, 1996. Winner 1997 3D Design Big Kahuna Awards, Print Category.

ATR: What slows you down?

Bryan: I find that when I'm confronted with a huge dialog box filled with a ton of text entry fields, it will tend to interrupt my creative flow.

Copyright Bryan Ballinger, 1998.

Copyright Bryan Ballinger, 1998.

Sport Guys. Copyright Bryan Ballinger, 1998.

Trouser. Copyright Bryan Ballinger, 1998.

F-CURVE WINDOW OPTIONS

Along the top of the F-curve window is a series of small abbreviated commands that do clever things to help your workflow and enable you to stay within the F-curve window while editing (see Figure 5.25).

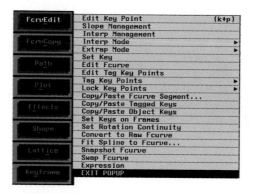

FIGURE 5.25   *F-curve commands.*

EDITKEY AND SETKEY

EditKey and SetKey are two ways to add and delete points on the F-curve spline. If you click the EditKey button and check the Status Bar, you'll discover that you can use the left button to move points, the middle mouse button to insert new points, and the right mouse button to remove unwanted points. If you want to precisely control the frame and value parameters of a point, click SetKey and pick a point. The Set Key dialog box with edit options then shows you every point on the curve and the values each point has (see Figure 5.26).

SWAP AND SNAP

Swap and Snap enable you to experiment without fear of screwing up your animation. Think of Swap and Snap as controllable undos. When you edit a spline in the F-curve window, the previous state of the curve is saved into the swap buffer, and a thin, dashed line shows you what the F-curve used to look like. If at any point in your work you decide that the old F-curve was better, simply click the Swap button to recall the old curve and place the new one in the swap buffer. If while editing you decide to save an intermediate F-curve before exploring further, click the Snap button, which replaces the saved F-curve in the buffer with the current F-curve but does not replace the current F-curve as the active F-curve.

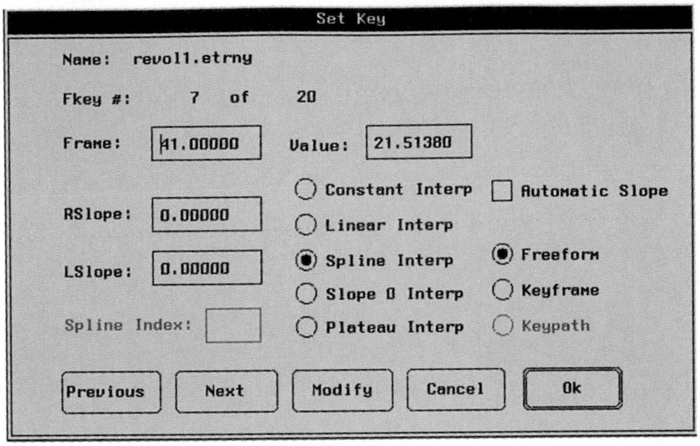

```
                          Set Key
   Name:   revol1.etrny

   Fkey #:      7   of     20

   Frame:   [41.00000    Value:  [21.51380 ]

                       ◯ Constant Interp    ☐ Automatic Slope
   RSlope:  [0.00000 ]  ◯ Linear Interp
                       ◉ Spline Interp      ◉ Freeform
   LSlope:  [0.00000 ]  ◯ Slope 0 Interp    ◯ Keyframe
   Spline Index: [    ] ◯ Plateau Interp    ◯ Keypath

   [ Previous ]  [ Next ]  [ Modify ]  [ Cancel ]  [ Ok ]
```

FIGURE 5.26   *The Set Key dialog box.*

SLOPE

Slope is a critical tool because it controls a parameter's rate of change in and out of Control points, which is a fancy way of saying that it controls the timing of the actions being animated. Because the normal functions of the Bezier control handles keep the two sides even (with the same tangency), the default Bezier curve is not suited to any motion that changes from acceleration to deceleration (or changes direction entirely) at a single Control point.

The Slope key allows you to *break* the slope, which means that the tangency control handles now operate independently of one another. A good example of when you might want this option is when your ball bounces on the floor. As the ball approaches the floor, it accelerates due to the force of gravity, but at the instant of contact that acceleration should become deceleration as it bounces up against gravity, slowing down. Try breaking the slope of the bouncing ball Y translation F-curve at the point when the ball hits the ground by choosing the Slope command and then clicking the point you want to break with the middle mouse button (see Figure 5.27).

The Slope command also allows you to *unify* the slope, meaning that the control handles are once again connected. Unifying the slope by clicking on the point with the left mouse button again makes the animation completely smooth.

CPTAG

CPTag enables you to copy tagged groups of points and paste them elsewhere on the function curve. For instance, if you perfected the Y axis curve for a single bounce, you could copy it and paste it again and again to create additional bounces.

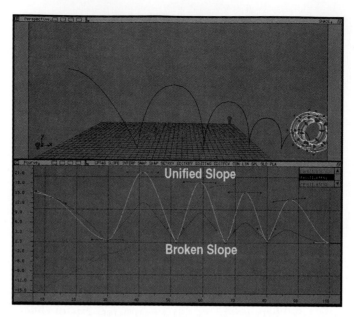

FIGURE 5.27   *Breaking the slope.*

SPLINE, LINEAR, SLOPE, AND PLATEAU

The Spline, Linear, Slope, and Plateau controls adjust the method of interpolation used between points. Because the default Bezier spline curve isn't always the best choice for all kinds of animation, the F-curve window offers some other types of curves that might better suit your specific needs (see Figure 5.28).

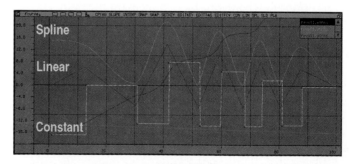

FIGURE 5.28   *F-curve splines.*

Choosing the Linear command causes the interpolation between each point to become a straight line. Linear is an excellent choice for animating lights and colors, where ease in and ease out are not so important. Using Linear interpolation on movement creates a mechanical, robotic look.

Slope equalizes all the Bezier control handles for tangency so that there is equal ease in and ease out for each point.

Plateau, very useful for character animation, retains the ease in and ease out attributes of the Bezier curve, but it uses a linear segment between two points on the curve with the same value. Ordinarily, a Bezier curve going through two points adopts a somewhat serpentine path through the Control points, which can cause backsliding, foot dragging, and other unwanted behavior in characters. Using Plateau means your characters stay where you put them but still move fluidly.

Spline changes the F-curve interpolation back to the default Bezier spline method.

INTERP

The Interp command (short for interpolation) allows you to have sections with different interpolation in the same F-curve. Clicking two adjacent points changes the interpolation between them. An F-curve can then mix and match sections with different interpolation to create motion effects, mixing sharp changes in action with more gradual ease in and ease out.

SCALING AND TRANSLATING F-CURVES

You can, if in OBJ mode (not TAG mode), also translate and scale the entire F-curve. Translating an F-curve in the X axis has the effect of moving the whole animation in time, either earlier or later depending on which way you go. By looking at the frame values on the X axis, you can easily synchronize action in the F-curve with a specific frame.

Translating the F-curve in the Y axis has the effect of changing all the values in that F-curve by the same amount. You can make the ground plane that the ball bounces on higher or lower by translating the TransY F-curve in the Y direction. Try it out.

DELETING F-CURVES

You should be wondering at this point how to *remove* animation from an option— you know, make it quit moving. That seems like a tall order in Softimage because so much is geared towards actually *adding* animation, but it's really quite simple. The F-curve Reset menu cell allows you to remove all the animation associated with an object, or just one of the many F-curves you might have set. Save your bouncing ball scene and try it out.

CREATING A CYCLE WITH EXTRAP MODE

Sometimes you want an object to have a repetitive motion, such as a wheel spinning or the pendulum of a clock swinging back and forth. In the F-curve Edit→Extrap Mode menu, you find the commands required to accomplish what you need.

CYCLE

F-curve Edit→Extrap Mode→Cycle repeats the section of the F-curve you have active from the first Control point to the last Control point. If the first and last points do not have the same value, you may see some jumping in the animation as the object snaps from the last frame back to the first.

CONSTANT

F-curve Edit→Extrap Mode→Constant finds the slope of the last two points in the F-curve and simply continues on at the same slope indefinitely. This type of motion is great for objects that constantly spin. Both of these effects update automatically if you change one of the points on which they depend, so you can change the cycle or slope at any time as your needs change.

TUTORIAL: SHOOTIN' HOOPS 2

Now let's use the F-curves with the scenes you created earlier in the chapter to get a better idea of just how F-curves can help you. Load the Shootin_Hoops2 scene that you saved earlier (or load the Shootin_Hoops2 scene from the courseware database). Remember you are interested in the differences between explicit translation, path translation, and trajectory translation.

1. **Examine the Explicit Translation F-curves.**

   Choose the explicit translation ball and look at the F-curves with the F-curve→Select→Object→Explicit Translation command. You should see three curves that look familiar: the TransX, TransY, and TransZ curves. As before, the vertical axis of the graph displays Softimage units, the horizontal axis time.

2. **Adjust the F-curve Points.**

   Because you know how to change the timing of an action by sliding the points on the F-curve earlier or later, adjust the timing of the first ball so that it looks more natural as it falls towards the hoop and bounces to the floor.

3. **Adjust the Path Translation Timing.**

Select the second ball, the path translation ball, and select the F-curve→ Select→Object→Translation menu cell. You should now see the function curve for the path translation. While the horizontal axis remains the time in frames, the vertical axis has changed to a decimal from 0 to 1. The vertical axis now represents the proportion along the path where the object is, at a given frame in time represented by the X axis. In other words, 0 in Y is 0 percent along the path, 1 is 100 percent along the path, and 0.5 is 50 percent along the path (see Figure 5.29).

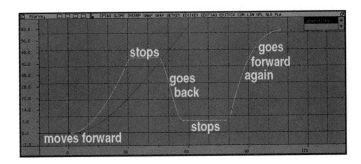

FIGURE 5.29 *Adjusting the timing.*

Even better, you can change the timing of the ball along the path very easily by adjusting the vertical level of the Control points. When the two Control points at different times have the same value and the slope between them is flat (set to 0), the object won't progress along that path at all. When the slope becomes negative, the object moves backwards along the path. The angle of the Bezier control handles even determines how the ball accelerates and decelerates to each point along the path.

4. **Mimic Realistic Ball Motion.**

Adjust the points along the path and the Bezier control handles to give the ball a satisfying basketball motion, accelerating into the floor with the force of gravity, slowing to a halt gradually at the top of each arc, and then accelerating downward again.

5. **Convert the Last Ball to a Trajectory.**

The last ball is currently using an Explicit Translation, but you want to convert it to the last type of translation, a trajectory. Along the way you'll find out how to convert back and forth between path and explicit translation.

Now convert that explicit translation into a trajectory by using the Path→Conv to Trajectory command. A Trajectory is a special kind of F-curve with a value at every frame. In this way, the timing of the curve is locked into the same data as the position, and neither is very editable at all.

A Trajectory can be thought of as raw data sampling the value at each and every frame, not so much as a spline that approximates the change in a value over time. Another term for this kind of F-curve is a Raw F-curve. Raw F-curves can be converted back into splines with the F-curve→Edit→Fit to Spline command, which does a best fit within a given tolerance to create a spline that matches the overall shape of the raw data, smoothing over small variations. In general, path translation and explicit translation F-curves are more useful than trajectories.

These three kinds of translation each have their strong suits, and it's important for you to understand the differences and advantages between them.

PATH TRANSLATION

Path translation is so useful that it deserves its own menu cell in the Motion module, called the Path menu. You already know how to create a motion path for an object by setting keyframes, but you can perform the same animation another way, by drawing the spline first, and choosing the Path→Pick Path command.

The Path→Pick Path command gives you the Path Timing dialog in which you choose the frame to start the object along the path and the frame in which the object should reach the end of the path. Clicking the Ok button then creates the translation F-curve for the object and assigns the object to the path. In the Schematic view, you may activate the Motion options and see the relationship between the object and the path you've drawn represented by a line segment connecting the two.

If you wish to remove the object from the path, you may delete the path or use the F-curve→Reset→Translation command, which cuts the object free but leaves the path in the schematic window.

If you wish to assign the object to a different path with a new translation F-curve, simply choose Path→Pick Path again and assign the object to the new path. However, this deletes any edits you made to the translation F-curve, such as easing in or out. To keep the translation F-curve while swapping paths, use the Path→Substitute command.

The Path→Timing command recalls the same Path Timing dialog box that appeared when you first attached the object to the path, allowing you to change your mind about the starting and ending frames. Another occasionally used set of tools is the Show and Hide Path and Show and Hide All Paths commands, which toggle the visibility of all the spline paths currently assigned as paths to objects in your scene. These tools do help clean up complex scenes.

TUTORIAL: HORSE RACE

Practice your newfound path animation expertise with the following tutorial. Use the horse race scene in the courseware database, or build your own scene imitating a carnival horse race game with small cut-out figures of horses attached on tracks to a vertical board. Suckers (oops, I mean contestants) place small wagers on each horse, and the race operator starts a motorized chain that drags the horses along the tracks. Along the raceway are many fits and starts, with the winning horse coming in just a nose in front of the other racers, and winning a stuffed animal for his trouble (see Figure 5.30).

FIGURE 5.30   *The horse race.*

1. **Set the First Horse's Path.**

   In the scene, there are three horses and three paths (see Figure 5.31). Select the first horse and connect him to the first path with the Path→Pick Path command. Set the start and end frames to 1 and 90, respectively. Repeat the process with each horse, attaching each to a unique path with the same start and end frame timing. Now play your animation.

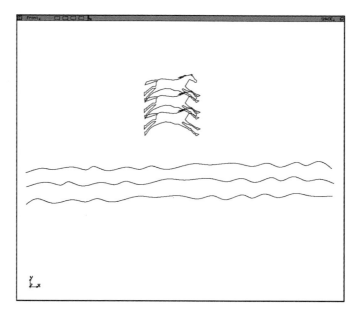

FIGURE 5.31 *Connect each horse to a path with the Path→Pick Path command.*

2. **Pick a Winner.**

   Change the timing on the second horse with the Path→Timing command so that he completes his journey along the path at frame 85, becoming the winner. Play your animation (see Figure 5.32).

3. **Change Horse 3's Timing with Sequence→Selection.**

   Select the third horse and use the Sequence→Selection menu cell (lower-right corner of the interface) to change the timing of that horse. The Sequence menu cell evenly changes the timing for a selected object or all the objects in a scene. It can shrink or enlarge the animation timing by a percentage or offset the whole animation by sliding the F-curves earlier or later in time. For Horse 3, offset the timing by 5 frames (making it late out of the gate), and scale the sequence by 90 percent to make him run faster (see Figure 5.33). Now play your animation.

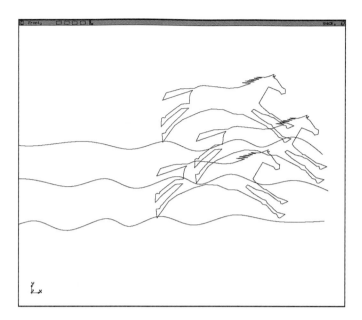

FIGURE 5.32 *Make Horse 2 the winner with the Path→Timing command.*

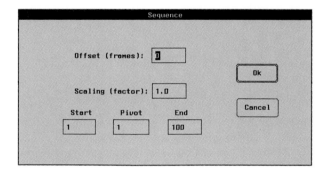

FIGURE 5.33 *The Sequence dialog.*

4. Change Horse 1's F-curve.

Select the first horse and bring up his path translation function curves with F-curve Select→Object→Translation. Use the EditKey command (in the F-curve window) to add in several more Control points to the path timing, and drag them up and down so that the curve has a serpentine shape. Whenever the slope of the path translation timing F-curve becomes flat, the horse stops. When the slope becomes negative, the horse goes backwards. Try it out by playing your animation (see Figure 5.34).

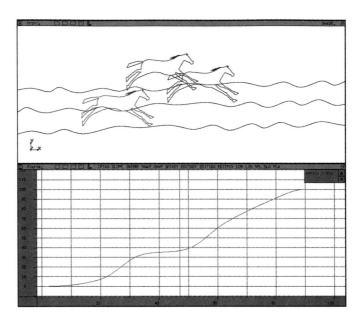

FIGURE 5.34   *Edit Horse 1's F-curve into a serpentine shape.*

5. Try a Linear Curve.

Select the second horse and add similar Control points to the path timing F-curve. This time, use the LIN command (in the F-curve window) to convert the spline curve into a linear curve. When you play the animation now, the horse motion should be somewhat jerky (see Figure 5.35).

6. Render a FlipBook.

Pick a winner on your own and edit the translation F-curve so that the horse you picked gets to 100 percent along the path (a value of 1 in the Y axis of the F-curve window) sooner (in fewer frames) than the others. Play it back, then pick a camera position by using the O, Z, and P supra keys in the Perspective window, and render a 100 frame FlipBook at a resolution of 320 × 240 pixels. Play your rendered FlipBook and save your scene as Horserace2 for future use.

In the Horserace tutorial, you learned how to use the path timing to change the effect of a path translation. You also learned how to directly edit the change in a value over time with a function curve. These two skills are critical for riding your animations to a photo finish!

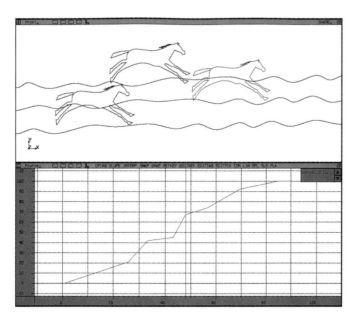

Figure 5.35 *Using a linear curve instead of a spline curve makes the motion less smooth.*

Animating Material and Texture Attributes

The process of animating materials and textures starts a little differently than animating objects. *All* the attributes that you set in the Matter mode, Material Editor, and Texture Editor create animation function curves when you click the Key button in those dialog boxes. You can keep these dialog boxes open while you set keyframes, which makes for an easy and productive workflow.

Tutorial: Changing Colors

The following tutorial is just a simple example of setting material keyframes. See Chapter 12, "It Looks Pretty: Materials and Textures," for more detailed examples of how to use the materials and textures dialogs to create and animate color and texture on your objects.

1. **Make a Stoplight.**

   Get the Stoplight scene from the CD-ROM or build your own simple traffic signal, like the one in Figure 5.36. Next switch to the Matter module and turn the Perspective View window to display in Shaded mode.

FIGURE 5.36 *The rendered stoplight.*

Select the sphere that makes up the lowest light in the stoplight, named Red in the Schematic view (see Figure 5.37).

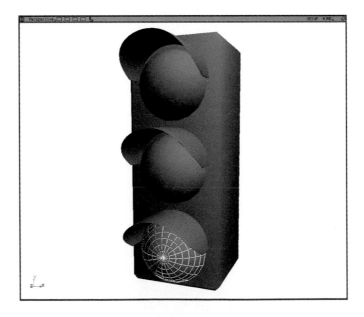

FIGURE 5.37 *The stoplight with the lower red light bulb selected.*

Call up the Material Editor by clicking the Material menu cell. If you move the Material Editor dialog box so that it doesn't obstruct the Perspective view (by dragging the title bar with the left mouse button), you can see (in Shaded mode) the effects of your work interactively, without closing the Material Editor.

2. **Go to Black.**

Select a black material color for the object, press R, and the scene refreshes, showing the new color. Set a keyframe for this color by dragging your Time Slider to frame 1 (don't close the Material Editor dialog yet) and by pressing the Key button in the Material Editor dialog (see Figure 5.38).

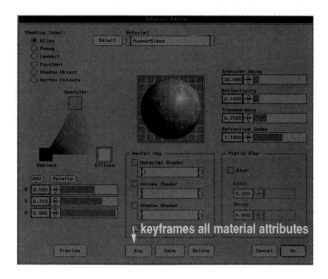

FIGURE 5.38 *The Material Editor dialog.*

3. **Turn Red.**

With the Material Editor still onscreen, move the Time Slider to frame 10 and choose a red color for the sphere. Click the Key button to set another material color keyframe.

4. **Watch the Light Change.**

With the Material Editor still onscreen, drag the Time Slider back and forth across the Timeline. Note how the color bars change as you go, and how the color gradient changes as you go, showing you the precise value of the Color parameters as they change over time. Close the Material Editor.

5. **Check the Material F-curves.**

Enter the Motion module and choose the F-curve Select→Material→All command. The resulting F-curve view shows all the material function curves for the object, including specular color, ambient color, diffuse color, reflectivity, transparency, index of refraction, and Blur parameters. You cannot, however, animate the shading algorithm. All the material F-curves can be edited in the usual ways.

6. **Add Keyframes.**

Set additional keyframes for the red light that turns to black from frames 30 to 40. Select the top light sphere, named Green in the schematic, and add keyframes for a black material at frames 1 and 30, and a green material at 40.

You can now play your animation in the Shaded mode to see the light change from red to green.

ANIMATING TEXTURES

All the Texture parameters can be animated in precisely the same way as the material attributes. You simply set keyframes with the Key button in the 2D Texture File or 3D Texture File dialog boxes (see Figure 5.39). Like the Material Editor, the 2D Texture File dialog can remain present onscreen while you drag the Time Slider and set multiple keyframes.

The secret to animating multiple textures is to animate the Blend portion assigned to each texture. For instance, if you want one texture to morph slowly over time into another, set the blending of Texture A to 100 percent at frame 1, and set the blending of Texture B (using the Next button) to 0 percent at frame 1. Remember to use Key for both sets of values, and then drag the Time Slider to frame 100. Now set Texture A's blending to 0 percent and Texture B's blending to 100 percent. Then set the keys for both. This accomplishes a crossfade between Textures A and B.

All the texture attributes for both 2D and 3D textures create regular F-curves that you can edit and manipulate in the normal way. Take a look at the F-curve Select→Texture 2D and F-curve Select→Texture 3D menu cells for all the F-curves available there.

More information on how to animate textures can be found in Chapter 12.

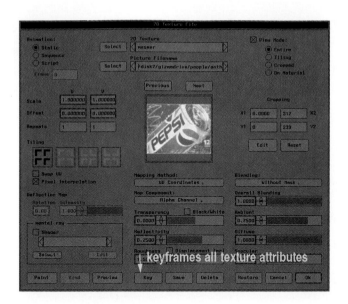

FIGURE 5.39 *The 2D Texture File dialog.*

ANIMATING WITH CLUSTERS AND CLUSTER CENTERS

Clusters are, at the most basic level, a way to name a group of vertices or Control points on an object, and then use that named group in an animation. You create clusters on an object by tagging a group of Control points (with the Tag Rect menu cell or the T supra key). A polygon mesh or patch object can have as many clusters defined as you need, and, unlike shapes, the clusters can be named, so that selecting them later isn't such a chore.

Usually a cluster is formed of vertices that are in a contiguous area, so that area of the mesh is deformed by one cluster. However, there is no rule that says you can't assign every other vertex on a mesh to one of two clusters, and animate the mesh shape that way. In fact, there is no rule that says that vertices can belong only to one cluster. This means that clusters can overlap somewhat.

You can define tagged points on an object as a cluster by choosing the Shape→Set Cluster command from the Motion module. When you do, the Cluster List dialog box immediately appears onscreen and allows you to change the name of the current cluster, making it more understandable. For example, you could change Cluster0 to LeftCornerMouth instead.

Once a cluster has been defined, it joins the other clusters present in the Cluster List for that object (see Figure 5.40).

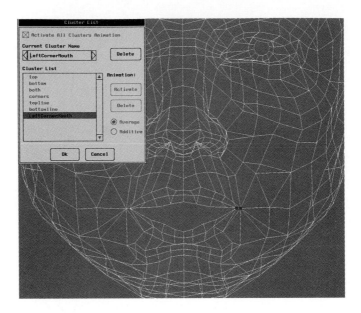

FIGURE 5.40   *The Cluster List dialog.*

Clusters themselves can be animated with a Cluster Key so that all the vertices that make up the cluster move, scale, or rotate together. This means that an object can have groups of one or more vertices that change position over time, just like a shape animation.

The difference is that while a shape animation saves position data for each point in the object, resulting in a lot of animation data, animating with clusters makes each point in the cluster located relative to the *cluster center*. Doing so then stores only vector data for one local center per cluster. This method saves computation time and memory for large models, while accomplishing some of the same tasks as shape animation.

For instance, another way to animate a patch-based face object would be to tag and create clusters for each eyebrow region, the nose, the corners of the eyes, and four points around the mouth. Then the clusters could be translated around to deform the skin at those positions and keyframes could be set with SaveKey→Object→ ClusterKey.

Clusters may or may not have a cluster center. By default (and in older versions of Softimage) the software would automatically define a cluster center to be in the spatial middle of the group of tagged points, and the location of that center would not be readily editable. This meant that there was no way to control the hinge around which the cluster was animated or the point from which it scaled.

In the current version of Softimage 3D|Extreme, you can create your own cluster center by checking the Create Center option box. If you do, Softimage adds a null object to your scene (visible in the Schematic view). In Center mode (CTR), you can move that center to any position you want. Scaling the center (in Normal Object mode) causes all the points in that cluster to move either to or from the location of the cluster center. This is a useful tip for animating muscle bulges, facial deformations, and breathing actions.

CONSTRAIN OBJECTS TO A CLUSTER AND VICE VERSA

Clusters have another useful purpose—they can be pinned to other objects, and other objects can be pinned to them. This solves a very thorny problem in character animation, which is how do individual objects stay attached to another object that is deforming without deforming themselves?

A great example is a cartoon character with a coat having many buttons down the front over the character's belly. When the belly grows, stretches, and shakes, the buttons need to move apart realistically but stay with the belly as it swings back and forth. The buttons could be separate objects constrained to clusters set on the surface of the belly (see Figure 5.41).

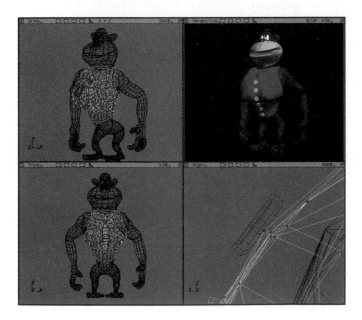

FIGURE 5.41 *Using clusters, you can ensure the character's coat buttons move realistically when his belly moves.*

Conversely, what if the character has a pierced ear (or other body part) and the animation calls for the earring to be pulled away from the character, stretching the ear lobe? The ear cluster could be pinned, or constrained, to the earring so that the cluster moves exactly with the earring, stretching and deforming as the earring swings (see Figure 5.42). Accomplishing this feat of magic is simple enough.

FIGURE 5.42 *Because it is constrained to the earring, the ear cluster stretches when the earring moves.*

To make an object connect to a cluster and follow it wherever it goes, first select the object with the target cluster, and activate the cluster you want to attach. Open the Cluster list with Shape→Cluster List, and select the cluster of choice from the text list of names. Then select the slave object and choose the Constraint→Constrain Object to Cluster command. Pick the target object (the one with the cluster) to complete the command.

The slave object should now move to the target cluster, with the local center of the slave object and the cluster center of the active target cluster co-located in space.

To make a cluster follow an object, simply activate the cluster of your choice with the Shape→Cluster List command, choose Constraint→Constrain Cluster to Object, and pick the object.

TUTORIAL: RUB-A-DUB-DUB

To demonstrate and practice cluster animation, the following tutorial will use a more complex scene of a bathtub filled with water animated by a wave. On the wave bobs a rubber ducky (connected to the water with Constrain Object to Cluster), and sitting on the ducky's back is a bar of soap, also constrained to the duck with Constrain Object to Cluster. The duck's tail will be animated as a cluster to wiggle a bit. The duck's head will be a cluster that bobs up and down automatically as the duck rolls on the wave by constraining it to a null hanging in space. Along the way you'll learn how to use the Wave animation tool (see Figure 5.43).

FIGURE 5.43 *The rendered bath scene.*

SECTION ONE: MODELING

In the first set of exercises, we'll create the tub, the water, the duck, and the soap. Those of you who have not completed the modeling section can load the scene called TheBath, which has all the elements already made, and then skip to Section Two of the tutorial. If you have completed the basic modeling chapters or already have some practice modeling in Softimage, you should create the elements of the scene from scratch.

1. **The Tub.**

   Although there are lots of ways to make the tub, the fastest (and therefore usually the best) is to start with a simple revolution shape and make a few modifications. Visually imagine making a perfectly circular tub and then stretching it like taffy until it looks like the bathtub in your house.

   In the Model module, choose a NURBS curve to draw with (Draw→Curve→NURBS) and in the Front view draw a profile of the tub as if you cut through the wall of the tub with a hacksaw, right at the drain. Take a look at Figure 5.44 to guide you and make the profile in such a way that the edge of the drain is close to, but not on, the Y axis. The wall of the tub should have some thickness to it, which will help hide flaws in the water animation later on.

   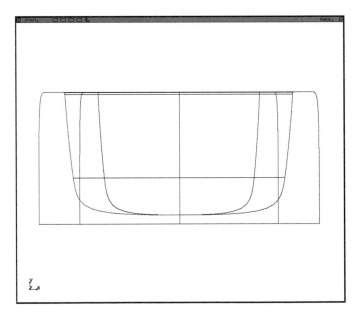

   FIGURE 5.44 *The revolved tool profile.*

   Now create a revolved surface from that profile with the Surface→Revolution tool, specifying a 360 degree revolution with 12 steps about the Y axis, made of a cubic NURBS curve in the Revolution dialog box. The results should look like Figure 5.45.

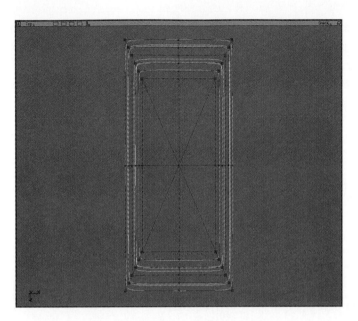

FIGURE 5.45   *The tagged and stretched tub revolution.*

Using the Top view and the Side view, tag all the points on the circular tub that are to the left (in positive X) of the drain, which should be created around the Y axis. Go to TAG mode, and translate the tagged group in positive X to make the length of the tub, stretching out the circular surface you started with until the proportions please you. Deselect the tagged group with the T supra key and the middle mouse button.

Select all the points on one side of the tub from the drain using the Top view and translate them in Z to stretch the tub's width to a proper size. Unselect that tagged group and do the same with the other side, until the proportions of the tub look big enough for a person (or two) to sit in.

2. **The Water.**

The water will be a patch surface, with sufficient subdivisions in it to make for good waves.

The best way create the water is to make a radial grid by drawing a NURBS curve from the Y axis out to the middle of the tub outer wall, with Control points at each Softimage 3D|Extreme grid unit (you can turn on Grid Lock if you wish, but the spacing is not crucial). Revolve the curve you just made into a 360 degree closed NURBS surface with Surface→Revolution.

Reshape the circular grid by tagging points and scaling them until the grid shape matches the bathtub perfectly, with the edges of the grid hidden by the thickness of the bathtub walls (see Figure 5.46). The wave moves the edges a bit, so leave plenty of overhang to avoid a gap between the water and the edge of the tub.

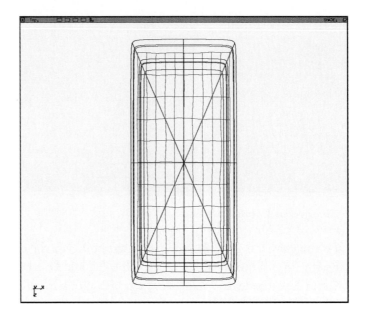

FIGURE 5.46 *The tub and water.*

Untag the grid, name it water by double-clicking it with the left mouse button, and for extra credit, randomize the surface point locations slightly with Effect→Randomize to make the water surface a little uneven.

3. **The Wave.**

The wave effect is a venerable Softimage 3D|Extreme custom effect that displaces geometry (and whole objects) according to a wave propagating through space. You have control (via F-curves) over the wave amplitude, period, and decay.

You create a wave effect by itself and then attach it to nodes or hierarchies of objects. You start by drawing, in the Front view, a cross-section of the wave desired with a Cardinal curve. It can have as many ups and downs, positioned as high or low as you wish, to create a complex wave set (surfers may wish to make seven small waves followed by a big one). The only rules are that the wave cross-section cannot self-intersect (cross over itself), and the start and ending points must meet at the exact same Y value. Use the Y Grid Lock to assure meeting this last criteria (see Figure 5.47).

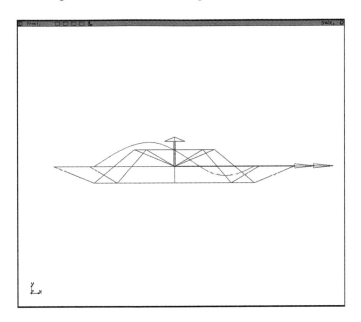

FIGURE 5.47   *The Wave effect spline curve.*

Try a curve like the one drawn here. Now with the curve selected, choose the Effects→Wave→Create command from the Motion module. The resulting dialog allows you to set many different parameters. Accept the defaults.

When done, click the OK button to create the wave. Softimage creates a new icon and places it in your scene. This is the epicenter of the wave, and if you animate its location, the wave center moves around. You can also change the scale of the wave and the rotation to affect the waves' orientation as they travel through space. Finally, attach it to the water object by selecting the wave icon and choosing the Effect→Wave→Attach→Node command.

Play back the animation to see the effect. You can make the wave bigger or smaller, move it in space, or edit the Wave→Decay F-curve to tune the wave to your liking.

4. **The Rubber Ducky.**

A simple rubber ducky can be sculpted out of a NURBS sphere without too much difficulty.

Create a NURBS sphere with 16 subdivisions. Rotate the sphere so that the poles of the sphere lie along the X axis and freeze the transformations of the sphere. The poles, where all the curve parameters that make up the surface meet, become the mouth and tail of the duck. Tag the first pole and drag inside the sphere to pull in the mouth. Untag all, then tag the second, third, and fourth rows of points, and translate them in X to form the bill. Scale them in Y to flatten them and move a few points on the end to widen the smile. Tag two new rows and position and scale as the duck head.

Continue this method to model the entire duck, by tagging cross sectional rows of points, and then translating and scaling them to form the body of a stretched out rubber ducky (see Figure 5.48).

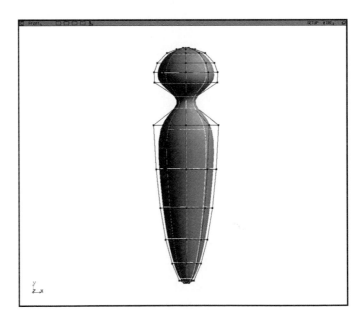

FIGURE 5.48   *The stretched ducky.*

When the stretched ducky is complete, you can bend the duck into an S shape, by again tagging and moving points, or by using a spline curve deformation to form the ducky into the familiar S-shape.

If you choose the Curve Deformation method, start first by drawing, in the Right view, a curve to represent the curve of the spinal column that the finished rubber ducky would have, if it had a spine. Try using a Cardinal curve for this purpose, drawn from bottom to top with Draw→Curve→Cardinal.

Then select the entire ducky object and deform it to the curve by choosing the Deformation→Curve→Node→Create command. Rescale the now deformed ducky with the Scale Transformation menu cells and slide it along the spline with the TransY menu cell until it looks right. Then convert the ducky back to a regular object, retaining the spline deformation, by choosing Deformation→ Curve→Node→Freeze, which removes the ducky from the curve. Now freeze the location of all the vertices into their new positions. From here, you can model further by pushing and pulling points.

Tag all the points along the bottom of the ducky and scale them until they form a concave base for the ducky to float on.

Finish the ducky by pulling some points on the nether pole to form a duck tail, pointed up in a jaunty fashion. Save your work (see Figure 5.49).

FIGURE 5.49   *The duck with a bill and tail.*

5. **The Soap.**

The final modeling phase is to create a bar of soap for the ducky to carry on its back.

Get a primitive cube and scale it in XYZ mode to form a rectangular soap-shaped object. Add the rounded corners with the Effect→Rounding command in the Model module. Try the default Rounding value of 25 Softimage 3D|Extreme units, and increase if necessary to achieve the desired effect. You may also use the Effect→Bevel tool for this job.

SECTION TWO: ANIMATION

In the current scene, the wave is already animated. We want to attach the rubber ducky to the surface of the water, the soap to the ducky's back, animate the shape of the tail, and make the head stay fixed in space, stretching the neck as the duck bobs around. We'll do all this with clusters, and Softimage will do most of the hard work for us, keeping everything together and moving the ducky consistently with the water wave action.

1. The Tail.

    We want the tail to wiggle a bit from side to side as if the ducky is shaking his tail as he floats along. We'll accomplish this by setting a cluster that includes all the Control points in the tail, and giving it a cluster center to rotate around that is located in the body of the duck.

    First tag the points that make up the tail of the duck. Then choose Shape→Set Cluster from the Motion module, and in the dialog that pops up, name the cluster tail, and choose to add a cluster center by checking the Create Center option box. Click the Ok button to seal the deal. Locate the cluster center, in either the View windows or in the Schematic view, and position the cluster center in the body of the duck, in front of the tail section. This location assists in making the motion believable and appealing.

    Now rotate the cluster center around the Y axis, which wags the tail to one side of the duck. Save a key for the cluster center at frame 1 with the SaveKey→Object→Rotation. Alternatively, you could select the duck object, rotate the tagged points, and then set a key with SaveKey→Object→ ClusterKey or Shape→Save ClusterKey.

    Move to frame 10 in your animation, rotate the tail to the other side of the duck body, and set a keyframe. Continue this process five more times at decreasing frame intervals to create a nice tail-wagging animation cycle. To make the duck wag his tail indefinitely, cycle the animation by selecting the F-curve for the action (either F-curveSelect→Object→Rotation or F-curveSelect→Object→ClusterKey, depending on the animation method you used) and choose the F-curveEdit→ExtrapMode→Cycle menu command.

Play back your animation and save your work.

2. The Soap.

The soap needs to ride on the ducky's back, keeping it relatively dry for your use in the tub. To do this, use the Constrain Object to Cluster command.

First define a cluster on the duck's back by tagging a point and using the Shape→Set Cluster command. Name the cluster "back" and do not give it a cluster center. Now select the soap, and in Center mode (CTR), move the soap object local center to the bottom of the soap. Then go back to Object mode (OBJ) and choose Constrain→Object to Cluster. The status line directs you to pick the object with the cluster you wish to constrain to. Pick the ducky with the active "back" cluster and the soap jumps to that location. Scale the soap as needed to fit the duck. Position the soap by returning to CTR mode and translating the local center, which offsets the soap.

Back in OBJ mode, try translating the ducky to see that the soap now follows.

Add small black spheres to the duck head in the location where the eyes should be to create pupils, giving form to the face. Use the same method as the soap to attach them to clusters set on the duck head so that they remain attached no matter what (see Figure 5.50).

FIGURE 5.50   *The ducky with its facial features and the soap attached.*

3. The Ducky.

The ducky itself bobs on the surface of the water, with just a little of the ducky beneath the waterline.

To do this, first tag a point on the surface of the water patch object, create a cluster with Shape→Set Cluster, and name it "ducky." Then move the local center of the ducky object to almost the bottom of the ducky, and center it in the body. This will be the point that attaches the ducky to the water, so for realism the point should be in the center of the contact patch between the ducky and the water. Back in OBJ mode, select the ducky and choose the Constraint→Object to Cluster. Pick the water as the object with the cluster you wish to constrain to. The ducky (and the attached soap) should snap to the water.

Play back the animation to see how the wave action transmits to the water patch object, then to the cluster on the water, then to the duck, and then to the soap!

4. The Duck Head.

The last step is to add the secondary action, the action that occurs as a result of the main animation action. Good secondary action gives complexity and appeal to the animation. In this case, we will imitate a natural behavior of birds, the behavior of keeping the head stationary while the body moves. Exaggerating the motion past what a duck would normally do will make the action more cartoonish.

Tag the points of the duck head, ending at the first row of the neck, and assign it as a cluster using Shape→Set Cluster. Name it head and add a cluster center (see Figure 5.51). Look in the Schematic view to locate the cluster center. Now get a null object (Get→Primitive→Null from the Model module) and place it in 3D space right where the cluster center currently is.

Finally, select the cluster center and constrain it to the location of the null you created with Constraint→Position. This locks the position of the head cluster to a given position in space, no matter where the rest of the body goes.

Play back the animation to examine your handiwork. Modify it as needed, and then add materials and render.

FIGURE 5.51   *Constraining the ducky.*

You can check your work against the QuickTime movie included on the CD-ROM called, you guessed it, RubADubDub.

CONCLUSION

Animation is the core of Softimage 3D|Extreme. The animation options available stretch throughout the entire package—this chapter is just a start. From here on out, every chapter will add to the list of animation features you now know how to use. In this chapter, you just scratched the surface.

You learned how to:

- Set keyframes for object motion and interpolate between them.
- Look at your animation in Wireframe previews, with fast playback, in Shaded view, and as rendered images.
- Set up path animation, explicit translation, and trajectories, and convert between them.
- Examine and edit F-curves to easily modify animation and timing.
- Animate colors and textures.
- Use cluster animation with cluster centers.
- Use constraint-based animation.

MODELING

3D image by Anthony Rossano and Mesmer Animation Labs. "Drop Zone" painting by Gary Faigin,
1995, used by permission of Academy of Realist Art, Seattle.

CHAPTER 6

THE MODEL SHOP—ALL ABOUT MODELING

With the basics of animation theory and a solid understanding of the Softimage interface behind us, it's time to move on to the Model module, where all the objects that populate your scenes are built.

This chapter, and those that follow in Part II, introduce you to the modeling tools and strategies found in Softimage 3D|Extreme. In this chapter, you will

- Build organic models by manipulating points
- Use curves to create surfaces
- Extrude text and other shapes
- Create revolved surfaces
- Create skinned surfaces
- Generate four-sided patch models
- Animate with relational modeling

Softimage 3D|Extreme has a remarkably complete and functional set of modeling tools for working with patches, NURBS, polygons, and, as you'll see in Chapter 10, "Meta-Clay Modeling." Objects can be generated from curves; surfaces can be trimmed, merged, and blended; and most of the time the modeling effect can be animated to change over time.

You can use the hierarchy in Softimage to connect and group components into more complex models or merge individual parts into a single complex object. Softimage has a full suite of Boolean tools, which you'll discover in Chapter 9, "Boolean Modeling," and the Boolean operations can be applied to hierarchies and even animated over time. The Model module Effects menu includes a number of custom effects (plug-ins developed by other companies and included in Softimage 3D|Extreme), and many more can be found on the Softimage Web site or elsewhere on the Internet.

Although Softimage has many tools for creating the objects you see around you, it falls well short of the mark in drafting tools. If you have an engineering or architectural background, you are likely to find the dearth of CAD tools in Softimage 3D quite frustrating. If, however, you are a sculptor or an artist, you will likely enjoy the more free-form expression of modeling in Softimage. Many high profile game development companies use Softimage 3D|Extreme for modeling their game environments and real-time actors because of the high degree of control provided by the Softimage polygon modeling tools and the polygon reduction toolset.

Because Softimage 3D|Extreme is an integrated package that includes all aspects of the computer animation process, you will find a high degree of synergy between the modeling tools, the Animation tools, and indeed all the modules. In Softimage you can mix and match animation and modeling as you create your scene.

For example, you can use such modeling tools as relational modeling to create animation effects and use such animation tools as Animated Duplicate and Spline Deformation to create new models. Although the capability to go back and forth so easily is empowering, it can also become overwhelming and lead to a lot of down time as you explore new interactions in the program. It is a good workflow policy to organize your project into discrete stages and stick with the plan. Usually that means modeling is the first step.

Modeling is defined as the action of creating all the objects that form the set for your production. Each object that is seen in your finished animation has to be manufactured in the computer before you can use it. This means that the walls and windows must be designed and constructed; the glasses, plates, and silverware must all be made; and the light switches, light fixtures, and light bulbs have to be modeled. In short, everything you want to see you must first create. Unless you plan to use nothing but 3D clip art (a practice that will not get you far), you will certainly have to become a proficient builder of objects.

OPEN YOUR EYES

The first step in mastering the art of modeling is to observe. Look at the objects that surround you and inspect their construction. Note which of them is symmetrical around one axis or cut from a flat sheet of metal. Look at how more complex objects are made up of many more simple objects. Begin to classify the stuff that makes up your surroundings by how it is constructed. Make lists of which are revolved objects, which are extruded, and which are sculpted or cast.

In general, greater attention to detail will make your work more interesting visually. For instance, a room detailed in modern spartan cubist furniture often looks less appealing and more "computery" when rendered than a drawing room outfitted in Victorian fashion with an ornate fireplace and grandfather clock.

One drawback to detail is that good modeling requires skill and time to complete. Another is that as you model in more detail, you generally increase the amount of polygonal and patch geometry, and your computer becomes less responsive, taking longer to render images of the scene. As an artist, you have to choose where to add the detail, where detail isn't needed, and where detail can be added with texture maps.

MODELING WORKFLOW

Before you sit down at the computer, look at the script or storyboards you have for the scene you are building. Next make a list of all the models that need to be built for the sets in your scene. Make a simple drawing of each model and consider how it will be constructed using the Softimage 3D|Extreme modeling tools. Include on the drawing some measurements of relative scale, so that the models fit the scale of the scene.

Finally, sit down at the computer and make each model separately to the predetermined scale. As you complete each model, assemble and name the model hierarchy and then save that hierarchy separately into your active database, using the Save→Selected Element command.

Organizing your work into individual tasks that you can repeat on long lists of objects makes it possible for you to tackle and complete demanding projects. Without this planning and organization, you are likely to flounder around in the software and find it difficult to complete your work.

ORGANIC MODELING: MOVING POINTS

Because all polygonal mesh objects and patch surfaces are defined by the vertices and Control points that make them up, you can, of course, change the shape of the object by moving those points around. This fundamental concept is the basis of *organic modeling*. When you simply push and pull points on the surface to create the shape you desire, you have the ultimate degree of control over your results. Think of organic modeling as sculpting with clay without the mess. In both cases, your talent and dedication are all that stands between you and a masterpiece.

Because polygonal meshes are usually composed of a great many vertices, sculpting in this way is not often possible (unless you are building low-polygon game characters, which is quite challenging). Patch-based surfaces normally have fewer Control points and form nice, smooth transitions between parameters, making sculpting them much easier and more productive. Start with a patch surface that has enough subdivisions for the detail you want to model into the object, but not more than you need, because too much detail tends to be confusing and difficult to work with (see Figure 6.1).

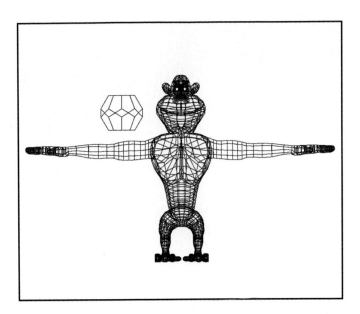

FIGURE 6.1   *Julian, an organically modeled character, and the primitive he sprang from.*

Often you will start with a primitive object that shares form with the object you want to end up with. For example, you could start with a cube and fashion a pyramid or start with a sphere and end up with a human head. Use the Get→Primitive menu to retrieve a primitive object that has something in common with the object you want to make.

SHOWING POINTS

If you can't see the vertices or Control points that make up an object, manipulating them is pretty hard. If you select an object but still don't see points at the intersections of the surface edges and parameters, look to the Show menu cell to see if the points are hidden (see Figure 6.2).

MOVING POINTS

You can move individual points on a surface interactively by choosing the Edit→Move Point command. When Edit→Move Point is active and you click a specific point in one of the View windows, you can drag the point to a new location. The number of the selected point in the Vertex List and the point's current XYZ coordinates are displayed in the Status Bar. Because this command is so useful, it has a supra key, M, assigned to it.

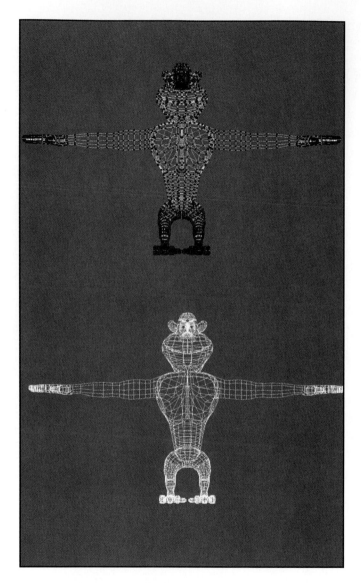

FIGURE 6.2 *Julian, with and without tagged points.*

In production work, you will want to keep your menu selections to a bare minimum because it takes your eye off the object you are working on. Practice holding the M key with your left hand while picking and transforming vertices until it is second nature.

TAGGING POINTS

Sometimes you will want to operate on more than one point at a time. *Tagging points* is a method of adding points to a selected group of points that can be moved, rotated, and scaled together, relative to the center of the selected object. Remember that you must be in TAG mode (click TAG in the Mode box) to operate on these points (see Figure 6.3).

FIGURE 6.3   *The Tag menu cell.*

The most common method of adding points to the tagged group is the use of the Tag→Rect command. Tag→Rect allows you to draw a rectangular marquee in any View window while holding any of the mouse buttons. The points that lie inside the marquee are added to the tagged group if you use the left mouse button and are removed from the tagged group if you use the middle button. If you use the right button, the selection is toggled inside the marquee, untagging those points that were tagged, while tagging those points that were not. The Tag→Rect command does not detect which side of the model is facing you, so it operates on both the front and back faces of the selected object. Tagged points show up in red on the model. The supra key for Tag→Rect is T; use it instead of the menu cell (see Figure 6.4).

Experiment at your leisure with the other methods of choosing a tagged group found in the Tag menu cell: Tag→Points selects single points or entire U or V rows of points on the object. Tag→Clear and Tag→Inverse match the functionality of the T supra key with the middle and right mouse buttons, respectively.

TRANSFORMATIONS ON TAGGED POINTS

When you enter TAG mode, all regular transformations and many other modeling effects operate only on the points in the tagged group. The translation keys move the selected group of points in the axis you choose, the Rotate menu cells revolve the tagged points around the local center of the object, and the Scale menu cells grow or shrink the tagged points by moving them in or out from the object local center. This all means that the location of the local center is critical to the effect you get by transforming the tagged points.

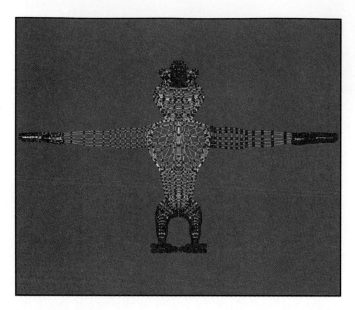

FIGURE 6.4 *Julian's arm tagged.*

Feel free to first enter CTR mode and move the local center to a logical hinge point for the model. For instance, if you want to model a cartoon head and make several shapes for the jaw in the open and closed position, you could move the local center of the head mesh to the lower portion of the head where the jaw would hinge, then tag all the points in the jaw and use TAG mode to rotate them around the local center, creating a cartoony "jawing" motion (see Figure 6.5).

PROPORTIONAL MODELING

Proportional modeling solves a tremendous problem with organic modeling. Often a polymesh object has hundreds of points, so that simple changes, such as in the facial expression of the model, require manual manipulation of a great many points. It would be great if you could grab just one point and have the others in the area stretch to follow the selected point, like grabbing the edge of a rubber mask to distort the features. Proportional modeling accomplishes this feat. When you move one point, all the points in a vicinity (set by you) are also affected. Closer points are affected more than distant points, and the rate of falloff can be changed with a spline curve profile. You begin by choosing the settings you want to use by summoning the Proportional dialog with the Edit→Proportional Setup command (see Figure 6.6).

The three top buttons in the Proportional dialog set predefined falloff curves: Linear (a smooth falloff), Exponential1, and Exponential2. In addition, you can manually drag the points in the Falloff Chart window to define your own falloff curve.

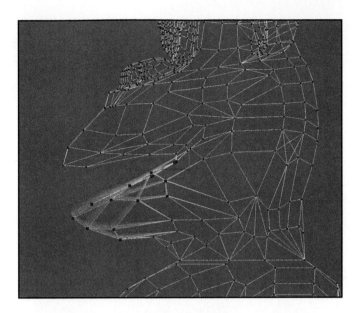

FIGURE 6.5 *Julian's tagged jaw.*

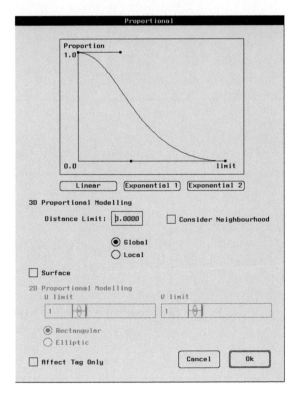

FIGURE 6.6 *The Proportional dialog box.*

The Distance Limit is the radius in Softimage units that will be affected by Proportional modeling. This is the most critical setting, as it determines how far the effect reaches and therefore how rubbery the object will be while you are editing it.

With the settings chosen, close the dialog box and check the Edit→Proportional menu cell to make certain that the effect is toggled on. Now simply use the M supra key to drag points on an object! (See Figure 6.7.)

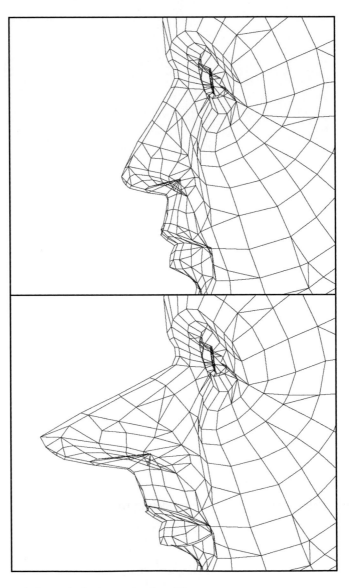

FIGURE 6.7 *Face before and after Proportional modeling.*

GRID LOCK AND MAGNET

If you are using the organic modeling tools to make objects that need to have accurate corners or exact snaps to other objects in the scene, Softimage 3D has tools to help you out.

The first, Grid Lock, snaps your points to regular intersections of the grid that you set up in the Layout dialog for a given View window (see Figure 6.8).

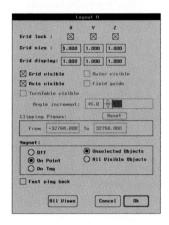

FIGURE 6.8   *The Layout dialog box.*

With the Grid Lock turned on, when you use the M supra key to move a point, it snaps to the nearest grid point. This is tremendously useful for drawing architectural kinds of spaces where you need walls and floors to line up exactly. As you move the point, look to the Status Bar to give you a readout of the current point location. This way you can exactly place points to a predetermined scale quickly and easily.

The second tool, Magnet, enables you to snap points of your current object to vertices on a totally separate, unselected object. If you need a window frame to fit perfectly within a hole cut in a wall, for instance, you could use Magnet to make sure that the window frame matches the space cut for it.

CLIPPING PLANES, THE RULER, THE TURNTABLE

The Layout dialog holds a few more modeling treats that can make you more productive. The Near and Far Clipping planes determine how much of your scene is visible in the one axis perpendicular to a given View window. This allows you to cut out a lot of the confusing and complex geometry from a view, so you can focus your work on an object right in front of you. The smaller the distance to the Far Clipping plane, the less you can see of your scene. You can even set it close enough so that only the near side of an object shows, and you can see the points close to you but not those on the far side of the object. When you can't see points, you can't edit them.

The Ruler Visible toggle box enables a ruler display on the View window, again to help in dimensioning objects and keeping an accurate scale.

The Turntable spins the View window about an axis running top to bottom, so you can see the object you are working on in an orthographic view from all sides.

Working with Curves

In a broad sense, the majority of the modeling commands in Softimage 3D are for working with curves. The concept is simple enough: By drawing curves and connecting them together, you can create surfaces. Because of the rich variety of curve shapes, you can make an infinite number of unique surfaces with this method. Four major categories of surfaces are created from curves in Softimage, which are described by their construction method:

- Revolutions
- Extrusions
- Skins
- Four-sided patches

Each is made in a different way and works better for certain kinds of models, but they all rely on curves as a basic construction element.

Drawing Curves

The Draw→Curve menu cell (see Figure 6.9) contains the commands for drawing curves of various types: Linear, Bezier, B-spline, Cardinal, and NURBS. After those initial curves have been laid down, however, more can be accomplished.

First, the direction in which the curve was drawn is important. When Softimage 3D creates a surface from a curve, it makes an assumption about which side of the resulting surface is the outside and which is the inside. If Softimage 3D gets it wrong, the surface will be inside out, and the lighting of the surface will look wrong compared to the rest of the scene.

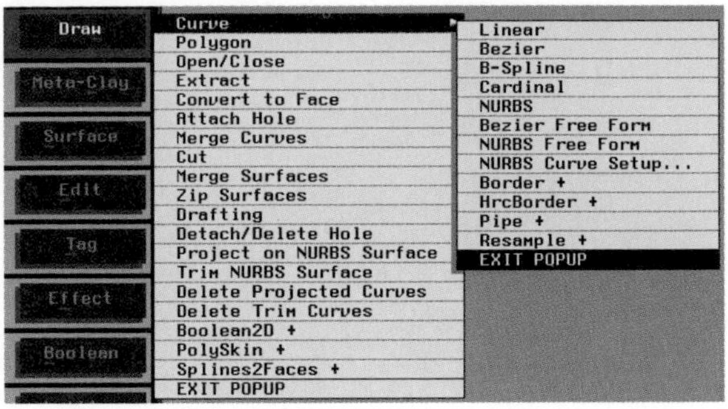

FIGURE 6.9   *The Draw→Curves menu cell.*

The general inconsistency of how Softimage 3D chooses to make surfaces is one of the most annoying aspects of working with the program: NURBS curves must be drawn clockwise for good surfaces, but all other curves must be drawn counter-clockwise. Softimage can even get the surface inside out when extruding a primitive circle, but fortunately the fix is easy enough. The Effect→Inverse command reverses a curve or a surface, so that a curve starts from the other end, and the normals of a surface face the opposite direction from before. Get used to this command because you will use it a great deal.

DRAW→OPEN/CLOSE

Because curves are drawn from one end to another, there must be a way to connect the start and end to create a closed curve for objects that are closed loops or closed surfaces. Draw→Open/Close adds a segment to the currently selected curve that connects the staring and ending points (see Figure 6.10). You do not have to manually add another point collocated with the first point to use this tool; Softimage takes care of that for you. If the curve selected is already closed (like a circle), the Draw→Open/Close command breaks the curve at the *edge flag* (the first point in the curve).

DRAW→CUT

The Draw→Cut command exists to trim curves down into several segments (see Figure 6.11). Linear, Cardinal, Bezier, and B-spline curves can be cut at a Control point only: Select the command from the menu cell and then point at the Control point where you want the cut. As usual, Softimage 3D does not destroy the original curve but adds two more objects to the scene, the two halves of the cut curve. Look in the Schematic view to find the new segments, and then use Display→Hide to hide the original unbroken curve.

FIGURE 6.10   *The Draw menu cells.*

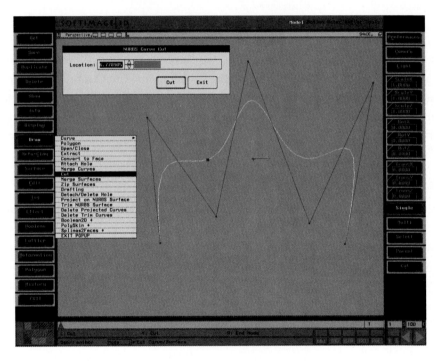

FIGURE 6.11   *A spline being cut with the Draw→Cut command.*

On NURBS curves you can cut a curve at any point along the span. Using the Draw→Cut command on a NURBS curve brings up a small dialog in which you drag a slider to move the cut point (represented by a small pink dot) along the span of the curve. This is a fundamental difference and advantage of NURBS over other kinds of curves.

The Draw→Cut command can also be used with surfaces to trim them along parameters—or anywhere, if the patch is a NURBS patch.

DRAW→MERGE CURVES

The opposite of cutting a curve into smaller segments is merging two curve segments into one. For this, you need Draw→Merge Curves. Use this tool by selecting one curve, then invoking the command and picking the second curve. The end of the first curve is then connected with a blend region to the beginning of the second curve. The Merge Splines dialog pops up, allowing you to choose between different merge options, depending on the kind of curves selected. As usual, this effect is non-destructive and actually creates a new curve segment while leaving the original two segments alone. You will want to either delete or hide the original segments when you are satisfied with the results of the merge.

If you pick the curves in the wrong order, or if the curves aren't aligned so the end of the first is near the start of the second, the resulting merge may look like a pair of crossed wires. Invert one of the curves to fix the problem with the Effect→Inverse command.

DRAW→CONVERT TO FACE

When you draw a curve and close it with Draw→Open/Close, or get a primitive circle and then view it in the renderer, you will see…nothing. That's because curves don't render.

An object must have surface geometry to become visible to the renderer, and a curve is not a surface. To convert a closed curve (it must be closed) to a surface, the curve needs to be marked as a *face*. The Draw→Convert to Face command turns any closed curve into a visible face, with a front side and a back side (see Figure 6.12). You can change the order of the sides with Effect→Inverse.

Faces have perfectly smooth, spline-based edges, which must be broken down into triangles (tessellated) to be seen. If the face is too complex, with too many points around the edge, it may have tessellation artifacts, which look like strange triangular striations in the surface. This typically appears in the OpenGL Shaded mode, and almost never in the render. You can reduce the complexity of the face by looking in the Info→Selection dialog and reducing the Face Step, creating fewer triangles during tessellation.

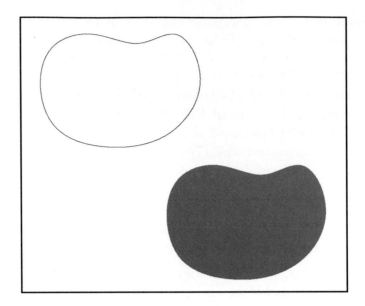

FIGURE 6.12   *A closed spline, with and without a face.*

DRAW→ATTACH HOLE

Okay, so you have a closed curve, but you want to poke some holes in it so you can make a smiley face. That is kind of like a Boolean operation on a face, where you can define regions within the closed area to be emptied of geometry. This is accomplished by drawing another closed curve, of the same curve type as used for the face, within the space enclosed by the face. Then you select the face and execute the Draw→Attach Hole command. The Status Bar prompts you to select one or more new closed curves, which become holes in the face. There can be many holes in a face, but as the number and complexity of the shapes increase, the chances of problem geometry increase (see Figure 6.13).

You can remove holes with the opposite command: Draw→Detach/Delete Hole.

DRAW→EXTRACT CURVE

Sometimes you may want to reuse a curve from an existing object in your scene. For example, if you were modeling a car body and finished the hood, you would want the front-right corner panel to match the curve of that portion of the hood exactly.

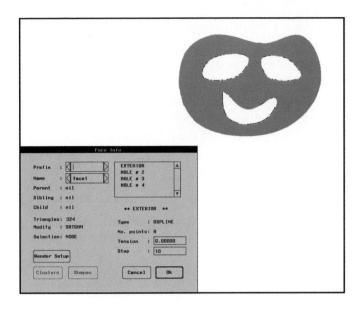

FIGURE 6.13 *A face with attached holes.*

Draw→Extract Curve gives you the power to copy a curve right out of any surface by simply clicking it. Select the object from which you want to take the curve, then invoke the command, and pick the curve you want in the Wireframe view (see Figure 6.14).

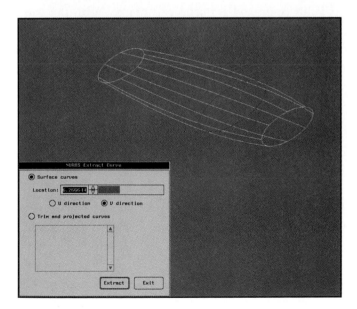

FIGURE 6.14 *An extracted curve taken from a surface.*

If the object is a Linear, Cardinal, Bezier, or B-spline patch, you can extract only curves that are exactly on the parameters of the surface between existing points. If the surface is a NURBS patch, the command Draw→Extract Curves brings up the small NURBS Curve Cut dialog box that allows you to slide a pink parameter line in the U or V direction to any position on the surface and extract a curve that matches that precise contour. Advantage: NURBS.

Editing Curves

After a curve has been drawn, you can go back to it and add more points to either end or in the middle. With NURBS curves you can even change a point's weight, which determines how it influences the curve. The place to edit curves is the Edit menu cell (see Figure 6.15).

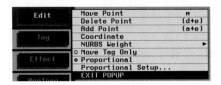

Figure 6.15   *The Edit menu cells.*

Edit→Add Point

The Edit→Add Point command performs this magic. With the command active, the Status Bar informs you that the left mouse button adds points to the end of the curve, the middle mouse button adds points to the inside of the curve, and the right mouse button adds points before the first point. In addition, you can use Edit→Add to add detail to a patch surface that has already been created. The Edit→Delete command removes points from a curve.

When you need to precisely position a point with great accuracy, the Edit→Coordinate command brings up a dialog in which you can enter values directly for a point you click.

Edit→NURBS Weight

On a typical Cardinal or B-spline curve, the curve itself is evenly influenced by the points on either side of the span. That means that it is impossible to mix curved and straight line segments in the same curve (or surface). This lends itself to smooth organic characters, but not to architectural or industrial designs where smoothly curved and linear shapes are found in the same objects. On a NURBS curve, each point can influence the curve to a different degree, so that one point in the middle of a curve can have a sharp angle, while the next has a smooth curve into the following point. This is accomplished by weighting the points on the curve (see Figure 6.16).

FIGURE 6.16 *NURBS Weight influences the line sharpness in and out of Control points. Surfaces pull sharply to more heavily weighted points.*

The easiest way to weight points is with the Edit→NURBS Weight→Point command. While it is active, you can click a point and drag with your mouse to change the weight, and see immediate visual feedback of the new curve shape. You can numerically change the weight for some or all of the points on a curve with the Edit→Coordinate dialog box. Points on a NURBS surface can also be weighted to create transitions between smooth curves and sharp angles.

RELATIONAL MODELING

Relational modeling is not a command, but rather a setting in the Preferences menu (see Figure 6.17).

When the Preferences→Create Modelling Relation toggle is on and you make a surface from a curve, the resulting surface is permanently related to the generator curve. Thus, if you then change the shape of the curve, the shape of the surface made from it changes also. This is a profoundly useful tool, because it means that you can refine the shape of your surfaces after they have been made, when you can see whether or not they look like what you had in mind when you drew the curve.

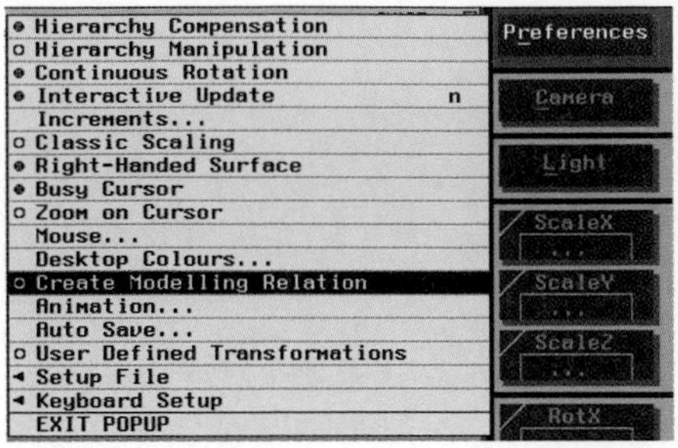

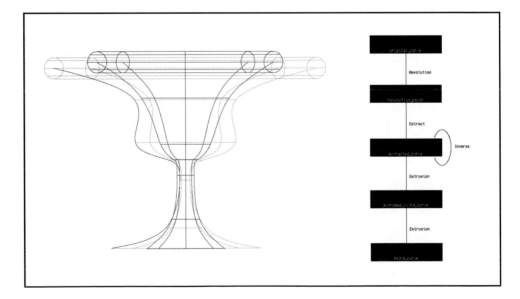

FIGURE 6.17   *The Modelling Relation toggle in the Preferences menu.*

In 3D modeling, the more iterations you make between the design and the completed shape, the better the model is going to look. It also means that when your Art Director or client comes in to look over your work and wants to make changes, you don't have to start from scratch. Relational modeling makes your life easier.

Softimage 3D|Extreme can keep a complex chain of relational links between different operations, so that the results of changes at any step are automatically sent down the chain to the finished model (see Figure 6.18).

FIGURE 6.18   *Relational Modelling in action.*

For example, if you turned on Relational Modeling, drew a curve and revolved a surface from it, then extracted a curve, inverted it, and extruded a third curve along the extracted curve, all those steps would be stored in a Relational hierarchy. You could go back to the original curve and change it, and the results would ripple through the revolution, the extraction, the inverse, and the extrude along a curve to change the final product.

Relational modeling is also a potent Animation tool. If you were to save different shape keyframes for that original curve at different points in time, the resulting modeled surface would animate over time as well.

Sometimes you want to cut the relation between a generator curve and the surface you made from it. That's where the Effect→Freeze→Modelling Relation command comes in. When you select an item that was constructed with Modelling Relation and run the Freeze command, the link is cut and the object stands entirely on its own. There is no way to restore the modeling relation once it has been cut. We'll use relational modeling later in this chapter when we start building surfaces.

TUTORIAL: CONSTRUCTION CURVES FOR A GUITAR BODY

In this tutorial, you use some of the Curve Manipulation tools to create a more complex set of curves than could be used to build a surface object, an acoustic guitar. You will draw individual curves, modify their shapes, merge them together, convert to face, attach holes, and learn some other useful curve functions along the way (see Figure 6.19).

1. **Draw Half of a Guitar Front Face.**

   Use the Draw→Curve→NURBS command and place your points in the Top view using the grid as a guide to place the points, starting from the bottom of the guitar and drawing to the top. The point at the bottom of the guitar should lie on the Z axis. The top of the curve can be slightly away from the axis, because we want a flat, straight segment here, where the neck of the guitar will attach. Use the M supra key to adjust the points to your satisfaction.

2. **Create the Second Half.**

   Create another identical curve on the other side of the Z axis with the Effect→Symmetry command, using the YZ plane as the plane of symmetry. (See Figure 6.20.) To easily figure out what plane is correct for symmetry operations, imagine placing a mirror so that you can see the reflection of the object where it needs to be in space. The plane where you would put the mirror is the correct plane of symmetry.

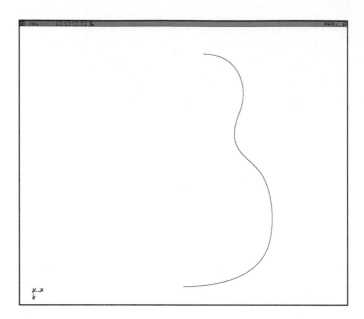

FIGURE 6.19   *Curves to form the top face of a guitar body.*

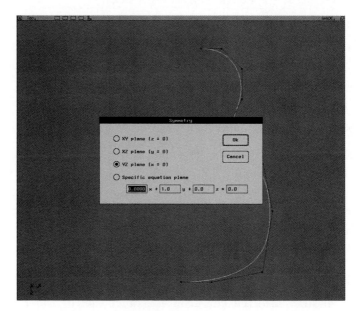

FIGURE 6.20   *Create an identical curve for the other side of the guitar.*

Connect the two halves together with the Draw→Merge Curves command, which connects the top of the guitar body. The order in which you pick the curves to merge determines whether the blend area is at the top of the curves or at the bottom, but it doesn't matter here because we are going to close the rest of the curve anyway.

When you choose Draw→Merge Curve, the Merge/Blend dialog pops up. (See Figure 6.21.) Here you can choose whether you want to keep the curved segment between the two merge curves or use a linear segment. Use a curved segment at the bottom of the guitar.

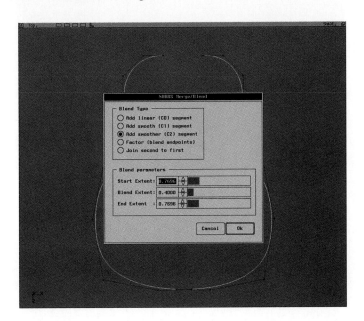

FIGURE 6.21   *The NURBS Merge/Blend dialog box.*

3. Close the Top.

The guitar body is still open at one end, the top end. Close it with the Draw→Open/Close command. Use a linear segment for the top of the guitar (see Figure 6.22).

4. Make the Guitar Base.

Open the Schematic view and take a look at the contents. Softimage keeps the two side curves and the new merged, closed curve. Hide the original side curves with the Display→Hide→Toggle command.

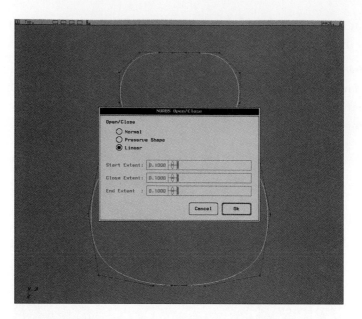

FIGURE 6.22   *Use Draw→Open/Close to close the gap between the two curves.*

Select the new closed body curve and use the Info→Selection command to name it "bodytopcurve." Duplicate it with the Duplicate→Selection command and translate the new body curve in negative Y to be an appropriate distance for the depth of a guitar body. Rename this new lower curve by double-clicking the icon in the Schematic view and changing the name to "bodycurvebottom."

5. **Add the Hole.**

In the Top view, draw a circular NURBS spline for the hole in the top of the guitar. Close it with Draw→Open/Close (see Figure 6.23).

6. **Convert to Faces.**

Select the bottom curve and convert it to a face with Draw→Convert to Face. Do the same with the top body curve. Now with the top body face selected, use the Draw→Attach Hole command, and pick the hole you drew. Take a look at your work in the Shaded Perspective view to see the top and bottom of the guitar with the attached hole.

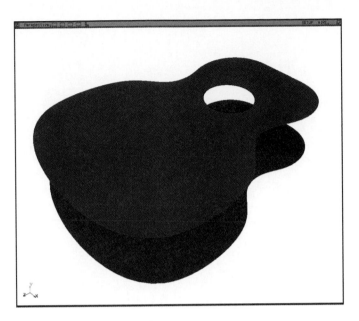

FIGURE 6.23 *The top and bottom guitar faces.*

7. **Shape the Neck.**

   In the Front view, draw an arc with a flat top for the contour of the guitar neck at the fattest point where it connects to the guitar body. Translate it in Y and Z to connect to the top of the guitar, and stick it out above the top face just a bit. Duplicate the curve and translate it in several Z Softimage units to where the end of the neck would be, and scale it down slightly so the neck has a graceful shape (see Figure 6.24).

8. **Extra Credit.**

   Create some more closed curve profiles for the bridge at the base of the guitar face.

These basic guitar curves could later be skinned together to form the surfaces needed for the solid guitar body. Save them for later practice!

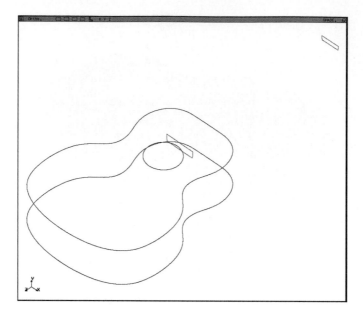

FIGURE 6.24   *Guitar with neck profiles for skinning.*

EXTRUSION BASICS

The four basic surface creation tools, Extrusion, Revolution, Skin, and Four Sided, are all located in the same menu in Softimage 3D: the Surface menu in the Model module (see Figure 6.25).

Surface	Extrusion
	Revolution
	Skin
Edit	Four Sided
	Bevel +
	Blending +
Tag	GuidedExtrude +
	HrcBevel +
	PolyBevel +
Effect	TBranch +
	EXIT POPUP

FIGURE 6.25   *The Surface menu cells.*

The first surface creation tool in the Surface menu, and possibly the most useful, is the Surface→Extrusion command. Extrusions can be performed on open and closed curves, faces, and polygons (see Figure 6.26). Extrusion takes a generator profile and extends it into the third dimension along an axis or another curve to create a surface object (see Figure 6.27).

FIGURE 6.26 *Different kinds of extruded objects.*

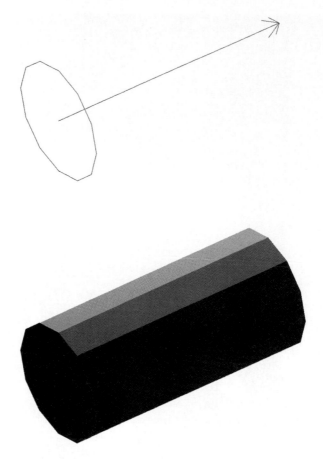

FIGURE 6.27 *A simple extrusion.*

Using the extrusion process is easy to think of as using a pasta machine (or a Play-Doh machine if your inner child is still stronger than your inner yuppie). The shape of the extrusion profile determines the shape of the object that gets pressed through it. Keep in mind that like pasta, extrusions in Softimage do not have to be rigid; they can follow curved extrusion paths.

Look around you right now and analyze the objects you see. Those that are symmetrical around one axis make good candidates for extrusion. Try looking at objects end-on from different sides to see if you can visualize the extrusion profile. Sometimes extrusions are used to give a flat 2D object a little depth, such as a hinge plate on a door or a wall plaque. The most overused extrusion example is flying text. (See Figure 6.28.)

FIGURE 6.28 *Extruded text.*

THE EXTRUSION DIALOG

Let's take a good look at the Extrusion dialog box and walk through the many options. Start by drawing a NURBS extrusion profile in the Front view (try something simple, like a swirling curve). Then draw a NURBS extrusion path in the Top view. Finally, select the original swirling extrusion profile, and choose the Surface→Extrusion command from the Model module (see Figure 6.29) to summon the dialog.

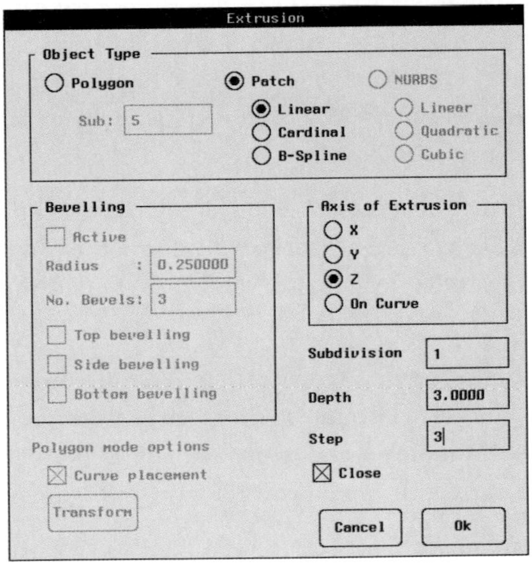

FIGURE 6.29 *The Extrusion dialog box.*

At the top of the dialog, you can choose whether the resulting surface is made of a polygon mesh, a spline patch, or a NURBS patch. To create a NURBS extrusion, the original extrusion profile you draw must be a NURBS curve.

If you start with NURBS curves, you can make a resulting surface of any type. If you choose Polygon, you can set the Polygon Subdivision, which determines how many polygons are added between each curve parameter, affecting the smoothness of the final object. If you choose Patch or NURBS, you can later make the object more or less smooth by setting the Step in the Info→Selection dialog box.

The Axis of Extrusion determines the direction that the profile is pushed to create the shape. If you choose X, Y, or Z, the extrusion is a rigid object symmetrical around that axis. If you choose On Curve, you can then select the extrusion path and make a more organic, floppy-looking extrusion.

The Subdivision number adds parameterization (or more detail) on the resulting surface in the direction of the extrusion. If you choose On Curve, the object automatically has one subdivision for each point on the extrusion path. Increasing the step increases the smoothness along the Axis of Extrusion.

Depth specifies, for X, Y, and Z axis extrusions, how far along that axis the shape extends. You can change this later by simply scaling on that axis, so you don't have to worry about getting it right now.

The Close check box determines whether the final surface has caps on the two ends, which makes it look like a solid, or whether it does not have caps, which makes it look like an empty tube. If you choose to make the final object a NURBS or patch surface, the two caps are separate faces, linked in a hierarchy to the extrusion. If you choose polygon, the extrusion is one closed object.

Make any choices you want, and close the dialog by clicking on the Ok button in the lower right corner. If you chose an axis to extrude on, the command will be completed. If you chose to extrude along a path, you may now pick the path to complete the extrusion.

Finally, a word about beveling in Softimage: The Beveling option here works only for polygonal meshes and creates a rounded shoulder between the edges of the extrusion. It works very poorly, however, and results in bad geometry when the extrusion profile includes detail smaller than the Bevel Radius (see Figure 6.30).

Sometimes the Beveling option does other weird stuff, particularly when beveling hierarchies of text faces, such as making abstract polygons connecting letters to the global center. The Bevel Direction is also dependent on the orientation of the curve, and if the curve is inverted, the bevel is made inside out. Invert the extrusion profile to correct this problem. More effective Beveling tools are available in Softimage, so don't use this one unless you have to.

FIGURE 6.30 *A bad text extrusion with incorrect polygons, creating garbage in the fine detail of the letters.*

If you choose X, Y, or Z as the Axis of Extrusion, just close the dialog to execute the command. If you want to extrude along a path, close the dialog and then pick the extrusion path to complete the command.

If Preferences→Modelling Relation is on, the final extrusion shape will be related to the extrusion profile and the extrusion path, so try editing those curves to see the extrusion update automatically as you move points on the curves.

I mentioned earlier that you could extrude from polygonal shapes. This is an extremely important tool for low-polygon, real-time game modeling. If you create a polygon model, enter POL mode, and then select one or more polygons on the surface with the raycasting option (supra key G), you can choose Surface→Extrusion to extrude that polygon.

Julian, the gorilla character shown earlier in Figure 6.1, was created entirely by this method from a primitive dodecahedron shape. When in Polygon mode and Local Transformation mode, the Extrusion mode uses X and Z as the height and width of the polygon and the Y axis as the normal direction of the polygon. If more than one contiguous polygon is selected, the group Y is the average of the normals.

You can also create interesting effects by extruding polygons along a curve and transforming the resulting polygons along the path. Look to the Ganglia tutorial later in this chapter for details.

TUTORIAL: EXTRUDING TEXT

In this short tutorial, you will learn how to make and animate a flying logo for a broadcast news show.

When creating the text for the logo, you can use either splines or faces. Although the splines may be more useful if you plan to edit the letter shapes, the faces are generally easier to extrude into text. This is because some letters, such as "B," have holes in them. Splines can't be defined to include such holes because they have no surface area for the hole to be in. Faces, however, can be defined to include holes, and Softimage does this automatically when you create text.

1. **Enter the Call Letters.**

   Call up the Text dialog box with the Get→Text command and enter the first line we want, KNBC, into the text entry area. Choose the Verdana Bold font near the bottom of the font list. For the Model Generation option, choose Faces. Make the slant 20.00, which slants the text 20 degrees as if it were italicized. Finish the command with the Ok button (see Figure 6.31).

NOTE

The extra command in the box, Generate Character Set, creates a face or spline hierarchy for each and every character in that font, including upper and lower case, punctuation, and special characters. This can be very useful when choosing fonts, because it's the quickest way to see what all the letters look like.

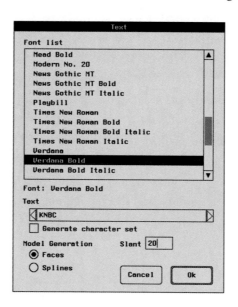

FIGURE 6.31 *Create some text splines to extrude.*

2. **Study the Hierarchies.**

   Take a look at the hierarchies created by the Text command in the Schematic view. The easiest way to scale the Schematic to completely show everything in it is to point your mouse into the window and use the A supra key, which means frame all (see Figure 6.32).

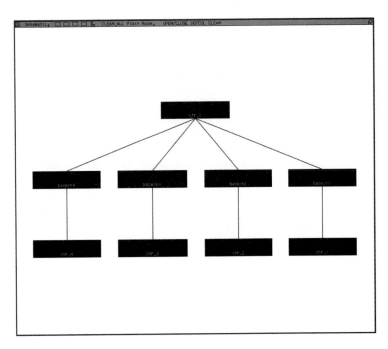

FIGURE 6.32   *The Schematic view of the text splines.*

The Text command creates a hierarchy of text, with each letter at the bottom, parented to a null object positioned on the baseline. Then all the baseline nulls are parented to one top null. This is so the entire tree can be manipulated or each letter can be rotated individually.

The faces are visible in the Shaded Perspective view, but they have no dimensionality to them. Correct this by invoking the Surface→Extrusion dialog box in the Model module.

3. **Add Dimension.**

In the Extrude dialog, make the resulting objects out of a patch composed of linear splines. The Axis of Extrusion should already be Z, which is correct. Change the Depth to be three Softimage units, make sure the Close box is checked so the letters have front and back faces added, and click Ok.

In the Perspective view, again frame all and orbit around to see the depth of the letters. In the Schematic view, frame all to see the organization of the hierarchy (see Figure 6.33).

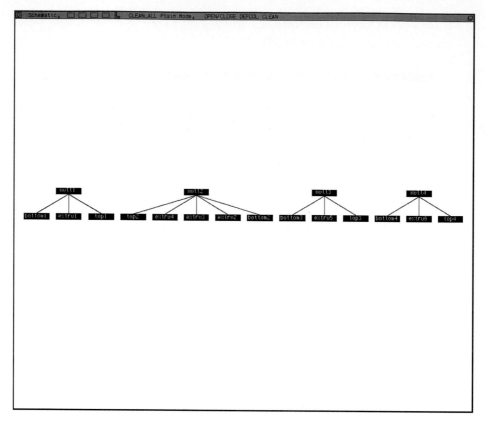

FIGURE 6.33 *The hierarchy of the extruded letters.*

Each letter is now an individual hierarchy, with the baseline null as the parent, and one node for the front face, the back face, and each of the extrusions. The hierarchy of faces is still there as well, so you should select it as a tree and hide it with Display→Hide→Toggle & Desel Hidden. To make your life easier, create a primitive null with Get→Primitive→Null and make it the parent of all the baseline nulls, so the entire extrusion hierarchy can be transformed together.

4. **Make News.**

Repeat the above steps to create a new text hierarchy with the letters "NEWS." Extrude them, combine them into a new hierarchy, and then move them under the letters "KNBC."

Drag the Time Slider to frame 100, then select each hierarchy as a tree, and save a translation keyframe for it with SaveKey→Object→Explicit Translation→All. This saves the final position of the letters square to the camera plane. Now repeat for the orientation of the letters by saving a keyframe with SaveKey→Rotation→All (see Figure 6.34).

FIGURE 6.34 *The KNBC flying logo.*

5. **Let It Fly.**

Drag the Time Slider back to frame 1 and translate the KNBC hierarchy vertically in Y until it is well off the screen in the Perspective view. Save a keyframe for its explicit translation.

Select the NEWS hierarchy, translate it –500 units in Z, and then rotate the whole hierarchy 80 degrees in Y. Save keyframes for both the explicit translation and the rotation in all axes.

Back at frame 100, pick a jaunty skew for the camera position by orbiting and rolling the camera, and by playing back your animation until you are happy with the results.

6. **Extra Credit.**

Because this piece is destined for broadcast, set it up properly by changing the Camera→Format setting to NTSC aspect ratio (1.33 times as wide as the frame is tall).

> **NOTE**
>
> Remember that if you choose to create the text from splines, you would have to convert each letter to a face before extrusion, and letters like P and O that have holes in them would need the holes attached with Draw→ Attach Hole.

Check to make sure your title isn't outside the title safe area of the TV screen by going to the Layout dialog for the Perspective view, turning on Field Guide, and viewing in Wireframe. Keep your action inside the inner black rectangle to make sure it isn't cut off by some television monitors.

Finally, in the Matter module, go to the Render dialog and choose the correct render settings for CCIR 601 video. Make the resolution 720×486 pixels with a pixel aspect of 0.9. Turn antialiasing on with a Max filter of at least three steps. Also turn on Field Rendering and specify Odd Field Dominance. Lastly, click the Script Post-Frame button to select a script that combines the now separate filed frames into one interlaced image. Choose the Inter03 script, located in the Softimage/3D/tools/scripts directory, within the location where you installed Softimage 3D.

Whew! That's a bunch of specific settings that matter only if you are going to use this work in broadcast video in the U.S. You can ignore these settings for all other uses.

This simple logo extrusion animation is typically called a *flying logo*. Flying logos account for a fair portion of the work in the 3D world today.

TUTORIAL: MAKING ROLLER COASTER TRACKS

A slightly more complex use of extrusion is the creation of roller coaster tracks. Roller coaster tracks are a symmetrical cross section that is swept along the path taken by the roller coaster car. It's a great use of extrusion along a path, because the other ways of making tracks would be so time consuming and difficult (see Figure 6.35).

1. **Design the Path.**

   Make the path taken by the coaster car. Start with a primitive circle, made out of a Cardinal spline with 16 steps and a radius of 20 Softimage units. Cardinal splines are good for paths because they go directly through each point, making it easy for you to control exactly what the curve does between points.

   Rotate the curve 90 degrees in X to make it flat in the Top view, and freeze the rotation with Effect→Freeze→Rotation in the Model module. Show the points with Show→Point if they are hidden and drag some of them up and down to make a convincing roller coaster path similar to the one in Figure 6.36. This will be the path taken by the roller coaster car. We need now to make two more splines, one on either side, to be the tracks.

2. **Lay the Tracks.**

   The problem is, if we just duplicate the path and offset it, that won't be entirely accurate. The tracks aren't actually the same, because one is inside the other and, therefore, is shorter.

FIGURE 6.35 *The rendered roller coaster.*

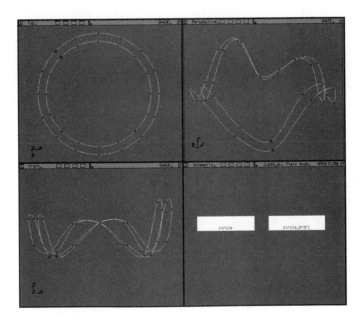

FIGURE 6.36 *The roller coaster paths.*

Softimage has a handy tool for this called Draw→Curve→Border, which makes a new spline inside or outside another by a specified distance.

Call up the Draw→Curve→Border dialog box (see Figure 6.37), and set the parameters for the outside path. Linearize Spline should be off, but Preserve Number of Points and Thorough Checking should be on. Set the Step Size to 5 and the Distance At Border to 0.35. Dismiss the dialog with the Ok button and pick the center path to complete the effect.

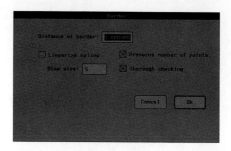

FIGURE 6.37   *The Border dialog box.*

Repeat the command again with a border distance of –0.35 to make the inside track.

3. **Create the Rail's Extrusion Profile.**

Zoom in tightly in the Front view and make a rail profile like the one in Figure 6.38 from another Cardinal curve. Then close the spline. It should be about 0.3 Softimage units wide.

4. **Extrude the Rails.**

With the Extrusion profile selected, choose the Surface→Extrusion command again to bring up the Extrude dialog box. Choose to make the extrusion object out of a Cardinal patch, and then select the On Curve option and deselect the Close option. Close the dialog and complete the command by picking the inner rail you made.

Repeat the process using the same Extrusion profile and the outer rail as the Extrusion path.

5. **Make Relational Changes.**

If you used relational modeling, you can now edit the profile or make it bigger or smaller as needed to fit the model.

In addition to its straightforward use in the tutorial, extrusion along a path can be an Animation tool. You can set Shape keyframes for both the Extrusion profile and the path it is extruded along (see Figure 6.39).

FIGURE 6.38   *The rail extrusion profile.*

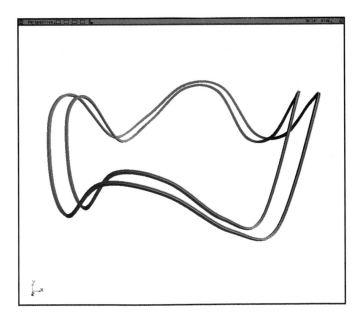

FIGURE 6.39   *The extruded rails.*

TUTORIAL: GUIDED EXTRUDE—LIPS

Another form of extrusion along a curve is the Guided Extrude Custom effect. With a Guided Extrude you have an Extrusion profile and two Extrusion paths, one for each side of the profile. As the profile extrudes along the two paths, the profile gets bigger or smaller as needed to connect them together. We'll use it here to make a set of lips like the ones in Figure 6.40.

FIGURE 6.40 *Completed lips models.*

1. **Trace the Lip Edges.**

   Run your finger along the top edge of your lip, and then draw that shape with a B-spline in the front window. This shape becomes the left Extrusion path. Now trace your bottom lip edge, and draw that as well, starting from the same side as before. Your splines should now look like an outline of a pair of lips (see Figure 6.41).

2. **Draw the Extrusion Profile.**

   Draw the contour of the lips to be the Extrusion profile. Think of what your lips look like at the middle, from the side, and draw the contour so that the gap between your lips faces up, in positive Y. This is important because the effect has to decide which direction should be pointing out in the extrusion, and it chooses positive Y as the default. The splines should look like Figure 6.42.

FIGURE 6.41 *The outline of the lips.*

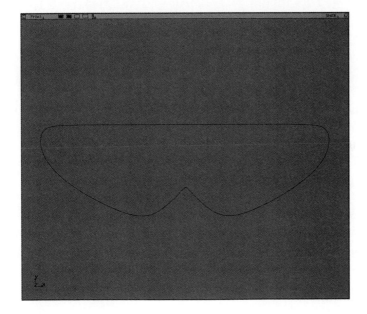

FIGURE 6.42 *The contour of the lips.*

3. **Extrude.**

Choose the Surface→GuidedExtrude command. In the dialog box, opt to scale width and height, and turn off Capping.

Click Ok and finish the command by picking the profile, then the left path, and finally the right path. The Status Bar helps you remember the order. After the last path is picked, the command executes and creates the lips (see Figure 6.43).

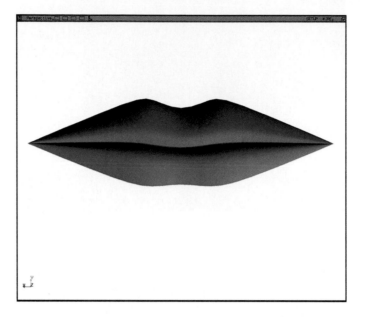

FIGURE 6.43 *Completed, shaded lips.*

Guided extrude is a fantastic and very underappreciated tool. Explore using it for boat hulls, paths, and other elements that are basically extrusions but may need different left and right extrusion paths.

TUTORIAL: EXTRUDE BEVELED TEXT WITH POLYGONS

In the previous text extrusion tutorial, we ended up with some fairly plain-looking text, serious enough for the evening news. But what if we need to create more ornate text for the Academy Awards—text with rounded edges and gold trim? For that we'll have to make the flying text out of polygonal meshes (see Figure 6.44).

1. Type the Text.

Call up the Get→Text dialog and type "Academy Awards" into the text entry box. Choose the Vivaldi Italic font and make the model out of faces.

FIGURE 6.44   *Rendered, beveled text.*

2. **Set the Bevel.**

   With all the text still selected, call up the Surface→Extrusion dialog box and make a few changes. Set the Object type to Polygon and leave Subdivision at 5, which means that there will be five polygons between each of the faces' Control points. Increasing that number gives you smoother edges at the cost of more polygons.

   Make the Axis of Extrusion Z.

   Make the Depth 2.

   Turn on beveling by checking the Beveling Active check box. You can bevel the front of the text by checking the Top Beveling option and leaving the sides and bottom unbeveled.

   Bevel Radius determines how wide the bevel is. If the bevel is too wide, however, the risk of creating bad polygons near the corners of letters becomes more severe. Keep the Bevel Radius under 0.2 Softimage units.

   Number of Bevels determines how many times the edge is subdivided. Increasing the number to five gives you smoother bevels.

Finally, click the Ok button to execute the command, and look at the results in the Perspective view (see Figure 6.45).

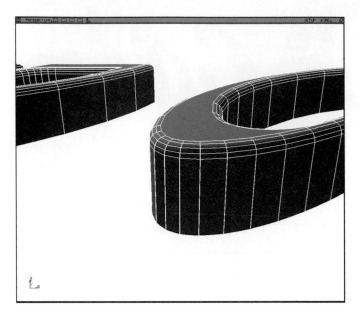

FIGURE 6.45   *The beveled text in Wireframe.*

3. **Combine the Letter Objects.**

Each letter has been extruded separately, which is a hassle to work with. Combine all the text into one polygonal object with the Effect→Merge command in the Model module.

Do this by switching to Multi mode and then selecting all the newly extruded letters in the Schematic view. Then choose the Effect→Merge command. Leave the parameters in the Merge dialog unchanged, click the Ok button, and a new object is created in the Schematic view. Select everything else with the Select→Toggle command and hide it all. Switch back to Single mode before you go on.

Examine your handiwork in the Perspective view. If there are problems with the beveled letters, you can go back and make them again with a smaller Bevel Radius setting. Sometimes beveling the letters individually instead of all together helps as well.

When you learn about materials, you discover that a different material color can be applied to the body of the letters and the beveled edges. This creates the popular gold-trimmed look for ornate beveled flying logos.

TUTORIAL: A DUNGEON FLOOR PLAN

Another very common use for extrusion as a modeling tool is the creation of walls and floors for buildings, mazes, dungeons, and other spaces. Particularly when working on games, keeping the polygon count as low as possible is pretty important, and extruded shapes tend to be quite lean. We'll use relational modeling to create a Doom-style maze (see Figure 6.46).

FIGURE 6.46 *The completed dungeon.*

1. **Draw a Line.**

   In the Top view, turn on the Grid Lock to keep your walls square.

   Execute the Draw→Curve→Linear command to start working on a floor plan, and draw a straight line in the Top view with at least two points.

2. **Extrude the Wall.**

   Check Preferences→Modelling Relation to make sure relational modeling is on. Then use the Extrude command to extrude the line segment you just drew into a wall in the Y direction eight Softimage units high with three subdivisions (see Figure 4.47).

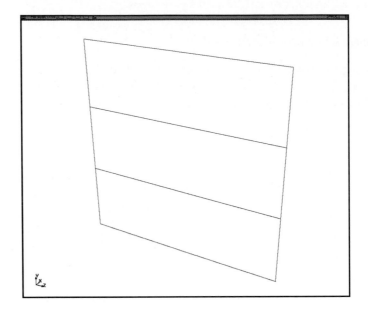

FIGURE 6.47 *A single wall element.*

3. Design a Dungeon.

In the Schematic view, select the curve you started and choose the Edit→Add Point command. Now you can continue to add points to the line you started. Draw out a maze-like dungeon shape. As you add points in the Top view, watch the Perspective view to see the walls taking shape.

When you have a good-looking dungeon, use the Draw→Open/Close command to close off the floor spline. Make the floor solid with the Draw→Convert to Face command (see Figure 4.48).

This sort of contruction technique is particularly useful in creating spaces for real-time games, where the interior must be interesting to look at yet light in polygons. By making your walls extruded with several subdivisions, you can apply different Texture maps to the top, middle, and lower sections of each wall to add detail.

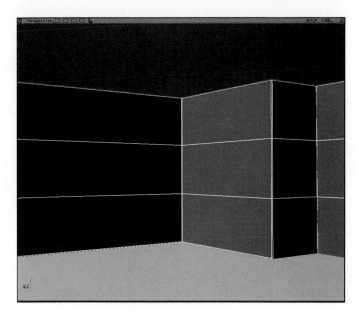

FIGURE 6.48 *The relational walls of the dungeon.*

REVOLVED SURFACES

The next surface creation tool to master is revolution. No, this isn't a political statement; it's a modeling tool. A revolution is a surface that is symmetrical around a central axis. Think of a revolution as the kind of surface that comes out of a lathe or as
the shape of a pot thrown on a pottery wheel. They're pretty darn easy to make and
work with (see Figure 6.49).

THE REVOLUTION DIALOG

Any kind of curve, Linear, Cardinal, Bezier, B-spline or NURBS, can be drawn in
any view and then revolved around any axis. By default, Softimage uses the global
axes as the point of revolution, so making your objects in the global center is a good
idea.

Simply draw a Revolution profile and invoke the command with the
Surface→Revolution menu cell (see Figure 6.50). The Revolution dialog (see Figure
6.51) comes up, giving you some parameter choices.

FIGURE 6.49   *Different kinds of revolved surfaces.*

Surface	Extrusion
	Revolution
	Skin
Edit	Four Sided
	Bevel +
	Blending +
Tag	GuidedExtrude +
	HrcBevel +
	PolyBevel +
Effect	TBranch +
	EXIT POPUP

FIGURE 6.50   *The Surface→Revolution menu cell.*

FIGURE 6.51   *The Revolution dialog box.*

Under Object Type, you can choose whether the Surface object is made from polygons or a patch. If you drew the Revolution profile with a NURBS curve, you can make the surface from a NURBS as well. If you choose Polygon, you can determine the Polygon subdivision, which smoothes your surface by adding more polygons.

The Axis of Revolution is where you pick which axis to revolve the surface around. I tend to build my revolutions in the Front view, next to the global Y axis, and revolve them around Y. Other interesting shapes, such as car tires, can be made by revolving a shape in the Front view around the X axis.

If your relational modeling is active, you can choose to revolve the profile around a free axis, with the Free Axis option in the Revolution dialog. This option creates another spline in the Schematic window and revolves around it. You can use the M supra key to move the points on either end of the free axis and change the revolved shape.

The last axis option, Around Curve, enables you to define your own Axis of Revolution by drawing a two-point curve of your own to revolve around.

The Degree of Revolution determines how far around the object is lathed. If you choose 360 degrees, it will be completely circular, and the edges in the U direction become closed together. If you revolve less than 360 degrees, the U parameter will be open (see Figure 6.52).

Subdivision determines how many rows of Control points will be in the surface created, while Step determines the surface parameterization for tessellation into triangles. If Modelling Relation is active, you can set shape keyframes for the Revolution profile and cause the resulting shape to animate over time.

FIGURE 6.52 *Different degrees of revolution.*

TUTORIAL: VIRTUAL GLASSBLOWING

In this tutorial, we'll make a tray full of different glassware and a paintbrush (see Figure 6.53). Why is glassware often such a good candidate for a revolution? Because that's how glassblowers make it in real life. The hot lump of glass comes out of the oven and is rolled over a metal surface, making a shape that is symmetrical around the axis of the glassblower's pipe. Pottery is also usually symmetrical because it's revolved on a pottery wheel.

FIGURE 6.53 *Rendered glassware, all made of revolutions.*

1. **Revolve a Martini Glass.**

   Turn Preferences→Modelling Relation on, if it isn't already. With a Linear spline, draw a profile of a martini glass, with the stem about half a Softimage unit from the Y axis. Revolve it to make a full glass, with the surface made of polygons. You can move it to the side with TransX, so you can see the original profile, and edit that profile with the M supra key to get it just so (see Figure 6.54).

2. **Try a Wine Glass.**

   The problem with the martini glass is that it has an infinitely thin surface and won't render refractions and reflections very accurately. Let's make another glass. This time design a wine glass by drawing another NURBS profile on the Y axis and keeping drawing points to make an inside and an outside surface. Use Draw→Open/Close to connect the edges together into a closed curve.

   Revolve it, this time out of NURBS, to make a smoother surface (see Figure 6.55).

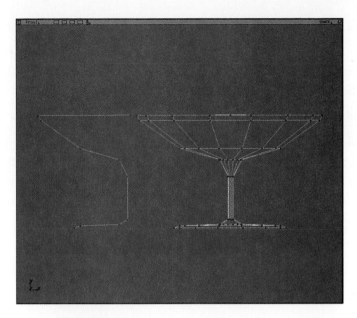

FIGURE 6.54   *A very thin martini glass.*

FIGURE 6.55   *A wine glass, this time with thickness.*

3. Add a Perfume Bottle and Stopper.

Make the profile of a perfume bottle, this time out of Cardinal curves, and revolve it. Make a stopper for it as well, and lay it at the base of the bottle.

4 Make a Mason Jar.

Make a Mason jar by drawing a spline revolution profile and revolving a surface out of B-splines, then tag all the points on a side, and scale them in towards the center of the jar just a bit to flatten the sides.

5. Use Polygons for a Paintbrush.

Draw the profile of a paintbrush in the Front view, parallel with the X axis, and revolve the surface out of polygons, using the X axis as the Axis of Revolution. Tag the polygon vertices at the end of the brush and scale them to be a little flatter, like a paintbrush. When done, translate it and rotate it to sit in the Mason jar (see Figure 6.56).

FIGURE 6.56 *Other glassware.*

6. Revolve a Tray.

Make a tray for them all to sit on. Draw a profile of a tray edge with a circular lip (as in Figure 6.53), and revolve it 360 degrees around Y out of B-splines. Freeze the relational modeling on the object so you can edit it further with the Effect→Freeze→Modelling Relation command. Scale it in X so that it is oblong instead of circular. You can also tag parts of the tray and deform the tags by scaling and translating them.

7. **Extra Credit: Assign Material Attributes.**

If you have already explored the Material dialog, assign some material attributes to the surfaces with transparency, reflectivity, and refraction. Arrange all the elements on the platter and render a preview. If you haven't yet worked with materials, skip this step.

Now in the Preview Setup dialog, set Raytraced Depth to 6, so that the renderer follows six ray bounces between the objects as light travels through and between them. Render another preview and examine the difference (see Figure 6.57).

FIGURE 6.57   *The glassware on the tray.*

Revolved objects are extremely easy to create and are quite commonly found in the real world. Keep an eye out for objects made of revolutions as you go through your day, and when you find one, consider the axis it was revolved on and what its cross section would look like if it were cut in half.

SKINNED SURFACES

Some shapes in the real world aren't symmetrical around any axis at all. These shapes can't be made by revolving or extruding a Profile curve, but they can be made by imagining a series of cross sections slicing through the object. In fact, almost all shapes, including revolutions and extrusions, can be visualized as a series of cross-sectional closed curves, sampled at a number of points along one axis of an object. (See Figure 6.58.)

FIGURE 6.58 *Different kinds of skinned objects.*

To visualize this, imagine a carrot. Lay the mental carrot down on an imaginary cutting board and, starting at the top, cut it into slices about a half inch thick. Each individual slice is a cross section of the carrot. When the carrot is all cut up, imagine carefully stacking the slices back together and wrapping a sheet of plastic tightly around them. That's what a skinned surface is, a spline patch stretched over a series of cross sections.

Another good visualization of a skin is the manufacture of a boat hull. First the cross sectional ribs of the hull are constructed, and then a surface is stretched over them to form the watertight surface.

Human shapes can also be made from skinning cross sections. Visualize the cross-sectional shape of your leg, starting at the thigh and moving down the leg about six inches at a time. A skin created from circles made in the shape of the cross sections of your leg would look just like your real skin stretched on your frame.

NOTE

Polygons cannot be skinned with the Surface→Skin command, although they can be skinned with the Draw→ PolySkin command. The PolyShrink and PolyGrow effects in the Motion module are also helpful.

THE SKINNING PROCEDURE

To create a skinned surface, start by drawing at least two cross sections from the spline of your choice.

If you choose to use any spline but NURBS, the cross sections must each have the exact same number of Control points. That's because the Patch surface is made by connecting each Control point with a U parameter, while the cross sections themselves make up the V parameters.

If you choose to use NURBS as the cross sections, each can have a different number of Control points and the skin still works. Advantage: NURBS.

When you have drawn a few cross sections and placed them apart from one another in space, choose the Surface→Skin menu cell to activate the command (see Figure 6.59). You must now pick each of the cross sections in order, from first to last, with the left mouse button.

FIGURE 6.59   *The Surface→Skin menu cell.*

If you accidentally pick a cross section out of order, use the middle mouse button to un-pick it and go on. If you forget which mouse button does what, look at the Status Bar to see how to choose the cross sections. When all the cross sections are picked, use the right mouse button to finish the command and bring up the Skinning dialog box (see Figure 6.60).

FIGURE 6.60   *The Skinning dialog box.*

As usual, you can choose the resulting Object type from polygon mesh, patch, and NURBS. The NURBS options are available only if you construct the cross sections from NURBS as well.

You can specify a step, changing the tessellation of the object into more or fewer triangles for rendering, and you can close the surface. When you close the dialog, the skinned surface is made.

TUTORIAL: SKINNING A BOAT HULL

Let's take a moment to make a simple boat hull with a skinned surface (see Figure 6.61).

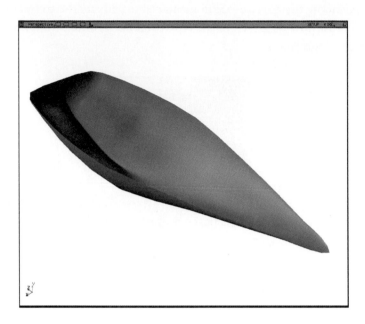

FIGURE 6.61   *The shaded, skinned boat hull.*

1. **Shape the Hull Cross Section.**

   To make a perfect arc shape, use the Primitive Arc curve with Get→Primitive→Arc. Set the curve to be a B-spline with a radius of five units, beginning at 180 degrees and ending at 360 degrees, and with eight steps or Control points.

2. **Drag Points for a Keel.**

   Use the M key to pull the center point down just a bit, and drag the point on either side of the center point towards the center by about one Softimage unit, which will hint at a keel in the finished shape (see Figure 6.62).

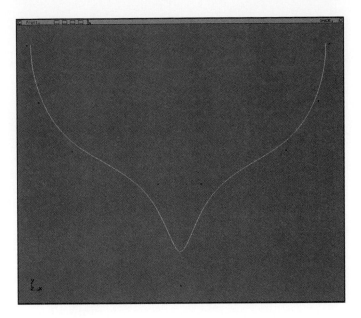

FIGURE 6.62 *The arc of the keel.*

3. **Add Cross Sections with Repetitive Duplication.**

   We now want a number of similar shapes at regular intervals. To make them, choose the Model module's Duplicate→Repetition command, which can make duplicates of an object while performing a transformation on each one. We'll start with the rear (stern) of the boat, which should remain broad, yet sweep up to the fan tail.

   In the Repetitive Duplication dialog box, set the Number of Duplicates to four and change the scaling in X to 0.9 (the hull narrows a bit) and in Y to 0.75 (the hull becomes more shallow). Change the translation in Z to three, making the four duplicate cross sections four units apart.

   Click Ok to complete the command, and examine the new cross sections (see Figure 6.63).

4. **Make the Bow.**

   Now create another cross section with the same settings in the Get→Primitive→Arc command as you used in the first hull cross section and translate it –6 units in Z (towards the bow). Make five duplications of this cross section, with 0.6 for Scale in X and Z, 0.45 for Scale in Y, and a Translation in Z of –7. This creates a nice sweeping bow (see Figure 6.64).

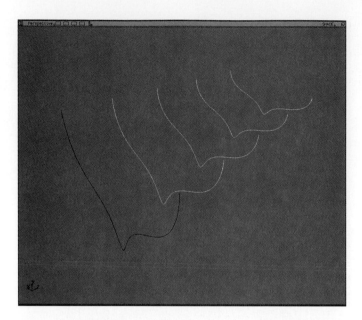

FIGURE 6.63 *Multiple aft hull ribs (skin cross sections).*

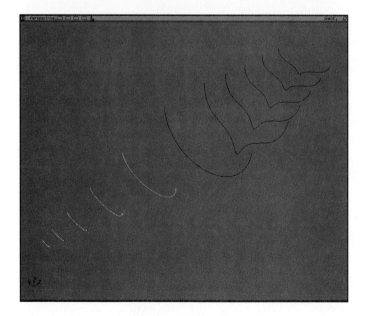

FIGURE 6.64 *All the hull cross sections.*

5. **Skin the Hull.**

Now zoom out of the Perspective view until you can see all the cross sections easily. If the grid gets in the way, you can turn it off in the Layout icon. Make sure that nothing is selected by using the Select→Clear command. Start the Skin command with the Surface→Skin menu cell and pick each cross section in order from the stern to the bow. When all are picked, use the right mouse button to call up the Skin dialog. Make the skin a Cardinal patch, with a Step of two, and make sure the Close box is unchecked, or off (see Figure 6.65).

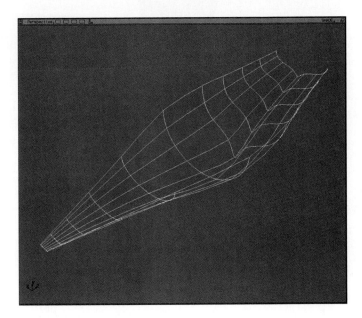

FIGURE 6.65   *The completed hull skin.*

6. **Fix the Leaks.**

If you look at the hull carefully, you will notice that the bow and stern are open (the U parameters are unclosed). This boat would sink pretty fast. To close the parameter, call up the Object Info dialog with the Info→Selection menu cell and check the boxes for Top and Bottom Capping in just the U direction.

There you go—a perfect boat! With Relational Modelling on, you can edit the cross sections and see the effect on the surface. Try reshaping or translating the cross sections to make a more unique hull design.

TUTORIAL: SKINNING A HUMAN LEG

The same skinning technique can be applied, with a few extra tricks, to making human body parts for a model. We'll begin with a leg (see Figure 6.66).

FIGURE 6.66 *Completed, rendered leg skins.*

1. **Sketch the Leg.**

   Start by giving yourself some visual cues to model to. Expand the Right view until it fills the screen. Here we'll sketch the outline of the human leg, so we can match the cross sections we'll make to the proper proportions of a leg.

   A great tool for sketching with a NURBS spline is Draw→Curve→NURBS Free Form. With this command activated, drag with the left mouse button to sketch the side profile of the inside of a human leg. When you release the mouse button, the command converts the path into a NURBS curve.

   Start sketching curves for the rounded areas of the leg, the thigh, the inside of the knee, and the calf. You don't have to make a complete path all along the leg at first, just make little strokes that show the leg's shape.

   When you get some you like, draw a final path along the shape from top to bottom. Repeat this for the front side of the leg profile, down the thigh, over the kneecap, and down the shin. Then look at the finished curves in the

Perspective view and correct any errors of proportion by moving points (see Figure 6.67).

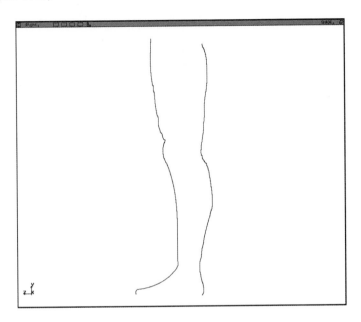

FIGURE 6.67   *Leg guide profiles to help scale cross sections.*

2. **Fit a Circle to the Leg Guides.**

   In the Top view, get a primitive B-spline circle and place it over the leg guides you just made. Rotate it 90 degrees around X so that it is oriented correctly to become a leg cross section (see Figure 6.68).

3. **Set the First Thigh Cross Section.**

   This first cross section is the shape of the leg at the top of the thigh. Translate it in Y until it rests at the top of the leg guides. Scale it to the same proportion as the leg guides, and move its points until it looks like a cross section of your own thigh.

4. **Add More Cross Sections.**

   Duplicate the cross section with the D supra key and translate it a third of the way down the thigh. Scale it so that the front and back points of the cross section lie exactly on the guides. This method ensures that the cross sections are placed and scaled accurately according to the outline of a human leg. Now in the Top view, move points with the M supra key to make the cross section slightly different from the first. Imagine the contours of the muscles under the cross section, and bulge that part of the cross section circle.

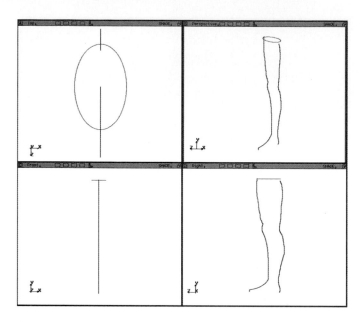

FIGURE 6.68   *The Top view of the thigh cross section.*

Repeat the steps above for as many cross sections as you want to make, extending down the leg, past the knee, down the calf, through the ankle, and into the foot. For each cross section, check it against the position of the guides at that point on the leg, and in the Top view for the size of the cross section, so that cross sections at the thigh are bigger than those at the knee, and so on (see Figure 6.69).

5. **Use Surface→Skin.**

Skin the cross sections together with a B-spline surface (see Figure 6.70). Make sure that the Close box is unchecked, or your skin turns inside out on itself.

If relational modelling is active, you can edit the cross sections after the leg is skinned to refine the musculature and perfect the shapes.

6. **Mirror the Leg.**

Use Effect→Symmetry to make a mirror image of the leg, so that you have two in a matched left/right pair. Save your scene for later animation practice.

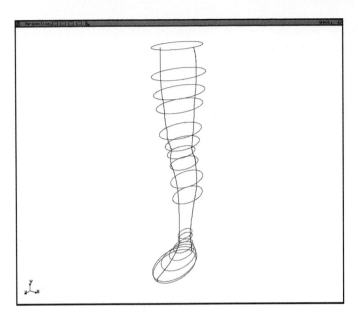

FIGURE 6.69 *All the leg guides and the cross sections drawn to them.*

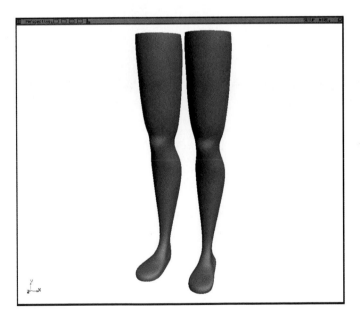

FIGURE 6.70 *The skinned legs.*

This versatile skinning technique is also a great way to make human faces. Look in a mirror and imagine drawing lines from the center of the top of your head down your face and under your chin, about half an inch apart. Then imagine these lines on their sides. The shape of each line is the contour of your face at that longitude; the top of your head and under your chin are the poles.

Another method is to locate one of the poles inside your mouth and the other at the rear of your head, and imagine the contour lines coming from inside your mouth and over the top of your head to the back (see Figure 6.71).

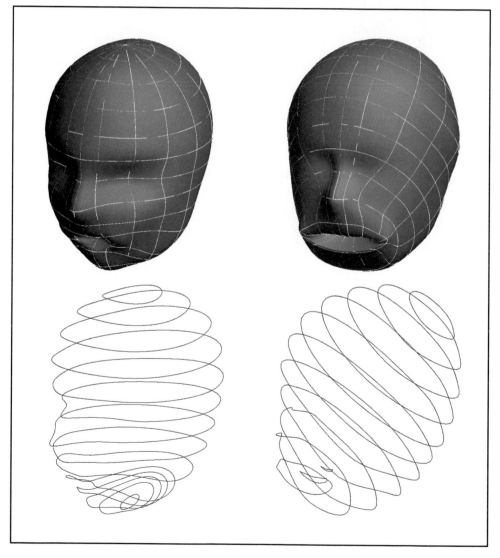

FIGURE 6.71 *A skinned head and the curves used to create it.*

The integration in Softimage 3D|Extreme between the modeling and animation tools is so tight that often there is no way to say where modeling leaves off and animation begins. Usually the modeling tools are used to create animation, but occasionally the animation tools can be used to make models. We are going to explore one of those occasions here by creating a saxophone with a skin. The secret lies in the cross sections.

When you are ready to animate, the sax can come alive with personality by merely saving Shape keys for some of the cross sections (see Figure 6.72).

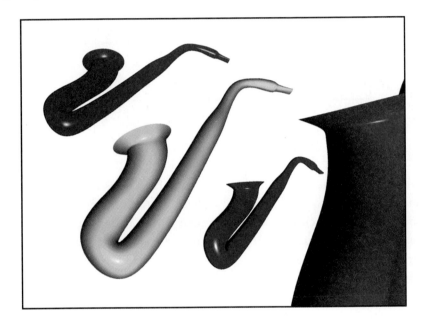

FIGURE 6.72   *The completed saxophone shapes.*

1. Outline the Sax.

Turn on Preferences→Modelling Relation. Then in the Right view draw a curve for the overall shape of the saxophone with a B-spline. Refer to Figure 6.73 for the general idea.

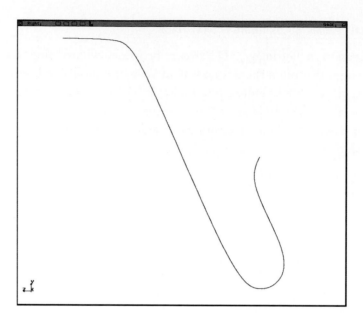

FIGURE 6.73 *The sax body curve.*

2. **Make a Circular Sax Cross Section.**

Make a primitive circle, out of B-splines, with a radius of 0.5 units. Rotate it in Y 90 degrees, so that the circle is facing you in the Right view. You need the local axis of the circle to be oriented so that X runs in and out through the center of the circle, because later we plan to use a constraint based on the X axis orientation. Use Effect→Freeze→Rotation to freeze the local center at the same orientation as the global center.

Check the scale of the circle against the size of the saxophone. It should be as big around as the reed at the mouthpiece of the sax. Scale the circle as needed to make it so.

3. **Animate the Circle.**

Put the circle on the curve of the sax body with the Path→Pick Path command in the Motion module. The default duration, 0 to 100 frames, is fine. Now the circle travels along the path, but it doesn't stay oriented correctly relative to the path it is on.

Fix that by selecting the circle, using the Constraint→Tangency command, and picking the path. Now the circle should travel along the path and change direction as it does so to remain facing along the path at all times (see Figure 6.74).

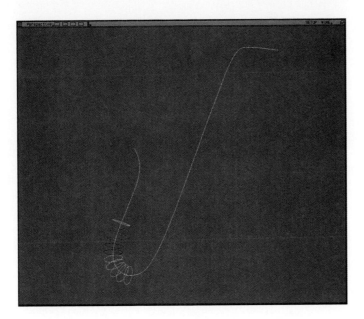

FIGURE 6.74   *The first extrusion profile on the sax path.*

4. **Set Keyframes.**

   Set some size keyframes at different points in time as the circle is at different locations along the path. Start with frame 1, saving a key with SaveKey→Object Scaling→All. Move the Time Slider along to the frame at the top of the first bend, and set another keyframe with the same scale.

   Now drag the Time Slider until the circle is at the lowest part of the sax, the bell. Scale the circle up to be three times as large. Set a keyframe. Drag the Time Slider to the end, scale the circle up some more, and set a last keyframe. Now the circle travels along the path and changes size as it does so (see Figure 6.75).

5. **Duplicate the Cross Sections.**

   Now we are ready to create all the skin cross sections. Select the circle. From the Duplicate menu cell in the Motion module, choose the Duplicate→From Animation command. This tool makes a number of new circles based on the transformations and shape of the circle at different points in time. We can either specify a certain number of copies or a frame increment at which a new copy is made. Choose the Number of Copies option and set it to 20. Click the Ok button to create the copies. Now 20 new cross sections are placed and sized precisely for the sax.

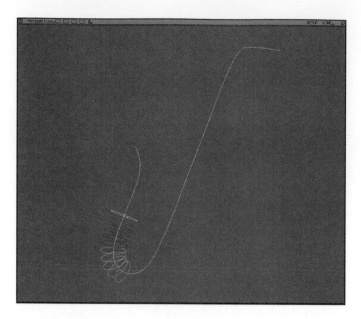

FIGURE 6.75 *The extrusion profile traveling along the path.*

6. **Skin the Saxophone.**

Select nothing and then activate the Surface→Skin command in the Model module. Pick all the new cross sections in order from first to last. Use the right mouse button to finish the shape and make the surface object a B-spline (see Figure 6.76).

Check out the results! This technique also works if you change the shape of the circle over the course of the animation, creating a less smooth-looking sax.

You can also use this method to create a few different sax skins with different shapes, and then use the shapes to create a Shape List for shape animation.

Four-Sided Patch Surfaces

The Four Sided tool is the most underused of all the Softimage patch modeling tools. It is designed to create a UV patch from four different splines, which represent the four sides of a UV patch. Each one of the splines can be a different shape. If you use non-NURBS splines, however, each pair of sides must have the same number of points. If you use NURBS, each spline can be different. Advantage: NURBS (see Figure 6.77).

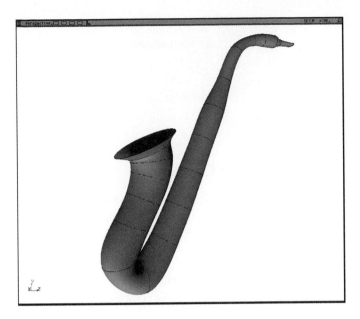

FIGURE 6.76   *The completed sax skin.*

FIGURE 6.77   *Kinds of shapes that are patches.*

Why is this important? Imagine that you are modeling the body panels of a sports car for a TV commercial and that you are working on the hood. The window line at the windshield end of the hood, the two edges at the corner panels, and the edge at the bumper end are all complex curves, and the surface needs to connect them all perfectly smoothly (see Figure 6.78). To accomplish this, you could use the Draw→Extract tool to extract the precise curves from the panels that border the hood, and then use them in the Four Sided command to make a surface that precisely fits within the other parts.

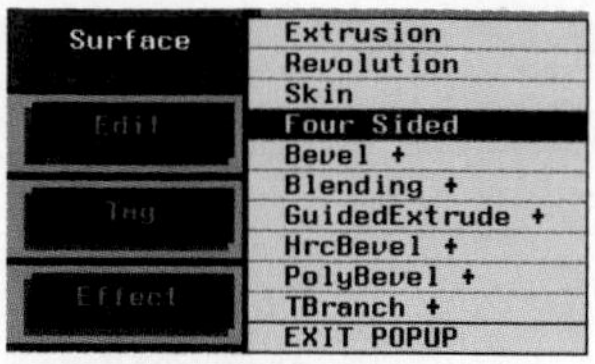

FIGURE 6.78   *The Surface→Four Sided menu cell.*

THE SURFACE→FOUR SIDED COMMAND

Using the tool is easy. Draw the four sides out of separate splines, and try to at least get the end of one side close to the start of the next curve, so that Softimage can correctly guess which end of the curve to connect to the next one. The direction you draw the curves is not important.

Finally choose the Surface→Four Sided command from the Model module, and pick each of the four sides in a consistent order, clockwise or counterclockwise. If you pick the sides in the wrong order (for example, one side, then the opposite side, then the next pair of opposite sides), the patch will be mangled.

When you pick the last curve, the surface is created unless you use NURBS, in which case the Four Sided Surface Setup dialog appears, enabling you to choose the NURBS parameterization type for your surface. The default, Non-uniform, is adequate unless you plan to precisely texture the patch, in which case Chord-length parameterization is a better choice. When you click the Ok button, the surface is completed!

TUTORIAL: RELATIONAL PATCHES AND RIPPLING FABRIC

A great use for animated four-sided patches is in the creation of a curtain for a movie theater or stage. The surface of the curtain needs to have creases and folds running vertically down the fabric, and it needs to bunch up and fold convincingly as the curtain rises. Plus, if you make two sides for the curtain, it needs to be able to tuck up just one end, leaving nice folds running diagonally down to the other, lowered side of the curtain. That's a recipe for using a four-sided patch, with some careful placement of object centers to aid in animating the shape and transformations of the curtain (see Figure 6.79).

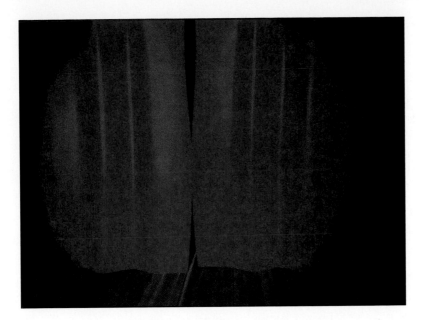

FIGURE 6.79 *Completed, rendered curtains made with the Four Sided tool.*

1. **Draw the Top Edge of the Curtain.**

   In the Top view, draw a Cardinal spline that represents the shape of the folds in the curtain as viewed from the top. Refer to Figure 6.80 for an indication of the shape. The curtain should have 8 to 14 points to get a nice smooth curve with a fair number of wrinkles.

2. **Duplicate and Translate the Spline.**

   In the Front view, raise this spline to 15 units in positive Y, and duplicate it with the D supra key. Translate the duplicate down to 0 in Y to form the bottom of the curtain. Use the M supra key in the Top view to move some points on the bottom curtain profile so that the curtain doesn't hang perfectly straight. Translate the whole bottom profile backstage in negative Z one unit to help the curtain hang nicely when the bottom is raised.

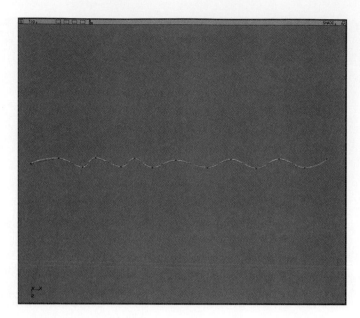

FIGURE 6.80 *Top view of the curtain spline.*

3. Make the Curtain's Side Edges.

Now in the Front view create a Cardinal spline for the left edge of the curtain. Use fewer points, maybe four, to make a smooth curve that is easy to animate and adjust later. Too much detail here might make the curtain look odd and will certainly be more difficult to animate. Try to make the curve sway gently back and forth, so the curtain doesn't hang too straight. Imagine Martha Stewart gently adjusting the curtain so it looks like it has been hanging in a musty theater for a long time.

Translate this curve to the left edge of the curtain's top profile. Switch to CTR mode and translate the local center of the left profile to the top of that spline, so that we can use a scale transformation on it later to make it shorten as if a string is being pulled up from the bottom to the top. Back in OBJ mode, duplicate the left edge, translate it to the right side, and again use the M supra key to adjust the points so they aren't too symmetrical (see Figure 6.81).

FIGURE 6.81   *All the curtain profile curves.*

4. **Make the Patch.**

   First check that Preferences→Modelling Relation is turned on, so you can animate the curtain by saving key shapes for the curves if you desire. Choose the
   Surface→Four Sided command, and then pick each edge of the curtain in a
   clockwise fashion, starting with the top edge. When you pick the last edge, the
   curtain is completed.

5. **Create the Second Curtain.**

   Translate the complete curtain patch to the side a few units in X so you can
   again see the curves. This will be the curtain on the right side of the stage.
   Make another patch with exactly the same method to form the curtain for the
   left side of the stage. Rotate it 180 degrees in Y, and translate it so that it sits
   next to the other curtain along the X axis.

6. **Open the Curtains.**

   You can animate each spline that forms an edge of a curtain to change the
   shape of the curtains. To see this in action, use the Schematic view to locate the
   spline that runs vertically, forming the edge of the curtains where they are closest together. Select the spline and set a keyframe for its shape at frame 1. Drag
   the Time Slider to frame 80, and move points on the spline with the M key to
   make it shorter. Set another shape keyframe.

Now select the spline that forms the bottom of the curtain, and save a keyframe at frame 1 for the starting shape. Drag the Time Slider to frame 80 and manipulate the points on the curve to form a graceful arc rising from the edge that remains full length to the shorter edge. You could use the M supra key and translate each point, or set up and use proportional modeling to make your life easier. Save a keyframe at frame 80.

When you play your animation, you should see a complex folding curtain changing shape as if it were gracefully bunching up at the top to reveal a screen (see Figure 6.82). Martha would be proud.

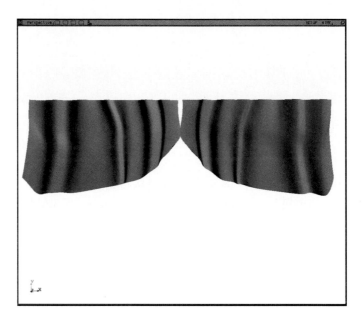

FIGURE 6.82   *The bunched-up curtain.*

CONCLUSION

Modeling is an art form, and these tools are just the basic elements you will use to practice your craft. Each can be combined with other, more specific tools in Softimage 3D to perform unique functions. Some techniques work miracles in some circumstances and don't work at all on other occasions. The key is to find the combination that works best for you.

In this chapter, you learned how to

- Push and pull points on a surface.

- Work with curves, including Linear, Cardinal, Bezier, B-spline, and NURBS.

- Create extruded objects, extrude polygons, and extrude along one and two paths.

- Produce revolved objects and animate the Axis of Revolution.

- Skin complex profiles together to form mechanical and human shapes.

- Make four-sided patch surfaces and animate them.

From the LucasArts CD-ROM game "Grim Fandango." Courtesy of LucasArts Entertainment Company, LLC.

CHAPTER 7

POLYGON MODELING

A subset of Softimage's Modeling tools, the Polygonal Modeling tools enable you to manipulate objects made of polygons, as well as individual polygons themselves. Sometimes using the Polygon Modeling tools is just the easiest way to make the objects you need for your rendered scenes, but other times Polygonal Modeling is the only way to precisely control what you get. Using the Polygon Modeling tools, you can draw each polygon precisely where you want it, control the exact location of every vertex, and keep total control over the number of polygons in each model (see Figure 7.1).

FIGURE 7.1 *Several models with different levels of polygonal detail.*

Every polygon in Softimage can be transformed separately, colored and textured individually, and even animated individually. The POL mode restricts all the Transformation menus to work only on polygons, and the Polygon menu cells add even more polygon-specific functionality.

In this chapter, you will

- Create and edit polygons, point-by-point and edge-by-edge
- Model from poly primitives
- Copy, duplicate, and transform polygons
- Extrude polygons
- Make polygonal terrain models
- Round and bevel poly objects
- Perform Polygon reduction

Making an entire scene by drawing and connecting individual polygons is like building yourself a house out of toothpicks, or knitting a car out of steel wool. Sometimes that's what it takes!

POLYGON MODELING FOR GAMES

For real-time 3D scenarios, however, all this possible detail can be too much of a good thing. Polygonal modeling has become increasingly important over the last few years with the popularity of real-time 3D games and VRML (Virtual Reality Markup Language). When a game or VR simulator needs to display a 3D environment interactively to the user, so the user can move freely about the 3D space, the computer rendering the scene must be able to redraw the scene very rapidly, typically 24 to 30 times each second. Because the computer must evaluate and perhaps draw each polygon in the scene every single time the scene is refreshed, keeping the polygon count low is critical to smooth gameplay and good computer performance (see Figure 7.2).

In game development, the programmers who build the code engine typically perform tests to determine exactly how many polygons the engine can draw per second, on a reference machine that the game players are likely to have. Then the game designer sets the frame rate at which the game must refresh for smooth action, and the total engine performance number is divided by that frame rate to deliver the *polygon budget.* The polygon budget is how many polygons can be on screen in each frame, before the game engine begins to choke and can't draw them all in time. After the polygon budget has been determined, the game designers list all the elements that need to be onscreen at one time, and divide the polygon budget up into a budget for each element.

For example, if my game engine can draw 90,000 lit, textured triangles per second, and I want the game to play at 30 frames per second, the polygon budget is 3000 triangles per each frame. If I assign 1000 triangles to the terrain, 200 to the backdrop, and decide that five enemies can be onscreen at once, each with 200 triangles for the enemy and 100 triangles for weapons, shots, and so on, that leaves me with 300 triangles for the main character.

Modeling an attractive, convincing main character in less than 300 triangles isn't easy, but it can be done by creating your character from scratch with the Polygon Modeling tools.

NOTE

For those of you interested in video game technology, there is usually a *texture budget* as well. A typical game engine can draw a polygon without a texture in about 10% of the processor cycles required for the same polygon with a texture, so reducing texture usage can help performance.

Also, as the textures get larger, the time required to map them onto polygons and the memory used to store them increase. Texture maps in video games are often very small, ranging from 32 pixels wide by 32 pixels tall to 128 pixels square for really big ones. (See Figures 7.3 and 7.4.) Some game engines even store multiple sizes of each texture to assist in drawing the textures at different scales, called MIP mapping (see Figure 7.5).

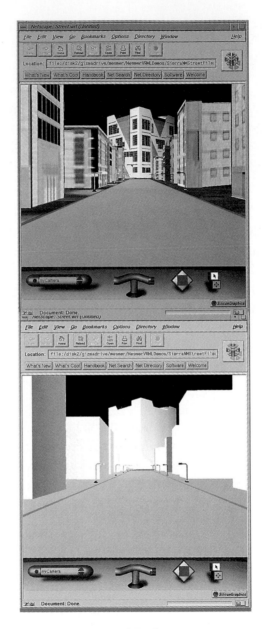

FIGURE 7.2   *A real-time image and the geometry behind it.*

FIGURE 7.3 *A very small texture sheet used to texture Microsoft low poly models for the Microsoft Combat Flight Simulation game. Texture map painted by David Choi. Copyright 1998 Microsoft Corp.*

MAKE MINE PINK: SELECTING POLYGONS

The Polygon Selection methods are listed in the Polygon menu cells (see Figure 7.6). Those polygons selected on a given object are highlighted in a translucent pink shade in the Wireframe views (see Figure 7.7). When you switch to the POL mode, only the selected, pink polygons are transformed by the Scale, Rotate, and Translate menu cells. Many other commands are likewise restricted to the selected group of polygons.

> **NOTE**
>
> A typical PC game texture budget is calculated by examining the video memory of the target machine, currently about 2 MB. That video memory must store the screen area, (about 302KB), an offscreen draw buffer of the same size, and finally the texture memory. That limits texture memory for the entire scene to about 1.4 MB, or the size of a floppy disk. The textures are mapped into the screen area by choosing which pixels of the texture to copy into which area of the screen memory, an operation usually performed by the video card itself.
>
> Because texture space is at a premium and takes longer to draw to the screen anyway, clever use of material color is a must. One technique is the use of vertex shading. Each vertex of a polygon may, in fact, have a different color, and when they are drawn to the screen, the shading engine creates a gradient between the vertices with different coloration. This method is growing in popularity and is completely supported by Softimage. Softimage can even convert a texture map on a polygonal mesh into vertex colors.

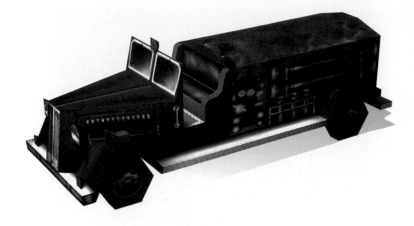

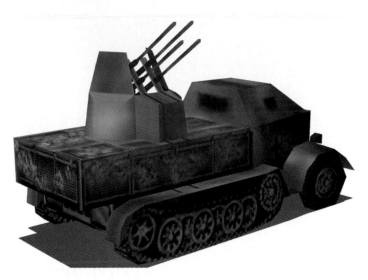

FIGURE 7.4 *Two low-poly vehicles, with 256 × 256 pixel Texture maps, from the Microsoft Combat Flight Simulation game, modeled and textured by David Choi. Copyright 1998 Microsoft Corp.*

You can select polygons by tagging the vertices of the polygon desired and executing the Polygon→Tag Vertex command. I do not find this command useful, however. A more popular method is the Polygon→Select by Rectangle command (supra key Y), which you use by dragging a marquee around a polygon or group of polygons. When you drag with the left mouse button, those polygons entirely within the marquee are selected and shown in pink in the Wireframe view windows. If you use the middle mouse button, those within the marquee are deselected, and if you use the right mouse button, they are toggled to the opposite of their previous state.

FIGURE 7.5   *A real-time texture library with many textures in a single file.*

	Vertex
Lattice	Edge
	Polygon
	Select by Tag Vertex
Deformation	Select by Rectangle y
	Select by Raycasting g
	Reference Frame
Polygon	Breakup +
	Coplanar +
	Eater +
History	Equalize +
	Fractalize +
EXIT	MergeGeometry +
	Mosaic +
	PolyOrder +
	PolygonDetach +
	PolygonInvert +
	SelectPolygon +
	Stitch +
	Wakeup +
	Weld +
	EXIT POPUP

FIGURE 7.6   *The Polygon menu cells in the Model module.*

The Select by Rectangle method selects polygons on either side of an object, so be sure to check that only those desired are highlighted before you transform the selected group.

The newest method, appearing in version 3.5, is Polygon→Select by Raycasting (supra key G). When Select by Raycasting is active, hold down the left mouse button to select the polygon directly under your pointer. Only polygons with normals pointing toward you are selected, so polygons on the back side of an object are not added to the selected group of polygons. If no polygons become selected when you use the G supra key, the normals may be inverted. When you raycast with the middle mouse button, you deselect polygons, while the right mouse button toggles polygons.

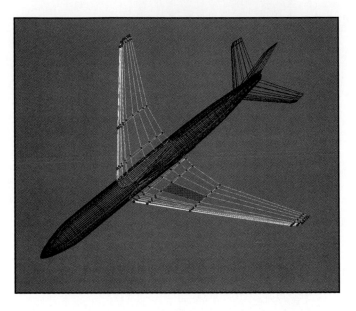

FIGURE 7.7 *A model with selected polygons highlighted in pink.*

STARTING FROM SCRATCH: MAKING YOUR OWN POLYGONS

Although it is certainly faster to make objects from a spline with an extrusion, a revolution, a skin, or a four-sided patch, and it is easier to make polygons from a primitive polygon object, you can draw your very own polygons, one point at a time. We'll cover this method first, on the theory that you must crawl before you learn to walk. A firm understanding of polygon terminology and practice in creating polygons will certainly serve you well as you go forward.

To recap from Chapter 6, "The Model Shop—All About Modeling," a polygon is a geometric construct composed of at least three *vertices* positioned in space and connected by straight line segments called *edges*. Each polygon has a front face and a back face, indicated by which direction the polygon normal is pointing (see Figure 7.8).

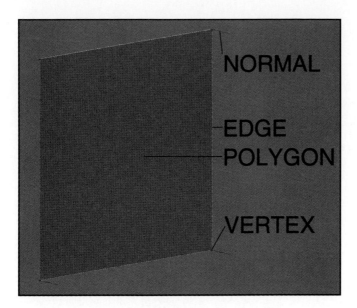

FIGURE 7.8 *Polygon basics.*

THE DRAW→POLYGON COMMAND

The Draw→Polygon command in the Model module is the place to start drawing your first polygon (see Figure 7.9). The Draw command doesn't just draw single polygons; it starts by creating a new polygonal mesh object, visible in the Schematic view. You can then attach additional polygons to the first one, sharing vertices and edges.

Because Softimage attempts to keep polygons within the same mesh consistent in their normal orientation, the direction you draw a polygon is important. The default method is to draw polygons counterclockwise. After the first polygon is placed and confirmed, the command automatically changes to the Attach mode.

With Draw→Polygon active, you can click in any View window and hold down the mouse button to place the first vertex. It's a good idea to draw polygons in an orthographic view instead of the Perspective view, because you can keep the polygons planar. You can place additional vertices with the left mouse button, or add vertices between existing ones with the middle mouse button. You can add as many points as you wish to the polygon, but it's a good idea to keep the number of points in a polygon under 255 so it can be stored in a single byte. When you are done with the polygon, click the right mouse button to end the Polygon Add mode and enter the Polygon Attach mode (see Figure 7.10).

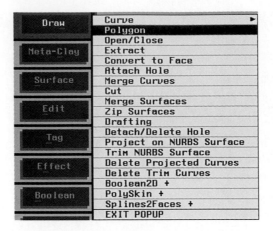

FIGURE 7.9   *The Draw→Polygon menu cell.*

FIGURE 7.10   *Drawing and attaching new polygons.*

In the Polygon Attach mode (also found by itself in the Polygon→Polygon command), you must pick two existing vertices on the polygon to define the shared edge between the old polygon and the new one. You then add additional vertices that belong only to the new polygon, by clicking in space with the left mouse button.

If you select the first two vertices for the shared edge in a way that would lead to the new and old polygons having different normal orientations, Softimage gives you an error message in the status line and makes you repick. This refusal to allow bad polygons seems like a hassle, but it prevents rendering and redraw problems later.

When you are done with the new polygon, click the middle mouse button to accept it as done and add another. Use the right mouse button to end the mode. In this manner, you can add one polygon to another, carefully defining the shape of the object.

ADDING AND REMOVING VERTICES

What if you have a polygon already made that needs to be subdivided to create more detail? You can add more vertices to any polygon, in places where additional edges would help you create more polygonal detail. Then you can add edges to subdivide the polygon into two smaller ones, and further subdivide those smaller polygons as needed. This is the process most often used to create polygonal detail for faces, fingers, and musculature on low-poly characters.

You add vertices with the Polygon→ Vertex command, found in the Model module. Clicking the left mouse button adds a vertex to an edge at the spot under your mouse pointer. If you click an edge with the middle mouse button, the vertex is added at the exact center of the edge, which makes it easy to keep lines straight when adding polygonal detail for buildings, and so on (see Figure 7.11).

FIGURE 7.11   *A polygon with some added vertices in the middle of edges.*

To remove vertices that are no longer needed, click the offending point with the right mouse button. If the vertex is redundant, it simply goes away, but if there are other edges defined by that vertex, the edges go away as well, and so will the polygons that rely on those edges, leaving a hole in your model. Be careful.

ADDING AND REMOVING EDGES

After adding vertices to a polygon, you can connect them with an edge to subdivide the one previous polygon into two. Simply choose the Polygon→Edge command (see Figure 7.12), pick the first vertex, and then the second. Softimage adds an edge (see Figure 7.13), unless the operation creates adjacent polygons with different normal orientations. In this case, the error message "Bad edge orientation" appears in the Status Bar and you must pick the vertices in the opposite order.

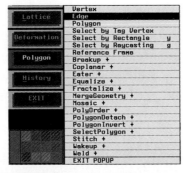

FIGURE 7.12   *The Polygon→Edge menu cell.*

FIGURE 7.13   *The polygon from Figure 7.11 with edges added between the new vertices.*

Edges can only be added within a single polygon. This means that if the vertices you want to connect belong to different polygons, you cannot add an edge. You have to find an edge between the two vertices and add an intermediate vertex, making two more edges to connect the points. Using the middle mouse button allows you to connect a series of vertices with shared edges. The right mouse button removes edges, which removes the polygons dependent on that edge, and may create a hole in your model.

ADDING POLYGONS TO A MESH

The Polygon→Polygon command has the same functionality as the Attach mode of the Draw→Polygon command, and it can be used by itself to either fill holes left in polygons or add new polygons that share edges with the current mesh. Polygons can only be added to open edges, so that no more than two polygons can ever share an edge. You can show the open edges of a mesh with the Show→Edge flags command (see Figure 7.14).

After executing the Polygon→Polygon command, pick at least two vertices to attach a polygon. If you are adding a new polygon, then click somewhere off the mesh to place a new point in space, and continue to place new points until you have defined the polygon you want. To complete the polygon, click the middle mouse button.

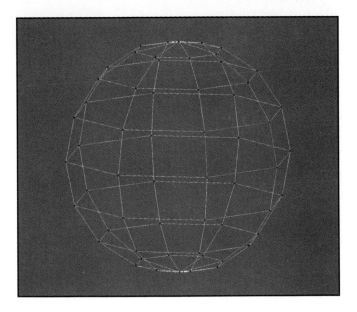

FIGURE 7.14   *A polygonal mesh with holes showing the edge flags.*

If you are patching a hole in a polygon, continue to select only existing vertices until you have plugged the hole. Then use the middle mouse button to complete the polygon.

TAKE A SHORTCUT: WORKING FROM A PRIMITIVE

Now that you know how to start from scratch, making your own objects out of nothing but ambition and the Polygon menu cell, I should tell you that it is almost always easier to start out with a simple geometric polygon primitive and use the polygon duplication and transform tools to create the object you need. From one polygon, you can make many by duplicating the original and transforming it in a number of interesting ways. Many types of angular, precise-looking objects can be easily created this way, such as buildings, machines, ovens, and all manner of other manufactured devices. But before we dive in, first a word about the polygon transformations and the Polygon Local Coordinate system.

POLYGON TRANSFORMATIONS AND LOCAL COORDINATES

When you are in the POL (polygon) mode, remember that only the selected polygons are acted upon by the Transformation menus' cells and a number of other commands, including Duplicate and Delete. This means that the object stays as it is, and only the pink polygons are translated, scaled, rotated, and so on (see Figure 7.15). Don't forget to return to OBJ mode when you want to work on the entire object and not just the individual polygons.

When you transform a polygon, it needs to have its own local axis to which to transform relative (unless you are in GBL mode). By default, if you select a single polygon and Show→Centers is on, you will observe that the center is in the geographic middle of the polygon, with the X and Z axes oriented towards the edges of the polygon, and the Y axis pointed outwards along the normal. This is very useful, because you can now use the Y axis to move the polygon in and out along the normal, and you can scale X and Z to make the polygon smaller or larger.

However, if you select more than one polygon and they share an edge, the center is located in the middle of the group, and the orientation is the average of all the polygons in the group (see Figure 7.16). Although this does give the group a center for transformations, it might not be a very meaningful one. (You could create your own center with Cluster Centers.)

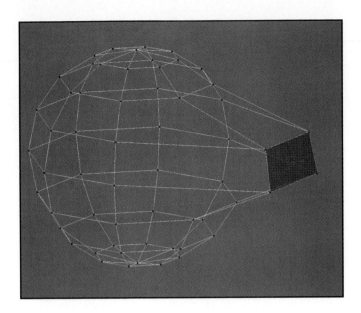

FIGURE 7.15   *A polygonal object with selected polys translating on their own axes.*

If none of the selected polygons in the group shares an edge with another selected polygon, each polygon has its very own center, aligned with just that polygon. This fact makes it possible to transform polygons in large groups instead of individually. Pay attention to the centers on the groups of polygons you transform, or their behavior will make very little sense to you.

When you are in POL mode, the Transformation menu cells operate only on the selected group of polygons, causing the polygons to move in space relative to the object to which they belong. If you want to animate this change of transformation, use the SaveKey→Object→Shape command, not the SaveKey→Object→ Translation command, because you are really adjusting the location of the points that make up the surface. The Rot menu cells rotate the polygons around their local axes (see Figure 7.17).

The Scale menu cells make the polygons larger or smaller in X or Y (see Figure 7.18).

You can make more elaborate transformations to a polygon by simply moving the vertices around with the M supra key.

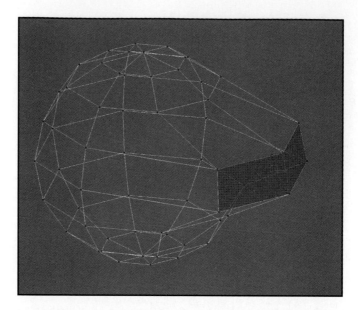

FIGURE 7.16   *A polygonal object with grouped polys translating on a common axis.*

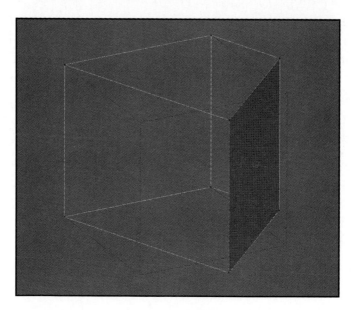

FIGURE 7.17   *A polygonal object with polys rotated about Y (the normal).*

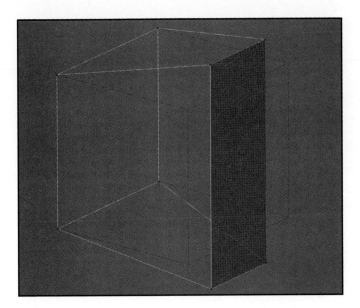

FIGURE 7.18 *A polygonal object with selected polygons scaled in X and Z.*

DUPLICATING POLYGONS

When you duplicate a selected polygon by using the Duplicate→Selection command while in POL mode, a bunch of special things happen. You might expect that another polygon would be made on top of the last, but that's not what happens. The original polygon is cut into a number of new polygons, one for each edge, and connected to the new polygon that takes over the shape and location of the original (see Figure 7.19). In other words, a border of new polygons is made, all connected by shared edges to a new central polygon.

If this new central polygon is translated away from the object, the new border polygons connect it to the other polygons in the object. If the new center polygon is scaled, the border polygons create a bevel. You should also remain in the Model module while using polygon duplication.

> **TIP**
>
> Duplicating polygons is a fabulous method for creating windows with window sills. Simply select the central polygon that will become the window pane and duplicate it. Scale it down slightly in X and Z to create a window frame. Duplicate it again but this time translate it in negative Y so that it becomes recessed into the frame (see Figure 7.20).
>
> Select the polygon at the base of the window frame and duplicate it. Then translate it in positive Y so that a window ledge extends a short distance from the base of the window.
>
> If you have a bunch of windows on a building face, select every other window and execute these commands on them as a group. It works because none of the polygons shares an edge with another. Then go back and repeat this for the windows you excluded the first time around.

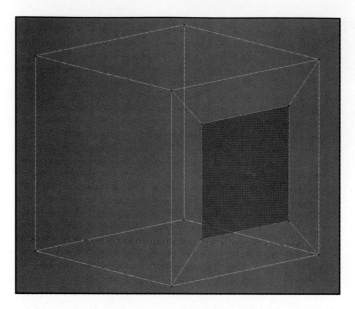

FIGURE 7.19 *The selected polygon is duplicated and then scaled slightly smaller. Note the bordering polygons.*

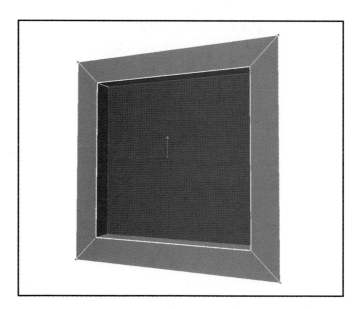

FIGURE 7.20 *A simple polygonal window with frame and sill.*

DELETING POLYGONS

Of course, you sometimes want to remove a polygon while keeping the vertices and edges that it shares with neighbors.

When in POL mode, choosing the Delete→Selection command permanently removes the selected polygon from the object (see Figure 7.21). The edges it used to share now become open, and you can build new polygons to share them. This polygon delete function is a great way to knock holes in an object.

FIGURE 7.21   *The Delete→Selection menu cell.*

WARNING

Remain in the Model mode while deleting polygons, or the entire object disappears.

EXTRUDING POLYGONS

Individual polygon shapes can also be extruded, often with interesting results. To accomplish this task, you must be working in POL mode, have some polygons selected on an object, and then use the standard Surface→Extrusion command in the Model module. When in POL mode, all the extrusion details in the Extrusion dialog apply only to the selected polygons on the selected object. You can extrude polygons along a path, and you can apply a transformation to the polygon at each step of the extrusion, making the resulting polygons smaller, revolved slightly, or offset in space (see Figure 7.22).

The polygon Extrude Along a Path option in the Extrusion dialog gives you the power to draw a path, and then have the Y direction of the polygon (the normal) oriented along this path during the extrusion.

TUTORIAL: MAKING GANGLIA

It's finally time to put all this polygon theory to work. In this tutorial, we'll use Polygon Extrusion to create a nerve cell, called a ganglia (see Figure 7.23).

1. **Start with an Icosahedron.**

   Draw a wavy curve in the Front view, starting at the origin and heading up in positive Y. Use a B-spline for easy control.

   Now get a primitive icosahedron and leave it at the global center where it came into existence (see Figure 7.24).

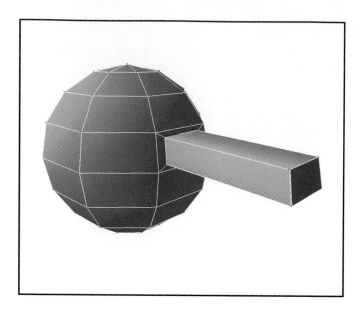

FIGURE 7.22 *An object with some polygons selected and extruded.*

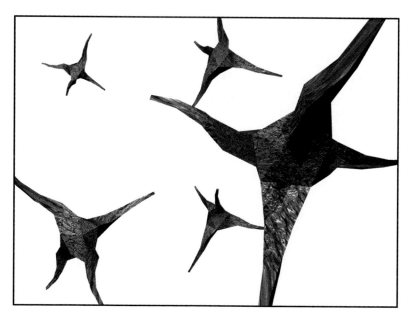

FIGURE 7.23 *Completed, rendered ganglia.*

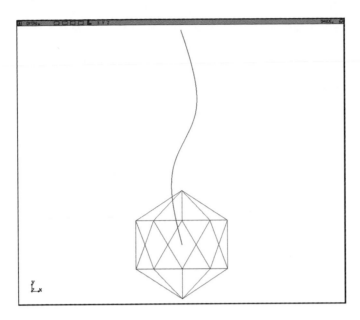

FIGURE 7.24 *The icosahedron and the extrusion path.*

Switch to POL (Polygon mode) and select four of the faces with the G supra key, making sure that you choose non-contiguous (not touching) faces (see Figure 7.25).

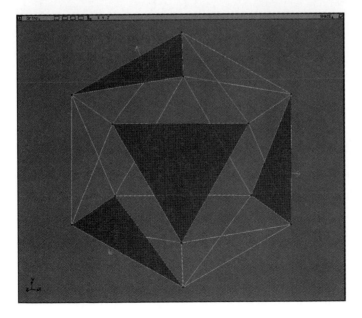

FIGURE 7.25 *The icosahedron with four faces selected, showing the centers.*

When non-contiguous polygons are selected, each one gets a local center with the Y axis oriented along the normal of the polygon. We'll use this local center as a local coordinate system to extrude each polygon in a different direction.

2. **Extrude Some Arms.**

With the icosahedron selected, bring up the Extrusion dialog box, and see that the On Curve option is the only option available. Click Ok and then pick the extrusion path you drew to complete the command. Arms should sprout from the selected faces of the icosahedron (see Figure 7.26).

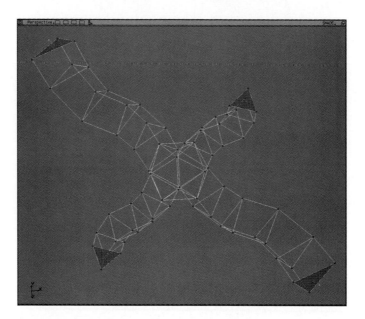

FIGURE 7.26 *The icosahedron with straight extruded arms.*

3. **Set the Transform Options.**

Undo the last command by holding the U supra key and clicking anywhere with the left mouse button, until the arms go away. Now invoke the Surface→Extrusion dialog again. This time turn on Curve Placement and click the Transform button to show the transformation options (see Figure 7.27).

Set the Scale in X, Y, and Z to 0.8, which makes each successive polygon 10 percent smaller than the last.

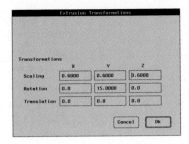

FIGURE 7.27 *The Extrusion Transformations dialog, set for the ganglia.*

Set the Rotation in Y to 15 degrees, which makes the arms twist around the direction of the normal as they move out.

Close the dialog, and execute the command to create the armed ganglia (see Figure 7.28).

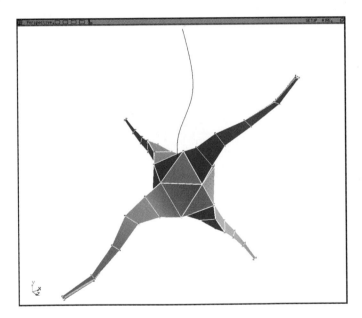

FIGURE 7.28 *The ganglia with spiral arms.*

As you can see, extruding polygons can yield some interesting results. Extruding polygons along a path is useful for making fingers on low-poly hands and also for other path extrusion effects, such as tree branches and roads. As an extra bonus, being able to transform a polygon at each stage of the extrusion adds in functionality, such as that found in the repetitive duplication tools.

Eric Ingerson

Senior Animator

LucasArts Entertainment Company, LLC

Jessica Forys

Technical Manager for the Art Department

LucasArts Entertainment Company, LLC.

Anthony: How does Softimage 3D|Extreme play a part in your day?

Eric: I spend the most (and happiest) time animating, and Softimage 3D is all I've been animating with lately. I'm pretty partisan about keeping it that way. It's quirky and maddening at times, but using any of the other animation packages we have here is, by comparison, like animating with a bag over your head.

The software is so flexible that I think everybody who has used it creatively for a while will do things in slightly unexpected ways. I think most of the best "word-of-mouth" techniques you hear about are clever twists on the intended uses for the tools.

Anthony: What were the other skills you had before you met Softimage 3D|Extreme that meshed with the program and helped you get work done?

Eric: Stop motion and 2D experience was the basic and necessary groundwork, as well as film school, which was invaluable. Some dabbling in drama helped my sense of staging and gave me a way to approach varied character action. And, of course, figure drawing. I'm very rusty at drawing now, but the sense of "the natural pose" stays with you.

Just animating well takes a lot perseverance—a lot of grueling, mind-numbing hours spent adjusting animation. When you're learning, it's even more severe, especially as an unpaid student.

Anthony: What's the most frustrating part of the process for you?

Eric: Having something that looks good but does not suit the scene is pretty frustrating, but by far the

biggest ongoing frustration is coaxing the software to perform. That's why it's so painful to change software packages, because it takes a long time to build up a good repertoire of techniques and workarounds. I haven't touched particles yet, because I'm not really interested in creating special effects. I'm sure I'll eventually be called on to use it, though, and I hope it's fully integrated by then.

Anthony: What special methods have you developed to make Softimage renderings look distinctively yours?

Eric: I use a lot of overlapping movement all over the hierarchy, and I try to get the elbows and the knees just right when using IK by animating the chain roots. I use "plateau" spline interpolation almost exclusively and avoid long, sweeping "spliney" motions by breaking it up with velocity adjustments, pauses, and overlaps. A little motion peppered throughout a relatively static shot goes a long way, as long as something's always moving, or is about to move, just a little. If you watch old Ray Harryhausen films like *Seventh Voyage of Sinbad* or *Jason and the Argonauts*, those models are continuously writhing about. That's a little extreme for most situations, but in computer or stop motion 3D, keeping things moving is very important. Also, if you can find a excuse to plant a hand on a table or column, you can get a lot of the complex overlap and interplay to come automatically with IK. Seeing the first test render when the character seems to have finally "woken up" is the really rewarding part of the process The rest is just polish.

Anthony: What are the film or television effects that really blew your mind?

Eric: Most recently the parts of Starship Troopers done by Tippet Studios. It was the best sci-fi film compositing I've seen, and the creature animation blew me away.

From the LucasArts CD-ROM game "Grim Fandango." Courtesy of LucasArts Entertainment Company, LLC.

From the LucasArts CD-ROM game "Grim Fandango." Courtesy of LucasArts Entertainment Company, LLC.

Anthony: What do you suppose is the next frontier for computer graphic imagery?

Eric: In general, the standards for animation, modeling, and compositing will keep getting higher, and some of the stuff you see now that audiences accept as "okay" will eventually strike audiences the way old Flash Gordon movies strike us. A big hurdle for 3D effects is realistic and manageable animated hair and fire. I haven't yet seen a convincing animated CG campfire, with all the whirls and billows correctly animated.

Anthony: If you had one wish for the next version, what would you implement?

Eric: Better implementation of animated constraints, including being able to edit them in the dopesheet as easily as regular keyframes.

Anthony: Jessica, what can you tell us about your job?

Jessica: I was hired by LucasArts in 1996 as the UNIX system administrator and then promoted to the art department one year ago. In a nutshell, most technical issues that affect the art department usually land in my lap in some manner.

A great deal of sheer perseverance is a critical skill for my job. Working with new technology comes with its share of headaches. Deadlines, budgets, and buggy software complicate the already difficult business of producing 3D art. There are those moments when you know it should work and a great deal of time can be spent debugging something. I have become a very patient person.

I have a background as a programmer, network administrator, and UNIX system administrator. I learned to filter through a multitude of variables that could have been causing problems.

From the LucasArts CD-ROM game "Grim Fandango." Courtesy of LucasArts Entertainment Company, LLC.

Anthony: How does Softimage 3D|Extreme play a part in your day?

Jessica: Setting up render farms and SGIs, reviewing render logs and license servers, and installing plug-ins, patches, and shaders can take up a modest part of my day. I spend a good deal of my time performance-tuning SGI system and memory allocation, in addition to making sure plug-ins (ours and third-party) are working properly.

I spend a lot of time with rendering in a few areas: /var/tmp/soft.status, ray.irix5 outputs, and the flexlm license logs. That is my triple header for debugging what could be going on with Softimage renders. I have set up all our systems so they are cross-mounted locally throughout the project and on our render server. This way they could create their textures and scenes locally (which was much faster than working off the network for us). In order to ensure that everything was working smoothly, most of the team wrote out .mi files and rendered from the command line. This allowed us to quickly pinpoint any problems that the system was having. Every artist who was rendering has lots of swap space, plenty of memory, and a "slave" machine (SGI R10ks) to render to, and over time we added a multiprocessor server. This was not even enough and we could have used at least double the rendering power we had, but there are always budgets and economic realities to contend with.

Anthony: What's the most rewarding part of the process for you?

Jessica: Knowing that I can turn a situation that appears to be desperate and futile into a success. I generally use a combination of technical and creative skills to come up with a solution. There have been a few projects that sometimes ran into overbearing brick walls where I was able to create a door.

Anthony: How do you explain what you do to your parents?

Jessica: I don't—I still like them to believe that I am working on the new *Star Wars* movies and that George consults with me often!

TUTORIAL: MAKING A POLYGON HEAD

Low polygon modeling is also an easy way to create a human head, perhaps for a real-time game. Starting with a primitive cube, you can add vertices and edges until you end up with a head similar to the one in Figure 7.29.

FIGURE 7.29 *The completed polygonal face.*

1. **Get a Cube.**

   Start with a primitive cube. Enter POL mode and choose the Polygon→Vertex command with the middle mouse button to add vertices to the middle of the edges on the front face. Then use the Polygon→Edge command to connect the four vertices (you'll have to add one more to the line that bisects the head) to divide the head into four equal quadrants (see Figure 7.30).

   The face will lie below the middle line, with the vertical division as the center of the nose.

2. **Add the Facial Features.**

   Add more vertices and edges to form the eyes, nose, and mouth as shown in Figure 7.31. Because the face is largely symmetrical, facial features can be easily roughed in by bisecting each line and adding a new vertex at the midpoint of lines with the Polygon→Vertex command and the middle mouse button.

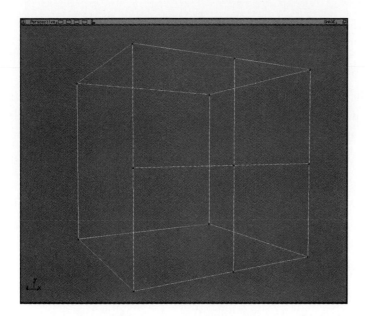

FIGURE 7.30 *The bisected cube.*

Ignore the top two quadrants, which will become rounded as the forehead and hair are added later.

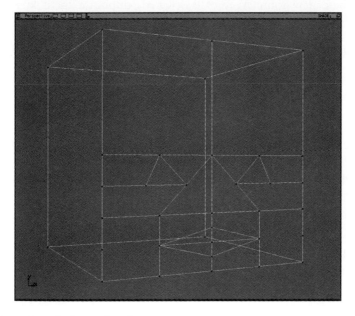

FIGURE 7.31 *A simple face on the cube.*

3. Give the Nose and Chin Depth.

The facial features all currently lie in a single plane. Some, such as the nose, need to extend from the face, while the eyes need to recess.

Tag the nose point and translate it in Z forward to make the nose poke out. You can also tag and scale the points on either side of the nose to make it less broad and geometric.

Add a new vertex under the nose, and connect it side to side with two new edges.

The points in the center of the head under the nose extending to the chin can be tagged and translated in Z to create a chin, and the points on the side of the head can be translated in Z and scaled inward in X to round the face.

4. Make the Eyes.

Select the eyes with the G supra key and duplicate them. Scale them down in X and Z to make a smaller polygon for the eye ball, and translate it slightly in Y to recess it into the face. The eyeballs are now triangular but could be more round, so add a few new vertices to the middle of each edge and translate all the vertices with the M supra key to make a rounder eyeball.

With these new rounder eyeballs selected, duplicate them and scale them smaller in X and Z to make the irises (see Figure 7.32).

5. Shape the Skull Shape.

The head is currently very square, so tag the bottom rear points and bring them in to make a jaw line. You can also tag and scale the points on the top of the head in X and Z a bit to round the shape of the head.

Finally, tag the top points and the rear points (no points on the face), and choose the Effect→Rounding command. Set the Round to 0.25 (25% of the line width between points), and execute the command to see the finished face.

There you have it: A simple, painless, low poly face (mine has 69 polygons), suitable for VRML, simulation, or 3D game building (see Figure 7.33). The completed head, in different stages of construction, can be found on the courseware CD-ROM, in a scene entitled "polyface."

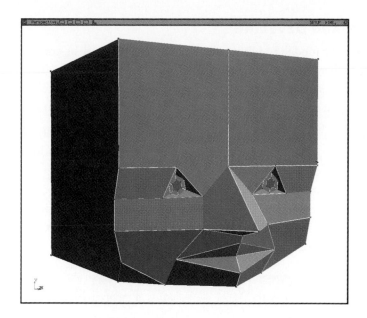

FIGURE 7.32 *The face takes shape with depth and eyes.*

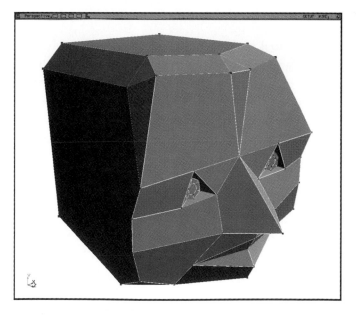

FIGURE 7.33 *A completed head shape and low poly face.*

ROUNDING AND BEVELING

One side effect of modeling with polygons is that you tend to create models with sharp edges. Other times, if you create shapes that should be rounded, you will see facets when the final is rendered, which doesn't look good. The Bevel and Rounding tools can help you smooth the edges of objects after they have been made.

The Bevel tool, located in the Model module in the Effect menu cell, adds one polygon between each edge, effectively rounding the sharp edges by adding detail (see Figure 7.34). This command can even be performed locally on tagged vertices only, if you are in TAG mode. The size of the bevel in Softimage units can be set in the Bevel dialog box that opens when you choose the Effect→Bevel command. Although this tool seems like it's designed to bevel the edges of text, it can be used to round any polygonal object.

FIGURE 7.34   *The Bevel dialog box.*

The Effect→Rounding tool performs a similar function, but where the Bevel tool places the new edges a given distance away from the old edges, Rounding subdivides each polygon, giving you the option of deciding how evenly the subdivision is made (see Figure 7.35). Setting Rounding to 1 divides each polygon exactly in half and places the new polygons exactly midway between their neighbors in location and angle. Setting Rounding to 0.5 divides the previous polygon into two, one-half the size of the other (see Figure 7.36).

FIGURE 7.35   *The Round dialog box.*

SUBDIVISION

Many times in Polygon modeling you wish you had more detail on an object, even if just temporarily, so that you can deform the object more cleanly, or perhaps to work on some of the new, smaller polygons to add detail. The manual method of adding vertices and edges would take a long while if, for instance, you wanted to add 500 new polygons to the sides of a building to model the exterior shape.

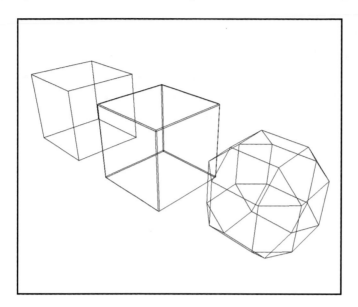

FIGURE 7.36 *The effects of beveling and rounding.*

The Effect→Subdivision tool, however, takes care of adding new polygonal detail for you. When you execute the command, a dialog pops up allowing you to choose how many additional subdivisions will be created on your model in each axis (see Figure 7.37). Leaving an axis at 0 does not subdivide the model in that direction at all, while a subdivision of 1 adds a new edge exactly in the center of the object.

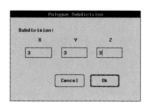

FIGURE 7.37 *The Polygon Subdivision dialog box.*

For instance, if you start with a primitive cube with six sides and six polygons, and use Subdivision on it with a setting of 3 in X, 3 in Y, and 3 in Z, the cube is divided in thirds in each axis, resulting in a cube with six faces but 27 polygons. Subdivision does not change the actual shape of the object at all; it just adds more polygons by chopping the current polygons into smaller pieces. You can then manipulate each of the smaller pieces to add surface detail to the model.

CLEANUP

The Cleanup command is a complement to the Subdivision command, because it can remove unneeded polygonal detail from a model. After you use Subdivide to add windows and ledges to a building, for example, you could use Effect→Cleanup to get rid of all the excess polygons that remain in the model, keeping only those that add detail.

Cleanup does this by examining the edge between each pair of polygons in the model, looking at the angle between the two. If the angle is 0, then the two polygons are coplanar, and there is no detail being added by that edge, so it is removed, creating one larger polygon where two smaller polygons once were.

You can set the angle at which the Cleanup command decides to get rid of the edge by entering an angle in the "Merge polygons if angle smaller than" entry box.

If, while removing edges, any vertices are left without any connecting edges, those vertices are removed. By removing both edges and vertices, this tool also performs a simple method of polygon reduction, and should be the first tool you reach for when your models need to lose weight.

The Cleanup tool can also merge vertices that are close together, which welds and cleans slightly inaccurate vertex placement. It can improve model fidelity from some lower-end, less polygon-accurate programs, such as 3D Studio.

Unconnected vertices can be connected, also improving model fidelity, and the new polygons can be reordered, making the model more orderly and more likely to work well with other effects.

TUTORIAL: ERECTING A POLYGON BUILDING

In this simple tutorial, you will use the Polygon Duplication and Transformation tools to create a believable polygonal building simply and easily (see Figure 7.38).

1. **Start with a Primitive Cube.**

   Get a primitive cube and scale it to be twice as tall as it is wide. Then use the Effect→Subdivide command to chop it into more polygons that you can use to model in detail. Set the Polygon Subdivision to 8 in X, 0 in Z (we don't need detail on the side of the building), and 16 in Y to create a lot of top to bottom detail. These settings will create many new polygons we can duplicate and transform to make windows, exterior detail, doors, and so on.

FIGURE 7.38 *The completed polygonal building.*

2. Add Roof Detail.

Use the G supra key (Select by Raycast) to select all the polygons on the top, front row of the building, but not the roof (see Figure 7.39).

Make sure you are in the Model module and enter POL mode to work on selected groups of polygons only. Choose the Duplicate→Immediate command to make a new group of polygons, and then activate the TransY menu cell. Set the Translation mode to LCL (Local mode) so that the polygons translate on their local axis, where Y is along the normal.

Translate the group so that it extends in front as a roof overhang.

When done, select the top row on the next side of the building and repeat. Create a ledge along the top of each side.

Now we'll create a stepped roof line. Deselect all the polygons with the Y supra key and the middle mouse button, and select only the top roof polygons. Deselect the single polygons on the left and right edges of the roof.

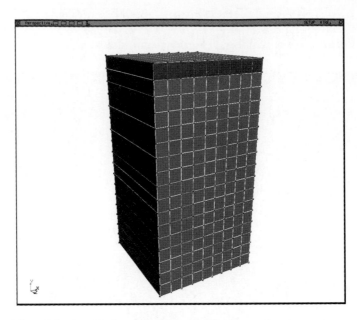

FIGURE 7.39 *The scaled cube with the subdivision and roof polygons selected.*

Translate all the selected roof polygons up a few units above the roof ledge, creating an angle at the left and right edges.

Duplicate the selected polygons and translate them up in Y a bit to form a roof step. By selecting fewer roof polygons and then alternating between translating them up with and without duplicating them first, you can make a pattern of sloped and stepped roof segments as in Figure 7.40.

3. **Add Front Detail.**

Deselect all the polygons, and then select a strip of polygons running top to bottom along the front of the building, two polygons in from the left edge. Select a symmetrical strip two polygons in from the right edge.

Duplicate the selected polygons and translate them in Y to extend a solid concrete detail along the front of the building.

Add a similar strip of exterior detail in the exact center column of polygons if you want.

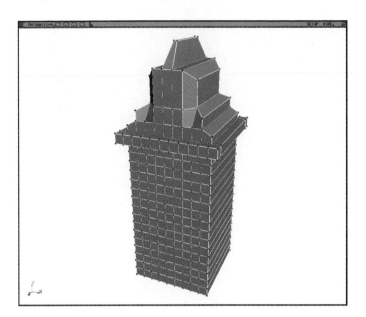

FIGURE 7.40 *The building with a polygonal stepped roof line.*

4. Add Windows.

Start by selecting only every other polygon in the rows between the edges of the building and the exterior detail you just made. Don't select polygons that touch each other or share a vertex.

Dolly in (supra key P) in the Perspective view to be tight on one window so you can precisely adjust your work.

Use Duplicate→Immediate to create new polygons around the windows, and then scale the selected polygons in X and Z to become slightly smaller, leaving a window frame. Translate the selected polygons slightly into the building.

Duplicate them again, but this time only translate them into the building to recess the windows into the face of the building (see Figure 7.41).

Dolly out to see that the changes you made to the polygon you viewed were also made to all the other selected window polygons. This means that you can add detail to a great number of polygons at once, saving time and effort. You may wish to turn smoothing off to see your building more accurately; do so by entering the Info→Selection dialog and clicking the Faceted radio button.

FIGURE 7.41 *One window, duplicated and recessed.*

As with any construction site, your building is finished but a mess. To remove all the unneeded polygons in the building, use the Effect→Cleanup command. In the Polygon Cleanup dialog box that it brings up, check the "Merge Polygons if angle smaller than" option and hit Ok (see Figure 7.42). You can check your work against the scene named PolyBuilding on the courseware CD-ROM.

POLYGON BREAKUP

Ordinarily, neighboring polygons are always connected at each edge because they actually share that edge, like Siamese twins perpetually joined. In some cases, however, you may want each polygon to have its very own edges, unshared with any other polygon in the mesh. Reasons for this include a desire to offset some polygons, remove some polygons, or scale some polygons, leaving gaps in the model. An even more common purpose is that when you plan to blow up a polygon model with the Explode tool, each polygon must be disconnected from its neighbors so that it can fly apart on its own as the mesh blows into small bits.

The Polygon→Breakup tool in the Model module fulfills this role. When it is activated, you can pick a polygon mesh. The mesh flashes a different color to indicate that the effect has run, and a new object is created with the same polygonal structure as the original, but with no shared edges (see Figure 7.43).

FIGURE 7.42 *The completed wireframe building.*

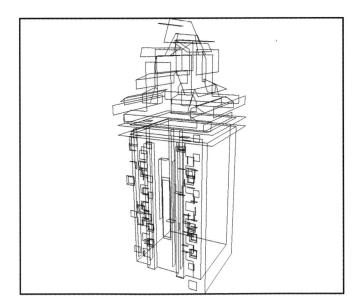

FIGURE 7.43 *The building model, after breakup, with all polygons translated in Y to show the Exploded view.*

POLYGON REDUCTION TOOLS

Sometimes it is easier to model with patch or Meta-Clay tools, even when you need to end up with low poly models. Sometimes you will be given large, heavy models that need to lose weight for use in your current project. In both cases, you need to take models with lots of detail and a lot of polygons and reduce the polygon weight while striving to retain detail and model quality.

Softimage has a complete complement of world-class Polygon Reduction tools to remove polygons from models while maintaining quality, using a variety of different methods. In general, as you reduce the number of polygons in the model, the detail in the model begins to degrade. The smaller the model gets, the worse it looks. Polygon reduction, like so many operations in Softimage, is not a science but an art—the art of finding the perfect balance between detail, shape, and number of polygons (see Figure 7.44).

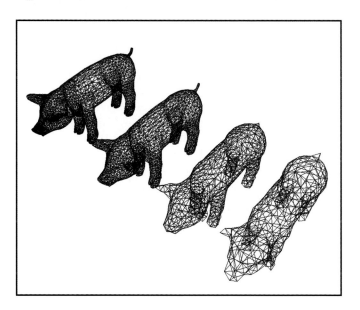

FIGURE 7.44   *The same model, in several stages of polygonal reduction.*

It must be said, however, that the Softimage Polygon Reduction toolset is not very popular, perhaps because it looks so darn complicated. In reality, it is simple to operate once you know the tricks. Here I'll show the basic functionality of the toolset in a way that will enable you to explore the features more fully. Check the Softimage documentation for a complete explanation of all the features.

The Effect→PolygonReduction command brings up a large dialog box, divided into four different areas (see Figure 7.45). The top area contains the options used to operate the Polygon Reduction command itself. The three lower areas are all different toolsets in their own right, and each operates independently of the others. Only one can be active at a time, set by clicking the radio button next to the section names, Rule Based, Optimization Based, and Filter.

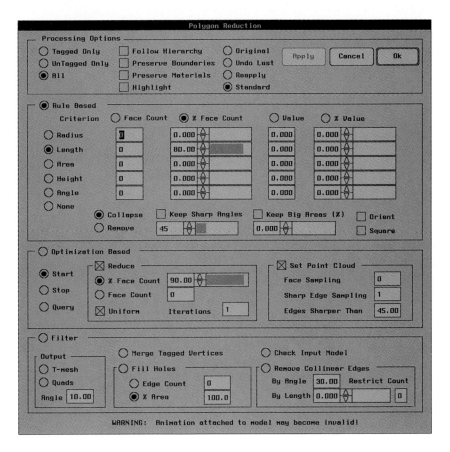

FIGURE 7.45 *The Polygon Reduction dialog box.*

THE RULE BASED METHOD

The trick that usually stops users cold is that the effect must first be attached to an object, and then iteratively adjusted for optimal results. After the first application, a new cone icon appears in the scene, representing the Polygon Reduction tool. You can then select that icon and edit the parameters of the command with the Effect→Custom→Edit Parameters menu cell. This two-part method allows you to make a great many small changes to the model very rapidly, trying things out, undoing the changes, trying different things, and trying combinations of things to get exactly the right balance for each different model. It works like this:

1. Tessellate the Model.

   Select the model and tessellate it into triangles with the Effect→Convert command.

2. Adjust the Radio Buttons.

   Use the Effect→PolygonReduction menu cell to call up the Polygon Reduction dialog. Check the top of the box in the Processing options. Set the All radio button to apply the effect to the entire object, and the Standard radio button to start the default operation. The other options in this area are special cases for hierarchies of objects and objects with materials. You can ignore the other options, because they won't operate yet. Click the Ok button to start the effect, dismiss the dialog, and then pick the target mesh you want to reduce.

3. Modify the Effect.

   An icon appears in the scene, representing the effect. Select this cone icon and begin to modify the Effect commands with the Effect→Custom→Edit Parameters menu cell (see Figure 7.46).

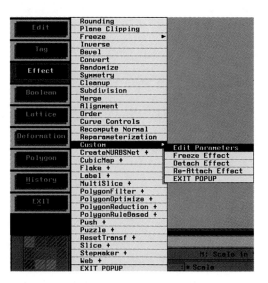

FIGURE 7.46 *The Effect→Custom→Edit Parameters menu cell.*

The dialog comes back. Move it on the screen so that you can see your original model in the Perspective view while you modify the effect, so that you can observe changes in the model (see Figure 7.47).

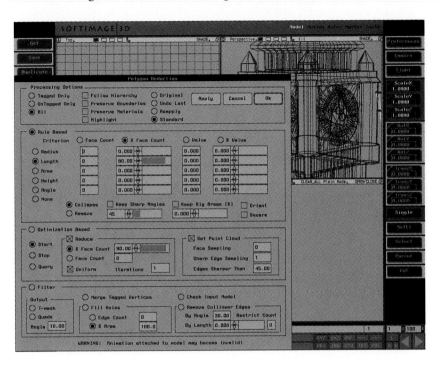

FIGURE 7.47 *The interface, with the Polygon Reduction tools up.*

4. Make the Rule.

Choose the method of Polygon Reduction and start in. The first tool to try is the Rule Based method, which allows you to reduce the polygons in an object either by a percentage or until a target number of polygons is reached, based on a number of different factors.

In general, the effect looks at each polygon in the model and ranks it according to the value of a factor. It then places all the polygons in a list sorted by that value, and begins to remove them one at a time from the smallest to the largest, stopping when it reaches the number you set:

● *Radius* examines each polygon to see how big a circle can be placed within each one. Those polygons with the smallest circles are removed first, on the theory that they are smaller and less important.

- *Length* ranks the polys by the length of the longest edge, again removing smaller polys first.

- *Area* calculates surface area, and again removes smaller polys first.

- *Height* examines each vertex and looks at its height above the plane formed by the neighboring vertices. The Remove button must be on for this option to work. When polygons are removed by height, small bumps in the surface detail go away first, leaving larger, flatter areas on the model.

- *Angle* examines the angle along edges between polygons, just like the Effect→Cleanup command. This is a simple, fairly foolproof method.

   Choose one of these methods and set the slider for % Face Count to the percentage of polygons you want removed. Start small, like 20%, and work slowly.

5. Reduce the Model.

   Click the Apply button to reduce the model. The effect runs and the model onscreen changes. The dialog remains up, allowing you to change the % Face Count, choose a different method, and run the effect again. Continue this method of stepwise enhancement until you are satisfied with the results. If you go too far and the model is hashed into a small crumpled ball, you can change the Processing Option from Standard to Undo Last, and click Apply again to undo the last command. You can then change back to Standard to try another setting.

When you are happy with the results, click Ok to dismiss the dialog. Remember you can always go back and do it some more.

The Optimization Based Method

The Optimization Based approach is a more complex method that actually spawns another background process to work on the model, allowing you to get back to work on other parts of the scene, while the poly mesh slowly cooks down. The Optimization method uses a point cloud representation to retain the form of the original mesh and can do a great job, with adequate practice.

The secret to it is to select the Start radio button, then click the Apply button to kick off the calculation, and spawn the new process. Then you use the Query radio button and Apply to check on the progress of the model. Use the Stop radio button with the Apply button to stop the process before your model cooks down into a crumpled ball.

THE FILTER METHOD

The Filter method cleans up models, closes holes left when bad polygons are collapsed, and removes redundant collinear edges. Just make selections as to the function you want applied to the model, and use the Apply button to perform the filter. Unlike the other portions of the Polygon Reduction toolset, the Filter method does not reduce the number of polygons in the active model.

CONVERTING PATCHES TO POLYGONS

When you have a model that has already been created as a patch surface, it is simple to convert it down into polygons.

First check the level of detail that will be created by checking the Info→Selection command's dialog box for the selected object. The dialog shows you how many polygons and triangles are required to tessellate the patch surface to the current level of detail (see Figure 7.48).

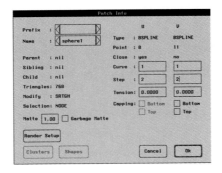

FIGURE 7.48 *Set the detail needed in the Patch Info dialog box.*

Reducing the step of the U or V parameterization reduces the polygons required. When you have set a reasonable degree of subdivision for the model, close the Info Selection dialog and choose the Effect→Convert command in the Model module (see Figure 7.49).

Effect→Convert first converts the patch into polygons. If you recall the command with the middle mouse button, it then converts the quad polygons into triangles. You can also use Effect→Convert to change patches into NURBS and NURBS into polygons and change the degree of curves.

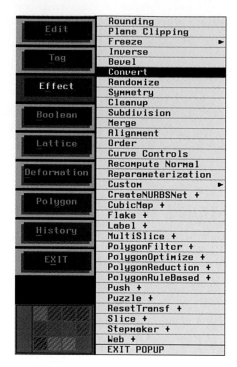

FIGURE 7.49   *The Effect→Convert menu cell.*

MAKING TERRAIN WITH POLYGON EFFECTS

There are two different ways to use polygonal geometry to form more complex terrain models for animation and games geometry. The first, Polygon→Fractalize, creates imaginary landscapes based on fractal algorithms. The second, Deformation→BumpMap, uses an image you paint to create a topography (see Figure 7.50).

THE FRACTALIZE METHOD

Polygon→Fractalize is a simple tool that creates sufficient results for many uses. It can take a long time to run and can generate a great many polygons if you are too liberal in your settings, because it includes some recursive functionality. The Fractalize command looks at each vertex in a triangulated grid and moves it according to a fractal calculation, either in positive Y or in the normal direction. The grid can be automatically subdivided by the command to generate finer detail, and the changes can be applied interactively to amplify the effects.

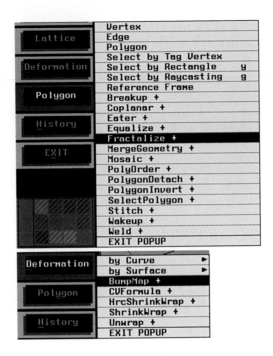

FIGURE 7.50 *The Fractalize and BumpMap menu cells.*

To design a landscape, start by creating a polygon grid and converting it to triangles with the Effect→Convert command (see Figure 7.51). You can use Proportional modeling at this point to add some major features to the land if you wish.

Execute the Polygon→Fractalize command. The Fractalize dialog (see Figure 7.52) appears, where you may set a number of parameters, then after you dismiss the dialog, pick the grid to complete the command.

- *Positive Offset* makes sure that the vertices are always moved in a positive direction, never negative. Best results occur with this option on.

- *Normal Offset* uses the normals of the grid to determine the direction that the vertices are pushed. If you start with a completely flat grid, leave this off. If you bump up your surface a bit and want your work considered by the fractal algorithm, check this on.

- *Additive* forces the changes to accumulate as you run more iterations. This generates bigger changes in your terrain—peaks and valleys instead of random noise on the floor of a jungle.

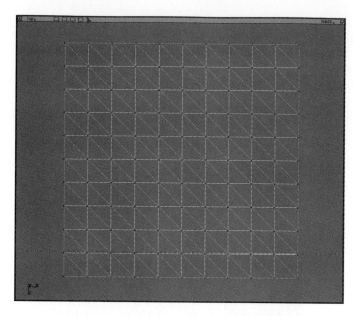

FIGURE 7.51 *The starting mesh, triangulated.*

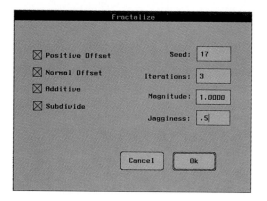

FIGURE 7.52 *The Fractalize dialog box.*

● *Subdivide* divides each triangle into *four* triangles every iteration when it is checked on. This creates smoother geometry, but beware of setting iterations too high for your machine memory and processor. When the setting is too high, the command takes an extremely long time. Imagine that if you start with a 10 by 10 grid, convert it to 200 triangles, and then run five iterations, you create 200×4^5 triangles, or 204,800 triangles. Seven iterations give you just over three million triangles, which brings your machine to a halt.

- *Seed* is a Randomization value that makes sure the fractalization algorithm comes up with different results given different seed values. Experiment to see what happens at different seeds.

- *Iterations* sets the number of times to subdivide the model and repeat the offset process. As mentioned earlier, keep it under 6 unless you have a long lunch break coming up.

- *Magnitude* is a value, expressed in Softimage units, that sets the range for each possible offset. Increasing it gives you more treacherous terrain, while low numbers give you grasslands.

- *Jagginess* determines the scale of the fractal and can be used to set the sharpness of the average angles between polygons. Low numbers (under 0.4) give you gradual rolling changes, and higher numbers give you cliffy craggs, eagles nests, and so on.

Set the parameters to your liking, and complete the command by picking the mesh to be fractalized. Softimage then creates a new object in the Schematic, showing you the results of your choices.

THE BUMPMAP METHOD

The second method, Deformation→BumpMap in the Model module, uses a more sophisticated and challenging technique to determine the height of each polygon in a mesh.

To start, you paint a 2D imagemap, using the Softimage Paint program, Adobe Photoshop, or a similar image tool. The file should be a color image, where darker tones represent lower areas of geometry and lighter tones represent higher areas (see Figure 7.53). By painting a pattern of changing color values, you can precisely control the topography that is constructed.

> **TIP**
>
> Being able to stop Softimage is often useful if a calculation seems to be running away from you, or if the software has become non-responsive and you suspect that it has crashed. In IRIX, if you start from a command shell with the Soft command, you can close the shell to terminate the programs that started from it.
>
> If you did not start from a command shell, open a new shell window and examine the running processes with the PS -E command. Look for the soft process, and note the process ID number printed with it. Then give the command "Kill 1234," where 1234 is the process number you noted. The command "Killall Soft" will do it as well.

FIGURE 7.53 *A good starting image, with different hues indicating changes in topography.*

The BumpMap tool can use changes in hue between the red, green, and blue channels to change the topography generated, as well as changes in the alpha channel. So feel free to paint different things in the R, G, B, and A channels to make a more complex landscape.

TIP

The more detail the starting mesh has, the better looking the results will be. Particularly nice landscapes can be made by creating a Cubic NURBS grid with 15 cells in U and V, and moving groups of points manually to set the major features of the landscape before applying the BumpMap effect to fill in minor detail (see Figure 7.54).

Convert the image to a Softimage PIC file if you use a separate tool, or just save it if you use the Paint program within Softimage 3D.

Next create a starting mesh object. The target mesh object should have enough detail to deform cleanly into the terrain shape, and can be either a polygon MES or a patch, including NURBS.

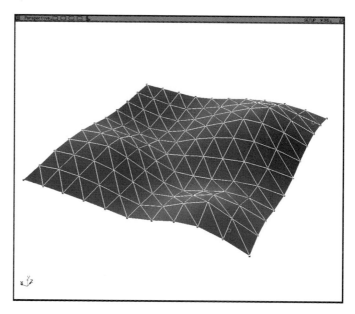

FIGURE 7.54 *A good starting mesh, with points raised to create major landmarks.*

Invoke the Deformation→BumpMap command and set the parameters as you wish in the dialog box (see Figure 7.55).

Start by directing the tool to the picture file you want to use with the Browser button. Then pick the projection plane for the image to be mapped onto the surface. If the mesh is in the default XZ plane, visible from the top in the Top view window, use the ZX projection. The UV projection doesn't seem to work, so avoid it.

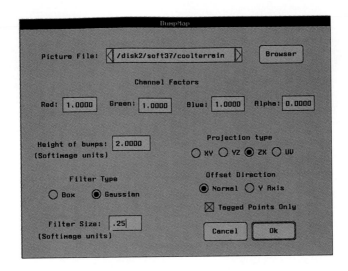

FIGURE 7.55 *The BumpMap dialog box.*

The Height of bumps control sets the overall amount of deformation applied by the effect in Softimage units. The contribution to that amount for each channel of the image (Red, Green, Blue, and Alpha) can be adjusted by setting Channel Factors from 0.0 to 1.0, where 0.0 is no influence at all and 1.0 is all the influence possible for that channel. (Setting the numbers higher than 1 has no effect.)

The Filter Type determines which filter is applied to smooth the map between vertices that fall between pixels, and Gaussian should yield more accurate results.

You can choose to deform all the vertices on the mesh or only the tagged ones, and the vertices can be moved in a positive Y direction, or along the average of the neighboring normals. While moving along the normals yields more accurate and interesting results if you deform the surface manually before applying the effect, you will need less main bump height.

Click the Ok button to close the BumpMap dialog, and then pick the mesh to complete the effect.

The BumpMap tool is a very professional method for painting and then modeling complex surface terrain for later use in 3D worlds, and it was used to create the amazing island landscapes in Cyan's incredible game Riven (see Figures 7.56 through 7.59).

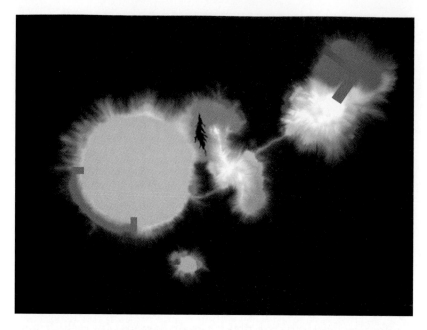

FIGURE 7.56 *A grayscale displacement map painted to create an island for the Cyan CD-ROM game Riven. Printed courtesy of Cyan, Inc. Copyright 1997.*

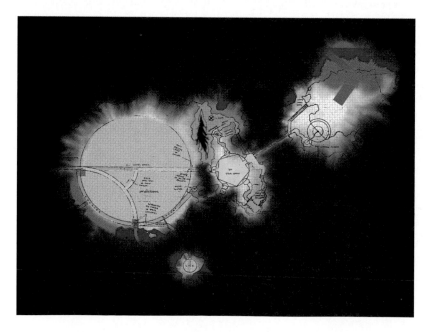

FIGURE 7.57 *The island displacement map with the map of the island superimposed on it showing features. Printed courtesy of Cyan, Inc. Copyright 1997.*

FIGURE 7.58 *The island displaced with a custom version of the BumpMap command, rendered without textures in the mental ray. Printed courtesy of Cyan, Inc. Copyright 1997.*

FIGURE 7.59 *The finished, textured island. Printed courtesy of Cyan, Inc. Copyright 1997.*

CONCLUSION

Experiment with all these tools on your own before you use them in production. It will save you time and help you produce more impressive work for your clients.

In this chapter, you learned how to

- Create and edit polygons, point-by-point and edge-by-edge
- Model from poly primitives
- Copy, duplicate, and transform polygons
- Extrude polygons
- Make polygonal terrain models
- Round and bevel poly objects
- Perform Polygon reduction

"Mayor Willie Brown" © Lunarfish 1997

© *LUNARFISH. Image courtesy of Lunarfish.*

CHAPTER 8

NURBS MODELING

One of the distinctions between a sophisticated modeling tool, such as Softimage 3D, and other lower cost tools has always been the inclusion of NURBS modeling tools in the product. NURBS are very complex mathematically, so adding in NURBS modeling functionality is a complex, time-consuming, difficult, and expensive area of software development. NURBS, however, offer tremendous advantages in the construction of complex and accurate models (see Figure 8.1).

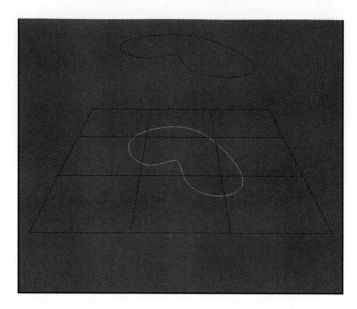

FIGURE 8.1   *A four-sided, trimmed NURBS patch with a projected hole.*

Even when texturing a model, NURBS offer more control than other modeling methods. On normal patch surfaces with a UV-mapped texture, the texture conforms to the contour of the surface, like a decal on a model airplane wing. However, the decal is mapped on equally between each span of parameters, ignoring how close or far each parameter is. This can cause texture pinching and stretching in models with uneven parameterization.

On a NURBS surface, you can control the parameterization of the surface, choosing from Non-Uniform, Uniform, Chord length, and Centripetal methods of measuring the area covered on the model between spans of the U and V parameters. This gives you control over how your textures are UV mapped onto complex NURBS surfaces, such as people and dinosaurs.

As usual, the additional benefits come at a cost. The NURBS tools are more complex than the other patch options, and models made of patches are more difficult for the software to display as you work, making for slower interactive refresh. Also, when modeling with NURBS, it's easy to make really heavy models. In many cases, however, the benefits outweigh the costs, making NURBS a valuable part of the modeler's toolbox.

In this chapter, you will learn

- Why NURBS are better than patches
- Adding rows to NURBS Patches
- Projecting curves onto a NURBS surface
- Merging NURBS surfaces
- Blending NURBS surfaces
- Using Relational modeling with NURBS

PATCHES VERSUS NURBS

The first step towards using NURBS is to understand how they are made and how they differ from normal patches.

Normal (rational) patches based on Linear, Cardinal, Bezier, or B-spline curves (Quadric curves) are composed of sets of 4×4 Control points organized into U and V parameters, running perpendicularly to each other (see Figure 8.2). The position of these parameters is determined by the location of the Control points in the original curves used to generate the surface.

FIGURE 8.2   *A single four-sided patch, showing U and V parameters.*

More complex surfaces (surfaces with more than four Control points in either U or V) are made by stitching together more than one 4×4 quadric patch (see Figure 8.3). Once made, these patches can only be modified on exactly the pre-existing U and V parameters. Another way to say this is that on a non-NURBS curve, the curve can be cut or modified only at a current Control point. This means that you can't trim a curve arbitrarily; you can cut it to the nearest point only, but that's not very accurate. This is because the math used to define the surface only knows what the surface is like at the intersections of the parameters.

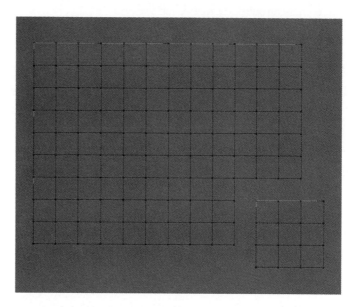

FIGURE 8.3 *Many single four-sided patches, quilted together to form a more complex surface.*

Another problem is that patches can only be joined together into a single patch if they have the same number of Control points in the parameter being joined. The Merge function simply connects the dots between the surfaces, and that doesn't work if there are differing numbers of dots (see Figure 8.4). NURBS do away with all these limitations.

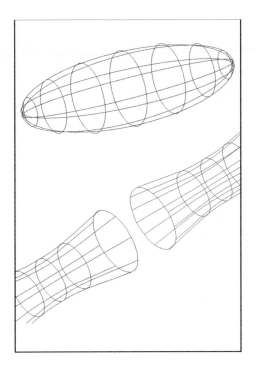

FIGURE 8.4 *This patch can be cut only at a parameter and can't be joined to another patch with a different number of Control points.*

NURBS IN THEORY

A NURBS curve is defined in such a way that the software can find a point at any position along the curve, even if the location desired is between Control points. This means that NURBS can be blended, cut, trimmed and merged at any point on the surface, not just at the intersection of control parameters. Unlike patches, which are based on cubic polynomials only, NURBS can be defined by a B-spline equation with any number of exponents. The number of exponents used is called the *degree* of the NURBS.

NURBS DEGREE

Softimage directly allows you to create linear NURBS (often marked C0 or zero-order continuity), Quadratic NURBS (C1 or first-order continuity) and Cubic NURBS (C2 or second-order continuity) (see Figure 8.5).

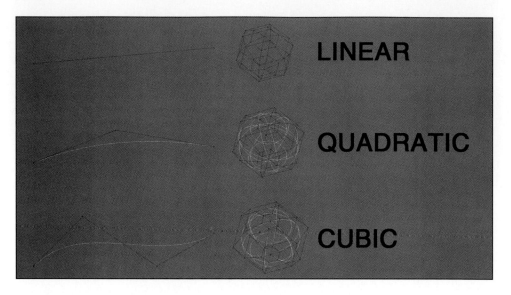

FIGURE 8.5 *C0, C1, and C2 NURBS curves and surfaces.*

In Softimage, more complex NURBS curves and surfaces are made by joining together a number of NURBS curves. On a Linear NURBS curve or surface, the last Control point of one NURBS is collocated with the first Control point of the next one, ensuring that the line stays connected (see Figure 8.6).

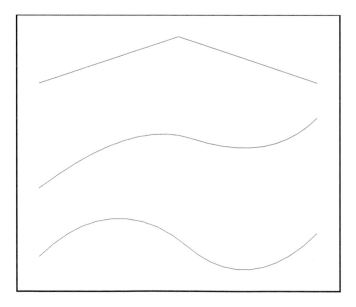

FIGURE 8.6 *Overlapping segments showing C0, C1, and C2 continuity.*

The last two points overlap on a Quadratic NURBS, ensuring positional and directional continuity between the two segments. On a Cubic NURBS curve or surface, the last three Control points overlap with the next segment, guaranteeing positional, directional, and curvature continuity between the segments. The point at which the two NURBS segments meet is called the *knot*.

Linear NURBS give you a faceted, polygonal appearance; Quadratic NURBS are smoother, much like patches; and Cubic NURBS are smoother yet (see Figure 8.7). You can import NURBS curves of even higher orders, up to C21, but not all Softimage NURBS functions will work properly with them.

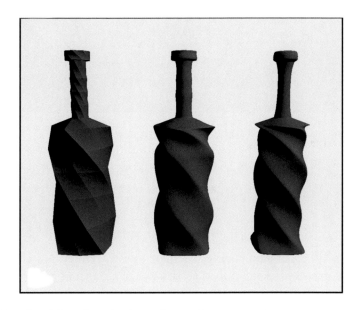

FIGURE 8.7   *Olive Oil Bottle in C0, C1, and C2 surfaces, respectively.*

NURBS PARAMETERIZATION

You can also control the *parameterization* of your NURBS surfaces. The parameterization is simply the organization of the surface into a *parameter space*. The parameter space describes the location of the surface at all points on that surface, as a pair of values for U and V (see Figure 8.8). The parameterization starts at one corner of the surface with U=0 and V=0 and stretches along the surface to the opposite corner, where U=1 and V=1.

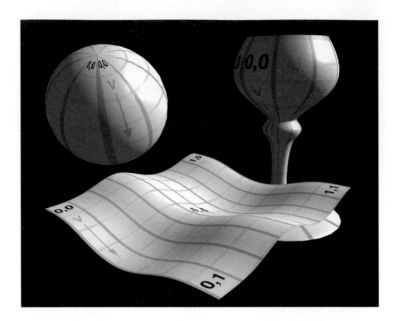

FIGURE 8.8 *Parameter space for a simple patch and a more complex one.*

That's simple, but the distribution of the parameter space doesn't have to be even all over the surface. In the Effect→Reparameterization menu cell, you can set the parameterization to:

- *Uniform:* Each U and V parameter gets an equal share of the parameter space.

- *Non-Uniform:* Each parameter gets a share of the parameter space based on the length of the curve segment for that parameter, calculated when you first draw the curve.

- *Chord Length:* Parameter space based on segment length, but dynamically calculated again for the segment if you edit it.

- *Centripetal:* Parameter space based on segment length, but completely recalculates the parameter space for the entire curve or surface whenever changes are made, ensuring even parameterization.

The greatest importance for parametization in Softimage 3D is in control of Texture mapping (see Figure 8.9). Uniform parameterization results in uneven UV texture mapping of NURBS surfaces. Centripetal provides the most accurate UV mapping, even if the shape of the surface changes due to animation.

FIGURE 8.9 *Different parameterizations change how textures map onto the surface.*

NURBS IN PRACTICE

This curve math lesson all boils down to three facts:

- You can cut a NURBS curve anywhere.
- You can cut a NURBS surface anywhere, even between parameters.
- You can connect NURBS curves or surfaces, even if they have different numbers of Control points, with a Blend or a Merge. This capability to merge NURBS surfaces means that you can construct one piece NURBS skins for animating with Inverse Kinematic (IK) chains, to avoid boundary and joint problems when animating (see Figure 8.10).

NURBS curves and surfaces can have points of different weights mixed in as well. This means that a NURBS can have both sharp and round segments in the curve and the surface (see Figure 8.11).

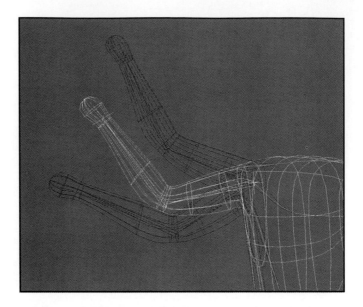

FIGURE 8.10   *A one-piece NURBS body with IK chains in it, showing seamless deformation.*

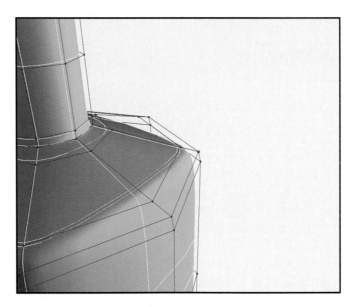

FIGURE 8.11   *Close-up of the bottle showing the effect of different weights on the surface.*

NURBS have one more fantastic advantage: NURBS curves of any shape can be projected onto another NURBS surface to form a complex boundary. These projected curves can be used for modeling, or the NURBS surface can be trimmed or expanded by them, much like attaching a hole to a face (see Figure 8.12).

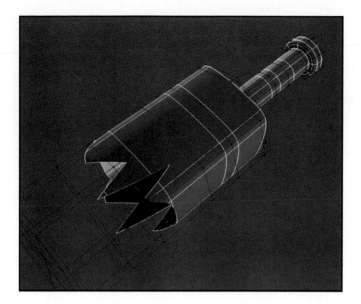

FIGURE 8.12 *The bottle surface trimmed out.*

ADDING DETAIL

The first and simplest trick in the NURBS grab bag is adding and removing detail on the surface. Imagine that you have constructed a human torso from a section of skins and you need to add some more detail to model in the musculature of the chest. The Edit→Add Point command gives you the power to interactively position a new parameter with Control points in either or both of the U and V parameters (see Figure 8.13).

Choose the Edit→Add Point command and pick the NURBS surface on, or near the area to which you want to add the detail. The NURBS Add Row/Column dialog box appears, which can be moved to a position onscreen, where you can easily see both it and your model, by dragging the title bar of the dialog box.

The dialog box has controls for picking the U or V parameter and a slider that smoothly rolls a thin, pink line over the contours of your surface. Position the line where you need to add detail, and press the Add button to add a new parameter and a row of points (see Figure 8.14). Add as many parameters as you need, then dismiss the dialog with the Exit button. You can now edit the location of the new points on the model with the M supra key, or by tagging the entire U or V parameter with the Tag→Points→Row in U or V command and transforming the tagged group.

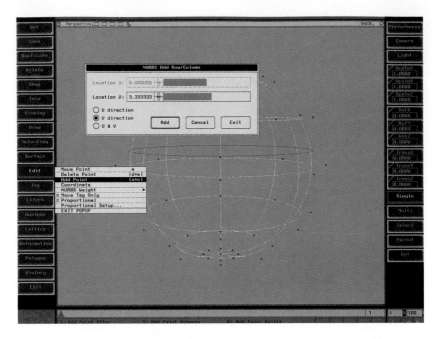

FIGURE 8.13   *The Edit→Add Point menu cell and the NURBS Add Row/Column dialog box.*

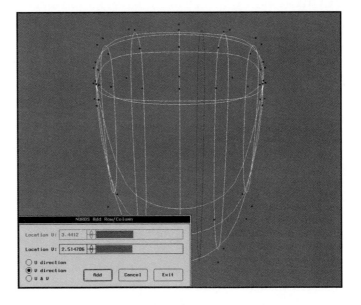

FIGURE 8.14   *Adding a parameter to a NURBS surface.*

Editing the entire parameter like this is particularly useful with organic models where the parameters are arranged around eyes, mouths, and so on.

WEIGHTING POINTS

One visual problem with patch surfaces is that, because they blend between all points equally, it is hard to create definition lines in the model. To add definition, you can weigh points on a NURBS surface singly or in a group. Use the Edit→ NURBS Weight→Point command to enter the NURBS Weight mode, and then click and drag any NURBS point to change its weight (see Figure 8.15).

To change the weight of many points simultaneously, tag a group of points (or use the Tag→Points→Row command) and then use the Edit→NURBS Weight→Tagged Points command.

If you want to directly enter the weight of a specific point, use the Edit→Coordinate command and then click a point to call up the Edit Coordinate dialog, where you can directly enter the location of the Control point, as well as the NURBS weight.

The Info→Points dialog box also gives you a command over the location and weight of points in a NURBS object.

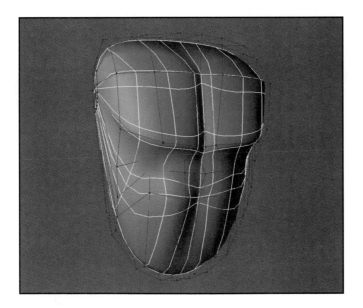

FIGURE 8.15   *Weighting the new parameter to define the musculature.*

In your hypothetical torso, we could use the Edit→NURBS Weight→Tagged Points command to weight the row of points at the base of the pectoral muscles, adding a sharper definition (see Figure 8.16).

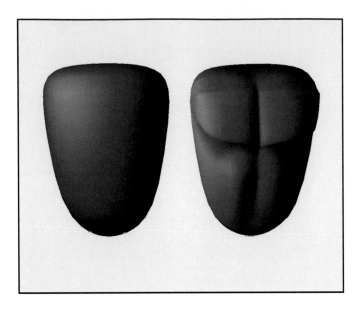

FIGURE 8.16 *The torso musculature before and after weighing.*

CUTTING NURBS CURVES AND SURFACES

Just like adding detail, you can cut a NURBS curve or surface at any location (see Figure 8.17). If you need to cut a curve to precisely fit your needs, use the Draw→Cut command and click the curve in question. The NURBS Curve Cut dialog appears, again with a slider that moves a small pink point along the contour of the spline. Position the point where you want the cut made, and click the Cut button.

If you want to cut a surface in either U or V, select the surface, choose the Draw→Cut tool, and click the surface near the approximate parameter on which you want the trim. Again the NURBS Surface Cut dialog box appears, allowing you to choose either or both of the U and V parameters to cut on. It also provides a slider to move the cut line to the exact location needed.

When you cut objects, the original is left whole and two more objects are created, one for each half. You will need to select and hide, or delete the unneeded parts. This insistence on retaining the construction curves during modeling seems at first to be a confusing hassle, but Softimage 3D likes to err on the side of safety. This way, if later on you become unsatisfied with what you have made, you can go back to the original curves and redo it.

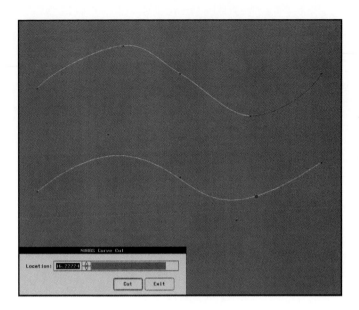

FIGURE 8.17 *Cardinal curves can be cut only at the knot. NURBS can be cut anywhere.*

Cutting should not be confused with trimming. Cutting slices the surface evenly along the U or V parameter direction, creating additional objects in the scene. Trimming can cut the surface along an arbitrary path that crosses back and forth across different U and V parameters, but it doesn't create additional objects in the scene.

REPARAMETERIZATION

The accuracy and parameterization of a NURBS surface can be changed as you work, enabling you to choose the level of detail that suits you during modeling, and then changed for animating or rendering (see Figure 8.18).

The Step setting determines how the space between major parameters is divided into smaller squares during tessellation, and then finally converted to triangles in the render. Often the Step on a NURBS surface is rather high, because the default parameterization for some construction curves is 10. This means that a simple shape, such as a wine glass, might end up with 6000 or more polygons when it gets shaded or rendered. The glass will be very smooth, but you may have trouble rendering. You can change the Step setting non-destructively at any time in the Info→Selection command's dialog box (see Figure 8.19). I tend to set it to the lowest possible setting of 1 while I work, which makes for very fast editing and refreshes, and then increase the Step when I render.

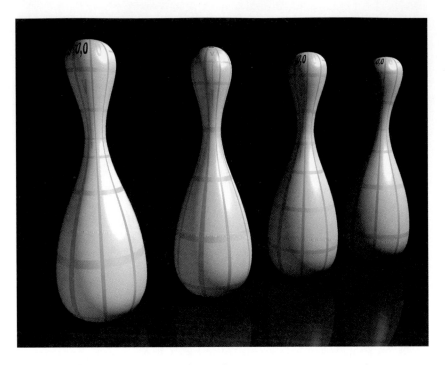

FIGURE 8.18 *Different parameterization changes the texture space.*

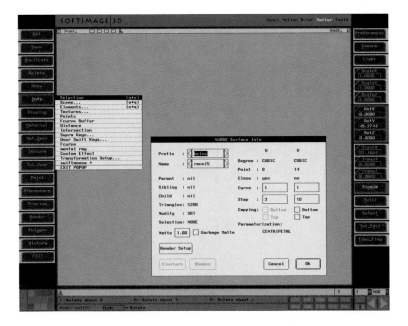

FIGURE 8.19 *Change the Step settings in the NURBS Surface Info dialog box.*

The NURBS surface parametization can be changed between Uniform, Non-Uniform, Chord Length, and Centripetal with the Effect→Reparameterization command in the Model module (see Figure 8.20). These settings determine how the surface is measured between parameters, and they can drastically change how textures map onto your models. The Uniform method is measured only once when the surface is created to determine the surface parameterization, so if your shape changes over time, the texture coordinate information may not stay as you want it.

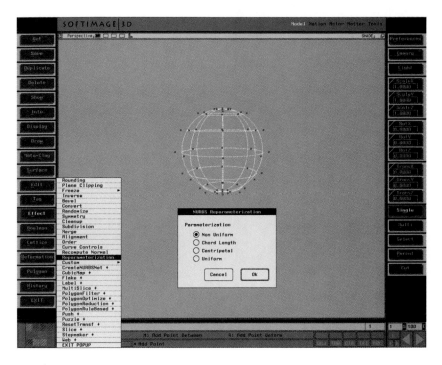

FIGURE 8.20 *The Reparameterization menu cell and dialog box.*

In the Uniform mode, the texture is bunched up where there are more Control points.

In practice, I find that the default method, Non-Uniform parameterization, and the Chord Length parameterization yield the best results when animating texture mapped NURBS surfaces.

PROJECTING AND EXTRACTING CURVES ONTO A NURBS SURFACE

Usually one single surface doesn't give you the complexity that you need. It's tough to find a modeling tool that makes a hand, for instance, out of a NURBS surface, because the hand has so many changes in topography. It's a complex part, and often the best strategy is to build a *complex surface* made of several different NURBS patches, each lining up exactly with the others to maintain the illusion that the object is one single mesh. The trick is fitting the pieces onto one another precisely—and that's what projecting and extracting curves is all about.

The theory is simple: A closed NURBS curve can be projected onto a NURBS surface, just like a slide projector shining an image onto a wall, so that it wraps around the surface and becomes measured in the parameter space of the target patch. It's an easy way to make complex curves that lie precisely on a NURBS surface (see Figure 8.21).

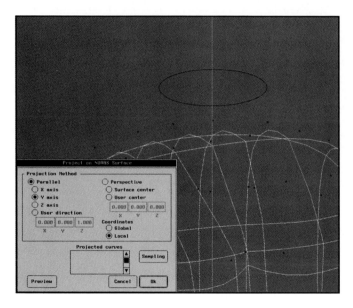

FIGURE 8.21   *The closed NURBS curve is projected onto the surface.*

Once projected onto a NURBS surface, the new curves can be *extracted* and used as construction elements for other modeling operations.

PROJECTING CURVES

For projecting, Softimage requires two elements: a NURBS surface and a closed NURBS curve (see Figure 8.22).

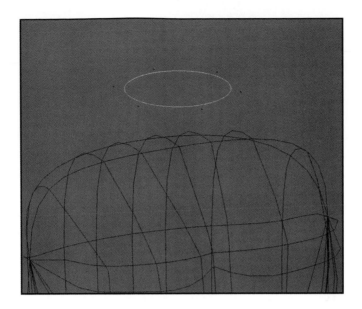

FIGURE 8.22 *A NURBS surface and a closed NURBS curve, ready to project.*

With the NURBS surface selected, choose the Draw→Project on NURBS Surface command from the Model module. Pick the curve to be projected, and the Project on NURBS Surface dialog appears (see Figure 8.23).

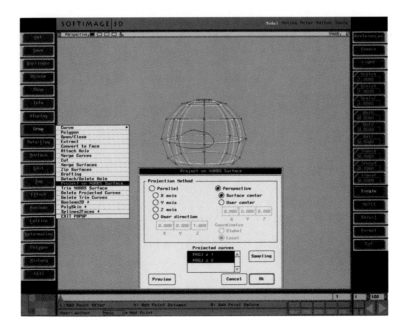

FIGURE 8.23 *The Draw→Project on NURBS Surface menu cell and dialog box.*

The first task is to select the Projection method. Usually the Parallel method, which projects perpendicular to a given axis, is what you want; pick the axis of projection, either X, Y, or Z.

You can also choose to project the curve into the center of the surface with the Perspective method that scales the projection curve down as it approaches the center.

After you make your choice, click the Preview button to see a quick representation in pink of the curve that will be created. If your surface is two-sided, the projected curve will land on both sides. You can select or deselect the preview curves in the Projected Curves list.

You can also control the sampling used for the new projection curves with the Sampling button. The default of 10 is too high for many uses, so I tend to set it to 5.

When the parameters for the projection are set, complete the command by clicking the Ok button. You will now be able to see the projection curve on the surface.

For NURBS surfaces with projected curves, Softimage lists the projected curves by name in the Info→Selection dialog. Projected curves can be removed from the surface after they are no longer wanted by choosing the Draw→Delete Projected Curves command and picking the curve you wish to delete.

EXTRACTING CURVES

When you extract a curve, any parameter curve on a surface can be copied right out of the surface, and added as a new object in the scene. All parametric surfaces can have curves extracted from them, but only NURBS can have curves extracted from the surface at any location in UV parameter space. Also, because you can project your own curves onto NURBS surfaces, you can extract them back out to get useful construction curves for additional modeling.

Choose the Draw→Extract command, and pick the surface from which you want to extract a curve. If the surface is a NURBS, the NURBS Extract Curve dialog pops up, allowing you to choose, via a slider with the familiar pink indicator, which curve to extract (see Figure 8.24). Select the projected curve in the Trim and Projected curves list; then click the Extract button to add the new curve to the scene.

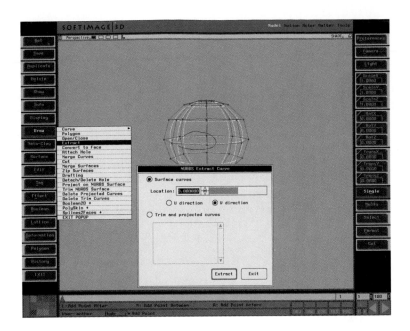

FIGURE 8.24 *The Draw→Extract menu cell and NURBS Extract Curve dialog box.*

Select the new curve and take a look at it in the Perspective window. It will have the outline of the projected curve and the shape of the surface! That means if you were to extrude a surface along the extracted curve, the resulting object would fit the surface perfectly (see Figure 8.25).

TRIMMING NURBS

Parts of a NURBS surface can be clipped away by another NURBS curve in a technique that works just like projecting a curve onto the NURBS surface. This technique is useful primarily for trimming off parts of a surface that overlap other parts of a model, the same way you would use a pair of scissors to trim excess paper.

Choose a plane to project the trim in, and then draw the trim curve in that View window. Make sure the curve is a NURBS, and that it is closed with the Draw→Open/Close command. Select the surface first, then the Draw→Trim NURBS Surface command, and finally pick the trim curve to bring up the Trim NURBS Surface dialog (see Figure 8.26).

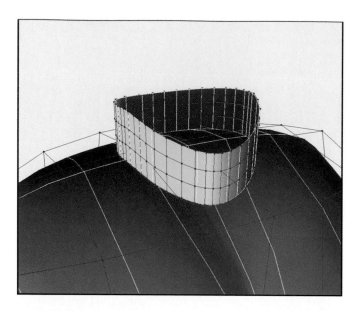

FIGURE 8.25 *One part fits the other perfectly.*

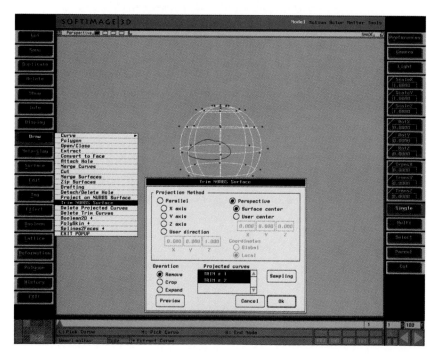

FIGURE 8.26 *The Draw→Trim NURBS Surface menu cell and dialog box.*

You can pick the Projection method and axis here, as well as set the Sampling and preview the trim curves, just like in the Project NURBS Curve dialog.

The Ok button completes the command and slices off whatever portions of the surface land inside the projection of the trim curve.

If you want to keep the portion of the surface inside the trim curve, choose the Crop option instead of the Remove option in the Trim NURBS Surface dialog.

You can add material back to the surface after a trim by drawing another closed NURBS curve that intersects the trimmed area of the surface, and executing the Draw→Trim NURBS Surface command with the Expand option in the Trim dialog (see Figure 8.27).

FIGURE 8.27 *The original surface, trimmed and then expanded.*

BLENDING NURBS WITH RELATIONAL MODELING

When animating a fully articulated character with Inverse Kinematics, the best possible geometry to work with is a single unbroken NURBS mesh. When using a single mesh, there will never be any hassles with joints between extremities, and there will never be unwanted gaps between parts of your model. The NURBS surface also has fewer Control points to modify and weigh until you get your character moving just the way you want it.

Sometimes when you need to animate a figure, it isn't possible to build the skin as a single NURBS mesh. In these cases, the next best method is to construct separate NURBS meshes for each body part, and connect them together with a blending segment that smoothly covers each gap between the body parts (see Figure 8.28). But how can you keep these blend segments perfectly aligned with the changing shape of the body as you animate it?

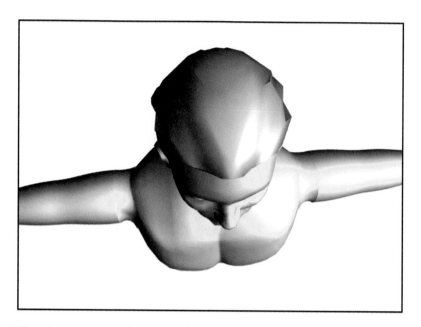

FIGURE 8.28 *A torso and arms showing blend segments.*

Fortunately, when you turn on relational modeling before you project and extract curves onto a NURBS surface, changes made to the original curve or the NURBS surface are automatically updated in the shape of the projected and extracted curves. This means that Relational modeling will keep projected curves accurately stuck to the NURBS surfaces they are a part of, even if the NURBS surface is being distorted by IK animation. When the blending skin is made, also with Relational modeling, the entire blend segment changes shape as IK chains deform the NURBS segments that make up the body parts.

TUTORIAL: BLENDING BODY PARTS

To see in a simple way this blending technique works, try the following tutorial.

1. Create the Geometry.

Open the scene named BlendBody from the CD-ROM, or construct two NURBS patches, one as the torso and one as the right arm (see Figure 8.29).

Ensure that Relational modeling is active in the Preferences menu by checking the Create Modeling Relation radio button.

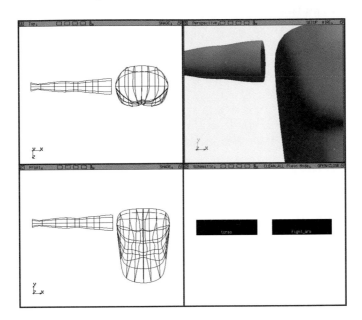

FIGURE 8.29   *Two NURBS patches, one as an arm and one as a torso.*

2. Extract the Curve.

Extract a curve from the end parameter of the arm to project onto the body: Choose the Draw→Extract command and pick the open end of the arm nearest the body. Exit the Extract dialog box.

Find the extracted curve in the Schematic view. Move it into the Schematic view so you know which object is the extracted curve.

Duplicate it and scale the duplicate 10% larger by setting the X, Y, and Z size to 1.1.

Duplicate the original extracted curve again, and scale the new duplicate up by 20% over the original size. You should now have three extracted circles of different sizes.

Arrange the extraction curves in the Schematic window from right to left in order of size, and name them SmallProjectionCurve, MedProjectionCurve, and LargeProjectionCurve, respectively.

3. **Project the Curve.**

Select the Body NURBS surface, choose the Draw→Project on NURBS Surface command, and then pick the first extracted curve (SmallProjectionCurve).

In the Project On NURBS Surface dialog box, choose to project on the side of the body closest to the arm by selecting the correct curve in the Projected Curves box.

Click Ok to complete the projection. A new Body NURBS object is created with the curve projected onto it. Hide the old body, and then repeat the procedure for the other two curves.

You will now have three curves of different sizes projected onto the body (see Figure 8.30). These three curves represent the extent of the blend from the arm to the body surface. You can change the blend later by making the curves larger or smaller, which moves them on the body surface.

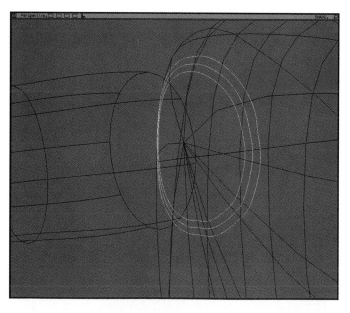

FIGURE 8.30 *The arm, torso, and projected curves.*

4. **Extract the Projected Curves.**

The goal here is to create profile curves for skinning the blend segment, so you need to extract the projected curves off the surface so they become separate curves in the Schematic view that you can skin from.

Use the Draw→Extract command to pull all three projected curves from the body surface, arrange them under the Projected curves in the Schematic window, and name them SmallExtract, MedExtract, and LargeExtract (see Figure 8.31). Now these curves are all controlled by both the shape of the projected curve and the shape of the NURBS body surface.

FIGURE 8.31 *The Schematic view of the extracted curves.*

5. **Skin the Blend.**

The next step is to create the new blend segment between the open end of the arm and the three curves that were first projected and then extracted from the body surface. Select the first, smallest projection curve (SmallProjectionCurve). Start the Skin command with Surface→Skin, and pick the three extracted curves in order from small to large.

When all four curves are active, click the right mouse button to call up the Skinning dialog (see Figure 8.32). Make the skin a Cubic NURBS patch with Non-Uniform parameterization.

FIGURE 8.32 *The Skinning dialog box.*

6. Fine-tune the Blend Segment.

The last step is the hardest. The blend segment connecting the two body parts needs to be adjusted to work well with your model. Arrange the Top view and Front view for an unobstructed view of your blends, and examine it.

If the blend seems to criss-cross in the middle, the first skin curve may need to be inverted. After inverting the curve, look at the parameters running down the length of the blend and see if they align with the direction of the blend. If they seem to be rotating as they go around the blend, the first skin curve may need to be rotated to align the parameters for a smooth blend. When you have adjusted the curves to form a good blend, your model is ready for animation (see Figure 8.33).

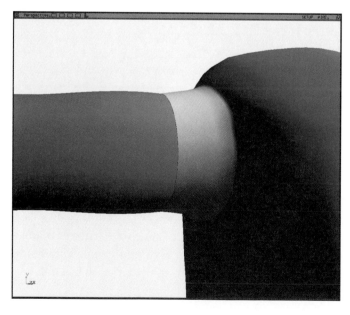

FIGURE 8.33 *Close-up of a good relational blend.*

The moral of the story is that blending NURBS with projected and extracted curves is difficult to do correctly. There is a new custom effect, called Blending, that takes away some of the pain. In versions of Softimage 3D previous to 3.7 sp1, it was an unsupported gift that you had to install yourself, but in the current version, it comes as part of the default installation. The Blending effect does exactly what we just went through in the blending tutorial, but it automates the process somewhat and consolidates the functions into one dialog box.

THE BLENDING CUSTOM EFFECT

The Blending custom effect isn't foolproof, but it eases the pain of blending NURBS surfaces somewhat. The theory is simple: You can blend two NURBS surfaces together by creating another blend object that stretches between the two surfaces. You can use an existing U or V parameters to attach the blend, or you can project a curve onto a NURBS to define the edge of a blend area.

TUTORIAL: BODY BLEND, TAKE TWO

To demonstrate how much easier the Blending custom effect is to use, let's try the arm-to-torso project again.

1. **Prepare the NURBS.**

   Create the original two NURBS surfaces that will be connected with the blend segment.

   Project a closed NURBS circle onto each one to define the areas where the blend will connect, or use the scene called BodyBlend2 from the courseware CD-ROM (see Figure 8.34). The Blending effect simply connects the projected curve from the Body surface to the open end of the arm surface.

2. **Run the Effect.**

   Choose the Blending effect from the Surface menu (see Figure 8.35). A new icon is added to the scene to indicate that a blend is present. You can edit the blend at any time after it is made by selecting that icon and choosing Effects→Custom→Edit parameters from the Motion module.

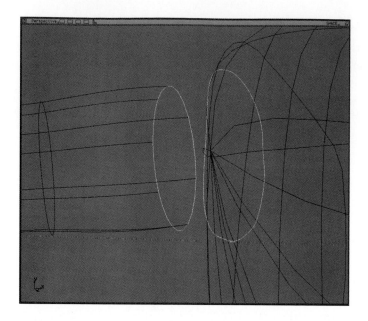

FIGURE 8.34 *The torso and arm, set up for blending.*

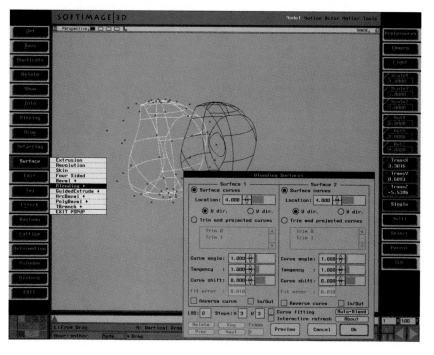

FIGURE 8.35 *The Surface→Blending menu cell and dialog box.*

The Status Bar now prompts you to pick the two surfaces to be blended together. Pick the left and then the right surface with your mouse. After the second surface is chosen, the Blending Surfaces dialog box appears.

Use the Surface Curves radio buttons and sliders to choose the right curve to blend on each surface. You will see the selected curves highlighted in pink in your View window to help you choose where you want the blend to connect on the surface.

Turn on the Curve Fitting option to simplify the blend geometry, and the Interactive Refresh option to get visual feedback from the dialog box to the display views.

3. **Fine-tune the Effect.**

   While looking at the blend segment in the Perspective and Top views, adjust the Blending options in the Blending Surfaces dialog to get a good blend (see Figure 8.36).

   First try clicking the Auto-Blend button in the lower-right corner of the dialog. Auto-Blend looks at your surfaces and makes a best guess about the proper settings. Usually it does a good enough job that you don't have to monkey with the controls manually. The Interactive Refresh option helps you see the results of your efforts without leaving the dialog box.

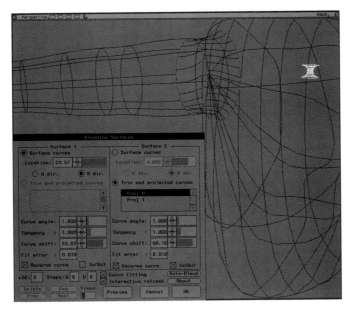

FIGURE 8.36   *Fine-tuning the Blend effect.*

If the blend seems twisted around, use the Curve Shift slider on either surface to help align the blend smoothly.

Adjust the Tangency sliders until the edges of the blend segment extend as a smooth addition to each of the surfaces, neither puffing out nor bending at too much of an angle. Technically you want the blend segment to be exactly tangent to each surface at the point where they connect.

The Curve Angle can be used to build the Blend parameters so that the blend is exactly the right size to fit into the gap.

If the blend seems completely twisted or deformed off the surfaces, try the Reverse Curve boxes to see if swapping the U and V parameters helps any.

The Reverse Curves boxes can also be used to invert the surface (Effect→Inverse won't work) if the surface in the Shaded view seems inverted.

4. **Complete the Effect.**

When the interactive display in your View windows looks pretty good, complete the effect by clicking the Ok button. Check your blend in the Shaded Perspective view. Note that when you move either surface the blend connects, Softimage automatically adjusts the blend to keep the surfaces together.

The blend segment keeps a smooth joint between your surfaces, even when you animate them with Inverse Kinematics.

The Blending custom effect is a lot easier to use than the manual Relational modeling with the Projected and Extracted Curves method, but it still isn't perfect (or easy). The best solution is a method, such as the Merge tool, that allows you to stitch different NURBS surfaces together into one single NURBS patch.

MERGING NURBS

The best way to construct a single mesh for a character' skin is to connect the different body parts into a single coherent mesh, with a single set of U and V parameters and a single parameter space for textures. This is the Holy Grail of NURBS modeling, because such a skin is extremely easy to weight and animate, and behaves very smoothly with a limited amount of geometry and few Control points. (See Figure 8.37.)

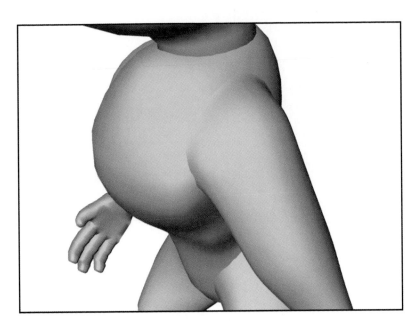

FIGURE 8.37 *Look Ma, no seams!*

Softimage 3D Extreme can meld several individual patches into a single patch surface, with the Draw→Merge Surfaces command (see Figure 8.38). The rules for merging two non-NURBS patches together are that they must be the same type of patch (Linear, Bezier, B-spline or Cardinal) and they must have the same number of Control points in the open parameter (the open edge) that will be merged. The Merge Surfaces command simply connects the Control points on one edge of the surface to the Control points on the selected edge of the other surface. The Merge Surfaces command connects either U parameter edges to other U parameter edges, or V parameter edges to other V parameter edges. You can think of it as making a single big quilt by stitching together many small squares.

Softimage 3D can merge NURBS patches with more flexibility as well. Although the NURBS must be of the same degree, they can have different numbers of Control points on the edge to be merged. That's important, because it's hard to make a torso with the same number of points as an arm. The alignment of the parameters on the two patches is extremely important for creating a good merge.

Once the two patches are correctly lined up and the edges match parameters, choose the Draw→Merge Surfaces command, then pick the edge of the first patch, and the connecting edge of the second patch. The NURBS Merge/Blend dialog box pops up, giving you some choices on how to merge the surfaces together (see Figure 8.39).

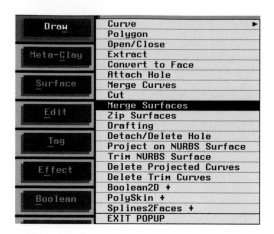

FIGURE 8.38   *The Draw→Merge Surfaces menu cell.*

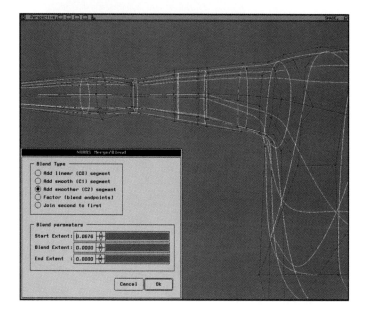

FIGURE 8.39   *The NURBS Merge/Blend dialog box and a merge in progress.*

The surfaces can be joined with a linear (C0) segment that shows as a seam, a fairly smooth (C1) segment, or a very smooth (C2) segment; the endpoints of the surfaces can be moved towards each other, or the second patch can be translated to the edge of the first patch and directly connected point by point. If you choose the smooth, smoother, or factor methods, you can adjust the set of sliders to modify how the blend between the two surfaces is created, thereby editing it interactively to meet your needs.

EDGE FLAGS

Because the U and V parameters of a surface need to be precisely aligned for the Merge Surfaces command to work properly, we must find out which direction the U and V parameters run on a surface. The Edge Flags provide us with that information. After you enable the Show→Edge flags option in the Model module, the starting U parameter is shown in red on the selected patch, and the starting V parameter is shown in green (see Figure 8.40).

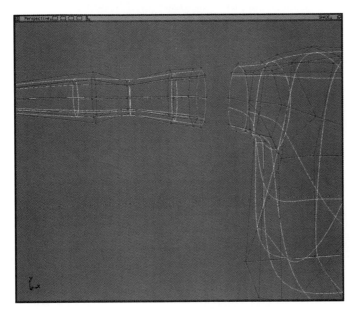

FIGURE 8.40 *The Edge flags show the U and V parameters and order of the surface.*

The point at which the red and green parameters intersect is the origin (0,0) or the parameter space for that patch. The diametrically opposite corner is the far extent of the parameter space for the patch, at 1,1 in U and V. On each starting U parameter, small green lines run perpendicular to the main edge flag, showing which direction the surface parameterization goes. On the first V parameter, small green lines run perpendicular to the main green edge flag to show the direction of increasing V parameterization.

These flags are important! For a merge to look good, the patches must be aligned correctly in both the U and V directions, according to two rules:

● *The patches should be arranged so that the beginning parameter of one patch connects to the ending parameter of the other.* For example, if you are merging the U parameters, the beginning U parameter of one patch should connect to the ending U parameter of the other. Likewise, the beginning V parameter of one patch should connect to the ending V parameter of the other, if you are merging the V parameters (see Figure 8.41). Think about it like Lego blocks: The top of one plugs into the bottom of another. This method keeps the patch, like the Legos, oriented in a consistent direction. Unlike Legos, patches can be connected along either of two axes, not just top to bottom.

FIGURE 8.41 *The end of one parameter plugs into the start of the other object.*

● *The parameters that aren't being connected should line up.* Specifically, the start of the U or V parameter on the first patch lines up with the start of the U or V parameter on the second patch, and the edge flags showing the direction of parameterization should be facing in the same direction. Otherwise, the object twists as the two surfaces come together.

CURVE CONTROLS

So what if you build your body parts, and the open parameters don't happen to be aligned properly to merge the surfaces? There must be a way to change the UV orientation of each edge, and even to swap the U parameters for V parameters should the need arise. Indeed, the Effect→Curve Controls command brings up a dialog that does all this and more for the currently selected patch (see Figure 8.42).

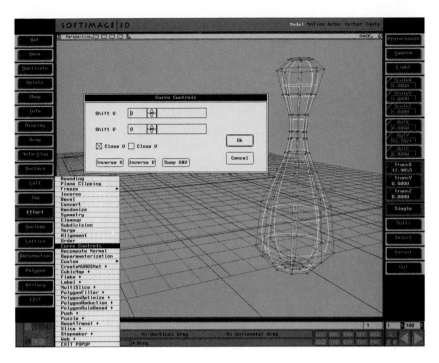

FIGURE 8.42   *The Effect→Curve Controls menu cell and dialog box.*

In the Curve Controls dialog box, clicking the Inverse U button reverses the direction of the U parameter, so that the parameter space starts at the opposite side of the patch. The Inverse V button swaps the orientation of the V parameter in the same manner. This is useful (following the earlier analogy) if you find yourself with Legos that you want to connect but they face each other top-to-top. The Inverse U bottom would invert one Lego, making the top become the bottom so they could be plugged together.

What if the open edge of one surface is the U parameter and the edge of the second surface that you need to connect is the V parameter? The Swap U&V button reparameterizes the selected surface so that the edge that was the starting U edge is now the starting V edge, and vice versa. This doesn't change the shape of the surface at all; it just rearranges the order of the points that make up the surface (see Figure 8.43).

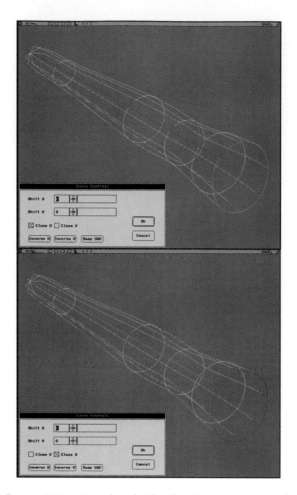

FIGURE 8.43 *A patch with Edge Flags showing inverted and swapped UV parameters.*

CAUTION

All the Curve Control commands change the parameter space, so any textures you have mapped on with UV mapping will now be oriented in a different way than you intended.

If your surface is open (in other words, an incomplete revolution), or is a patch where the starting U or V parameter doesn't exactly meet the ending U or V parameter, the Close U and Close V check boxes can close the edge by stitching the starting and ending parameters together. This is often useful for capping or closing shapes. The first and last rows of Control points can be moved, however, so it's a good idea to model in extra Control points if you intend to close the surface with this technique.

Finally, the starting U and V parameters can be shifted earlier or later on the patch with the Shift U and Shift V sliders. If the patch is closed in the parameter that you shift, the shape of the patch does not change. This allows you to shift the starting edge flag for a parameter to match the position of the same edge flag on the patch you want to merge, so that the section created between the two original patches doesn't twist from one to the other.

TUTORIAL: MERGING NURBS

The best way to learn how to do something is often to dive in and try it out for yourself. Let this tutorial guide you through the process of merging a body and pair of arms together. The general game plan is to evaluate the parameter alignment of the surfaces to make sure they line up correctly, and then merge the surfaces with the Draw→Merge Surfaces command.

You can call up the MergeNurbs scene from the courseware CD-ROM, or create your own torso by pulling and pushing rows of tagged points on a NURBS sphere, and an arm by skinning cross sections. Both should be Cubic NURBS patches (see Figure 8.44).

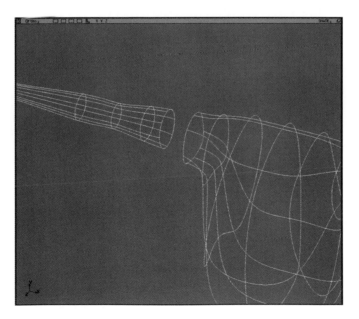

FIGURE 8.44   *The arm and torso ready to merge, with open parameters facing each other.*

1. **Set up the Views.**

   Arrange your View windows so that you have a clear Top view and Perspective view of the arm and the torso. Make sure that the Show→Edge Flags option is turned on, and use Multi mode to select both surfaces.

2. **Examine the Edge Flag Orientation.**

We'll be connecting the green (V) parameter of the two surfaces, so make sure that the start of the V parameter (the green line) on the first surface lies next to the end of the V parameter (no green line) on the second surface in the Top view. That way, the start of one plugs into the end of the other. If that isn't the case, use the Effect→Curve Controls dialog and the Inverse V button to swap one of the surfaces.

Next, look at the start of the U parameter (the red line) on each flag and make sure they line up in both the Top view and the Perspective view. If they don't, use the Curve Controls dialog to shift the U starting parameter on one surface to match the other. Also check the direction of the red edge flags to make sure that the surfaces are parameterized in the same direction. If they are not, use the Curve Controls Inverse U button to flip the direction of parameterization so the two surfaces match (see Figure 8.45).

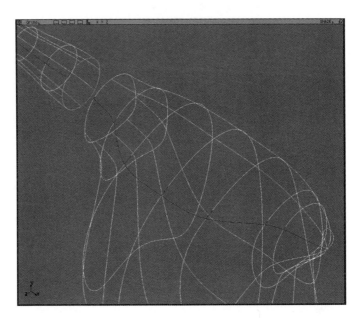

FIGURE 8.45   *The arm and torso ready to merge, showing proper edge flags indicating good UV orientation for a merge.*

3. **Merge the Parts.**

Physically align the two surfaces so that the openings are close to one another. Then invoke the Draw→Merge Surfaces command. The Status Bar instructs you to click first on the open edge of the first surface, and then on the open edge of the second surface. Once you do so, the NURBS Merge/Blend dialog pops up. Try the Factor (blend endpoints) method and adjust the Blend parameters while looking at the Perspective view to see the results of the changes you make. When the blend looks smooth, complete the command with the Ok button (see Figure 8.46).

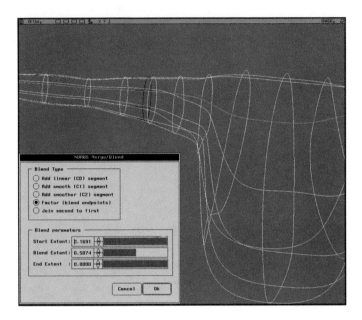

FIGURE 8.46 *Close-up of the merge, showing the blend extent and the NURBS Merge/Blend dialog.*

A new object is created, comprised of both individual surfaces and a new connecting blend, all in one consistently parameterized patch!

Hide the old parts and examine the surface in the shaded mode or preview a render.

Creating a proper merged NURBS surface is certainly easier than managing a relational blend, but conceptual care must be taken when making the surfaces that are used in the merge to build open U and V parameters where the merge takes place. If you can conceptualize a complex part being made of several smaller UV patches linked together, and model accordingly, you can create great models.

CONCLUSION

Working with NURBS can be complicated, but NURBS surfaces are worth the extra effort, particularly if you are working on film resolution projects or have complex characters that need to look photo-realistic. The ability to match the parameter space of the surface with a texture space to accurately wrap textures onto the surface is a huge benefit, and the NURBS project and extract features help you model more complicated and precise shapes. Finally, the ability to merge two or more surfaces together, even when they have different numbers of control points in each parameter, is what makes single skinned character modeling possible.

In this chapter you:

- Learned what makes a NURBS curve or surface different from other curves and patches.
- Learned what tools work better on NURBS.
- Saw how surface parameterization changes how texture mapping looks.
- Experimented with connecting NURBS surfaces with a blend segment.
- Worked to align the U and V parameters correctly for a NURBS merge.

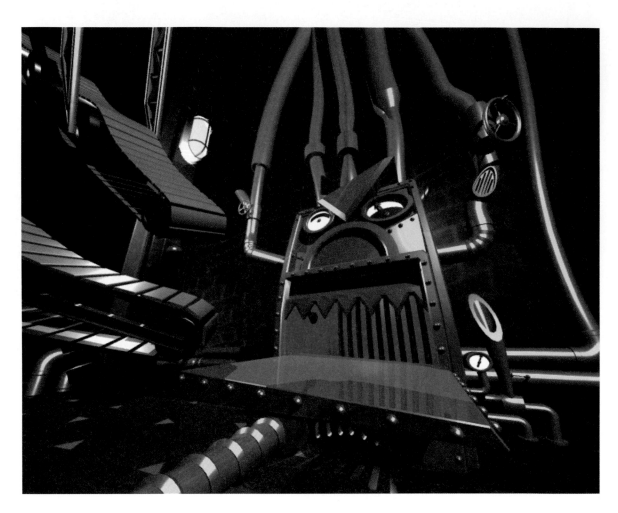

CHAPTER 9

BOOLEAN MODELING

So far the modeling tools in the SURFACE menu cell create only single objects. Many more complex models, however, require compound shapes, made by the interactions between two or more simple shapes. Sometimes you'll want to add two simple shapes together to form one object, or you will want to subtract the shape of one object from another. Sometimes you'll just want an object cut in half, so you can manipulate the parts independently. Or you may need to animate a cutaway view of an object, revealing the interior over time.

Boolean modeling is the way to easily accomplish many of these tasks (see Figure 9.1). In this chapter, you will

- Learn Boolean terminology
- Create unions, differences, and intersections
- Animate using the Boolean tools
- Clip and cut models in half
- Cut cross sections through models

FIGURE 9.1   *Different models made of Boolean shapes.*

In addition, you'll experiment with a few commands that cut objects along a given plane, like taking a bread knife or a cheese slicer to your models.

BOOLEAN BASICS

Boolean modeling takes its name from George Boole, the English mathematician of the early nineteenth century who articulated a deductive logical system for describing sets and their interactions in an algebraic manner. Boolean logic is simply a system of addition and subtraction of items in a given set. For our purposes, those items are the vertices on an object.

Each object is a set of vertices, and where the two sets intersect in 3D space, a new object can be created by either adding or subtracting those vertices in the intersection volume to create a new object (see Figure 9.2).

For example, you could use a cylinder object to poke a hole in a cubic object with a Boolean difference, or you could make a ball with flat spots by creating a new Boolean intersection between a sphere and a cube.

In Softimage 3D|Extreme, Boolean modeling works only on polygonal mesh objects. If you use a Boolean operation on a pair of patches, they are tessellated down to polygons for the operation, and the resulting object is a polygon. Similar effects to those possible with Boolean modeling can be achieved for NURBS surfaces with the NURBS trimming tools.

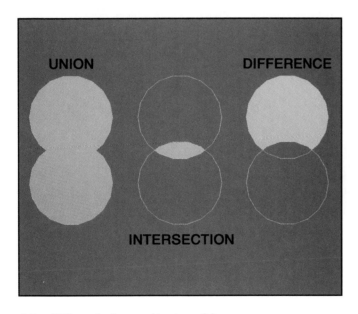

FIGURE 9.2 *Different Boolean combinations of the same set.*

> **NOTE**
>
> Software packages exist that allow new shapes to be constructed from the complex intersections of volumes defined by parametric surfaces (patches and NURBS). This technique is called *constructive solid geometry* and is a fascinating method of modeling. Constructive solid geometry programs (such as ProEngineer and Catia) are more often used in CAD/CAM and engineering work.

Boolean modeling has its own special terminology, which is the most daunting part of using the technique. Two starting objects are always required for a Boolean operation. The first object is called the A object, and the second is the B object. The resulting shape is the C object, which is either the union of A and B, the difference of A and B, or the intersection of A and B (see Figure 9.3). Once you understand what the terms "union," "difference," and "intersection" mean, you are home free.

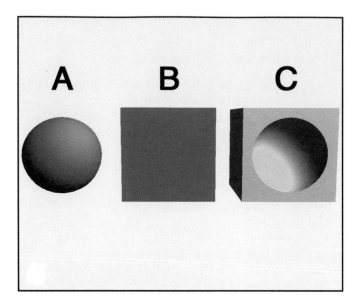

FIGURE 9.3   *The A object, the B object, and the C object.*

UNION

The union is the addition of both objects. The new C object has all the volume of space included in both the A object and the B object (see Figure 9.4). If the A and B objects overlap in 3D space, those vertices from A and B that end up inside the volume are removed because they are no longer necessary. If the two A and B objects don't overlap anywhere, the new object looks like a combination of the two.

DIFFERENCE

The difference is where the C object is the result of subtracting the volume of B from the volume of A. Visualize B taking a bite out of A and you have an accurate mental picture of the operation (see Figure 9.5). The C object has all the vertices of the A object, except those that are inside the B object when the command is executed, and it has new vertices from B where the B vertices are inside the A object. Confused? Then just stick with the B-takes-a-bite-out-of-A description.

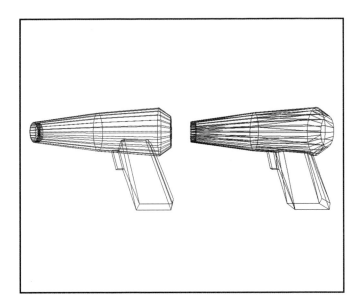

FIGURE 9.4 *A Boolean union of the handle and body.*

FIGURE 9.5 *A Boolean difference.*

A difference operation is a great way to trim out some detail from an object, making a complex surface, such as the pattern of grooves on a cut glass vase.

INTERSECTION

The intersection is the volume of space shared by both A and B (see Figure 9.6). If the A and B objects are apart in space and don't overlap at all, then the intersection will be nothing. Intersection is a very useful method for making shapes that are tough to model themselves but are bounded by two or more simple shapes.

FIGURE 9.6 *A Boolean intersection.*

STATIC BOOLEANS

Using Boolean modeling takes some getting used to, and you may have to do some prep work before invoking the command. If the objects are too small and have very fine detail, a Boolean operation may not do a great job. Sometimes the results can be improved by subdividing the A and B objects so the Boolean operation has more detail to work with. Because the Boolean tool examines the volume of space inside the two starting objects, if either is inside out, the results will be really wacked out. You must check the normal orientation on your starting objects before you use the Boolean command, making sure that the normals on each face out, so Softimage can correctly interpret the volume inside.

Once your starting objects are oriented correctly, you're ready to start the operation. Position the two objects so that they intersect in 3D space the way you want, and select the A object. The Boolean command is sensitive to the order in which you choose the objects for the difference calculation, but either object can be chosen first for the union and intersection operations. You will pick the B object later, after setting up the operation in the Boolean dialog box. Choose the Boolean→Static command in the Model module to invoke the Boolean dialog box (see Figure 9.7).

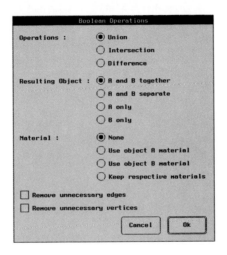

FIGURE 9.7 *The Boolean Operations dialog box.*

The Boolean Operations dialog looks daunting, but it's really pretty simple. First choose the operation you want: union, intersection, or difference. The Resulting Object radio buttons allow you to choose the makeup of the C object. Generally you want to keep the default, A and B together, so that the C object has vertices from both starting objects. If the A and B objects have material assigned, the C object can inherit either material on the entire surface, or the C object can have one material for A's vertices and another for B's vertices (see Figure 9.8). The two check boxes, Remove Unnecessary Edges and Remove Unnecessary Vertices, reduce redundant polygonal detail. Check them both on. When you are ready to move on, click the Ok button to dismiss the dialog, and then pick the B object with the left mouse button.

> **NOTE**
>
> Using the Resulting Object radio button, you can limit the C object to contain the vertices from only A or B, and you can make two C objects, one with A's vertices, the other with B's vertices. These options are rarely useful and can be very confusing to beginners, so don't use them until you are very clear on how the Boolean operations work.

The new C object is created in the same position as the originals, so you will need to locate the original A and B objects in the Schematic view and hide them to see the C object.

FIGURE 9.8 *A Boolean difference with the materials retained, showing what was A and what was B.*

TUTORIAL: MODELING THE CATACOMBS OF THE PANTHEON

The catacombs under the French Pantheon are interesting for two reasons. First, they're full of famous dead French people. Second, and more importantly, the hallways leading between the chambers are arranged in a torus, carved out of curved limestone blocks fit perfectly together. Straight hallways with domed ceilings cut straight through the torus, creating perfect vaults at the intersections. The shapes inside are beautifully perfect, and a great modeling challenge for Boolean modeling techniques. Although the layout here is not actually the layout of the Pantheon catacombs, it gets the idea across (see Figure 9.9).

1. **Create the Outer Ring Tunnel.**

   Get a primitive circle, Linear, Radius=3, 36 Steps.

   Tag the lower points that fall below the X axis, and in TAG mode, delete just the tagged points leaving a closed half circle.

Tag just the lowest two remaining points and translate them −4 units in Y. Name the spline doorway.

FIGURE 9.9   *The tunnels of the catacombs.*

Back in OBJ mode, scale the whole circle to 0.75 percent of its original scale in X to make it more proportionately attractive as a hallway with an arched ceiling. Move the circle 16 units in X, and revolve a surface (Surface→Revolution) around Y 360 degrees as a closed polygonal mesh with 36 subdivisions. Name this object torus (see Figure 9.10).

Move the doorway spline in front of the hall circle by entering 0 as the translation in X, and 20 as the translation in Z. This places the doorway in front of the torus, ready for extrusion through the torus.

Now use Surface→Extrusion to extrude the doorway in Z as a closed polygonal mesh, 40 units deep along the Z axis. Name the new object hallway1.

Duplicate hallway1 and rotate it 90 degrees around Y. You should now have two hallways cutting through the torus, looking like a Celtic cross from the top (see Figure 9.11).

Check the normals of the hallways to make sure they face out, because the Boolean command relies on the normal direction to evaluate volume. Use the Effect→Inverse command to invert the surfaces if they are incorrect, which they likely are.

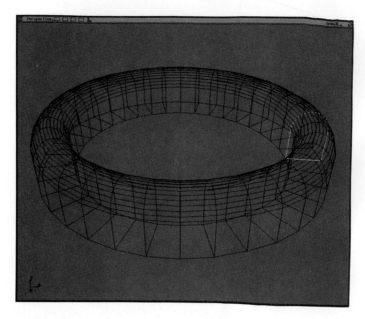

FIGURE 9.10 *The torus shape and the doorway used to make it.*

FIGURE 9.11 *The torus and hallways in the shape of a Celtic cross.*

2. Perform the Unions.

Create a Boolean union of the two hallways: Choose hallway1 and then the Boolean→Static command. Choose the Union option, and with A and B together and No Material, you can check the option boxes to remove unnecessary edges and vertices. Click Ok and pick hallway2 (see Figure 9.12).

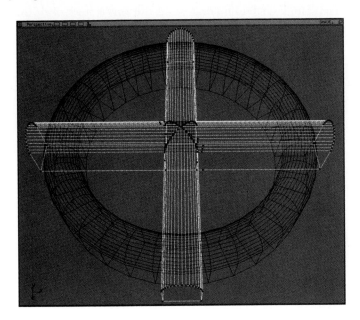

FIGURE 9.12   *The hallway assembly Boolean union object.*

After the new union object is created, delete or hide the old hallway objects and name the new object Newhallway.

Now create a Boolean union of Newhallway and the torus objects using the same settings. Name the new Boolean Hallwayassembly. Hide the old parts.

Examine the new object. See how it is now a single object made up of the space inside the other objects. Where the objects meet, Softimage creates complex jointed vaults.

3. Construct a Dome.

Get a primitive sphere, made of a polygonal mesh with 36 U and V subdivisions. Leave the sphere at the global center. Again tag all the points below the X axis and, in the TAG mode, delete them with Delete→Selection to create a half dome. Untag the remaining tagged points when you are done. Alternatively, you can use PlaneClipping, then rotate the dome back to the upright position, and freeze its transformations.

Get a primitive cube with a length of 1 unit per side. Starting with a one unit cube makes it easy to scale up to a precise size. Scale the cube to be 18 × 5 × 18 units. Translate it −1.5 units in Y, so its bottom is flush with the bottom of Hallwayassembly (see Figure 9.13).

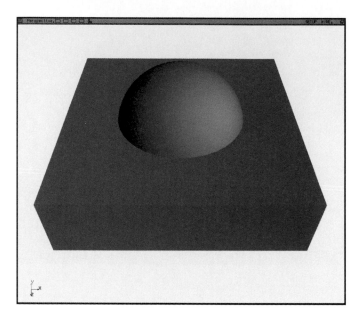

FIGURE 9.13   *The dome assembly.*

Create the dome assembly by making another Boolean union between the sphere and the cube. Name the new object Dome. Then hide or delete the old construction elements.

4. **Make the Last Boolean.**

Often the Boolean command creates unnecessary vertices along edges or ragged joints between objects. The more Booleans you do in a row, the greater these errors seem to become. It is therefore a good idea to clean up the model periodically. Freeze the transformations of each model. Then use the Effect→Cleanup tool on each of the two models, the dome and the hallway assembly, to remove unnecessary detail and clean the models. The default settings are good.

Finally, perform another Boolean union using the dome model and the hallway assembly model. Name the result Catacomb.

Hide the originals and again cleanup the new Boolean with the Effect→Cleanup command (see Figure 9.14).

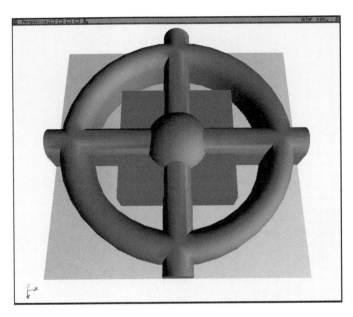

FIGURE 9.14 *The completed catacomb mesh object with the floor plane.*

Finally, add a floor plane with a primitive grid of 10 by 10 units, translated to –4 units in Y, and scale up four times to extend under the whole catacomb. You now have a complex catacomb system loosely modeled on the French Pantheon.

You're done—well, almost. As you've no doubt discovered, no project is ever totally finished because you can always think of another refinement. For extra credit on the catacomb system, try adding atmosphere, faceting, and tombs.

ATMOSPHERE

Place a few dim lights with hard shadows in the hallways and translate your camera inside the space to get the right spooky effect. A slightly reflective marbled texture on the floor and a brownish Lambert material on the walls really helps the look. If you render inside, either invert the normals of the entire object or turn off back culling so all the geometry is visible to the renderer.

FACETING

You can play with different effects by changing the automatic discontinuity in the Info→Selection dialog for the catacomb, which causes faceting that looks like the detail of the stone blocks used to construct the space. Try discontinuities of 9, 12, and 20 degrees and render after each setting to choose one you like (see Figure 9.15).

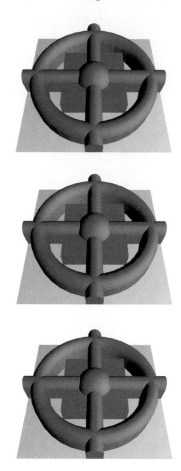

FIGURE 9.15   *The effect of different discontinuity angles on the render. Setting the angle below 5 degrees insures that most polygons will be faceted, while setting the angle above 90 guarantees that most will be smooth.*

THE TOMBS

Create a rectangular cube and place it so that it intersects the walls of the catacomb in the outer ring. Use Repetitive Duplication to make a bunch of them, evenly spaced around the torus. (Hint: rotate them in the Duplicate Repetition dialog.) Merge them into a single object and use that object in a Boolean difference to carve out tombs in the walls of the catacombs.

ANIMATED BOOLEANS

Softimage 3D|Extreme has a fascinating application for the Boolean operation in Boolean→Animation. Essentially, you can animate the transformations of the A and B objects over time, and Softimage dynamically recalculates the shape of the C object *at each frame*! This is pretty cool because it's actually the only way to create an animated object in Softimage that gains or looses vertices over time.

For instance, you could model a piece of cheese and animate it being eaten by another object shaped like a set of teeth, or animate a car chassis being constructed from nothing. You could also animate a cutaway of a machine showing its construction, or animate a lathe cutting wood, or a saw blade eating away at a model. Your imagination is your only limitation (see Figure 9.16).

The method is identical to the static Boolean command. Simply select the A object and choose the Boolean→Animation command from the Model module. Then choose your options and pick the B object to complete the command.

TUTORIAL: ANIMATED CUTAWAY

In this tutorial, we'll use Boolean→Animation to progressively cut away a model of an aircraft engine, while the turbine spins (see Figure 9.17).

1. **Make the Engine Shell.**

   Revolve the engine casing by drawing a NURBS curve as shown and revolving it to create a polygon mesh. Because the Boolean functions operate only on polygons, it's a good idea to start there. Draw the curve in the Front view, and make the NURBS closed to show the thickness of the turbine shell. When you revolve the spline around Y, give it at least 36 subdivisions to make a nice smooth surface. Name the object shell and then temporarily hide the object (see Figure 9.18).

FIGURE 9.16
Different stages of an animated Boolean cutaway.

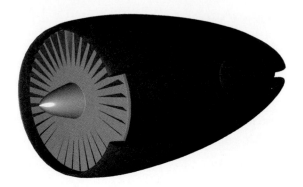

FIGURE 9.17   *The completed engine cutaway.*

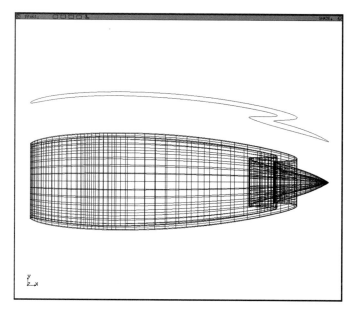

FIGURE 9.18   *The engine shell and the NURBS profile used to revolve it.*

2. Create the Turbine.

Next create the central axis on which the turbine spins, including the rounded nose cone. Make this object in the same way as the turbine shell, drawing the spline inside the spline used for the turbine shell to get the proportions right. Name this object spindle (see Figure 9.19).

Finally, create a single turbine blade with the Draw→Polygon tool, fitting from the spindle to the inside of the turbine shell.

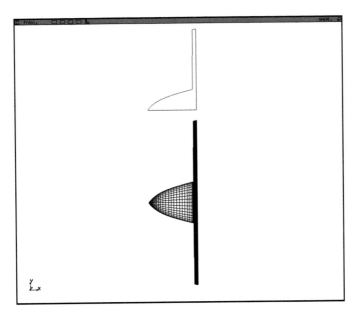

FIGURE 9.19 *The turbine spindle and the NURBS used to revolve it.*

Duplicate the single turbine blade 35 times with the Duplicate→Repetition Command, specifying a 10 degree rotation in Y. Merge all the blades together, including the original, using the Effect→Merge command, and then delete the original hierarchy of blades because we want to use the simpler merged object. Name the new merged object blades.

Next join the spindle and the blades with a Boolean union, and name the result turbine. (Remember to check your normals first!) You may wish to use the Effect→Cleanup command on the Boolean to reduce unwanted vertices and edges.

Set some rotational keyframes for the turbine assembly so that it spins rapidly for 200 frames about its axis.

3. **Carve Away the Engine Shell.**

   Get a primitive cube and scale it to be larger than the engine assembly. Rotate the cube 45 degrees on the Y axis, and translate it looking at the Top view so that the cube does not yet intersect the engine shell. This cube will become a knife that slices into the engine shell, revealing the turbine inside (see Figure 9.20).

FIGURE 9.20   *The cut cube carving out the shell.*

Name the cube shellcutter and set a keyframe for its current location with SaveKey→Object→Explicit Translation→All. At frame 200, move the cube so that it entirely surrounds the engine shell and save another key. If you want, you can change the material color on the cutting cube and the shell to show the cut edges more clearly.

Perform the Boolean. Select the engine shell first, and then choose Boolean→Animation. In the Boolean dialog, set the parameters to Difference and Keep Respective Materials.

Click the Ok button, and then pick the cutting cube object. Softimage creates a new object in the scene.

Hide the old engine shell and the cutting cube. Drag the Time Slider forward and check your model in Shaded view to see the shell being cut away.

4. **Cut the Turbine.**

Get another cube, and this time position it above the turbine. Color this cube red. Animate the translation of the cube from top to bottom, from frame 100 to frame 200.

Select the turbine assembly and perform another Boolean animation. Use the new cutting cube as the difference object, and then hide the cube and the old turbine assembly.

Position your camera for a good view of the inside, render a preview, and then play it back in FlipBook to get the idea of the motion.

If you wish to change how the cuts happen, simply set new keyframes for the cutting cubes and the animated Boolean will be automatically updated.

There you go! Animated cutaways have never been so easy—except in a solid modeler.

PLANECLIPPING

A very simple variation on Boolean modeling, PlaneClipping can be used to cut up polygonal models. Found in the Effect menu cells in the Model module, PlaneClipping chops an object in half, using the XZ plane as the cut plane. The portion of the model that extends above the XZ plane will be removed entirely. The object should be translated along the Y axis until the X axis is exactly where you want the separation to be. Then, with the object selected, just choose Effect→ PlaneClipping (see Figure 9.21).

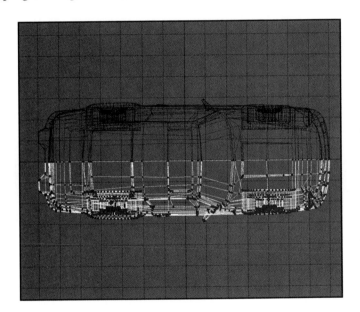

FIGURE 9.21 *A model cut with PlaneClipping.*

The effect also adds new vertices to subdivide polygons that lie on both sides of the XZ plane, so the cut is a smooth one. You can select the new object in the Schematic view, and translate it away from the original model to examine the results, or just hide the original object to see the new half.

SLICE AND MULTIANIMATEDSLICE

Slice is a similar effect to PlaneClipping, but with a great deal more flexibility and utility. With Slice, also found in the Effect menu cell in the Model module, you can cut an entire hierarchy of polygon objects (no patches or NURBS allowed) along any arbitrary plane. You can choose to get two pieces of the hierarchy, or a cross sectional piece, like a slice of salami, showing the interior construction of the hierarchy at the cutting plane.

You don't have to translate the hierarchy to the global center; instead you create a one cell polygon grid with Get→Primitive→Grid, and place and rotate it until it bisects the hierarchy at the location where you want the hierarchy divided (see Figure 9.22).

FIGURE 9.22   *A model and the slicing planes set up for the Slice effect.*

Choose the Effect→Slice command, and first pick the hierarchy to be chopped, then the grid that does the cutting.

The Slice dialog pops up, where you can set some parameters. Under Resulting Object, you can discard the cross sectional piece and place it into a separate hierarchy so you can move it independently, or you can have it merge into the resulting sliced geometry of the original hierarchy. Under Resulting Material, you can choose to assign the Material attributes of the cutting grid to the cross section with Keep Original Material. Or you could let the cross sectional slice pick up materials from the models it was made of with Use Material of Model. When you have made the choices, click the Ok button, pick the model to be sliced, and then pick the plane that will do the slicing to complete the effect.

As if that isn't cool enough, an even more powerful version of this tool is in the Motion module in the Effects menu called MultiAnimatedSlice. With MultiAnimatedSlice you can cut with several grid planes at the same time, by combining them into a hierarchy of cut planes. You can also animate the location of the cut plane to cut a model up into several pieces that come together over time. After the effect is assigned, you can re-edit the command with the Effects→Custom→Edit Parameters.

CONCLUSION

Although Softimage's implementation of Booleans isn't the easiest to understand, or the most reliable, Boolean modeling techniques are a valuable tool in any animator's bag of modeling tricks. They are a particularly good solution when you need to carve away part of a model, or when the shape you need is the combination of two other shapes that are easier to model.

In this chapter, you learned how to

- Create unions, differences, and intersections
- Create animated cutaway views
- Clip and cut models in half using PlaneClipping
- Cut cross sections through models using Slice

Image courtesy of Annesa Hartman and Mesmer Animation Labs.

CHAPTER 10

META-CLAY MODELING

Working with Softimage 3D\Extreme's Meta-Clay Modeling system is completely different from working with polygons and NURBS surfaces. The Meta-Clay system enables you to design organic, smoothly curving shapes by building a model out of many small, individual balls that all blend together, kind of like modeling with clay, as they come into contact with one another, creating more complex, "blobby" surfaces. (See Figure 10.1.) By combining many small metaballs together, you can create full human figures, hands, or other organic objects out of a single surface, which aids considerably in animation and rendering.

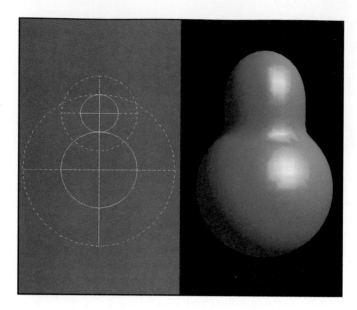

FIGURE 10.1   *Metaballs coming together to form a metasurface.*

The Meta-Clay Modeling method is a fantastically easy way to create blobby objects, and animating them is a snap, because they automatically regenerate their surface at every frame. A special kind of shape animation is also possible with metaballs, and this is the technique used to create the little green creatures in the movie *Flubber* (see Figure 10.2).

In this chapter, you will

- Learn how Meta-Clay works
- Learn how to set up Meta-Clay systems, called metasystems
- Make complex, organic shapes
- Group Meta-Clay elements
- Convert Meta-Clay to a polygonal mesh

FIGURE 10.2 *A Meta character.*

META-CLAY BASICS

Meta-Clay objects are organized into groups called *systems* or *metasystems*. Individual metaballs are also called *elements*. These elements are connected together in a standard Softimage hierarchy, with all the metaballs connected as children of one parent null. A single tree hierarchy of metaballs is one metasystem.

Each metasystem element (metaball) is made of a solid core and an area of influence that extends around it like a protective shield (see Figure 10.3). The balls can be visualized as solid objects, with a density changing from the surface to the outside edge of the area of influence, like an atmosphere around a planet. Where the atmosphere is dense enough, the metasurface forms. When the areas of influence from two metaballs come together, they merge into a smooth meniscus, forming a single solid object that comprises both cores and the area of influence shared by both balls. This is called the metasurface, and it smoothly surrounds all the metaballs in the metasystem.

FIGURE 10.3 *The metaball and the sphere of influence, represented by the dotted lines.*

You can alter individual metaballs in several ways. You can change the scale of an entire metaball by enlarging it with the Scale transformation keys, which makes the core bigger and the area of influence bigger too, keeping it in proportion to the core. You can also scale a metaball irregularly in X, Y, and Z to elongate it in one or more axes, making longer, thinner metasurfaces. Each metaball in a surface can also be given a different weight, so that it has more or less influence on the metaballs around it. You can even change a metaball's shape to be more square in one or more axes, instead of round (see Figure 10.4).

You can either leave completed Meta-Clay systems as is, or you can cook them down into a polygonal mesh when you have the shape you want. If you leave them as is, Softimage retessellates the metasurface down into triangles differently at every frame. If you cook the metasystem down into polygons, you can use the regular polygonal modeling tools to edit it further. If you leave the metasystem intact, it will always smoothly define a surface for you at render time, no matter what happens to the metaelements.

Like most of the tools in Softimage, Meta-Clay is a simple medium that, with vision, creativity, and artistic skill, you can sculpt into wonderfully organic shapes.

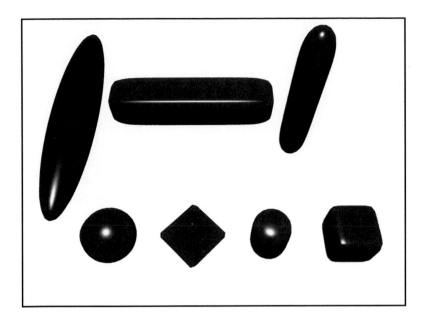

FIGURE 10.4 *Metaballs with different shapes.*

SETTING UP AND ADDING ELEMENTS

Start your Meta-Clay system by choosing the Meta-Clay→Add System command in the Model module (see Figure 10.5). In the Schematic view, note that a new object is added to your scene. This is the *root* of the meta system and all metaballs parented to this root will be blended together.

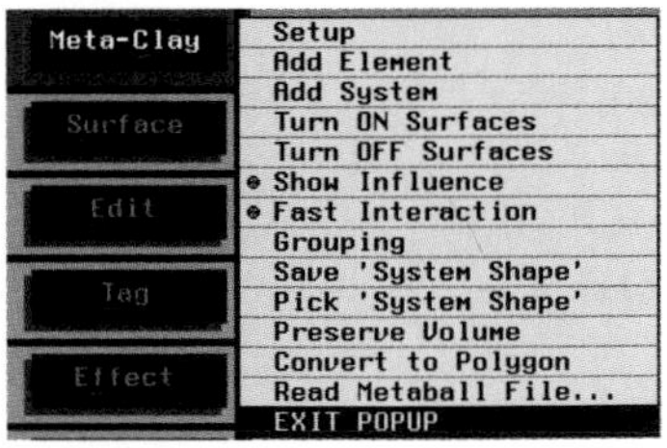

FIGURE 10.5 *The Meta-Clay menu cells.*

To add a metaball, choose the Meta-Clay→Add Element command. A single sphere, surrounded by a spherical dotted line, appears in your scene, as a child of the selected root. You can transform that metaball with the usual Scale, Rotate, and Translate menu cells.

To create another metaball object, either use the Meta-Clay→Add Element command again or duplicate the current metaball. Scale and translate this metaball into a different size and position, but make sure that the two metaballs's spheres of influence overlap in space. Check in at least two perpendicular views to be sure, or orbit the Perspective view to get the picture.

Next turn the Perspective view to the Shaded mode, and set the Shaded mode options to keep the view shaded at all times. Then experiment by moving one of the metaballs to observe the effects as the spheres of influence overlap. You may add as many new elements as you wish to make the shape you desire, but keep in mind that as the number of metaballs increases, so generally does the surface area of the meta-system, and up goes the polygon count during shading and rendering.

CHANGING THE INFLUENCE

Up until now, all metaballs have been created equal. That is to say, each has had an identical Influence Zone and the same core weight. Each has been perfectly elliptical as well. All these parameters can be changed, even animated, for each metaball in the system. To modify a metaball, just select it and choose Info→Selection to bring up the Meta Element Info dialog (see Figure 10.6). Here you can change a metaball's Weight, Core Ratio, Influence Zone, SuperQuadratic Exponent, and Negative Weight.

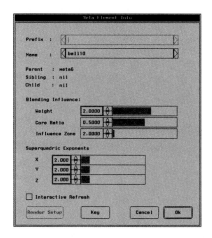

FIGURE 10.6   *The Meta Element Info dialog for a single meta element.*

WEIGHT

Weight is a measure of how powerfully the metaball acts on the whole system. Metaballs with higher Weights attract the metasurface to a larger area. Changing the Weight to a negative number makes the metaball subtract volume from the solid mass of the metasystem. Setting Weight to a negative number is also terrifically useful for etching grooves into surfaces, for creating hollowed out sections in metasurfaces to produce Mickey Mouse ears, for example, and for drilling smooth holes all the way through metasurface objects (see Figure 10.7).

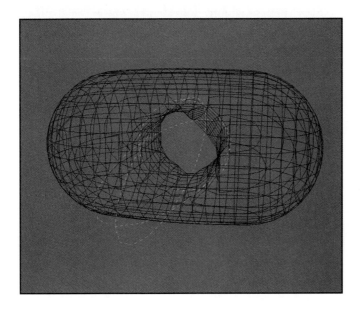

FIGURE 10.7   *A negatively Weighted element subtracts density from the system.*

Try it out by scaling a metaball in one axis so that it projects all the way through the metasystem and changing the weight to –10 in the Info→Selection dialog box. The Influence zone of that metaball turns blue to show you that it is a negative metaball. Now render the scene to see the effect.

CORE RATIO

The Core Ratio is the ratio between the size of the core and the size of the Influence Zone. The larger the gap between the core and the Influence Zone, the softer the transition into a metaball is when the surface is tessellated. A metaball with a small gap between the core and the influence zone will have a more distinct edge effect on the metasurface.

INFLUENCE ZONE

The Influence Zone slider scales the size of the Influence Zone independently of the core size. As the influence gets bigger, more falls within it and more metaballs are rounded together, becoming less distinct.

The Influence Zones of all the elements in the system are added together at each point in space to determine if the point is inside or outside the metasurface.

SUPERQUADRATIC EXPONENT

The SuperQuadratic Exponent squares off one axis of the metaball, turning it into more of a "metacube" shape. The SuperQuadratic Exponent can also be set to a negative number (see Figure 10.8).

FIGURE 10.8 *Different shapes caused with different settings of the SuperQuadratic exponent.*

ADJUSTING THE SYSTEM PARAMETERS

Fortunately Softimage offers a number of options that apply to an entire metasystem, which determine how easily you can work onscreen, as well as how smoothly the final object is rendered to the screen and to disk.

DISPLAY TOGGLES

So far we've worked with the metasurfaces in a simple spherical view, showing only the metaball and the sphere of influence, which means we had to render them to see how the actual metasurface looks. If you choose the Turn ON Surfaces command from the Meta-Clay menu cell, you'll get a simpler Wireframe-based surface approximation in the non-shaded view. This view shows us the detail we need without time-consuming renders or slow, Shaded mode screen redraws. You can toggle the surfaces off with the Meta-Clay→Turn OFF Surfaces command when you no longer need to see the surface in the Wireframe views (see Figure 10.9). The Show Influence toggle turns on and off the dotted sphere that shows the size of the sphere of influence.

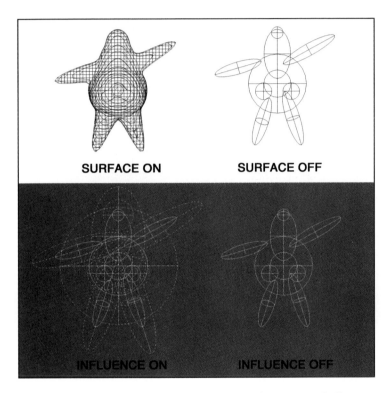

FIGURE 10.9   *The same system with surfaces on and off, and influences on and off.*

We can also use the Fast Interaction mode toggle in the same menu cell to speed the Wireframe display even further by turning off the surface display during editing, and only recalculating when the display is idle. This option is on by default, but I find that current machines are typically capable of working with the surface displayed and Fast Interaction off.

THE META-CLAY SYSTEM SETTINGS DIALOG

If you select the entire metasystem, by selecting any metaball as a tree with the Spacebar and the right mouse button or by selecting just the metasystem root in the Schematic view, you can use the Meta-Clay System Settings dialog to retrieve the settings for the entire system (see Figure 10.10). To call the dialog, use the Meta-Clay→Setup command.

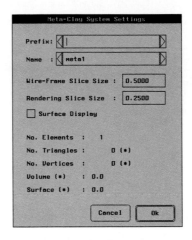

FIGURE 10.10 *The Meta-Clay System Settings dialog applies to the entire system.*

The metasurface is actually a mathematically defined perfectly smooth surface, but because everything must be tessellated down into triangles to display in Shaded view and to render, the metasurface must also be tessellated before we can actually see it.

We can use this dialog box to control both the Wireframe Slice (the detail we see in the Wireframe view) and the Rendered Slice, the detail used by the renderer (see Figure 10.11). By setting the Wireframe Slice to be quite a bit higher than the Rendered Slice, we can optimize the system for quick editing, while retaining the quality we need at render time. By default, the Wireframe Slice is set to 0.5 Softimage units, twice as large as the Rendered Slice of 0.25 units. These values may be too low for metasurfaces with a large surface area. The Wireframe surface display can be toggled on and off in this dialog as well.

TUTORIAL: MAKING A TEDDY BEAR

In the following tutorial, we'll use a simple subset of the Meta-Clay capabilities to model a convincing teddy bear quickly and easily. To give it some personality, we'll add black button eyes and a nose and use the mental ray Fur shader to apply a light fuzz to the bear (see Figure 10.12).

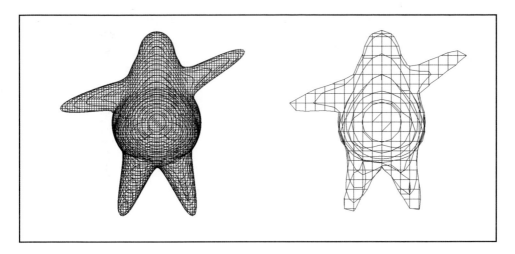

FIGURE 10.11   *The same Meta-Clay system with lower and higher Rendered Slice settings.*

FIGURE 10.12   *The completed teddy bear.*

1. **Set Up a System.**

   Use the Meta-Clay→Add System command to create a root for the metasystem.

Use the Meta-Clay→Setup command to turn on the Wireframe surface display and set the Rendered Slice to a rougher 0.5 units and the Wireframe Slice size to 1 units, so you can work rapidly in Wireframe and Shaded modes. Turn off Fast Interaction so the surface is calculated at all times. Now you'll be ready to work while the system keeps up with you and gives you the feedback you need to make good design decisions.

2. **Create the Body, Arms, and Legs.**

Start with one metaball (use Meta-Clay→Add Element) for the bear's largest feature, his stomach, by creating a metaball. Scale the metaball up equally in all axes to be about 10 units in X, Y, and Z.

Add a new metaball for the bear upper body, scale it to 6 units, and then translate it in Y to a position above the stomach, checking the wireframe surface to visualize a smooth transition between belly and upper body. Translate the upper body back in Z a bit so the belly sticks out in front.

Now create a new arm stub and position it where the bear's left shoulder would be, rotating it slightly about Z so the arm comes forward from the shoulder. Scale the arm in Y to about 7 su for the reach of the bear.

Create a new metaball for the end of the left arm and square the end off slightly by choosing the Info→Selection command and adjusting the X SuperQuadratic Exponent to make the surface look more flat on the end, like a teddy bear paw would be. Scale the metaball in the X dimension to make it a little longer and less round.

To create the right arm, select both the upper arm and the paw metaballs with Multi mode and use the Effect→Symmetry command to mirror them in the YZ plane, causing a new set to appear on the other side of the bear body.

Repeat this technique to create the legs, which are bending forward as if the bear is sitting on his rump.

You may add a bellybutton to your bear if you wish by creating a small (0.5 units) metaball, positioning it on the surface of the belly, and in the Info→Selection dialog adjusting its weight to be −2, subtracting a small divot from the surface of the tummy (see Figure 10.13).

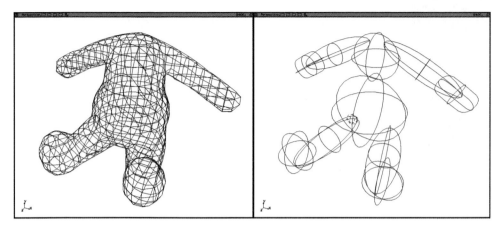

FIGURE 10.13   *The teddy body, arms, and legs.*

3. **Create the Meta-Head.**

   Make a new metaball, or duplicate an existing one, and move it into position for the head. Scale the head to a pleasing size for your bear. Add another ball for the base of the snout, flatten it to a disk, and then add a second, elongated metaball to finish off the snout. Add a regular primitive sphere as the small black nose at the end of the snout.

   Add ears, flattened into disks. Then subtract a hollow into each ear by duplicating the ear metaball, scaling it smaller and translating it forward, then adjusting its weight to be −1.

   Add two small flattened black primitive spheres to form the eyes (see Figure 10.14).

4. **Examine and Refine Your Work.**

   Turn on Shaded mode in the Perspective view so you can see a better, smoother representation of the surface you created. If it isn't smooth enough for you to judge aesthetically, use the Meta-Clay→System Setup command to reduce the Rendered Slice, and look at it again.

   Make any adjustments necessary to give the bear a pleasing shape, and then render a preview.

   Save your scene.

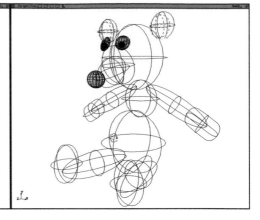

FIGURE 10.14   *The teddy head metaballs.*

5. Add Fur.

Fur in Softimage 3D|Extreme is added in the mental ray renderer as an output shader. The first step is to name your system by selecting the root and in the Info→Selection dialog naming it bearroot.

Next go to the Matter module and call up the Render dialog box. Change the rendering engine to mental ray in the drop box at the top of the dialog, and then call up the Render Options dialog box with the Options button.

In the middle of the Options dialog, note the area for assigning output shaders. Click the Select button to add one and locate the Fur shaders in the Shader_Lib database. Pick the fur_body shader, and then use the Edit button to edit the parameters for the shader in the Oz-Furry Postfilter dialog (see Figure 10.15). Click the Select button next to the object list to choose the name of your metasystem. This is the object on which the fur will grow.

You may adjust the parameters here to your liking, but be forewarned that setting the Fur Density or Length higher results in some lengthy render naps.

Finally render a single frame of your bear to see the effect. During the render, the mental ray first renders the surface of the bear. Only after the entire bear surface has been rendered will the fur be grown on the bear. This fur growth process can take some time and may run out of memory on machines with meager RAM and swap resources.

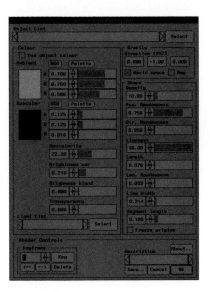

FIGURE 10.15 *The Oz-Furry Postfilter dialog in the Render Options dialog, set for the teddy bear.*

So there you have it—a simple way to make organic shapes with complex curves by combining groups of putty-like Meta-Clay elements.

CREATING GROUPS

As we've learned, all the elements in a given system are blended together when they come into each other's influence. But there are occasions where we will want to control which elements blend with which other elements, so we can create compound shapes that blend smoothly in some areas but don't in others. One example of this is a hand (see Figure 10.16). We want the fingers to blend smoothly into the palm, but if two fingers get too close together we don't want the skin between them to merge into some kind of webbing (unless the hand is attached to the Thing).

The solution to this dilemma is to create *groups* of elements within a metasystem and to specify which groups do not blend with which other groups. This is accomplished in the Meta-Clay→Grouping command's dialog box (see Figure 10.17).

The Meta-Clay Groups Settings dialog is composed of three list boxes: the current groups on the left, all the elements in the middle, and the unblended groups on the right.

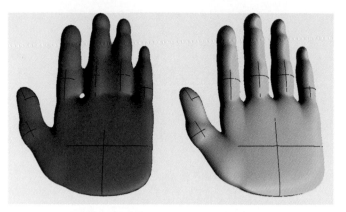

FIGURE 10.16   *A Meta-Clay hand, showing blending between the fingers.*

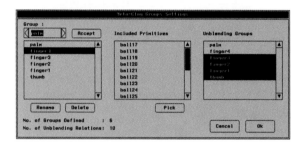

FIGURE 10.17   *The Meta-Clay Groups Settings dialog box.*

The methodology is to first create a new croup by typing in a new name and click-ing the Accept button. Then select each metaball that you want to add to that named group. For instance, you would name the palm group, the thumb group, the finger1 group, the finger2 group, and so on (see Figure 10.18). From the list in the middle, you select all these metaballs that belong to a single group. Next type in a name for the group in the Group entry field on the left and click Accept. The group is then listed in the left list box, and you can define the next group. Each metaball can be a member of only one group; you cannot share metaballs between groups.

Next select a group on the left side and choose which other groups on the right side are *not* to blend with it. By default, all groups blend, so the list on the right side is only for those groups that you don't want to blend together ever. Now the metaballs can move freely and only those not in unblending relationships combine to form the metasurface. Try this out by creating your own hand, which we will use later to demonstrate rigid envelopes in Inverse Kinematic systems.

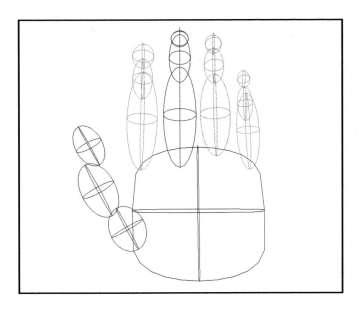

FIGURE 10.18   *The hand divided into groups.*

CONVERSION TO POLYGONS

Although it certainly is convenient to let the Meta-Clay system define its own surface dynamically at each frame, there are occasions when you want a Meta-Clay system converted down into a polygonal mesh. The Meta-Clay→Convert to Polygon command does this, using the Wireframe Slice size to determine how closely the surface is approximated. Once a metasystem is reduced to polygons, the new polygonal mesh can be manipulated with all the normal polygon tools.

When the command is executed, the old metasystem is retained and a new polygon mesh object is added to the scene, so you can go back and change the Wireframe Slice to get a polygonal mesh with a different level of detail. Reducing the Wireframe Slice will result in a polygonal mesh with many more polygons, while increasing the slice makes the resulting mesh lighter.

META-CLAY SHAPE ANIMATION

Meta-Clay systems have a special, sophisticated method for performing morphing shape animations. You can create a library of different metasystems, showing the shapes that the final system animates. These metasystems can have metaballs in different positions, at different scales, with different rotations, with different weights, and with different influences. Unlike any other animation tool on Softimage 3D, the metasystems may even have different numbers of elements, and the shape animation still works. This is the animation technique used to create a library of shapes for metacreatures in the movie *Flubber*, and to morph between them making believeable expressions on blobby creatures.

The shape animation process starts with you creating a single source metasystem and several target Meta-Clay systems that make up the library of different shapes to be added to the source system.

With the original source system selected, first choose the Meta-Clay→Save System Shape command to save all the transformations and metaball parameters for all the elements in the selected system. Then drag the Time Slider to a different frame in time, choose the Meta-Clay→Pick System Shape command, and pick the first target system to select it as the morph target for that frame. Immediately middle-click the original source system to call up the Meta-Clay Metamorphosis dialog box (see Figure 10.19).

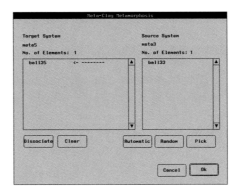

FIGURE 10.19 *The Meta-Clay Metamorphosis dialog box.*

The Metamorphosis dialog box is where you draw a connection between each element of the Source and Target systems, telling the shape animation which element will turn into which other element. You can assign them yourself here, or let Softimage automatically assign them based on the similarity of the shapes. You could also choose a randomization method that results in a lumpier, more weird-looking transformation. For some reason, it's necessary to choose the Meta-Clay→Save System Shape command again after you dismiss the dialog to save the new metamorphosis information.

You can then drag the Time Slider to a different frame and repeat the process until all the systems you created have been added to the list.

The Meta-Clay shape animation can then be easily controlled over time with the FcurveSelect→Meta-Clay→All F-curves. This more complex method of saving a library of meta shapes allows very close control over the manner of the metamorphosis. It is also incredibly useful for animating the metacreatures you make in lifelike and appealing ways.

CONCLUSION

We've just barely skimmed the surface of Meta-Clay modeling and animation in this chapter. Metasurfaces are often used for modeling and animation of organic characters and they can also be used with IK rigid envelopes. Take some time to explore the Meta-Clay menu cells, and try using them on your next modeling and animation assignment.

In this chapter you learned how to:

- Model complex surfaces with Meta-Clay systems
- Adjust the Meta-Clay parameters to create negative surfaces
- Group Meta-Clay elements to control blending
- Convert Meta-Clay to a polygonal mesh
- Set up a Meta-Clay shape library
- Morph between Meta-Clay systems of different shapes

Illustration © 1997 Nick Philip. ABSOLUT VODKA COUNTRY OF SWEDEN, Bottle design, Calligraphy and Logo are registered trademarks of V&S Vin & Sprit AB. Used by permission.

CHAPTER 11

DUPLICATES AND INSTANCES

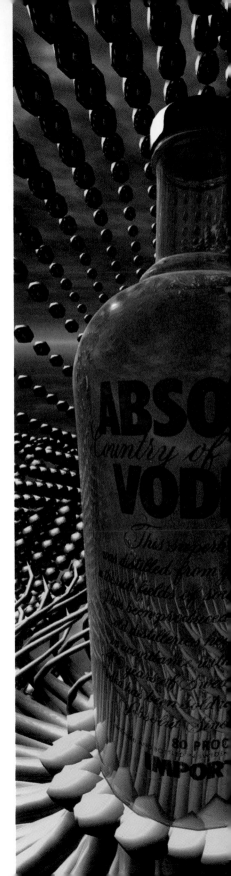

One of the great things about modeling objects in Softimage 3D is that all your effort goes into creating the first object. Once you complete a single model, you can easily make as many replicas as you want—almost instantaneously! What this means to modelers is that you are rewarded for reusing objects in your scenes. You can quickly duplicate master objects, and then you can modify these duplicates to look slightly different or to fit in a different part of your scene.

Softimage even offers tools to automate the duplication of models, so you can create hundreds of new shapes, varying them one at a time in rotation, translation, and scale. In this chapter, we'll explore the variety of tools that make use of duplicate models and their thinner second cousins, instances. Specifically, you will

- Learn the duplicate shortcuts
- Duplicate materials, lattices, animation, and other attributes
- Use repetitive duplication to create lots of models
- Use Duplicate by Animation to precisely place duplicates
- Use Duplicate by Surface as a Modeling tool
- Discover the power of instances

DUPLICATE BASICS

The simplest way to make one object into many is to select the original model and choose the Duplicate→Immediate command in the Model module (see Figure 11.1). You may select and duplicate entire hierarchies with this method, and you can use the Multi mode to select and duplicate groups of objects that are not connected into a hierarchy.

FIGURE 11.1 *The Duplicate menu cells.*

THE DUPLICATE SUPRA KEY

Because Duplicate is such a common function, it is blessed with a supra key: D. The best technique for using the D supra key in production workflow is to activate the Translate menu cells by clicking the gray border around them, then hold the D key, and click with the left mouse button on the object to be duplicated. Release the D key and drag with the mouse to translate the new duplicate object to another location in space.

DUPLICATE'S ATTRIBUTES

When an object is duplicated, by default it becomes another object in the Schematic view. It retains the materials and textures assigned to the original. Similarly, duplicate objects retain by default the original's clusters (although not cluster centers) and lattices.

An odd but useful fact about the duplicate operation is that if you duplicate an object that is deformed by a lattice, spline, surface, or other deformation, the resulting duplicate object has all its vertices cooked into the position resulting from the deformation, but the deformation itself is not duplicated. In other words, when you duplicate an object with a lattice deformation (or other type of deformation), the lattice is not present on the duplicate object, but it looks the same as the original. Master shape animators profitably exploit this fact when making libraries of shapes for shape animation.

When an object that has been transformed (with Scale, Rotate, or Translate) is duplicated, the Scale and Rotation transformations on the new object are reset to the default transformations: 0 for rotation and 1 for scale. The new object retains the translation of the original, which means it rests exactly on the original and has the same translation values for X, Y, and Z. The duplicate looks as if you took the original and performed a Freeze on all the transformations, cooking the vertex locations into a default state.

Objects do not, however, retain animation (unless you make the appropriate settings in the Duplicate Setup box, discussed in the following section). This means that if you animate a ball bouncing and then duplicate it, the new ball will be motionless. Duplicates never retain the constraints of the original, and this sad fact extends to IK constraints, such as the Preferred Axis constraint as well. Constraints are actually links to other objects that aren't in a hierarchy, so it makes some sense, but it does mean that you can almost never get away with duplicating your IK chains to make a right arm from a left arm.

THE DUPLICATE SETUP BOX

If you need to change the default behaviors of duplicates, you can modify them before you create them with the Duplicate→Setup command, which calls up the Duplicate Setup dialog box (see Figure 11.2).

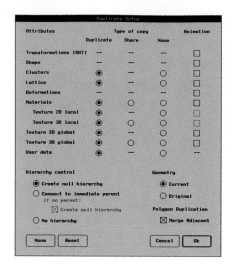

FIGURE 11.2   *The Duplicate Setup dialog box.*

In the Duplicate Setup dialog box, attributes of an object are listed vertically with four columns of radio buttons to set default behaviors for each attribute. The first column, Duplicate, lists those default attributes that follow from a master to a duplicate object. The next column, Share, allows you to choose whether material and 3D texture attributes are duplicated (creating redundant information) or are shared between the master and duplicate objects. The None column allows you to turn off attributes for the duplicate. The last column, Animation, determines what happens when animation information is present in the F-curve for the attribute.

If the animation attributes boxes are unchecked, Softimage copies no F-curves to the duplicate object. If you check the animation boxes, Softimage creates new F-curves on the duplicate for those attributes to match the original.

Another set of controls, the Hierarchy controls, allow you to determine whether multiple duplicates are all grouped together in a hierarchy (the default behavior), connected to the parent object, or let loose in the Schematic entirely without a hierarchy (a messy option).

When you model by duplicating polygons, Softimage keeps the edges of duplicate polygons connected with new polygons and shared edges by default. If you check off the Polygon Duplication Merge Adjacent check box, newly duplicated polygons each have their own local coordinate systems and do not share edges with neighboring polygons.

DUPLICATE REPETITION

If one duplicate is a good thing, then many duplicates are even better. That's the theory behind the Duplicate→Repetition command, which creates any number of duplicates from a single master object or hierarchy, each one transformed in space according to your instructions.

When you invoke the Duplicate→Repetition command, the program presents you with the Repetitive Duplication dialog box. Here you can specify the change in scaling, rotation, and translation for each axis that is applied to every subsequent model. In the No. of Occurrences entry box at the top of the dialog box, you select how many new objects are made. The transformations are made with the current settings in the Translation, Rotation and Scale mode boxes, so you can control whether objects are transformed relative to global or local axes, and so on.

Duplicate→Repetition helps make simple hierarchies of many objects, such as duplicating one place setting at a dinner table with a 90 degree rotation and three more occurrences to create four table settings, one on every side of the table. Or you could use the Repetitive Duplication technique to create hundreds of identical telephone poles stretching down the highway. Repetitive Duplication is good for creating cross sections for skinning, and also for creating precise geometric models, such as spiral staircases or courtyards ringed by columns (see Figure 11.3).

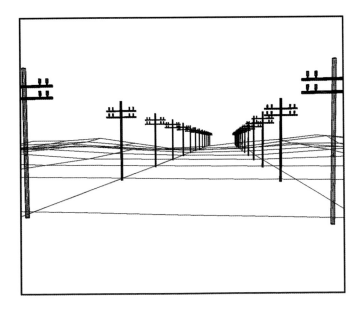

FIGURE 11.3 *Examples of duplicate repetition in use.*

DUPLICATING FROM ANIMATION

Often when creating scenes, animators require that many objects are precisely placed according to more complex sets of rules than can be produced through simple transformations in the Repetitive Duplication dialog box. In such cases, the answer is to use the Duplicate→From Animation function. The theory is that you first animate the object to be duplicated, moving it to the locations where it needs to be replicated, and changing its shape as needed for the replication. Then Softimage 3D leaves a new copy of the object at regular intervals along the animated life of the master object.

In practice, this is a fantastic construction method. You can make hundreds of railroad ties place themselves precisely between the railroad tracks by animating a single tie along a path between the rails, or you can create a complex pipe by animating the shape of a circle as it follows a path. You can even add rows of rivets to the surface of a ship hull by projecting a curve along the hull, and then animating a single rivet along that path and using the Duplicate→From Animation tool (see Figure 11.4).

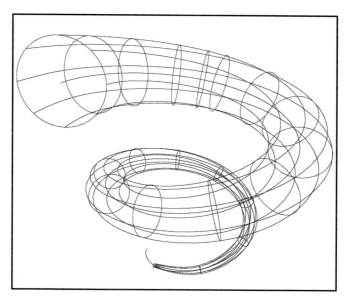

FIGURE 11.4   *An example of duplicating from animation.*

To use it, first animate the master object so that it changes over time as desired. Then invoke the Duplicate→From Animation command to get the dialog box you use to control the number of duplicates (see Figure 11.5). Frame Start and Frame End specify the first and last frames in the range that Softimage considers when duplicating your master object. The Copy Method can be either Frame Step or Number of Copies. If you use Frame Step, the object proceeds in increments of that number from the starting frame specified, making a copy at each increment until it reaches the end frame specified. The Number of Copies method allows you to choose precisely how many copies you want made. Softimage distributes that number of duplicates evenly along the animation from start to end.

For example, if you wanted to duplicate telephone poles along a road, you would place one pole on a spline that follows the side of the road and use the Duplicate→From Animation tool. If you specified Number of Copies, you could plant exactly 14 poles just by entering that number. If you didn't know how many poles were required, you could use Frame Step to plant a new pole at the location of the master pole on a given frame, such as every fifth frame or every eighth frame, until the master pole reached the end of the path.

FIGURE 11.5   *The Duplicate From Animation dialog box.*

When you accept the parameters in the dialog box by clicking the Ok button, Softimage creates all the new duplicates in the scene. They are linked together in a hierarchy under a single null object for easy manipulation.

TIP

Remember, if the object is on a path with spline interpolation, it moves more slowly at the start and end of the path, so duplicates are spaced more closely there than in the middle of the path. It's a good idea to set the F-curves for your animated object to linear interpolation before using this tool.

DUPLICATING BY SURFACE

Another interesting Duplication method, the Duplicate→Duplicator tool enables you to duplicate a single master object onto a polygon surface many times, placing the duplicate objects either precisely on vertices or randomly along the surface. You can arrange the duplicates on the surface to face one direction, or you can orient each one along the average of the normals on the adjacent polygons. An animated version of this tool, called Duplicate→AnimatedDuplicator, is available in the Motion module as well.

Duplicate→Duplicator is great for making objects with a regular surface covered by a great number of smaller, attached objects. With it, you can easily make pins covering a skin in acupuncture, teeth on a comb, hairs on a dog, jewels along a necklace, or an effect like the one in Figure 11.6.

FIGURE 11.6 *Julian with some spikes courtesy of the Duplicator.*

NOTE

The original object must be created at the global center, and the part of the object that protrudes above the X axis will be the part of the object that sticks out of the surface after duplication. As usual, the positive Y direction is converted to the orientation of the normal at each given point on the surface where a duplicate is made.

Using Duplicate→Duplicator is simple: Create the original object and the polygonal mesh that forms the guide for all the new duplicates.

Next choose the command, set the parameters in the dialog box to your liking, pick the surface that you want to duplicate onto, and choose the source model that you want copied (see Figure 11.7).

If you enjoy experimenting with this effect, also try the other duplicate effects located in the Model and Motion modules, Duplicate→Bridge, Duplicate→CopyGeometry, Duplicate→HrcCopyGeometry, Duplicate→VolumeDuplicate, and Duplicate→AnimateCenter.

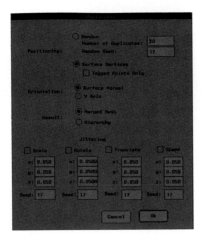

FIGURE 11.7   *The Duplicator dialog box.*

ALL ABOUT INSTANCES

Whenever a regular duplicate is made from a master object, the new object becomes a fully autonomous object in Softimage, with its own vertices or Control points, surface, and geometry. But this method has a few drawbacks. As you make many duplicates of complex models, the amount of geometry in the scene increases, as does the number of polygons that are tessellated for shaded and rendered views. As the scene becomes heavier, your machine response time slows down, and eventually it becomes difficult to work in the scene rapidly.

There is a better way, however, to duplicate from a master object. Using *instances* where possible can cut down the complexity of the scene. An instance is a like a copy of the original object. Unlike a regular duplicate, which creates another entire set of vertices and polygons, however, an instance is simply a pointer back to the original master object (see Figure 11.8). Therefore, instances are very light, requiring no actual geometry of their own, and they don't add any size to the RAM requirements of your scene.

In addition, if you change the master model from which instances are made, all of the instances automatically update their shapes to reflect the change in the master—kind of like relational modeling only better. Each instance can have its own local transformations, which means that it can be scaled, translated, and rotated independently of its master. Instances can also take their own materials and textures. An instance can be made of a single object or of an entire hierarchy. If an instance is made of a hierarchy, it shows up in the Schematic as a single object.

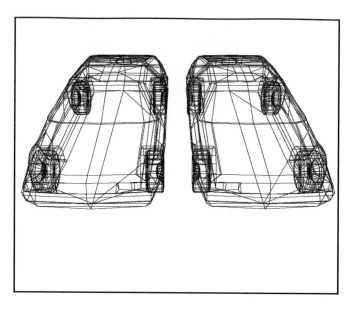

FIGURE 11.8 *A real object (left) and an instance.*

Instances don't ever show any Control points onscreen, and they redraw much faster than ordinary objects. Instances show up in the Schematic view as purple trapezoids, distinct from the other rectangular objects (see Figure 11.9).

FIGURE 11.9 *A real object and an instance in the Schematic view.*

Instances also take less RAM to render in the Softimage renderer (it is not clear that the mental ray retains them as instances at render time).

In general, instances are a good idea. In certain circumstances, however, they seem to slow down interactivity and can lead to problems saving and rendering scenes. Because an instance of a master hierarchy includes the entire hierarchy, you cannot create an instance and then make it a child of the master, because that leads to a circular reference within the definition of the instance. It is also possible, but not a good idea, to make an instance of an instance of an instance. Using this method seems to slow redraw onscreen as Softimage follows the links for each instance. I find it best to parent all instances to a single null, separate from the hierarchy of the master object.

USING INSTANCES

You can choose to create instances instead of duplicates by choosing the Duplicate→Instance command to create a single instance. For multiple instances, choose the Duplicate→Instance Repetition and Duplicate→Instance from Animation tools.

A good time to use instances is when you need many copies of a single object arrayed throughout your scene, and the copies must be placed accurately before the modeling of the object is complete. Consider the dinner setting example again. You could start by creating a plate model and instancing it for every place setting at the table. Then as you make each piece of silverware, simply place it next to the master, make it a child of the master, and an instance of the silverware magically appears next to each instanced plate. Continue modeling the placemat, the wineglass, the finger bowl, and the salad plates. As you make each a child of the master, new instances sprout up around the table.

SWAPPING INSTANCES

Another great thing about instances is that because they are just pointers to a master object, you can redirect the pointer to a new master object to change the shape of all the children. For example, you could model a stop sign to use in your video game geometry and place instances of that stop sign at each intersection of your virtual town. Later when your art director demands that the stop signs be replaced with yield signs, you can simply redirect the instance pointer from the stop sign master model to the yield sign master model, and all instances automatically take on the shape of the yield sign hierarchy.

The command required to perform this instance replacement is Duplicate→Swap Instance. To use it, select the entire master hierarchy (or single object), choose Duplicate→Swap Instance, and then pick the new object or hierarchy that will replace the old as the master of all its instances. Now all the objects that were previously instances of the first master object are converted to instances of the new master object.

EXPANDING INSTANCES

Of course, eventually you may want to replace the instances with regular models. You might wish to do this if you are fighting a weird rendering problem, because you now want to model each model to be slightly different from the master. Or it might just be time to cook all the models down to real triangulated geometry for export to your game engine.

In any case, the method is the same. If you select a single instance, you can convert it to a full, regular object on its own in the world by choosing the Duplicate→Expand command. If the master itself contains instances within it, they remain as instances. If you select a hierarchy of instances, the Duplicate→Expand command makes one new object or hierarchy for each of the instances.

If a master object itself contains instances, sort of a master built of instances of other instances of other models, Duplicate→Expand All converts every instance in the master hierarchy back into an expanded object. This way the newly expanded instance can't possibly have any instances under it in the hierarchy.

TUTORIAL: MODELING WITH PLACE HOLDERS

Let's practice what we've learned about instances by building a breakfast table with a number of place settings (see Figure 11.10).

FIGURE 11.10   *The completed breakfast scene.*

1. Make the Table.

Get a primitive cube and scale it to the correct proportions for the top of a breakfast table. If your breakfast table is round, use a cylinder. Leave it at the exact global center so we can use a duplicate repetition later to mirror objects around the table.

If you wish, you can add detail like an edge bevel to the tabletop with Polygonal Modeling techniques to make it more attractive. Add legs and parent them to the table top.

2. **Make the Placemat.**

The placemat will be the master of the instances and the top of the master hierarchy. Model it and place it on the table in front of where you sit (see Figure 11.11). Then Freeze the transformations of the placemat so that its local center goes to the global center, and it will pivot around the center of the table when you perform a duplicate repetition.

FIGURE 11.11 *The table with the master placemat.*

Now instance it for the other seating positions. If you have a table with four positions, you could use the Duplicate→Instance Repetition command with three copies and a rotation of 90 degrees around Y (see Figure 11.12).

3. **Add a Plate and a Juice Glass.**

Model a plate by revolving a spline around the global center Y axis. Then translate the plate to sit on your master placemat. Model a juice glass in the same way, and position it properly on the master placemat as well. Now select the master placemat and parent the plate and glass to it as children.

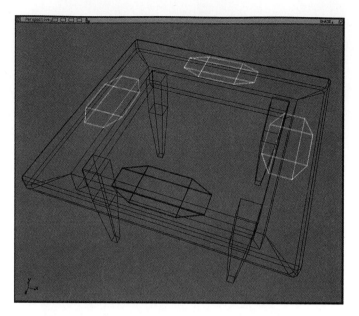

FIGURE 11.12 *The table with instanced placemats.*

See how the other instanced placemats suddenly got plates and glasses as well? That's because anything parented into the master hierarchy becomes part of each instance.

4. **Add Silverware and a Napkin.**

Model the silverware (modern Japanese stainless steelware is easier to model than Victorian silver designs), and place the pieces appropriately. Consult a waiter if you have problems with this step.

Parent the silverware into the master hierarchy (see Figure 11.13).

5. **Swap Out the Glass.**

You decide that it's not a weekday breakfast scene with a juice glass; it's a Saturday morning breakfast scene, and your drinking champagne mimosas! That calls for a different glass.

Model a champagne flute with a NURBS revolution and position it on the master placemat on the opposite side from the juice glass. Now select the juice glass, choose the Duplicate→Swap command, and then pick the new champagne glass. The instances are all now drinking champagne, not juice!

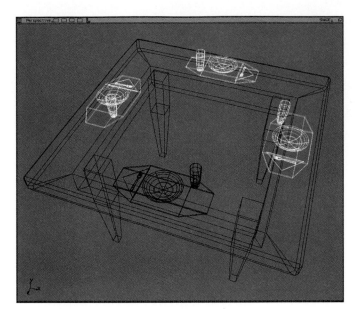

FIGURE 11.13 *The table with master place setting and instances.*

6. **Expand One Place Setting.**

If you decide that one place setting has to be different (the matching plate is dirty, for example, or perhaps you clumsily broke one of the champagne glasses on a mimosa binge), you can expand that instance into real models, and then edit them as usual. Select one of the instances and choose the Duplicate→Expand All command. Now examine that place setting in the Schematic view to see that it is now a hierarchy of real objects.

The most remarkable thing about instances is that adding new parts to the master model hierarchy adds them to the instances as well! As you can imagine, using instances can save you a great deal of time when modeling, especially when you suspect that there will be a great many changes before the project is completed.

CONCLUSION

Understanding duplicates and instances seems a little dry, but they are both an important part of getting the computer to do the work for you. That's really the beautiful part about computers: They don't mind doing mindless things again and again, over and over!

Automating your modeling process by using repetitive duplicates and animated duplicates is also a great way to get extra mileage out of your work by making lots of versions of your models that are slightly different, or placed in a different way.

In this chapter you learned how to:

- Duplicate objects and their attributes
- Use Repetitive Duplication to quickly create lots of models
- Duplicate from animation to precisely place duplicates
- Duplicate by surface as a Modeling tool
- Instance models to save time and speed up your workflow
- Swap the master of instances to instantly make far reaching changes
- Expand instances into free standing objects when you have made all the changes necessary

Looking at the boiler from the bridge in the lake. ©1997 Cyan, Inc.

CHAPTER 12

IT LOOKS PRETTY: MATERIAL AND TEXTURES

An object's appearance in the final render is always determined by four distinct factors (see Figure 12.1):

- Form
- Light
- Material
- Texture

FIGURE 12.1 *A fully rendered form shows shape, shade, and depth.*

Determined by the modeling methods you use, the form of the object provides only the object's outline, which the renderer fills. The form is nothing more than the shape of the model seen from the vantage point of the camera in the scene. It could just as easily be a flat cutout facing the camera, as long as the camera didn't move. In short, the form provides us with only the information our brain needs to match that form against the thousands of forms we hold in our heads and then to identify it with a name, such as "chair" or "house." This process of form pattern matching takes us less than 1/60th of a second for all the objects in a complete scene and can recognize hundreds of individual objects at a time. It's a massively parallel operation somewhere in our brain's visual cortex, designed to rapidly determine if that shape is something for us to eat or something to eat us. But after the form is identified, it holds very little interest for us. The model, therefore, is the least important element of the scene and holds the interest of the viewer for the shortest time.

The light in the scene fills the form in different ways. If the light is behind the object, the form is a black outline (see Figure 12.2). If the illumination is a bright light coming from where the camera is, the form may be a stark, white-filled shape (see Figure 12.3). With good lighting, the form becomes shaded, showing the direction of the light, and becomes dimmer as the light falls off around the form (see Figure 12.4).

FIGURE 12.2   *Backlit form shows only the shape.*

This shading is what finally brings depth to the form and makes it more than a cardboard cutout. Lighting can also be used to obscure the form, partially or completely. Partially obscured forms are more interesting to humans because our form processing wetware must work longer and harder to resolve the shape and identify whether the object is of interest to us or not. Lighting is a very important part of your scene.

But still, with just light and form, we would live in a perfectly smooth grayscale world. To bring an object alive, we need material and texture. Softimage 3D|Extreme realizes how incredibly important these aspects are, assigning them an entire module: the Matter module.

Material is the color information we get from an object, which tells us more about the surface: Is it blue or red? Is it smooth and shiny, or rough and dull? Where in the scene are the lights that shine on the material? Which side of the object is in the dark? Material includes reflectivity, transparency, and refraction attributes as well.

Material is just color information, spread across the object, but how the color changes answers many questions.

FIGURE 12.3   *Frontlit form shows only the shape.*

FIGURE 12.4   *Well lit, the shape takes on form and depth.*

Texture is the surface detail of the object. It can include color information; patterns of color, transparency, reflectivity, and refraction; and the roughness of the surface. Texture can be a simple thing, such as a floral pattern on a couch that repeats exactly across the fabric, or a complex thing, such as veins of color running consistently through hundreds of rocky bluffs in a Nevada desert, always different, never repeating (see Figure 12.5).

FIGURE 12.5 *The shape with material and texture takes on life.*

All four aspects—form, light, material, and texture—combine to provide us with a rich visual experience. We have, so far, covered the first two in some detail, but the last two have eluded us. In this chapter, you will learn:

- The shading algorithms Softimage uses
- The ambient, specular, and diffuse qualities of light
- How to use reflection, transparency, and refraction in a material
- How to set object texture attributes
- How to work with 2D Texture maps
- Different mapping methods for textures
- How to use 3D procedural textures

ALL ABOUT MATERIALS

Every other 3D package I've ever seen lumps materials and textures into the same dialog box. Generally, they are seen as individual aspects of how an object looks to the renderer. In Softimage, they are completely separate topics with separate dialog boxes, menu cells, and methods of control. As usual, this means you have to think ahead and have a plan for what you want to accomplish in Softimage because just poking around in one big dialog box isn't going to help you here. It also means that Softimage retains significantly more control over the precise material and texture attributes than do other programs, which is a great benefit. In 3D packages with less control but easier options, the result tends to end up looking colorful and fantastic, but well-textured scenes done in Softimage look more like real life. All this power, however, isn't exactly user friendly.

From the Material menu cell (see Figure 12.6) in the Matter module, you can access the Material Editor dialog box (see Figure 12.7). You will use the Material Editor dialog to apply material attributes to all objects in your scene.

FIGURE 12.6   *The Material menu cell in the Matter module.*

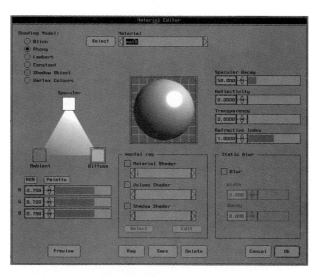

FIGURE 12.7   *The Material Editor dialog box.*

Materials can be applied to individual objects or it can be applied to the parent of a hierarchy (see Figure 12.8). If a material is applied to the parent, all the children inherit it, unless they have their own material applied. If a child has a material of its own, that material is used at render time.

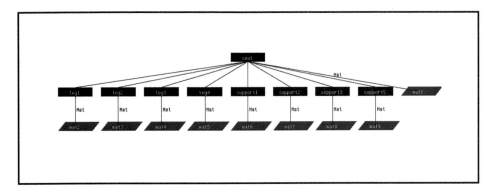

FIGURE 12.8 *The Schematic view showing materials assigned to objects in a hierarchy.*

Materials show up in the Schematic view when you click the small down arrow that represents the Mode menu and toggle on the Matter option. Materials appear as small blue rectangles, connected by a line to their objects.

Go ahead and select an object in your scene, and call up the Material Editor dialog in the Matter module (F4 on your keyboard) so that you can follow this discussion of the controls in the Material Editor dialog box.

CHOOSING COLORS

The Color triangle in the Material Editor shows the blending that will happen between the diffuse, ambient, and specular colors that you choose. When you click on one of the square Color tiles at the corners of the triangle, you can use the color sliders or the Color palette to choose a color for that leg of the Color triangle.

> **NOTE**
>
> For a thorough discussion of light and color theory, see Chapter 3, "Producing Your First Softimage Animation."

The most common system for picking colors in a computer is the RGB (Red, Green, Blue) system. By mixing these colors in the right proportions, it's possible to make almost any shade. But it's not easy. In fact, using RGB to pick colors is like running a marathon while carrying a bowling ball. For instance, you can't pick colors by spectrum. And if you do finally get a hue that you like, there is no way to keep the hue constant while you saturate or desaturate, or make the color brighter or dimmer. The best thing to do is never use the RGB system, and immediately convert to using the HSV system (my favorite) or the HLS system.

Softimage supports all three color systems, with a small button above each set of three color picker bars. By default it says RGB, but you can always switch by clicking the RGB button until it says HSV.

The first step in picking color the easy way is to crank the Saturation slider all the way up, which makes the hue you want easy to spot. Saturation is the proportion of hue to white in the color. As the saturation goes down, the color approaches white. As the saturation goes up, the color becomes more vibrant and intense. Next pick the hue you want by dragging the top Hue slider back and forth until you see the color you need. Now adjust the Value slider. *Value* is technically how much light is absorbed versus emitted by the color applied to a surface. As the value goes down, the color gets darker and darker, finally becoming black. Lastly, adjust the Saturation slider again to get the perfect tone.

You can use this slider method or the Color palette (see Figure 12.9) to select your object's diffuse, ambient, and specular colors (see Figure 12.10). The Color triangle (see Figure 12.11) shows the blending that happens between the diffuse, ambient, and specular colors that you choose.

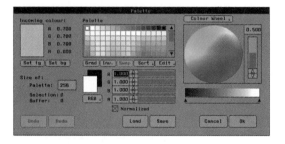

FIGURE 12.9   *The Color palette is another way to choose colors.*

As you remember from Chapter 3, the diffuse color is the primary color of the object surface. When you click the Diffuse Color tile in the Material Editor, all the changes you make in the sliders and the Color palette are immediately shown on the diffuse leg of the Color triangle.

Ambient color is the shading that reveals the back, unlit side of an object. When you click the Ambient Color tile in the Material Editor, you can use the Color sliders or the Color palette to set the ambient color. Unfortunately, Softimage by default adds about 30% gray ambient color to each material, which makes the objects look dull and lifeless. A better idea is to turn the ambiance off entirely (set the ambient color to black), which results in crisper, computery-looking scenes. You could also use a slight variance in hue with the ambiance, so that the color changes stay rich as the shading changes around to the back side.

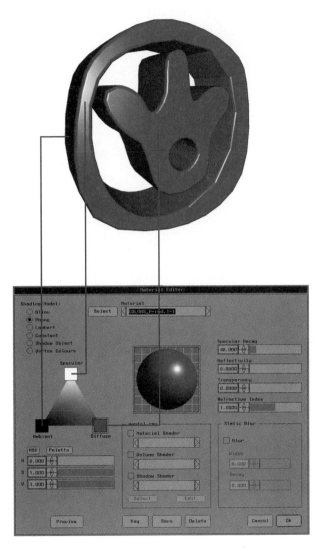

FIGURE 12.10 *Ambient, diffuse, and specular color.*

Specular color is the highlight that we see on shiny surfaces. It is really a slightly diffuse reflection from the light source (or light sources) in the room. Very smooth, shiny objects have a very small, precise specular dot, and rougher matte-colored objects have a broader, more spread-out specular smear. Metals, being both reflective and often rough, tend to have very broad and very bright specular highlights called *blooms*. The specular highlight is also a visual cue showing us the number and direction of the light sources. The specular highlight can be assigned its own color, which mixes with the light color to form the result. The size of the specular highlight, sometimes called the specular roll-off, can be adjusted with the Specular Decay slider in the Material Editor. The color of the specular highlight can be adjusted by selecting the Specular Color tile and manipulating the color sliders.

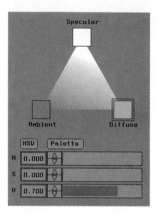

FIGURE 12.11   *The Color triangle and the HSV sliders.*

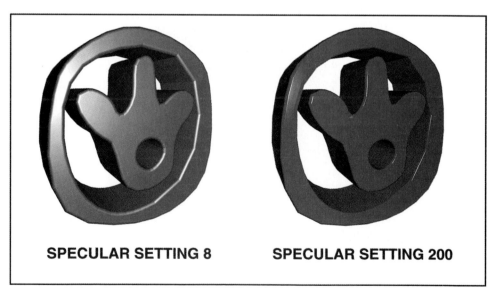

FIGURE 12.12   *A broad specular bloom (Specular Decay value of 8) and a small specular dot (value of 200).*

SHADING MODELS

When the renderer is instructed to draw an object to your screen, it uses a computer process called an algorithm, which is a plan for how the computer goes about solving a problem. In this case, the problem is how to convert an abstract geometric or mathematical representation of an object into a visual, 2D image. Many different shading algorithms determine how the surface of an object is colored during the render, and Softimage gives you the choice of five:

- Shadow
- Constant
- Lambert
- Phong
- Blinn

The algorithms differ in terms of how accurately they model the physics of light and therefore how well they can color an object. Usually the less accurate methods also render faster. You can choose the shading algorithm used for each object by clicking the radio button for that method in the Material Editor.

In general, the shading algorithms examine each location of the polygon that needs to be rendered and create a normal for each pixel that will be visible on the rendered image. Softimage then uses the normal to calculate the angle between the surface and the lights in the scene; the color of the surface material at each pixel is scaled by the value of each light and a factor based on the angle of the light to the surface. If the light is perpendicular to the surface, it has maximum effect. If it is tangent to the surface, it has minimum effect. If it is behind the surface (an angle to the normal of more than 90 degrees), then the light doesn't shine on the polygon at all (unless you have Back Culling turned off).

PHONG

Phong is the default shading algorithm, which smoothly interpolates between diffuse and ambient light and also calculates a specular highlight for each light source that illuminates the object (see Figure 12.13). Phong works very well for objects that are finely shaded, shiny, reflective, transparent, refractive, or reflective.

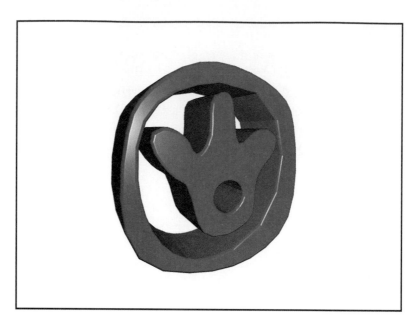

Figure 12.13   *A Phong shaded object*

Blinn

Blinn is the most sophisticated method and accurately displays the diffuse color, the ambient color, the specular color, and the size of the specular highlight (see Figure 12.14). Blinn is superior to Phong in some cases when the object is a smooth, metallic surface or has sharp edges that show a specular streak, or when the object has a light bloom (a large generalized specular area). Generally, Phong is just as useful.

Lambert

Lambert is a simpler algorithm that considers only the diffuse light and ambient light. Objects shaded with the Lambert algorithm appear to have a smooth matte finish with no specularity (see Figure 12.15). Lambert is best for materials that are natural, such as skin or bark, and have no specular highlight or reflectivity.

Constant

The Constant shading method fills in the entire object with the diffuse color. There is no interpolation of colors and, therefore, no shading at all (see Figure 12.16). Because the object has no shading, it appears to be perfectly flat and oriented directly towards the camera with a bright light on it.

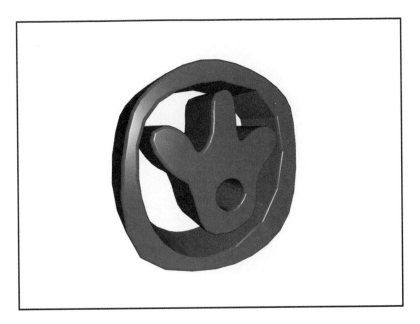

FIGURE 12.14   *A Blinn shaded object.*

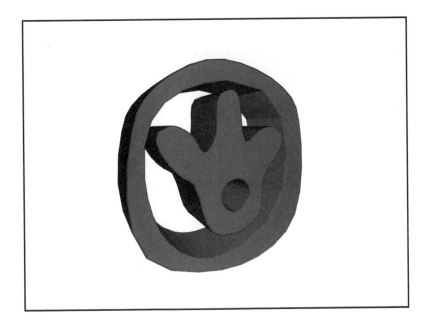

FIGURE 12.15   *A Lambert shaded object.*

FIGURE 12.16 *A Constant shaded object.*

SHADOW

The Shadow algorithm makes the actual object invisible to the camera object. The object, therefore, is invisible in your scene but still casts shadows where there are shadow-casting lights that shine on it (see Figure 12.17). If the shadow object is also partially transparent, it can color the shadows.

THE MANUAL METHOD: COLOR BY VERTEX

For many real-time applications, particularly game development, textured surfaces are too expensive (and time consuming) to render. One alternative to textures is to paint color directly onto each polygon by associating a color with each vertex. This method is often called *Color by Vertex*, and the renderer smoothly interpolates the colors across the surface of the polygon from one vertex to the next, creating a smooth blend (see Figure 12.18). This trick is used extensively in games such as "Super Mario Brothers" to create complex shading patterns without the use of large Texture maps. This option allows you to paint a color onto an object in the Softimage paint program, vertex by vertex.

FIGURE 12.17 *The Shadow shading algorithm.*

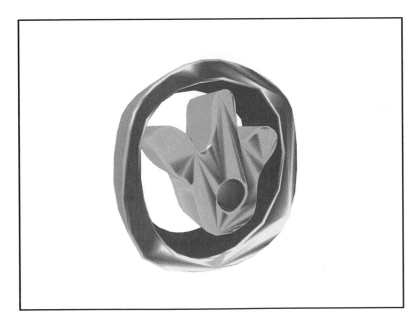

FIGURE 12.18 *An object colored by vertex.*

The Firemarble Press from Riven. Copyright 1998, Cyan.

JOSHUA STAUB

CG Production Director at Cyan, Inc., for Riven: The Sequel to Myst

Currently Art Director for Cyan, Inc.

Joshua: I think it would have to be a combination of all of those. Technique is definitely a part of the equation because I spend a lot of time trying to find creative solutions to solving big problems. The first question I always have for myself is, "How in the heck am I going to do this?" The solution becomes my technique, and hopefully I carry that into other problems. For Riven especially, the workload required a ton of elbow grease. (I think I could have started my own factory making elbow grease!) Working 14 to 18 hours a day (including weekends and most holidays) for years in a row is incredibly grueling, and there were many times during Riven that I could compare my job to working in a factory making car parts or something. Not very stimulating. The artistic part comes when I'm tweaking lighting, textures, and so on and perfecting the scene. That is the refreshing part that makes it all seem worth it. I suppose that is what keeps me going from one scene to the next.

ATR: How long have you been doing what you are doing?

Joshua: I've been at Cyan for four years now. Prior to that I was attending the University of Washington in Seattle. Before that, I did freelance layout/graphics work for various companies in the Bay Area.

I learned 3D graphics, modeling, animation, and so on on my own. I have never taken a single class on anything remotely related to this industry. I have known Robyn Miller (co-founder of Cyan) since I was about 12 years old and learned a lot from him just by watching him.

ATR: Would you characterize your work as art, technique, skill, elbow grease, or something entirely different?

ATR: How does Softimage 3D|Extreme play a part in your day?

Joshua: I spend the most time in the Modeling and Matter modules. Most of what I do deals with modeling, texturing, lighting, and rendering. I spend the least time in the Motion and Actor modules, although I am ultimately intrigued by Softimage's ability to do incredible animations.

In fact, it is really the only software package that I have for my SGIs. So except for post-production work (Adobe After Effects: Mac) and touch-up (Adobe Photoshop: Mac) I'm in Softimage for the majority of my day.

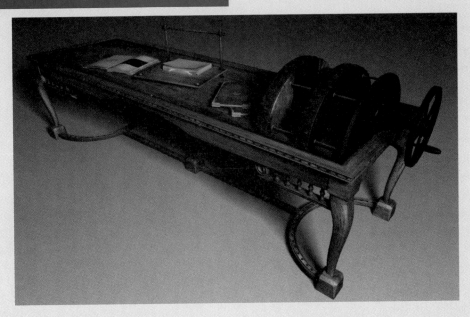

Gehn's book assembly table, from Riven, the sequel to Myst. Copyright 1998, Cyan.

All of my life I've wanted to create things that looked real; real enough to be mistaken for photographs. It's really what motivates me more than anything else. I remember when I was younger people used to tell me that I shouldn't even try to paint or draw realistically because absolute realism could never be achieved. Well, I don't think that I'm quite there yet, but using Softimage has allowed me to get closer than I ever have before. Perhaps the skeptics are right, but I'm sure as heck going to try and prove them wrong!

ATR: Do you ever feel like you use Softimage 3D|Extreme in ways that the designers never intended?

Joshua: Absolutely. I believe that it is pretty well understood that Softimage is a program specially designed to create realistic images, but with a slant towards animation. In other words, Softimage is great for a lot of things, but the ease and power of animating (IK and otherwise) is definitely its strongest point. Most of what I require from Softimage is the ability to create realistic still images, which for me includes handling very detailed and large scenes (2 million+ triangles) with lots of large textures (15,000+ textures) and lots of lights (200+ lights). I know that Softimage was not intended to do these types of computations because I don't believe anyone has ever been crazy enough to make scenes quite as complicated as ours—at least that's what Softimage told us!

Believe it or not, the speed still frustrates me. To be perfectly honest, I blame that on myself. I suppose I won't be completely satisfied until I'm working in my own home, with a huge display (like, 60 inches), working in perfectly realistic scenes that are rendered with radiosity in real time (sound possible?). For the majority of my work in a particular scene, things move very quickly. Unfortunately, the scenes get very large very fast, and inevitably I get bogged down by slow moving models or scenes that just don't render fast enough. A few scenes for Riven took my machine over two hours just to *load*, and up to five hours to *save*. In order to get anything done I had three SGI workstations in my office so that I could work with several scenes at once.

The most rewarding part of the process of working with Softimage is seeing the final rendering. There is still a certain magic to seeing a final image that looks convincingly realistic, complex, and beautiful at the same time.

ATR: What special methods have you developed to make Softimage renderings look distinctively yours?

Joshua: There are various things that I do before I even begin working with a scene that I'm sure a lot of other people do as well. I turn off all ambient lighting (I would rather create my own specific bounce lighting than have the computer just fill any dark areas). Because of that, my scenes tend to have a lot of light sources, most of which aren't actually represented by physical "lights" in the scene (lamps, and

Gehn's chair, from Riven. Copyright 1998, Cyan.

so on). Rooms can contain several dozen lights in order to create the desired effect. I spend a lot of time on textures in order to add realism. Virtually everything in the scene has a color texture (at least one, usually more) and at least one specific "bump map." I actually spend significantly longer on an object's texture than modeling the object itself. In my opinion, most models don't need to be very complicated at all, as long as the texture creates the necessary detail. It is so much more efficient to do it that way anyway.

This may sound boring, but I couldn't do what I do if I wasn't psychotically organized. The size of the scenes I have to work with are horrifying (example: Scenes in excess of 17,000 textures, 6,000 materials, 8,000 shaders, 20,000 separate models, 200 light sources, 2 million triangles, had enough?). Just naming scenes, lights, renderings, and so on is a huge chore. I won't even get into my Schematic views— I keep them meticulous, which takes me hours— because just thinking about them gives me nightmares.

ATR: If you had one wish for the next version, what would you implement?

Joshua: Can I have more than one?

One, the ability to have more than one camera. In other words, I would like to be able to duplicate cameras and place them separately all over the environment.

Two, the ability to duplicate, scale, and group light sources; basically, treat them like objects. I can't tell you how many times I have wanted to take a series of lights, group them (with other objects even!), duplicate them (with their interests) and rotate them around the room (for example: to the other walls).

Finally (although I have many more), I would like to be able to convert displaced (via displacement maps) into real geometry. I rarely use displacement maps, because I can't tell where the displacement extends in order to place objects, lights, and so on on the surface (at least without tedious checking and rendering)!

A typically big scene from Riven, on the Garden Island looking along the East path. Copyright 1998, Cyan.

Copyright 1998, Cyan.

SAVING AND BROWSING MATERIALS

Once you have set up a material just the way you like it, you can save it to use elsewhere in your scene or in another project. Click the Save button and assign a name for it that will be easier to find later, such as "porcelain" instead of "mat1.1-2.3," or whatever Softimage would name the material on its own.

You can also browse the pre-existing library of materials provided in the SI_Materials database by clicking the Select button at the top of the Material Editor dialog and navigating the DB list to that database (see Figure 12.19).

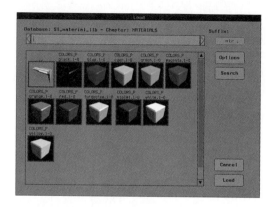

FIGURE 12.19   *The materials in the SI_Materials library.*

In the Material browser, use the Options button to change the view from the unhelpful text list to the more helpful Use Icons view, so you can see what you are choosing. You can also change the sort order of the materials displayed.

TRANSPARENCY, REFLECTION, AND REFRACTION

Each object in a scene might also have some combination of reflection, transparency, and refraction. Generally these effects require the use of Softimage's raytracing engine. The raytracer is automatically invoked at render time when a ray encounters an object with these properties.

Adding transparency with the Transparency slider makes an object progressively less opaque. A transparency of 0 means the object is entirely opaque, while 1 is entirely transparent (see Figure 12.20). As an object becomes less and less visible, so do its material color attributes.

Another important feature of transparency is that the color of the object acts as a filter on rays that pass through it; so placing a blue glass on a white tablecloth results in a blue shadow from light passing through the glass. Generally transparency doesn't look so good unless it is paired with reflectivity and refraction.

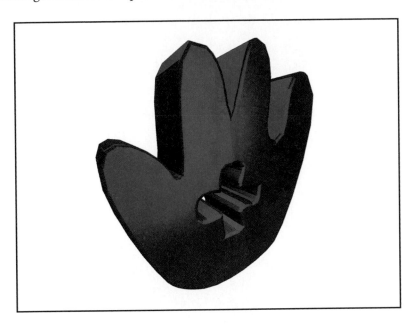

FIGURE 12.20 *Different levels of transparency.*

Adding reflection makes an object reflect those objects around it. When the renderer encounters reflectivity, another ray is cast, bouncing from the reflective surface to strike another object in the scene. The color returned by the reflective ray is then blended with the surface color to get the final image.

You can adjust the reflectivity of an object by changing the value with the Material Editor's Reflectivity slider. A reflectivity of 0 means no reflection, while a reflectivity of 1 means that the object is totally reflective like a mirror and shows no material color at all (see Figure 12.21). Rendering reflection requires the raytracer in either the Softimage renderer or the mental ray.

FIGURE 12.21 *Different levels of reflectivity.*

Refraction is a property that accompanies the property of transparency. When a ray passes from one volume of space (the air) into another volume of space (the object), the ray is bent slightly at the boundary of the two volumes (see Figure 12.22). This effect is most easily observed by sticking your finger in a glass of water. Notice how your finger seems to bend at the boundary between the air and the water. Each translucent volume of matter in the real world has a unique index of refraction that describes how much light bends at the boundary. An index of 1 means no bending at all and an index of about 2.3 is the highest boundary commonly found, which is in a cut diamond. Regular glass has an index of refraction of about 1.2, and cut crystal has an index of refraction of about 1.4. Refraction is a very expensive (time-consuming) effect to render and significantly affects your render times.

Accurate refraction must also be calculated many more times than reflection, because its effects are cumulative, and it must occur at each boundary between transparent objects. For instance, just for a water glass, there are four boundaries for any given ray:

- Air to the first side of the glass
- The inside of the glass to the water
- Water to the far side of the glass
- The far side of the glass to the air

You need to increase the ray depth of the renderer to the maximum number of boundaries you want used in the render calculations. This ray depth can be set at render time in the Options subdialog of the main Render dialog box (see Figure 12.23).

STATIC BLUR

The Static Blur option in the Material Editor is a cheap way to get a simple Glow effect from a polygonal object (see Figure 12.24). The Static Blur effect works by expanding the polygons in an object away from the object center along their normals by an amount you specify in the Width Entry slider. Keep this value low to start out, such as 0.5. Then each polygon is blurred, according to a Decay you specify. If your object has few polygons, this won't work well. Adding polygons with Effect→Subdivision is a good idea. This effect works best for small glowing lights, red dots, and other simple polygonal objects that need to seem self-illuminated.

FIGURE 12.22   *Three different levels of refraction on a transparent object.*

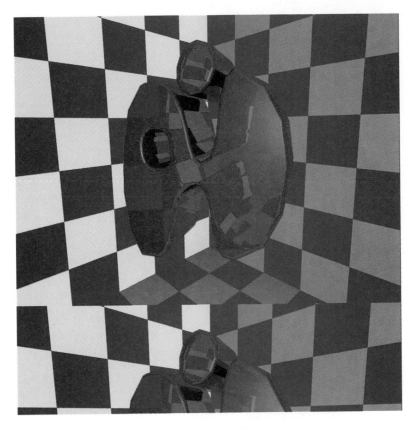

FIGURE 12.23 *The effect of different ray depths on the refraction.*

ANIMATING MATERIALS

You can animate all material attributes in the Material Editor. To help you, the attributes come with F-curves, which are located in the F-curve Select→Material menus (see Figure 12.25).

The process for animating a material is simple:

1. Select a frame.

    Select the object and drag the Time Slider to the frame where you want the Material value to be set. Open the Material Editor by clicking the Material menu cell in the Matter module. You can move the Material Editor out of the way of your Perspective view to get a good view of your scene by clicking the title bar and dragging the window to another corner of your scene.

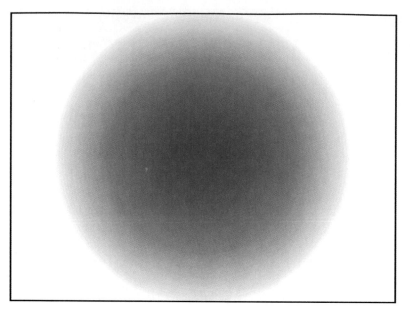

FIGURE 12.24 *Static blur on the knot.*

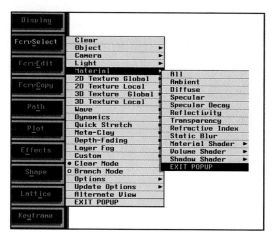

FIGURE 12.25 *The Material F-curve menu cells.*

2. Set the first keyframe.

Set the material parameters the way you want them and press the Key button to save a keyframe for all the attributes at that frame.

3. Change the parameters and set another key.

   Leave the dialog up and drag the Time Slider to a different frame. Change the diffuse color, the ambient color, the reflectivity, and the transparency. Then set another key by clicking the Key button.

4. Check how the values animate.

   Now with the dialog still open, drag the Time Slider back and forth to see the values animate in the Material Editor dialog box. If your Perspective view was shaded, you also see the changes in material color there, although the Shaded view cannot represent transparency, reflection, or refraction.

5. Examine the F-curves.

   Close the dialog box and use the F-curve Select→Material→All command in the Motion module to view the F-curves for the material attributes you keyframed.

GLOBAL AND LOCAL MATERIALS

So far, we have applied a material to a whole object at once. When an object has a single material that covers an object's entire surface, it is called a *global material*. Softimage has the remarkable power, however, to define a material for each polygon in the object or for any number of groups of polygons in an object. A material applied to less than the whole object is called a *local material* (see Figure 12.26).

NOTE

Local materials and textures are possible only for polygonal objects, not for patch-based objects that can use the UV parameter space to accomplish a similar effect.

Local materials can be very useful. Imagine that you want to give material colors to a single-skinned human model that includes the person's clothes and belt as part of the mesh. You could define a material for each area of the model that needs a different color, and then pick colors for denim, skin, leather, and gold as needed to color the skin and the clothes. The resulting model might look like it was composed of many different models cleverly fit together, but it would in fact be a single mesh object, which is much easier to animate.

To create local materials, you must first create a master global material for the whole object. Then and only then can you select a group of polygons and create a local material.

FIGURE 12.26 *Local materials are groups of polygons with different colors.*

The workflow for creating a local material follows three steps:

1. Use the Polygon→Select by Rectangle (supra key Y) or the Polygon→Select by Raycasting (supra key G) methods to select a group of polygons on the object.

2. Execute the Polygon→Assign New Material command in the Matter mode, which creates the local material in the Schematic view and attaches it to the selected group of polygons (see Figure 12.27).

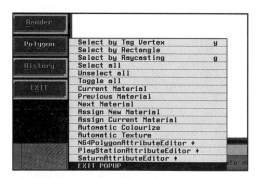

FIGURE 12.27 *The Polygon→Assign New Material menu cell*

3. In the Material Editor dialog that pops up automatically, choose the material attributes you want for this selected group of polygons.

In the Schematic view with the Matter mode on to show the materials and the relations between objects and materials, examine your new object (see Figure 12.28). The local material is connected to the object, just as the global material is. The local material is connected with a red line, indicating that it is the currently active material, the one that will come up if you use the Material menu cell in the Matter module.

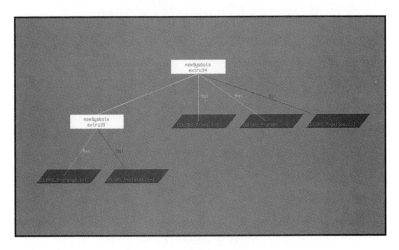

FIGURE 12.28   *When an object has a local material, it has more than one material icon in the Schematic view.*

If you deselect the current group of polygons, select another with the G supra key, and then use Polygon→Assign New Material to add another local material to the object, three materials will be attached in the Schematic view, and the red line will indicate that the new material is the currently active material.

LOCAL MATERIALS DEFINE GROUPS OF POLYGONS

Local materials aren't just a means of coloring objects in a more complex way; they are also a way to save selected groups of polygons on the object and then recall those groups later for other purposes. These saved groups of polygons can be used later for animating the shape of an object, for modeling purposes, or for attaching local textures (discussed later in this chapter). As is so often the case in Softimage 3D|Extreme, the actual use of the tool is left up to your imagination.

You know that you can save these groups of selected polygons with Polygon→Assign New Material, but you also need a way to toggle between the selected groups and activate the different groups of polygons. The Polygon→Next Material and Polygon→Previous Material commands rotate forward and backward through the groups currently stored on each object.

Tutorial: Spinning Top

In this tutorial, you learn how to apply local materials to color in a polygonal object with a pattern of different colors (see Figure 12.29).

Figure 12.29 *Completed spinning top.*

1. Model the Top.

In the Front view, draw the revolution profile of a child's top using a linear spline. When you intend to create polygonal models, the linear spline is a good spline to use because you can precisely control the size and placement of the polygons in the final model. Each linear span between points becomes the edge of one polygon.

Revolve the spline 360 degrees with 12 subdivisions around Y to create the finished top. Move the center of the top to the exact tip where it meets the ground plane using the CTR mode. That way, it spins and wobbles from the tip, not the middle, looking more realistic.

Create a flat surface for the top to revolve on by getting a primitive grid. Scale and translate it to fit just under the top (see Figure 12.30).

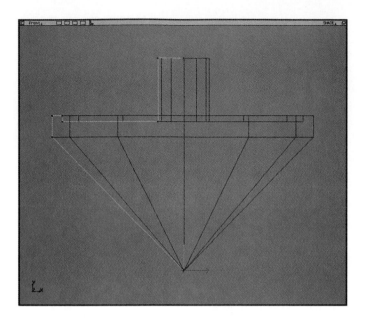

FIGURE 12.30 *The top revolution profile and surface.*

2. **Apply Materials.**

The goal is to paint the top in a pattern of bright colors that blend together as the top spins when finally rendered. First apply a base coat to the top by choosing a global material. Pick a neutral color for the base. Turn the Perspective view window on to Shaded mode, so you can see the color you put on the top.

Next, using the Y supra key, select just those polygons on the top of the toy's stem where you twist the top to start it spinning. Paint those polygons with a new material color by executing the Polygon→Assign New Material command in the Matter module and choosing a bright color, such as red.

Then deselect those polygons with the Y supra key and the middle mouse button, and use the G supra key to select a pattern of alternating polygons on the flat surface of the top by pointing and clicking in the Perspective view to select polygons by raycasting. Assign a new material to these polygons with the Polygon→Assign New Material command and make them yellow.

Continue on, selecting groups of polygons and assigning new material colors until you have painted the top just the way you want.

Examine your handiwork by orbiting the top in the Perspective view (see Figure 12.31).

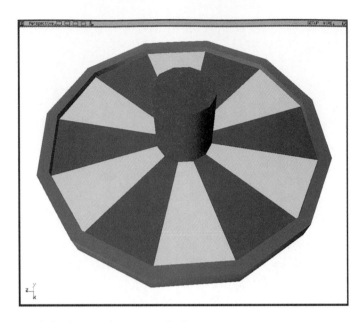

FIGURE 12.31 *Apply local materials to groups of polygons.*

3. Spin the Top.

At frame 1, set a keyframe for the top's rotation around the Y axis (SaveKey→Object→Rotation→Y). Drag the Time Slider to frame 100 and enter 3600 into the direct text entry area of the RotY menu cell. Then set another key for rotation around Y to animate the top spinning completely around 10 times in 100 frames.

Add a bit of wobble by dragging the Time Slider back to frame 1 and setting a keyframe for RotZ. Then move to frame 50, change the value of RotZ to 15, and set another keyframe. Drag forward to frame 80, set the RotZ back to 0, and then set another keyframe so the top comes back to true. At frame 100, rotate the top by hand in Z so that the edge of the top meets the ground plane, as if the top has fallen over and is at rest.

Play back your animation and edit as necessary to make a convincing effect.

4. Render the Top.

To convincingly render the top so that as it spins faster and faster the surface colors become less and less distinct, blurring together, we need to use Motion Blur. However, we need a special kind of Motion Blur. The regular Softimage renderer uses a less accurate method that blurs the object according to changes in translation of the object center, but our center isn't translating; it's rotating. Only the mental ray can solve this render problem for us.

With the top selected, choose the Info→Selection command and then click the Render Setup button in the Object Info dialog to bring up the render controls. Turn on Exact Motion Blur for this object and close the dialogs.

In the Matter module, set up a render using the mental ray. You won't need anti-aliasing, so keep the frame size small, such as 320 × 240 because rendering exact Motion Blur can be time consuming. Turn on the Motion Blur option and set the shutter speed to 0.7, which keeps the virtual shutter open for 70% of each frame except the first and the last.

Render and then take a look at the finished piece in the FlipBook. The completed spinning top illustrates how using local materials can help make a simple object more complex without additional modeling.

COPYING AND SHARING MATERIALS

Because each object in your scene can have one or more materials, a great many individual materials can clutter up your scene. You will need tools to manage this complexity, as well as to save time and energy by reusing the materials you create. The commands to manage and share materials are located in the Mat_Oper (Material Operator) menu cells (see Figure 12.32).

FIGURE 12.32   *The Material Operator menu cells.*

Many times in a scene you will want to use the same material on different objects. In Softimage, there are several ways to accomplish this; all have different advantages.

The simplest method is to name the material in the Material Editor and save the material to disk. When you want to use it again, you can browse the disk to find the saved material and reuse it.

A second method is to copy the material from the object to the new object that needs it (see Figure 12.33). This is accomplished by selecting the object without a material, executing the Mat_Oper→Copy Mat command, and then picking the object that does have the material you want copied. Then each object has an identical copy of the same material, each with different names, so that when you change one, the other is not affected.

FIGURE 12.33   *Objects in the Schematic with copied materials.*

In another commonly occurring situation, you have many objects in a scene that all need to share the same material (see Figure 12.34). Sharing a material means that they all reference the same material, so that when you change the material attributes on one object, all the objects sharing the material automatically change as well. Obviously planning ahead and sharing materials in this manner is a godsend during the editing and refinement portion of production work. To share a material between several objects, select the object without the material, open the Schematic view, and locate the icon for the material you want to share.

Choose the Mat_Oper→Associate command and then pick in the Schematic view directly on the material you want to share. A new line is drawn to the selected object to indicate that it too is using that material definition. As many objects as you want can share a single material in this way.

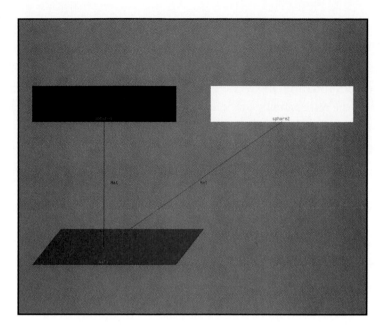

FIGURE 12.34 *Objects in the Schematic sharing one material.*

Sometimes while duplicating objects, or just in the normal process of modeling and animating, many materials are created that have the same attributes but are stored in different files under different names. In addition to cluttering your Schematic view, this slows scene loads and saves quite a bit and has a small impact on renders. You can merge all these similar materials into one, and their parent objects can then share the new material. To do so, use the Mat_Oper→Optimize All command.

If you want only certain models to have their materials optimized and therefore shared, select just those models and try the Mat_Oper→Optimize Selected command.

ALL ABOUT 2D TEXTURES

In Softimage 3D|Extreme, a 2D texture is a special combination of 2D images wrapped onto an object using a projection method, just as you might project an image onto a wall using a slide projector.

You can use any 2D image as a texture, including photographs taken with a digital camera, images you created in a 2D paint program, other rendered frames, or even natural materials, such as wood that you have placed on your scanner bed and scanned. The color component of the 2D texture can variably affect just the ambient color, just the diffuse color, just the specular color, or any combination of the three.

Unlike the slide projector, which projects color information only, 2D textures can also project information about the bumpiness of the surface, the reflectivity of the surface, and the transparency of the surface. This texture information can be used to add realism to a rough surface, to vary the pattern of reflectivity, or to cut away an object entirely, saving modeling time.

Most importantly, in Softimage 3D|Extreme you can layer as many different textures as you want onto the object to create the look you need. The information about the surface provided by the 2D textures is also blended on the object with the object material color and any 3D textures it might have as well. The blending can be done uniformly all over the object, or it can be varied across the surface using either the RGB intensities of the 2D maps or the alpha channel of the 2D maps to multiply the intensity of that texture component. Mental ray shaders can also be used as 2D textures, opening up a universe of procedural (algorithmic) texture options.

In short, the 2D texture controls in Softimage are tremendously robust and sophisticated, and they allow for the best texture work done in the 3D industry. As usual, the controls aren't user friendly, so keep reading to learn how they work.

PREPARING YOUR OBJECT AND CHOOSING A TEXTURE

Before we enter the 2D Texture File dialog, prepare your model for easy texturing. First apply a bright red material to the diffuse color in the Material dialog, so you can easily tell what is material color and what is texture color on the object. Apply a blue to the specular color and change the Specular Decay to 20, creating a large specular highlight. Add a green color for the ambient color. The object should now look similar to Figure 12.35.

Next select the object and frame it in the Perspective view with the F supra key to make it easier to see in the rendered preview. Then call up the 2D Texture File dialog (see Figure 12.36) with the Texture→2D Global command in the Matter module. This huge dialog has all the controls for everything that you can do with 2D textures all arrayed in one confusing mass. We'll break the dialog down into many smaller autonomous chunks, making it easier to deal with.

At the top, two text boxes labeled 2D Texture and Picture Filename rest next to a pair of matching select buttons (see Figure 12.37). These are the controls for loading pre-made textures and for adding new images to a texture you are creating. A 2D texture can contain many different pictures and lots of settings information. The actual images you see are stored in the PICTURE chapter of the database and are accessed with the Picture Filename select button. The *2D Texture file* is the overall master file for all the texture information on an object. Saved in the TEXTURES2D chapter of your database, it contains all the settings from the 2D Texture File dialog and the filenames of the pictures used on the object. Entering a name in the 2D Texture box enables you later to retrieve your combination of pictures and settings easily.

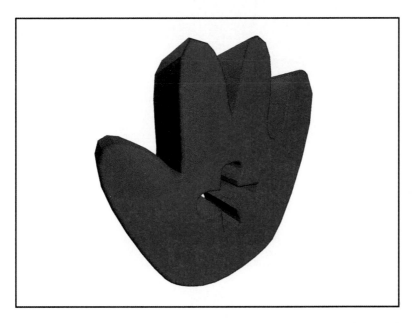

FIGURE 12.35 *The knot, ready for texture testing. The colors make the diffuse, ambient, and specular areas easy to identify.*

Click the Picture Filename select button to call up a file browser and navigate through your file system to locate the standard Softimage image library, called SI_Materials. Enter the PICTURE chapter and then choose a folder to see the contents of that portion of the image library. You can see the images in an Icon mode, which is much more helpful than the default Text mode, by clicking the Options button in the browser and choosing Use Icons (see Figure 12.38). Pick any image that strikes your fancy to apply it to the object and click the Load button to return to the 2D Texture File dialog box.

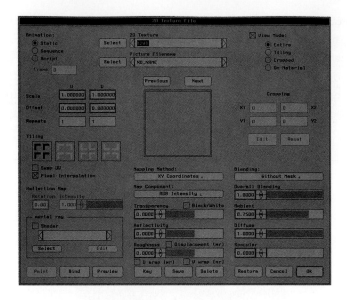

FIGURE 12.36   *The 2D Texture File dialog box.*

FIGURE 12.37   *Browse textures and pictures with the Select buttons.*

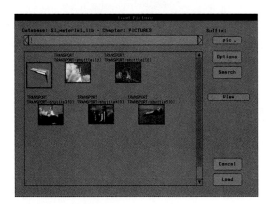

FIGURE 12.38   *Browsing picture files by icon.*

To see the new texture wrapped onto your object, click the Preview button in the lower-left corner. The Preview window appears over the dialog box. Render a preview using the renderer and set up your choice in the Preview Options dialog in the Matter module. Click all three mouse buttons at the same time to exit the preview and return to the 2D Texture File dialog box.

BLENDING

Our first step in understanding the complexities of 2D textures is to tackle the concept of Blending. Objects never arrive at the 2D Texture File dialog in pristine condition. They all have a material color (even if it's the default gray), and they may also have a 3D texture and potentially many other 2D textures. We need a way, therefore, to blend all of them together with great control. The lower-right corner of the dialog gives us that control, with the Blending controls (see Figure 12.39).

FIGURE 12.39   *The Blending controls in the 2D Texture Editor.*

With the first control, the Blending drop-down menu, we specify whether we want the texture applied to the entire surface of the object or masked by either the alpha channel or the intensity of the RGB color values of the map itself. Leave it at the default of Without Mask to simplify the learning process.

Next we determine how much we want this texture to count towards the color of the object by adjusting the Overall Blending slider. If the Overall Blending slider is at 1, no other material color shows through. If it is at 0, however, this texture adds no color information to the surface at all. By adjusting this slider in the intervening range between 0 and 1, you can mix this Texture map with other maps and with the material and 3D Textures (see Figure 12.40).

Overall Blending is the most simple Blending method. Within Overall Blending, you can emphasize or remove the ambient, diffuse, and specular colors (see Figure 12.41).

For instance, if you want the texture to appear mainly in the specular sheen of a highly waxed floor, you would leave Overall Blending at 1 but reduce the Ambient blending and Diffuse blending to 0. The object would then show the ambient and diffuse color from the Material Editor but would mix the texture in the areas of specularity.

In the same way, you could bring up the Ambient blending so that the material color is gradually replaced by the texture in the areas of ambiance. In this way, you can apply a different texture to each color component of the rendered image.

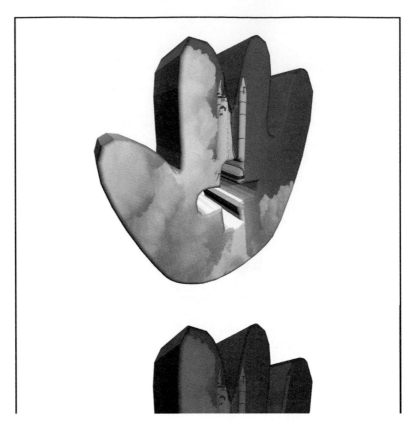

FIGURE 12.40   *Overall Blending at 1, .5, and .25 showing the material color blending with the texture.*

Experiment with different blendings on your test object to get the hang of it, previewing with the Preview button in the dialog's lower-left corner.

TEXTURES IN THE SCHEMATIC VIEW

When you close the 2D Texture File dialog, you still need to be able to tell if a model has a texture applied, and, if so, which one. The Schematic view can also show you textures, as well as models and materials, to give you visual feedback and help you organize your scene. In the title bar of the Schematic view, you can click the Plain mode down arrow to display the Schematic View Mode toggle menu.

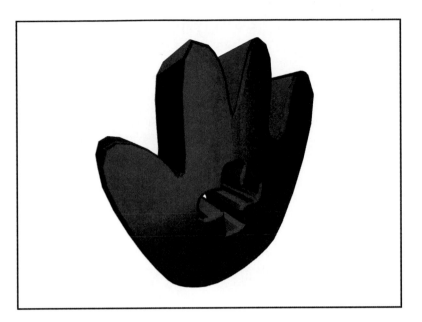

FIGURE 12.41 *With Overall blending at 1.0, but the Diffuse blending at 0, the texture shows through only the specular and ambient areas.*

If you toggle Matter on, you will see textures represented as blue trapezoids connected to the objects that they belong to with a solid line (see Figure 12.42). You can immediately edit the texture definition by selecting a texture icon in the Schematic view and using the Info→Selection command to recall the 2D Texture File dialog. The limitation with editing textures this way is that no preview of the model is available. You can also delete textures directly in the Schematic view by selecting them and using the Delete→Selection command.

You can copy 2D textures between items in the Schematic view, much like you can copy materials between objects. You can choose to copy all the textures from one object to another with the Txt_Oper→Copy All command, or just selected textures if the source object has more than one, with the Txt_Oper→Copy Selection command. Either way, the correct method is to select the object with no textures, then execute the Copy command, and then pick the object that has the textures you want to copy. This method can also be used to copy textures to selected polygons, and several other workflow enhancements exist for people who have to texture many polygonal objects day in and day out, such

> **NOTE**
>
> The Schematic View Mode drop-down menu indicator is prone to disappearing in certain common circumstances. If you run Softimage on a monitor with a resolution of less than the standard 1280 × 1024, it goes away (as does a lot of other stuff). If you toggle onmore than one Mode option, such as Motion and Matter, it goes away and the only thing that shows is a small down arrow mixed in with the Open/Close button. If you just know that it is there, you can still click it.

as 3D gamers. Check the manuals for the full details on the use of the other commands in the Txt_Oper menu cell (see Figure 12.43).

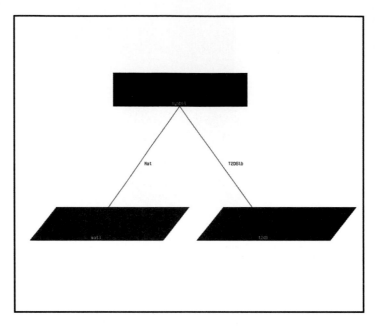

FIGURE 12.42   *Textures show up in the Schematic view if you toggle on the Matter option.*

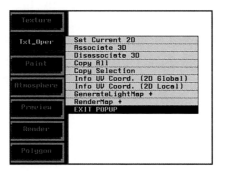

FIGURE 12.43   *The Txt_Oper menu cells.*

CROPPING YOUR TEXTURES

Sometimes the images you bring to the 2D Texture File dialog need to be cropped before using them. Perhaps this is because of an unsightly line around the edge of the image, or perhaps you just want to use a smaller portion of the image. There are three ways to crop the image. The toughest is to enter a crop amount in pixels directly into the numerical cropping feedback boxes. These boxes, X1, X2, Y1, and Y2, give the region of the image that is considered in the render. You can also click directly onto the fine cropping lines in the actual tile to drag them and select the area of the image to use.

The most accurate way is to enter the special Cropping dialog box by clicking the Cropping Edit button (see Figure 12.44). In the Cropping dialog, you can use the cropping lines to more accurately determine the area you want used, and you can save the results of your cropping as a separate file.

FIGURE 12.44   *The Cropping controls.*

MAPPING METHODS AND TXT MODE

Once you choose a texture, Softimage needs to know how to apply it to the object's surface. Remember the texture is fundamentally a 2D image, and the object is a 3D object, so Softimage needs some way to wrap the 2D plane around the 3D object to fix the texture onto the surface. That process is called *Texture mapping*, and Softimage supports several methods (see Figure 12.45). The simplest one, *Projection mapping*, is available for all objects, including both polygonal and patch-based surfaces. The more complex *UV mapping* method is available only for patch-based objects because it relies on the UV parameter space set up by the patch. The last method, *Reflection mapping*, is available for all surfaces but is used in a slightly different way to create more complex-looking reflective surfaces.

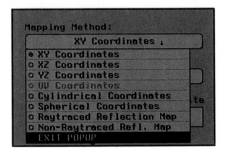

FIGURE 12.45   *The mapping methods drop-down menu.*

Texture mapping is so important that it gets its very own mode, the TXT mode. When you enter the TXT mode by clicking the TXT box in the mode box area of the lower-right corner onscreen (see Figure 12.46), all the Transformation menu cells apply only to transformations of Texture mapping. You will be able to scale, translate, and rotate the texture to fit exactly how and where you want it on the model.

When you use the TXT mode in the Wireframe views, you will see a red Wireframe representation of the Texture mapping method, but in the Shaded view you can get a live update of the Texture map projected onto the object by changing the Shaded mode setup to use Hardware Texture mapping and no display optimization.

FIGURE 12.46   *The TXT mode box on.*

PROJECTION MAPPING

Projection mapping is the method required for texturing polygonal objects, because polygonal meshes don't have a UV coordinate system to use as a texture space.

Without a UV coordinate system to use for mapping the texture onto the surface, the next best thing is to project a texture onto the surface, just like shining a slide projector onto the object and then recording how the texture wraps around the model. To use a Projection mapping method, use the Mapping Method drop-down menu to choose one of the three default planes of projection: XY Coordinates, XZ Coordinates, or YZ Coordinates. This determines the starting projection plane used to map the texture (see Figure 12.47). For instance, if you have a floor in your scene and want a tile pattern mapped onto it, the floor lies in the XZ plane, so the texture should be projected using XZ coordinates. If you project a texture correctly onto a flat surface, the texture maps perfectly without any distortion. If you choose the wrong plane to project it, the result will likely look like a striped mess.

PROJECTION PROBLEMS

In addition to user errors, Projection mapping has some severe problems. On a round object, the projection plane is correct only for the small spot on the front and back of the object that is flat to the projection plane. On all other areas of the object, the texture is progressively more and more distorted as the object surface gets perpendicular to the projection plane. On the side of the objects, the texture is badly smeared into streaks (see Figure 12.48). On an object with faces at right angles, like a cube, the distortion problem is particularly acute. Texture mapping is correct for only two of the six sides and looks terrible on the others.

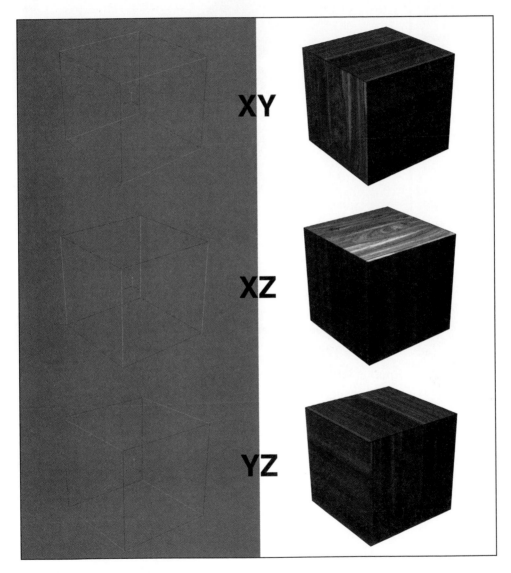

FIGURE 12.47 *The three Projection mapping methods.*

Real-time and game applications generally require that polygonal meshes with complex Texture mapping be used, so there are several ways to generate a fake UV mapping coordinate system for a polygonal mesh in Softimage. This new fake UV coordinate system can then be used to bind 2D textures flat to each polygon on an object, like pinning a poster onto a cube with thumbtacks at each corner of each face.

The old method of generating a list of UV mappings for each vertex was to use the TXT_Oper→Info UV Coord command on an object with a texture projection mapped onto it. This method was critical for animating characters that changed shape during animation because the textures would then stay on the areas of the object where they started out, even while the object stretched and deformed.

The new method is to use the more robust UV mapping tools in the Paint system, which includes lots of handy tools for game animators to affix textures directly to selected polygons and to paint directly on polygonal objects.

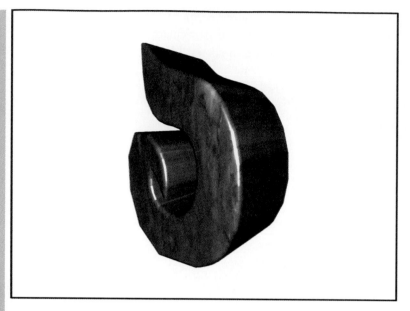

FIGURE 12.48   *Projection mapping smears on rounded objects.*

The only solution to this problem is to apply the 2D textures locally to each group of polygons that has a significantly different orientation, so you can match the projection plane needed for each group of polygons.

Another limitation of Projection mapping is that as the shape of an object changes in a projected texture, the part of the texture that shines on each polygon changes. Imagine holding your fist in front of a slide projector and then opening it, changing hand shapes. The patterns of light on your fingers changes, which wouldn't be what you want in most circumstances. Patch-based UV mapping doesn't have these problems, making ease of texturing another huge advantage of patch-based surfaces.

To modify the Projection method to fit your needs, choose the XY Coordinates mapping method, close the 2D Texture File dialog, and then click the TXT mode. Observe the rectangular red projection guide in the Wireframe Perspective view. You can now change the rotation of this projection guide with the Rotation menu cells to get a projection plane that isn't exactly lined up with the axes (see Figure 12.49). Slightly rotating the projection plane reduces the stretching artifacts that characterize planar

Projection mapping. You may also translate and scale the texture projection area to affect just the area of the model you want it to.

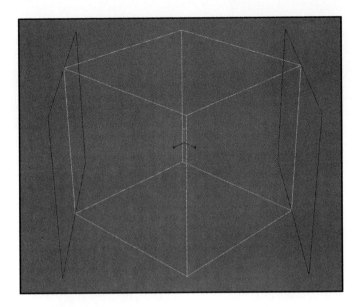

FIGURE 12.49 *Transforming the texture in TXT mode.*

NON-PLANAR PROJECTION MAPPING

Another option is to use the non-planar Projection methods also located in the Mapping Methods drop-down menu, which work better for some models.

Cylindrical mapping creates a cylinder around your object and projects the image evenly from the surface of the cylinder inward to the object (see Figure 12.50). A cylinder works well for objects that are rounded but still streaks at the flat top and bottom of objects where the surface becomes perpendicular to the cylinder. As usual, you can use the TXT mode to transform the projection to your liking.

Spherical mapping creates a ball-shaped projection around the object that evenly projects the image inward towards the object in the middle (see Figure 12.51). Spherical projection works well for very round objects, but pinching can be evident at the poles of the objects.

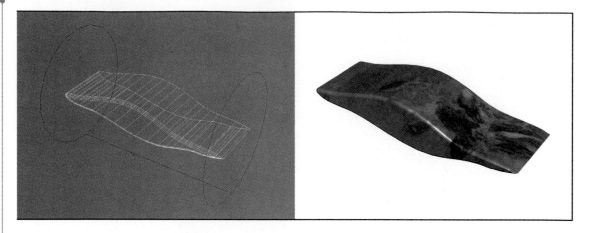

FIGURE 12.50 *The Cylindrical mapping method.*

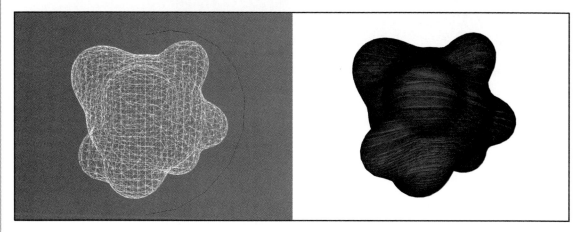

FIGURE 12.51 *The Spherical mapping method.*

UV MAPPING

UV mapping is a much easier way to exactly control how a texture is positioned onto a surface. However, because only patch-based objects have a UV coordinate system, UV mapping is available only in the Mapping Method drop-down menu for patch and NURBS objects.

When a texture is mapped onto an object using the UV coordinates, the parameter space is translated into a texture space for the surface. By default, the texture is placed so that the top-left corner of the image is pinned to the corner of the surface where the U and V parameters begin, and the lower-right corner of the image is pinned to the corner of the surface where the U and V parameters end (see Figure 12.52). This way the texture is guaranteed to stretch across the entire surface, but the texture can be located anywhere on the patch. It can also be scaled to any size and aspect by reassigning the location of the top-left and bottom-right corners.

FIGURE 12.52 *A rendered UV map.*

You can change the scale and location of the texture visually by leaving the 2D Texture File dialog and using the TXT mode to translate and scale the texture (see Figure 12.53).

The texture appears as a red rectangle projected onto the surface in the Wireframe view, and if Hardware Texture mapping is enabled, the texture is displayed in the Shaded view.

A UV map remains attached perfectly to the surface, as if it's spraypainted on, even if the surface changes shape over time. Sometimes this effect is called a decal map because the texture hugs the curves of the surface so perfectly. UV mapping is a perfect way to attach skin textures to objects that deform as they move. Read the reparameterization section in Chapter 8, "NURBS Modeling," for more information about how the parameterization of the patch surface affects how the texture looks when finally rendered.

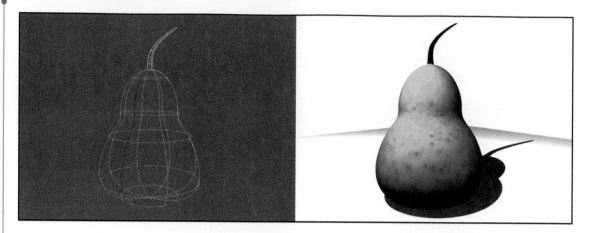

FIGURE 12.53 *UV mapping in the TXT mode.*

The only major problem with UV mapping arises when you apply a Texture map to an object and the texture is upside down or flipped 90 degrees from how you want it. If the texture appears rotated by 90 degrees, the texture aligns with the top along U when you want the top along V. You can swap this in the 2D Texture File dialog by checking the Swap UV check box. If the texture appears to be upside down, the problem is that the top of the image is mapped to the top U or V parameter when it needs to be mapped to the bottom U or V parameter. Unfortunately, there is no control to fix this in the 2D Texture File dialog, but if you leave it, you can invert the U or V parameterization with the Effect→Curve Controls dialog in the Model module.

REFLECTION MAPPING

Reflection mapping isn't just a Mapping method; it's a technique for adding realism to reflective surfaces (see Figure 12.54). One of the problems with reflective surfaces in a rendered scene is that there is usually not that much stuff to reflect compared to the real world. For instance, in the real world the reflections on a water glass seem beautifully complex, blurry, and indistinct at the same time because there is so much in the environment that surrounds the glass.

A Reflection map is another Texture map wrapped in a giant ball around the entire scene, like the sky wraps around the Earth. In such a map when a reflected ray bounces off the reflective object, it is guaranteed to hit something before it expires. This use of a Reflection map, sometimes called an Environment map in other 3D programs, adds greatly to the realism of reflective objects in scenes that have very little else in them.

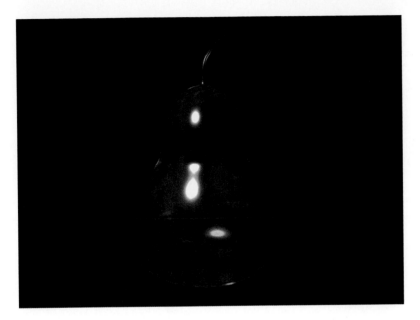

FIGURE 12.54   *Glass with Reflection maps.*

Reflection maps also can be used to simulate reflection without casting reflective rays. In this case, the Reflection map is mapped directly onto the object, just like a Texture map, but is projected in such a way that the texture shifts as the angle of the camera to the object changes. For instance, as the camera moves by a large plate glass window with a Reflection map of a street scene, the texture of the street scene shifts and distorts instead of staying stuck onto the surface of the glass. When a non-raytraced Reflection map is used, the object can be rendered with the scanline renderer instead of the raytracer, which can dramatically cut down rendering time. Non-raytraced Reflection maps are fast enough to be used in real-time systems, such as the N64 and the Softimage Paint system (see Figure 12.55).

You can add a Reflection map to the object by choosing the Raytraced or Non-Raytraced Reflection Map options in the Mapping Method drop-down menu.

To see the reflection, the object must have some reflectivity added in the Material Editor dialog. Keep in mind that if you choose Raytraced Reflection Map, the object will have a Reflection map and reflect the objects around it, while if you choose Non-Raytraced Reflection Map, the object will have only the Reflection map and will not reflect other objects in the scene.

FIGURE 12.55 *No Reflection map, raytraced Reflection map, and non-raytraced Reflection map.*

You can adjust the intensity of the Reflection map to gain more subtle effects by adjusting the Reflection Map Intensity slider. You can rotate the map to make it less square to the rest of the scene with the Reflection Map Rotation text entry box.

USING INTENSITY MAPS

Softimage does not have to apply a map evenly across the entire surface of the object. You can use an *Intensity map* to vary how much of a texture effect is shown at each location on the object. Imagine that you are drawing a stencil, for example, and you want the color, the bump, and the reflectivity to show on the object only in the area of the stencil. This is easy to do in Softimage once you understand how the Map Component and Blending drop-down menus work (see Figure 12.56).

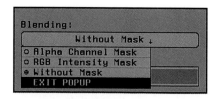

FIGURE 12.56 *The Blending method drop-down menu.*

In the final render, Softimage uses an Intensity map to multiply the value of a given effect. Multiplying by a low Intensity value results in very little of the effect, and multiplying by a high Intensity gives a greater effect. The Intensity map is a 256-value grayscale gradient from completely black to completely white with 254 shades in between. The question is, where do you get this map?

Softimage can use either the combined values of the Red, Green, and Blue channels in an RGB image to add up to an Intensity map, called the RGB intensity, or it can use the contents of the alpha channel, the fourth channel in a Softimage .pic file, as the map component (see Figure 12.57). If you want to use the Intensity map to control the blending of the color values (ambient, diffuse, and specular), you select either RGB Intensity Mask or Alpha Channel Mask from the Blending drop-down menu. If you want to use an Intensity map on the Roughness, Transparency, or Reflection map, you can choose which method to use with the Map component drop-down menu located just below the Mapping Method drop-down menu in the middle of the dialog.

BUMP MAPS, REFLECTION MAPS, AND TRANSPARENCY MAPS

In the middle of the 2D Texture File dialog, below the Mapping Coordinate drop-down menu, are the three sliders that control the Transparency, Reflection, and Bump (or Roughness) maps (see Figure 12.58). In addition to adding color to an object, Softimage's 2D textures can:

- Rough up the object's surface (a Bump map).
- Create patterns of reflectivity on the object (a Reflection map).
- Make parts of the object more or less transparent (a Transparency map).

These maps can add a great deal of detail and realism to a scene and they aren't all that hard to use.

BUMP

When you want to add some roughness to the object, just change the value of the Roughness slider. Generally a value in the range of −1 to 1 will suffice. Then when the renderer works on the object, it evaluates the areas of light and dark on the Texture map. It creates the illusion that the dark areas are depressed into the surface and the light areas are raised out of the surface (see Figure 12.59).

FIGURE 12.57 *The knot with Uniform blending, RGB Intensity Mask blending, and Alpha Channel Mask blending.*

FIGURE 12.58 *The Roughness, Reflectivity, and Transparency sliders.*

FIGURE 12.59 *A Bump map on the knot.*

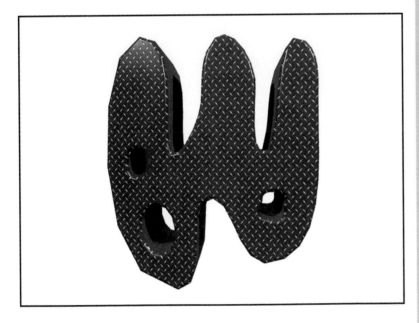

FIGURE 12.60 *A negative bump.*

NOTE

All the Texture sliders in Softimage 3D can be set to either positive or negative values, so there are no rules that light colors are bumped out or that dark colors become more transparent (see Figure 12.60). You can have it either way just by changing a positive value to a negative value or vice versa. This is extremely useful in production because half the time when you get a Texture map from a texture artist the map values are exactly the inverse of what you want.

The Softimage value sliders can be negative, but that doesn't matter! You can try it both ways. When people ask you how you want your masks in the alpha channel, say mysteriously, "It doesn't matter. In Softimage it's all relative!"

The Bump Mapping algorithm is a fake. The object's surface doesn't change shape; the renderer just lightens and darkens areas of the surface as prescribed (see Figure 12.61).

To understand, think of a concrete example. If you look at a dent or a divot in something like ice cream or styrofoam in a room with one light off to the side, and you cover one eye so you can't get any depth perception, you still have no problem seeing that a chunk is taken out of the surface. What you see is that the sides of the divot change shade according to their angle to the light. The back of the divot has more light shining directly on it, so it's lighter than the surface. The front of the divot (closest to the light) has less light on it because the angle to the light is less direct and because it is shadowed by the surface itself.

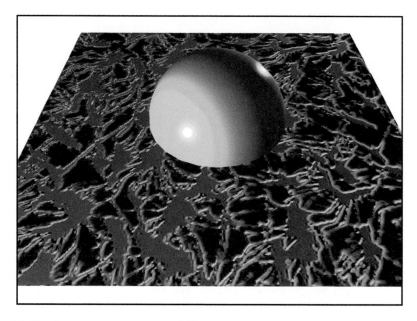

FIGURE 12.61 *Bump mapping is an optical illusion.*

This change in the shade, from light to dark, gives us the visual cue to see the divot as a depression in the surface. The problem is that it depends on the angle of the light to the divot. For example, remember those cool images of the surface of the moon showing craters and how if you looked at them long enough they started to look like bumps instead of craters? That's because you were looking at a 2D image of a bumpy surface with only one light source. It becomes ambiguous after a while whether the surface is bumped in with the light source to the right or bumped out with the light source to the left.

The Roughness slider in Softimage creates exactly this kind of optical illusion by examining the Texture map and using it to bend the surface normals of the object either towards or away from the light source (or light sources). Thus, the surface normals render areas of the surface either lighter or darker than normal.

The degree that the normals are bent, or perturbed, depends on the pixel value of the Texture map that is mapped onto that section of the surface.

You can use the combined values of the color portion of the Texture map to create the bumps by setting the Map Component dropdown menu to RGB Intensity. You can also use the contents of the alpha channel of the texture to bump the surface by setting the Map component to alpha channel.

> **TIP**
>
> You can use a mental ray 2D texture shader to generate alpha values for Bump maps, creating an infinitely large, never repeating, totally procedural Bump effect. Check the mental ray section for the details.

REFLECTION

You can use the 2D Texture map to create a pattern of reflectivity on the surface of the selected object by adjusting the Reflectivity slider. When you add reflectivity in the Materials dialog, you are making the entire object equally reflective, but in real life there are often variations in the reflectivity of a surface. A mirror may have rusted spots on the silver backing, making some areas less reflective than others. A shiny lamp may have areas that are tarnished and, therefore, less reflective. A tile floor may have some tiles that are shiny and reflective and others that are not.

With a Reflection map you can change the reflectivity all over the surface of the object to create more complex looks. Reflectivity values in the range of −1 to 1 are usually sufficient. You can use either the RGB intensity (see Figure 12.62) or the alpha channel to provide the reflectivity information.

A good complement to Reflection maps is a Specular map, which is used in the same way. Because specularity is really just a diffuse reflection of the light sources, the two attributes often go together. To create a Texture map that adds detail to the reflectivity and specularity of an object based on the RGB intensity (the grayscale value) of a Texture map, turn the Overall Blending up to 0.75 but the Diffuse and Ambient Color sliders all the way down to 0. Then bring the Specular and Reflective sliders up to 0.9 and render a preview to see the effect (see Figure 12.63).

FIGURE 12.62 *The knot with an Intensity map varying the reflectivity of the surface.*

FIGURE 12.63 *The knot with Intensity maps on the reflectivity and specularity.*

TRANSPARENCY

Softimage can use a Transparency map at render time to determine which areas of the image are visible and which are not. The Transparency map can also be used to make objects partially translucent and to vary the degree of transparency in transparent objects such as glass (see Figure 12.64).

FIGURE 12.64 *The knot with an Intensity map on the transparency.*

For instance, if you need to create a chain link fence in your scene, you could model or create it with a Transparency map. Modeling a chain link fence would be very challenging and one very heavy object when you are done, probably creating all kinds of rendering and workflow hassles. But you could also take a picture of a chain link fence with a digital camera and then use a paint program to fill the holes in the fence with pure black and everything else with pure white. This fence pattern could be applied to a simple grid as a Transparency map with the Transparency slider all the way up to 1, making the black areas completely invisible and the white areas completely visible at render time.

Transparency maps render fast enough to be used in real-time applications, such as video games, and can be used to dramatically cut down on the amount of geometry needed for some models.

Another great use for Transparency mapping is to create more complex and attractive transparent objects, such as thick hand-blown glasses. In natural glass, the material is not all consistently transparent. Areas of the glass are more or less transparent, more or less rough, and more or less reflective. By wrapping a 2D texture around a glass and applying the value not to the color but to the reflectivity, roughness, and transparency, you can make the surface look much more natural (see Figure 12.65).

FIGURE 12.65   *Better glass with Opacity map.*

Try this out by modeling a glass, applying a partially transparent and reflective material in the Material Editor, and applying a map to the glass with a Cylindrical Mapping method. Set the Overall Blending to 0 in the 2D Texture File dialog; make small incremental changes to the Transparency, Roughness, and Reflectivity sliders; and then preview it in Matter mode. For best results, place the glass in a scene with a few other objects and something behind it so the glass has objects to reflect and refract.

TILING

Very often you will have a texture, such as a wood pattern or a grass pattern, that you want to repeat indefinitely across a surface. This is easy to set up in Softimage 3D. The text entry boxes marked U and V for Scale, Offset, and Repeats provide the necessary controls (see Figure 12.66). If you want to limit the texture to appear on only a portion of the surface, you can adjust the scale and offset manually (the hard way), or you can use the TXT Mode Transformation menu cells to do the job (the easy way).

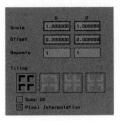

FIGURE 12.66   *The Tiling controls in the 2D Texture File dialog.*

Then you just set how many repeats you want in the U direction and in the V direction. The four tiles below the repeat entry boxes demonstrate the alternatives for rotating the tiles as they are laid down. Some tiles look better in different configurations and sometimes the seams between tiles can be minimized by changing the Tiling method. Click the Tiling radio button in the top-right corner of the screen to get an idea of how the Tiling patterns look, and then experiment by selecting different methods.

ANIMATED TEXTURES

You can, of course, animate all the parameters of the Texture dialog by setting keyframes at different points in the timeline with the Key button at the bottom of the 2D Texture File dialog box. All the F-curves for textures can be found in the Motion module under the F-curve Select→2D Texture Global or Local menu cells.

You can also apply a series of images to be mapped onto a surface, like playing a movie on an object within your animation. To accomplish this extraordinary feat, use the Picture Filename Select button to choose the first file in an animated sequence as the Texture map, and then click the Animation Sequence button at the top-left corner of the screen. When each new frame is rendered, the next frame in the sequence is used as the Texture map.

The lower option, Animation Script, is even more powerful and allows you to write a simple text file that contains the names of the files to be used in order. You can use this simple script file to animate loops and make other more complex decisions for each frame of the Texture map.

LAYERING COMPLEX TEXTURES

To create realistic textures you will often need to apply multiple 2D Texture maps to the same objects, layering them over and over each other while carefully adding in detail to the model's color, the specularity, the reflection, the transparency, and the bumpiness. Some models may require many different maps applied to different locations; some may require that maps be applied to the object and then painted to reveal details on the surface (see Figure 12.67).

Layering textures is an art form and there are no hard and fast rules for doing it. You need to look at the object, see what it needs, and then understand the texture controls well enough to add that lacking component back into the mix.

TIP

Using lots of textures to create super realistic surfaces is most effective in situations where the images can be viewed at high resolutions, such as CD-ROM games and film special effects. In TV work, textures are often a very bad idea because television (and demo reels in particular) are usually of such low quality that the textures will look very bad. In addition, because televisions scan every other line vertically and then go back to draw in the missing lines (the lines in each drawing pass are called fields), textures on TV and VHS tape tend to crawl, vibrate, and in general look awful. If you take a good look at professional TV graphics, such as those on the evening news, you'll notice that they never use textures, but instead rely on patterns of color and light to create visually stunning effects.

In Softimage, you can have as many 2D textures on each model as you wish. Each can be blended differently or applied to a different component of the image, and each can use a different Mapping method and Mapping component. For instance, you can use one texture for the color of the object, applying it to the diffuse and ambient colors, but apply another map entirely to the specular portion to create an iridescent look. Then you can apply another to add the roughness to the object and one more as a Transparency map to cut away part of the object, making it completely invisible. The sky is the limit and it is up to you to find your own style.

To layer several textures onto a single object, enter the 2D Texture File dialog by clicking the Texture→2D Global menu cell. Select the first texture by clicking the Picture Filename Select button, browsing the SI_Materials database or your own texture files, and loading the texture. Adjust the Mapping method to work with your object and then consider the matter of blending.

USING THE BLENDING CONTROLS

Generally, when layering textures over one another, you should apply them to different components of the image, but you can also blend the textures together into the same components by reducing Overall Blending to 0.5 or 50 percent. You can adjust the blending for the ambient, diffuse, and specular colors to get different effects (see Figure 12.68).

FIGURE 12.67 *Layering textures helps achieve realism.*

Once your first texture is to your liking, click the Next button above the image tile in the middle of the 2D Texture File. When you click the Next button, the current texture is saved and a new texture is created for the same object. You can now browse the SI_Materials database to select a new picture, assign it a new Mapping method, and decrease Overall Blending to allow the previous texture to mix with this one. Click the Preview button to see the results.

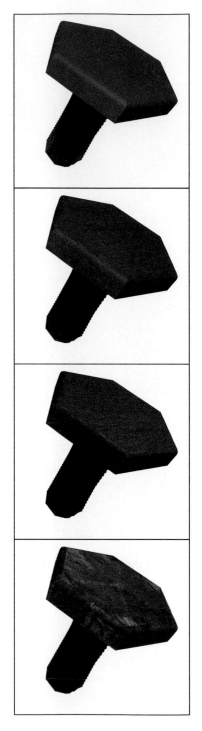

FIGURE 12.68 *With each texture layer, the nut looks more realistic.*

You can toggle back and forth between the two textures that you now have by clicking the Previous and Next buttons in the 2D Texture File dialog (see Figure 12.69). When you switch out of one texture for the first time, you are prompted to save the new texture.

FIGURE 12.69 *The Next and Previous buttons for blending multiple textures.*

The blending amounts are proportionate between textures, not absolute, so you can assign both textures an Overall Blending of 90% if you want. Remember to use the Blending controls differently on textures to bring out more of one texture in the diffuse, ambient, and specular portions of the image.

BLENDING WITH RGB AND ALPHA MASKS

Each texture can also have its own alpha channel mask, so you can limit one texture to display only within this mask by using the Blending drop-down menu.

If you apply a texture using the alpha channel blending mask and the texture doesn't have an alpha channel, nothing of the texture shows through on the object. You can exploit this by applying a texture with an alpha channel mask, and then painting the alpha channel mask directly on the object in the Softimage 3D paint module, causing the texture to show through on the object only where you make strokes with your 3D paintbrush.

If you don't want to go to the trouble of creating an alpha channel mask, but you still want the texture effect applied with some variation in intensity across the object, you can use the RGB intensity of the texture to blend the texture more or less. This works best when there are dramatic differences in lightness and darkness in the Texture map.

By cleverly combining textures, you can create completely different patterns of diffuse color, reflectivity, specularity, and more, either all over the object or just in specific areas.

GLOBAL AND LOCAL TEXTURES

Just like local and global materials, you can apply local and global 2D textures. Global 2D textures affect the entire object, but local 2D textures apply only to a selected group of polygons. In fact, the local 2D textures rely on the definition of the local materials to determine which groups of polygons a texture is mapped onto. Put another way, the local 2D textures are added onto the local material definitions.

An object can have any number of local textures (see Figure 12.70), but it is usually not a good idea to have a global texture on the same object unless the blending for that global texture is set quite low.

FIGURE 12.70 *Local textures on a single model.*

To apply a local 2D texture, first select the model and add a global material. Then use the Polygon Selection tools to select the group of polygons you want the texture on, and create a local material with the Polygon→Assign New Material command in the Matter module. Then check the Schematic view to see that the model has two materials on it and that the new local material is the active one, marked with a red line. (Remember, you can show materials and textures in the Schematic view by toggling on the Matter display option in the Schematic view.)

To apply a 2D local texture to the currently active local material, select the Texture→2D Local command to bring up the 2D Texture File dialog. From here, all the texture options for local textures are exactly the same as for global textures.

ALL ABOUT 3D TEXTURES

Softimage's final type of texture, a 3D texture, is a procedural texture, meaning it isn't defined by a two-dimensional picture but is rather the result of a three-dimensional algorithm that describes the texture as it moves through three-dimensional space. A 3D texture never repeats and never really has a starting or ending point on the surface. It never has a Mapping method and isn't restricted to a UV parameter space. It extends infinitely through the entire scene, described by a formula that is calculated only at render time. Because it is calculated in the renderer only, it is never visible in Wireframe or Shaded mode. You have to render to see the results (see Figure 12.71).

In real life, most textures are in fact 3D. When you examine the pattern of veins on a rock face, you know that they exist inside the rock as well, and if you flake off portions of the rock, you find that the pattern has changed underneath. Wood works the same way; as you cut through it you find different patterns of grain running through it.

In Softimage, three main algorithms are used to create 3D procedural textures: Wood, Marble, and Cloud. Each has a different look and each makes different patterns of color. Each also has a series of control sliders that you can adjust to change how the patterns change through space. You can also change the colors of the veins that run through the 3D texture. 3D procedural textures can be used to blend in the color of an object, including variable diffuse, ambient, and specular colors, the roughness, and the transparency.

To apply a 3D procedural texture, select the object and use the Texture→3D Global command to call up the 3D Solid Texture dialog box (see Figure 12.72). You can browse saved textures, including the library of prepared textures in the SI_material_lib database, by clicking the Select button at the top of the dialog.

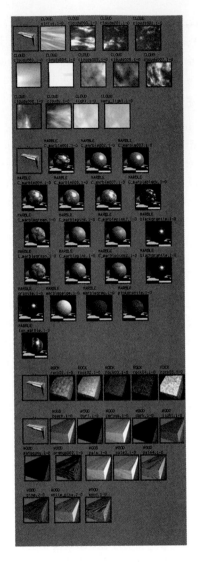

FIGURE 12.71 *Examples of 3D textures that ship with Softimage 3D.*

If you want to mix your own texture, start by selecting a texture type at the top from Marble, Wood, and Cloud. Then click each one of the color tiles in the Color Map section and change the color to your liking with the Color sliders or by selecting the color in the Color palette. You can also change the distribution of the colors in the Color gradient by clicking the small arrows that point to the gradient and dragging them left or right. Each vein in the texture may also have an associated alpha value. This alpha value is blended along with the color in the finished 3D procedural texture and can be used to make the 3D texture transparent, bumpy, or reflective. The

RGB intensity can also be used for Reflection, Transparency, and Bump maps. The alpha channel for each vein can be adjusted with the A slider.

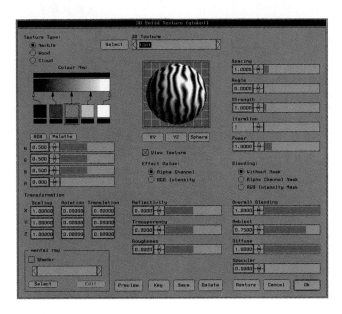

FIGURE 12.72 *The 3D Solid Texture dialog.*

The entire procedural texture can be transformed over the model by changing the Transformation Matrix located in the lower-left corner of the dialog. This is most useful for setting keyframes with different transformations, thereby causing the 3D texture to animate through time and space when rendered. This can create psychedelic patterns of shifting color or evolutions of shape in cloud patterns.

The sliders for Spacing, Angle, Strength, and Iteration all control specific variables in the 3D algorithms used to create the texture.

The Blending controls work exactly the same as the Blending controls in the 2D Texture File dialog. They allow you to determine which component of the 3D texture to pass through into the final image and whether to mask the 3D texture with the RGB intensity or the alpha channel. Unfortunately, you cannot layer more than one 3D procedural texture onto a surface.

TIP

As a short cut, a color can be copied from one tile to another by selecting the target tile with the left button and then clicking the target tile with the middle mouse button to copy over the color.

Reflectivity, Transparency, and Roughness sliders also work exactly the same as they do for 2D textures.

Of course, all the parameters can be animated over time by setting keyframes with the Key button. All the F-curves for these parameters are located in the F-curve Select→3D Texture (Global) menu cells.

CONCLUSION

The visual appearance of an object is affected more than anything by the material and textures you choose for that object. By carefully picking colors and textures, you can imitate the most realistic natural coloring or create fantastic visions of rioting color that could only come from a computer.

In this chapter you learned how to:

- Choose the appropriate shading algorithm for each model
- Choose the ambient, specular, and diffuse material attributes
- Use reflection, transparency, and refraction in a material
- Set projection texture maps onto objects
- Use 3D procedural textures

ANIMATION & RENDERING

Image courtesy of Annesa Hartman and Mesmer Animation Labs.

CHAPTER 13

ANIMATING WITH SHAPE ANIMATION

As you learned in Chapter 1, "Exploring the Softimage Interface," polygon meshes, spline objects, and patch surfaces are all defined by the location in space of the Control points, or vertices, that make them up. It follows that if you edit the shape of an object and save the location of the points before and after the edits, you can animate the shape of the object over time. Softimage 3D\Extreme performs exactly that trick, which is called, you guessed it, shape animation (see Figure 13.1). Shape animation is a fundamental catch-all term that applies to the generic method of saving the location in the space of every vertex in an object and then interpolating between those positions.

In this chapter, you build on the animation skills you learned in earlier chapters with:

- Shape animation
- Additive and Average shape interpolation
- Shape animation with Shape Weights
- Facial animation and lip sync

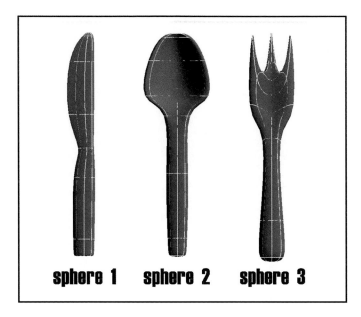

FIGURE 13.1 *The same sphere with three different shapes for shape animation.*

SHAPE ANIMATION BASICS

Because Softimage must save X, Y, and Z location data for each vertex in each model at each keyframe, a great deal of animation data can be created for heavy models with many keyframes. There are other, more efficient methods of handling the information for animating shapes.

Softimage sets keyframes for object shapes when you select an object and use the SaveKey→Object→Shape command. This command saves the location of every vertex at the frame you are on and also adds a named shape to the Shape List for later retrieval. Having this library of key shapes is extremely useful for character animation and other tasks requiring the surface geometry to change over time.

Because shape animation is so powerful, there are many different ways to use it. At the simplest level, you can push and pull points to create a series of explicit shapes through time with the SaveKey→Object→Shape command. Or you can create a series of models, each slightly different than the next, and use them to create a *shape library* with the Shape→Select Key Shape command. Once key shapes are created, you can retrieve them, add more, or delete unneeded ones with the Shape→Shape List command. Finally, when animating with key shapes, you can set them directly as a keyframe or manipulate the *Shape F-curve* (discussed later in this chapter) to precisely control the transition between shapes over time.

Tutorial: Mystic Symbols

To get a feel for shape animation, try this simple tutorial. The results should look like Figure 13.2.

Figure 13.2 *Animated symbols with shape animation.*

1. **Make a B-spline Circle.**

   Enter the Model module and get a primitive circle. Use a B-spline circle with 12 steps.

2. **Switch to the Motion Module.**

Now switch to the Motion module, where all the animation tools are located. Step 1's circle is your first shape, so move your Time Slider to frame 1 and save a keyframe for the shape with the SaveKey→Object→Shape command.

3. **Set the Keyframes.**

Move your Time Slider to frame 10 and tag every other point on the circle. Remember the supra key for tagging is T. Enter the TAG mode (so that transformations affect only tagged points). Use the Scale keys to uniformly scale the tagged points towards the center of the circle to create a star shape (see Figure 13.3). Set another keyframe for the shape by clicking the SaveKey menu cell with the middle mouse button.

FIGURE 13.3 *Scale the tagged points and set another keyframe.*

Drag the Time Slider back and forth from frame 1 to frame 10 to see how Softimage interpolates the points between the two shapes you saved.

At frame 20, scale the tagged points out and rotate them about the center 45 degrees (see Figure 13.4). Set another shape keyframe.

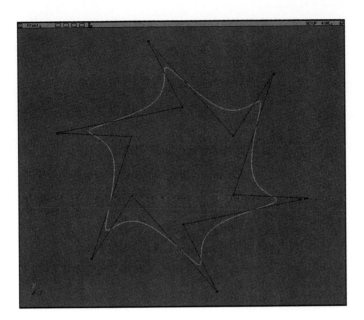

FIGURE 13.4 *Rotate the points and set another keyframe.*

In the Shape menu, select Shape→Shape List (see Figure 13.5). Click the dialog box at the top in the black title bar with the left mouse button, and drag the box out of the center of the screen into a corner, so that you can see both the dialog box and your shape. Each of the shape keyframes you set is listed in the box. When you select one by clicking the name, the name highlights and the shape updates in your view windows.

4. **Complete the Animation and Play.**

Move to frame 30 and recall the Shape List. Select the circle from the list (shape0) and dismiss the dialog box. Use SaveKey→Object→Shape to save the shape at that keyframe. Recall the Shape List with your middle mouse button on the Shape menu cell, and click through the items on the list. You will note that both shape0 and shape3 are the same shape, the circle. This is rather inconvenient because it means that if you continue to set shapes this way your Shape List will grow to include many duplicate shapes.

To finish the tutorial, drag your Time Slider back and forth to see your handiwork, and save your scene.

NOTE

The Shape List dialog box has a few drawbacks. As of this writing, you cannot replace the default names—shape0, shape1, shape2, and so on—with more descriptive ones, such as circle or star. Another potential problem is that all shapes set with SaveKey→Object→Shape are added to the list, even if they are redundant.

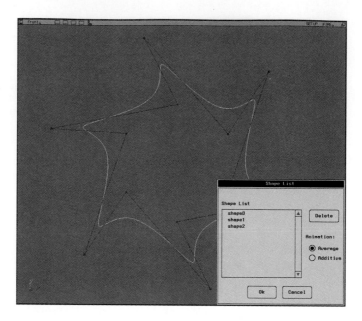

FIGURE 13.5 *The Shape List.*

To properly use shape animation, you should have only one copy of each shape in the Shape List, and then animate the transition from shape to shape by using the Shape F-curve or the Shape Weights Fructose (more on these later). However, there is another way to load the Shape List with the shapes you want to use: the Shape→Select Key Shape tool, which we'll explore in the next tutorial.

TUTORIAL: MAKING FACES

This tutorial uses the face model in the scene named Making_Faces found on the CD-ROM. If you're feeling industrious, you can create your own by starting with a B-spline primitive sphere (12 subdivisions) and pushing and pulling points and tagged groups of points to produce a face with large, expressive eyebrow ridges and lips.

1. **Organize Your Faces.**

   In the Front view, duplicate the head five times and line up the faces side by side.

2. **Add Some Expressions.**

   Edit the shape of the first face by tagging groups of points and translating them to form a smile. Edit the second face into a frown. Give the third face a raised eyebrow. Give all but one of the remaining faces new expressions of your choosing. Leave the last face unchanged, because it will become the master shape (see Figure 13.6).

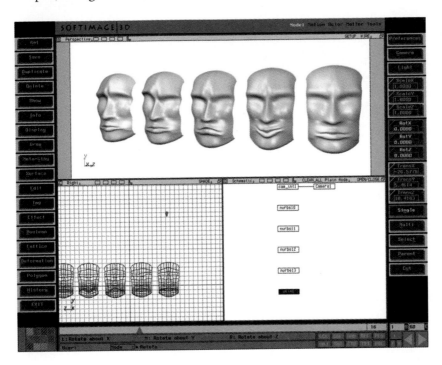

FIGURE 13.6 *The five faces.*

3. Prepare the Master Shape.

Select the master shape (the last, unchanged face) and translate it below the other faces to the center of your Front view. This face "contains" all the shapes of the other faces. You will save keyframes from frame –25 to 0 to prevent unwanted shapes from creeping into the final render, so set the start frame of the Time Slider to –25. Now move your Time Slider to frame –25 by directly entering that number into the current frame box. Save a keyframe for the shape with SaveKey→Object→Shape.

> **NOTE**
>
> Placing key shapes on consecutive, negative frames simply makes the workflow of setting key shapes more efficient, and makes using them easier when you are using the Shape F-curve. It is not a requirement for using the Select Key Shape command.

Click the Time Slider F button to put the Forward and Reverse buttons into frame-by-frame mode. Click the Forward button to advance one frame.

4. Combine the Faces.

Add all the faces to the master object's Shape List by first making sure that the master object is still selected and then choosing the Shape→Select Key Shape command. Now point to the first unused face object with your mouse and pick it with the left mouse button. The object you picked flashes red to indicate that you got it, a new shape is added to the master object's Shape List, and the master shape takes on the shape of the face you picked (see Figure 13.7).

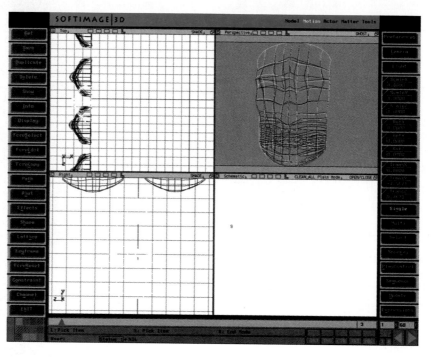

FIGURE 13.7 *When you add shapes to the master object's Shape List, the master object takes on the shape for each one you add.*

Simply click the forward button on the Time Slider to advance five frames, and pick with the left mouse button on the next face in the lineup. Repeat the process until you run out of faces.

This is a very clever way to generate a number of key shapes for an object. You can model them all at the same time, and then use the models to generate key shapes for the master object. Examine the Shape List for the master object to verify what you have done and save the scene for later use. Drag the Time Slider back and forth across the frames in the range –25 to 0 to see how one face interpolates into the next over time.

ADVANCED SHAPE ANIMATION

The tremendous utility of the Shape List and shape animation is not easy to use without a firm understanding of the Shape and Shape Weights function curves. My opinion is that the designers of the shape animation function never intended that animation be performed by using the SaveKey→Shape keyframing method, but always meant that command as simply a way to add shapes to the Shape List. For setting different shapes at points in time and controlling the interpolation between shapes (such as facial expressions), manipulating the Shape F-curves is the only way to go. But first, a little background.

HOW SHAPES ARE MADE

Each object in Softimage 3D|Extreme—splines, polygonal meshes, patches, and NURBS—is defined by a list of all the vertices (or Control points) that define the edges and curves of the surface. In most programs, an object has only one location for each point or vertex stored, and so the object remains in the same shape, rigid, throughout its life. Softimage, however, allows each object to have a Shape List. That means that each object can have more than one location for each vertex or Control point stored in a list, identified by a shape name.

For instance, one single rectangular mesh object could have several shapes, named FlagShape, CylinderShape, BowTieShape, and KleenexBallShape (see Figure 13.8). It's always the same object; it just has four different locations stored for each Control point, and depending on which shape is current, the object surface takes on a different form.

If different key shapes are set at different frames in time, Softimage has to interpolate the positions of each vertex over time to get the point from the place in 3D space where it starts to where it ends up. That makes the surface change shape over time!

Okay, now for the tougher part. On the object, vertex locations are actually stored as vector offsets from the local center. There's no easy way to describe a vector offset verbally, but look at Figure 13.9 and imagine that you are sitting at your desk with an apple and an orange sitting on the desktop. Imagine that you are the object and that your local center is in your chest. The fruit on your desk represents a few of the vertices that make up your surface. When you point to the orange, your arm forms a vector indicating the direction from your local center to the first point. The distance to the orange completes the information needed to place the vertex in space.

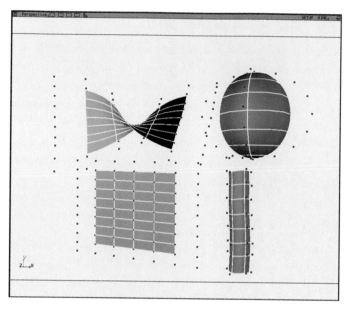

FIGURE 13.8 *Different shapes for the same patch.*

FIGURE 13.9 *How a hungry animator visualizes points in space.*

This method of storing the location of vertices relative to the center of an object makes it simple to move objects through space. It also makes it easier to calculate the other transformations (scale and rotation) with an algorithm that programmers call a *matrix transform.*

Now for the part relevant to shape animation. Each shape in the Shape List is really a list of the vector offsets for that shape. To interpolate between one shape and another, Softimage simply combines the two vectors proportionately, changing the proportion over time. You can choose between two methods—Average and Additive—to determine how the vectors blend. This choice is located in the Shape List and the default method is Average.

THE AVERAGE METHOD

Under the Average method, shapes merely blend from one into another. An object can never be a blend of more than two shapes and each shape blends into an earlier neighboring shape and a later neighboring shape.

The Shape F-curve shows a smooth gradient with time in frames along the traditional horizontal axis and the shape numbers rising along the Y axis. The Y value 0 is the first shape in the Shape List, the value 1 in Y is the second shape in the Shape List, and so on (see Figure 13.10).

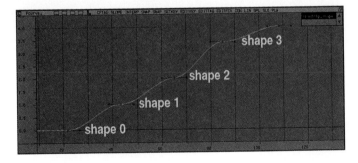

FIGURE 13.10 *The object shape F-curve showing Average interpolation.*

The Average method works only if you know beforehand the order in which the shapes need to be animated. Another way of saying this is that if you have nine shapes in the Shape List for a spline in the form of the numbers 1 through 9, and you animate the shapes by setting points in the shape animation F-curve to go from 0 to 8, the numbers animate in order, counting up from 1 to 9. If, however, you want the spline to go straight from 3 to 8, you are out of luck, because the spline can't get from 3 to 8 without traveling through 4, 5, 6, and 7.

Hollywood Squares, © Sony Television. Client/Agency: Sony Television & KingWorld. Image courtesy of Lunarfish.

Michael Carp, Director/Executive Producer

Lunarfish

Anthony: Tell me why you are working in film and animation.

Michael: I think in general that for anyone on the creative side, especially for people in film or animation, it's the ability to tell a story. The story could turn out to be anything. It could be cartoon, it could real, it could be surreal, and it is just an amazing ability and power to be able to do this. It's also an amazing feeling to do this with a small team, and then see your final product. We look back and say we did every single step of this, ourselves, right here, inside the software. It's a great feeling.

Anthony: I'm really fascinated by people who actually start a company. What led you to that decision?

Michael: I've been doing commercial productions for around 10 years now, and its always been on a freelance basis, working with other production companies.

About two years ago I decided to open up this company, so I went to my business partner (a friend at the time) Ed Davis, who worked at Softimage Corp. doing animation. Gradually I lured him away from the corporate realm, which took a while, and then we just jumped in!

I think the hardest thing is letting go of the money and risking the fact that you might actually lose money. People doing work in this business can make a great deal of money working for other people, which provides a simple comfort zone. For me, that's not very satisfying. The creativity can get lost up in there with making money and then making money becomes more important than anything else.

Storyboards for Hollywood Squares, © Sony Television. Client/Agency: Sony Television & KingWorld. Image courtesy of Lunarfish.

When you start your own company, nine out of ten times you have to go in with the mindset that you will not be taking income for a while, and that your employees will be making more than you. You need to go in with a mindset that you probably won't be making a ton of cash in the beginning, but you will be doing the kind of work that you like. Eventually, if you go about it right, you can define the income you want and still have a blast at work.

Anthony: What kind of work have you been doing recently that you really enjoy?

Wedgie Boy starting as a sketch, and then as a modeled wireframe. Wedgie Boy and all associated characters © LUNARFISH 1993-1998. Image courtesy of Lunarfish.

Michael: A lot of our time has been going to the development and production of Wedgie Boy, which is close to getting a deal. We also do a lot of work for Sony, including all the *Jeopardy* and *Wheel of Fortune* show openings and graphics. So everything you see at the front of the show is ours. We've done pieces for Intel. And we are working on the film, *What Dreams May Come* with Cuba Gooding, Jr. and Robin Williams.

Anthony: What characterizes your use of Softimage?

Michael: We spend a lot of time in taking full advantage of the unique animation capabilities and we do a lot of our rendering in mental ray. Ed Davis, Art Director and Lead Animator at Lunarfish, is the key guy on the animation side Our clients are constantly pushing us to find what's really difficult to do, and then all of a sudden they want to do more of that and define new ways of applying it to create a new or unique effect.

Anthony: What about the SGI versus NT hardware battle?

Michael: We've had good and bad luck with NT. We had an NT box here, actually a couple of them. But we typically do everything on the SGIs.

Basically, the one thing I look at is very simple. When you are in production, of course, there is a budget, but above all else you have to get the job done and usually within a crazy time frame. When it comes to commercial work and film, the clients just want the job done, whatever it takes. If we get caught up because a system isn't working correctly, it stops the job, and if it stops the job, then it kills our schedule and we're in trouble. There is a consistency with SGI that we have been able to rely on. If I'm buying a machine here and there I can plug them in and I know they are going to work. With NT machines, I think that we've had problems mostly with the lack of consistency from machine to machine. Not all NT machines perform the same, thus leaving more guess work and trouble-shooting for us.

Wedgie Boy rendered and then composited in a final shot.

Anthony: Tell me about Wedgie Boy.

Michael: Wedgie Boy is an internal project that we came up with to fulfill some of our company needs. We needed something productive for the animators to do when we're slow, when there was down time between tasks, something that was fun and would keep people busy. We wanted to have something to keep the juices flowing and have a lot of fun, the sort of project that is kind of twisted and quirky, where you hear people laughing and giggling in the back of the room. We wanted to have something to throw on the reel and to possibly sell in the market.

The character of Wedgie Boy was actually created about five years ago by a guy named Tom Tonkin, who is an illustrator out of New York. He has designed a lot of projects with us. We saw a character in his book that he had designed, thrown in with a bunch of other things, and I called him up and we talked. He then flew out here to San Francisco and we started working together. We just took his book, which was strictly 2D illustration, and we made everything in it 3D.

Wedgie Boy and all associated characters © LUNARFISH 1993-1998. Image courtesy of Lunarfish.

It's been going great, we've had offers from a few of the major networks and ongoing interest from a few other studios and investors.

Anthony: What's next for your company and where are you headed?

Michael: We are definitely going through growing pains right now. There are a lot of opportunities, and we need to find the best path for us and decide which avenues we should take. Of course, we want to continue on the commercial side, animation for TV and film. But if we pursue the film side, we could be locked up on projects for probably six months to a year or more at a time, which might pull us off the map for other things.

We're trying to weigh out these alternatives to see what makes sense. We might create separate divisions for TV and film work .

And, of course Wedgie Boy looks pretty good right now, too.

The bottom line at Lunarfish comes down to enjoying yourself. We surround ourselves with a lot of creative work and people who are willing to take risks creatively. We gradually have more and more ability to pick the projects we like, to develop our own projects, and that's what it's all about!

Wedgie Boy and all associated characters © LUNARFISH 1993-1998. Image courtesy of Lunarfish.

NOTE

Actually you can jump from 3 to 8 in the numbers animation by setting a keyframe for the 3 shape on one frame and setting another keyframe for the 8 shape on the very next frame. Because Softimage renders in even frames only, you never see the intermediate shapes, but they *are* there. This method also prevents the viewer from seeing the cool morph of the numbers.

THE ADDITIVE METHOD: SHAPE WEIGHTS

There is an even better method than Average. First, change the Shape List algorithm to Additive in the Shape List dialog box. This method makes it possible to add one shape to another, like pouring rum into a glass of Coke. Unlike the previous method, as you add in rum, you don't necessarily take away the Coke. The shapes become a mixture, which means that more than two shapes can be blended together into a frothy concoction, like adding some whiskey and some gin to the same glass of Coke. The proportion of each added liquid determines what the shape (or the drink) is like. Just like the drink, the resulting shape can become quite nasty if you don't exercise restraint in your mixology.

To mix the shapes, you must then go to the Shape→Shape Interpolation menu and change the interpolation method from Linear (the default) to Weighted. Now the F-curve Select menu's F-curve Select→Object→Shape Weights function curve shows the mixture between all the shapes in the Shape list. The Y axis shows the amount that each shape contributes to the mixture from 0 (nothing) to 1 (100 percent). If you want a shape really exaggerated, you can even mix a shape at more than 100 percent.

The fabulous thing about Shape Weights is that any shape can be added into the mix in any amount, at any frame in time by simply adding a keyframe with the EditKey command, and dragging the key up in Y to mix it in (see Figure 13.11). Think of a multi-track audio mixer as another analogy to explain what's happening, where each of the sliders is another shape, and the final look of the object is changed by simply moving the sliders up and down.

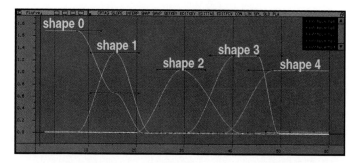

FIGURE 13.11 *Shape Weights curves.*

TUTORIAL: TALKING HEADS

Let's take a good look at how to use Shape Weights in an animation. The idea behind the Talking Heads animation is a simple one, but very hard to do in most animation programs. We want to animate lip sync so that a face model moves its lips convincingly over time to accompany a sound track. You'll use Shape Weights to interpolate between different face object mouth shapes you have saved in the Shape List (see Figure 13.12).

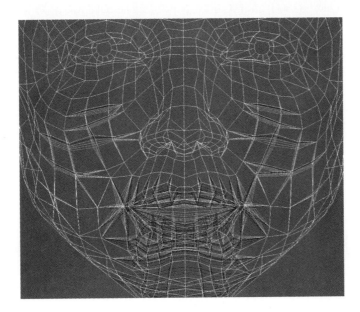

FIGURE 13.12 *Ghost view of the face changing shapes.*

Load the scene TalkingHeads from the CD-ROM, select the face model, and look at the Shape List (see Figure 13.13). Click each shape in turn and look at the face model. Each of the shapes is a *phoneme*, a building block of language. English words are spoken by connecting different phonemes together to form completed sounds. The phonemes in the Shape List are the "mmm" phoneme, the "eh" phoneme, the "zzz" phoneme (very close to the "sss" phoneme), the "ah" phoneme, and the "er" phoneme (see Figure 13.14).

The shape for each phoneme shows how a mouth should look when pronouncing that particular phoneme. Some shapes can work for several phonemes, because much of the sound of the phoneme comes not from the lips but the tongue and throat. Unfortunately, the shapes in the Shape List cannot be renamed, so they retain unhelpful names, such as shape0.

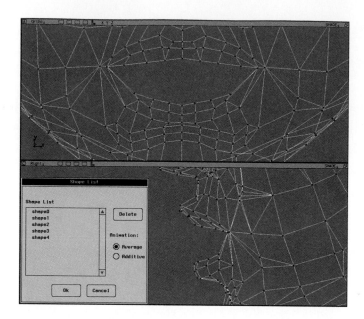

FIGURE 13.13   *The phoneme Shape List.*

FIGURE 13.14   *The phoneme mouth shapes.*

The scene on the CD-ROM is properly set up for Shape Weights animation. If you choose to make your own head with a Shape List, remember to change the interpolation in the Shape List to Additive, and change the Shape→Shape Interpolation to Weighted Interpolation, or you can't see the Shape Weights F-curves.

In the following tutorial, you string those phonemes together, one after the other, so that the face object pronounces the phrase "mesmerize me" when you play the shape animation.

1. **Find the Phonemes.**

   With the face object selected, open the Shape Weights F-curve via the F-curve Select→Object→Shape Weights menu cell. Look at the resulting curve (see Figure 13.15). Each shape has its own function curve and when the value of that F-curve is 0, none of that shape is added into the final appearance of the shape. Each of the Fructose stays at 0, except for one frame where it rises to a value of 1. Each shape is assigned five frames apart from frame –25 to –1.

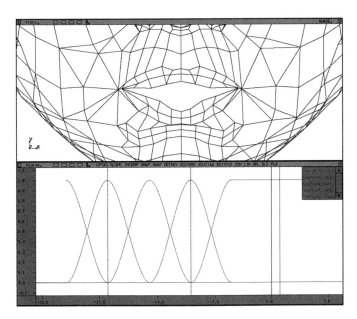

FIGURE 13.15 *Shape Weights for the phonemes.*

   Practice locating the phoneme you want by dragging the Time Slider back and forth to a facial shape you like, and then select the F-curve (in the F-curve window) that curves up to a value of 1 at that point in time. The phonemes are set as shapes in the order: mmm, eh, zzz, ah, and er.

NOTE

Adding the key shapes to the Shape List in the negative frames is an animation trick that keeps you from rendering them, and makes it easier to select the right phoneme when adding the keys for the actual animation.

2. Set the First Keyframe.

Start the animation by adding a key to the mmm shape (shape0) at frame 1 with the EditKey button in the menu bar of the F-curve window. Make the value of the key equal to 1, which means that the face has 100 percent of the mmm phoneme added in frame 1. Add another key to the curve on frame 4, also with a value of 1, and another at frame 5 with a value of zero. Play your animation. The face should go mmmmm for five frames and then stop.

3. Add a Vowel.

Locate the F-curve for the eh shape, by saying "ehhh" yourself in front of a mirror and dragging the Time Slider through the negative frames until you see a shape that resembles your mouth. Select the F-curve that rises to a value of 1 at that point, and use EditKey to add a keyframe to that F-curve at frame 4 with a value of 0, and at frame 5 with a value of 1. Keep the eh in force for two frames by setting another key at frame 6 with a value of 1, and then cut it off at frame 7 by adding a key with a value of 0.

4. Grab Some ZZZs.

Bring in some zzz for a few frames, overlapping with the eh for just a frame. Don't forget to start the shape a frame early with the value of 0, which prevents unwanted slurring (see Figure 13.16).

5. Finish the First Word.

Add in some mmm after the zzz for just three frames before you pull it back out, and blend the last half of it with the next phoneme, the er phoneme. Hold the er phoneme for four frames, then go to the ah phoneme for one frame, and finish the word with the zzz phoneme for a good long six frames.

Play your work in the Shaded mode while you look at your F-curve window to see how the face object changes the shape of the mouth as the Fructose rolls up and down. You may edit the points on the Fructose at this stage by using the M supra key to drag the point up and down, (adding more of that shape to the object) and dragging the point left and right (changing the timing of the phoneme, making it start or end earlier or later).

6. Start the Second Word.

After a pause of three to five frames, start the second word, Me. Use the mmm phoneme (briefly) and the eh phoneme to finish it off.

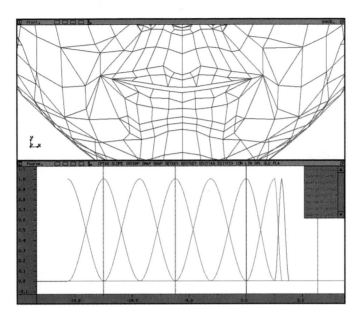

FIGURE 13.16   *Shape Weights for the zzz phoneme.*

7. Render and Record.

Render your work, and if you have access to a microphone on your workstation, record the audio track while watching the finished frames play in the FlipBook. Use a post production tool, such as Softimage Eddie, AW Composer, or Adobe Premiere, to mix the sound and images, and write out a QuickTime digital video file. (MediaConvert or MediaRecorder in IRIX will do the trick as well.) A completed movie file, titled Mesmerize.mov, is on the CD-ROM.

As you can see, the Shape Weights F-curve in Softimage gives you precise, easy control over the most complex of all animation methods: interpolating between many different shapes.

CONCLUSION

Versatile and powerful, shape animation is useful on many levels. You can quickly change a simple object over time (directly manipulate the points over several keyframes) or orchestrate a more complex project (build a Shape Library and tap into the Shape Fructose). Finally, shape animation controlled by Shape Weights gives you that extra edge. Use it for animating muscle deformations, mixing facial muscle actions to build complex and subtle expressions, cartoon squash and stretch, cartoon short takes (such as eyes bugging out, tongues unrolling to the ground, and so on), morphing between different creature types, and more. Remember, good use of shape animation will separate you from your peers using less powerful software.

In this chapter you:

- Set up shape animation and learned to work with the Shape List
- Worked with Average and Additive shape animation
- Used Shape Weights
- Performed lip sync and facial animation
- Explored the shape Fructose

1997 The Coca-Cola Co. Image courtesy of Little Fluffy Clouds, LLC.

CHAPTER 14

ANIMATING WITH DEFORMATIONS

Most things change shape. Animals, clouds, car tires, trees, and fish all regularly change shape on a second-by-second basis as the forces of nature act upon them. In Softimage, anything made up of Control points and vertices can change shape as well, but often directly manipulating all the points on an object to create different shapes for an animation is simply impractical. There may be so many vertices to edit on a complex model that shape animation is just too time-consuming when performed vertex by vertex. You may also want the object to change shape gradually over the entire surface, which is hard to do manually.

The solution is to turn to Softimage's Deformation controls. The Deformation tools enable you to displace all or some of an object's vertices in space—in other words, to deform the object. Generally, deformations apply to all the vertices or Control points in an object, and using the Deformation tools is much simpler than moving all the points on the object manually.

In this chapter, you will:

- Learn all about deformations in Softimage 3D|Extreme
- Learn to animate deformations, including both Node and Branch deformations
- Use the Deformation by Curve tools
- Use the Deformation by Surface tools
- Use the Deformation by Lattice tools

DEFORMATION BASICS

Deformations make all sorts of jobs easier. You can use deformations to stretch, bend, twist, taper, fold, spindle and mutilate objects. You can use deformations to move an object along a curvy path. You can use them to flatten an object against the surface of another object. Deformations can be used to simulate a skeletal system in objects to simplify character animation. You can use deformations as a modeling tool to bend and shape objects and then freeze the object in the new shape permanently. You can even animate all the Deformation parameters to create dramatic changes in the shape of objects over time.

Three primary types of Deformation tools are found in Softimage 3D|Extreme:

- Deformation by Curve
- Deformation by Surface
- Deformation by Lattice

Each tool deforms objects in a different way and has unique benefits (see Figure 14.1). Deformation by Curve can be used to move an object along a path while deforming all the object vertices, such as a snake slithering along a spline. It can also be used to implant a curve within an object that can act like a flexible IK skeleton, bending the object when the curve itself is shaped. Deformation by Surface can be used to stretch one object over another, like putting a rubber mask on your own face. Deformation by Lattice can be used to evenly stretch, bend, and twist objects smoothly to create rubber hose style animation effects.

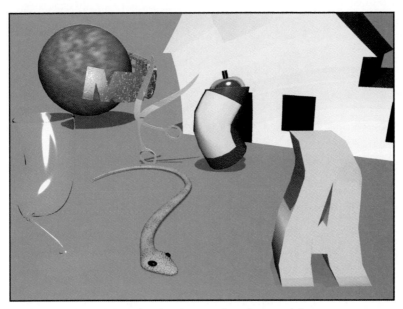

FIGURE 14.1 *Some objects deformed with Spline, Patch, and Lattice deformations.*

You can use these three Deformation tools on individual objects or on hierarchies. Deformations applied to individual objects are called *Node deformations*, and those applied to hierarchies of objects are called *Branch deformations*. Deformations can even be nested inside each other to create complex hierarchical animations.

DEFORMATION BY CURVE

Deformation by Curve is a simple, useful tool (see Figure 14.2) that can be used to animate creatures without legs, translate objects along a path, and add character animation to objects that don't have any clear limbs for IK skeletons (see Figure 14.3).

Deformation by Curve works by converting the X,Y,Z coordinate system of a model onto the U parameter coordinate system used by a curve. In this way, all the points on the model are placed in space relative to the curve (see Figure 14.4). When the curve changes, they change. When you translate the object along the curve, points on the object all deform to follow the curve.

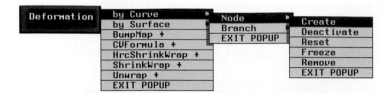

FIGURE 14.2 *The Deformation menu cells for deforming objects on a curve.*

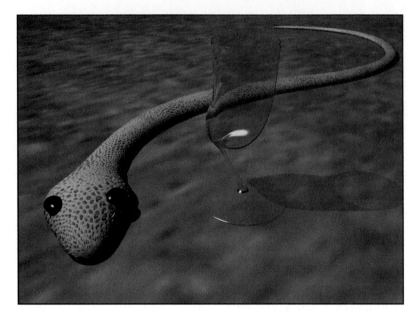

FIGURE 14.3 *Both the wine glass and the snake are deformed by a curve.*

To deform your models in the way you want, you must understand how the models and curves interact. Curves have a start and an end, and therefore have a forward direction, called the U parameter direction. The Y axis of the model is converted to the forward U parameter of the curve, called *Y up orientation.* The X and Z location of the model determine whether the model is deformed exactly around the curve or is offset in space from the curve.

It is always a good idea to build your model in the global center. Build the model so that the axis of the model you want facing forward along the curve is oriented up in the Global positive Y direction (see Figure 14.5). If you can't build your model in this way, translate and rotate the model until it is in the global center and faces up in positive Y. Then freeze the transformations of the model with the Effect→Freeze→Transformations→All command in the Model module.

FIGURE 14.4   *A curve has only one parameter, U, while an object has three, Y, Y, and Z.*

FIGURE 14.5   *The glass, the spline, and the glass on the spline.*

NOTE

The Effect→Freeze menu cells are tremendously useful in Softimage and are almost required for good deformations. When you freeze the translation of an object, the local center of that object is immediately moved to the global center, and every vertex in the object is therefore positioned relative to the global center. When you freeze the rotation of an object, the local center is returned to the same orientation as the global axes, and all the vertices are then located in space relative to the correctly rotated global axes. When you freeze the scale of an object, the Scale menu cells indicate that it is reset to a default scale of 1, and the vertices are located relative to the global center and are not affected by the scaling factor of the object. Using Effect→Freeze Transformations sets all these freezes and therefore puts all the object's vertices in a default state, minimizing the chance of hassles during the deformation process.

Next, draw the curve that the model is deformed by, placing the curve's start point where you want the base of the object to end up, and place the end point where you want the top of the object to end up (see Figure 14.5). This curve doesn't have to be located in or near the global center, and when the deformation effect is completed, the model is translated to the location of the curve.

Finally, select the model and choose the Deformation→by Curve→Node→Create command. The Status Bar prompts you to pick the curve that will deform the object. After you pick the curve, the object jumps to the location of the curve and is squashed down towards the base (see Figure 14.5).

TRANSFORMATIONS ON THE CURVE-DEFORMED OBJECT

Transformations on a deformed object are performed along the deforming curve. Give it a try: Click the triangular portion of the ScaleX (or Y or Z) menu cell to call the numerical entry box. Next, click the Set button to set the scaling back to 1 in X, Y, and Z. The object retains its former proportions and is only deformed along the curve! If you select the Scale menu cells manually, you can extend the object along the curve by scaling in the Y direction because Y for this object is now the U direction of the curve (see Figure 14.6). If you scale in X and Z, you can change the width of the object around the curve.

Translation for the object is now also made relative to the curve. When you select the TransY menu cell and drag the mouse, the object moves along the curve, undulating to follow the contours of the curve as it passes them.

Rotation of the object is, of course, also relative to the new curve-based coordinate system so that when you rotate the object around Y, it spins around the deforming curve.

TRANSFORMATIONS ON THE DEFORMING CURVE

Because an object's vertices are now defined in the parameter space of the deforming curve, whatever you do to the curve is reflected in the object. This applies not only to the shape of the object, but also to its transformations.

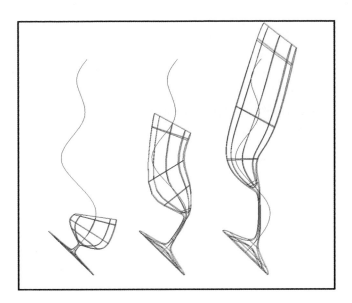

FIGURE 14.6 *Scaling a deformed object in Y stretches it along the curve.*

That's a fancy way of saying that when you move the deformation curve, the deformation object moves exactly with it! When you rotate or scale the deformation curve, those transformations also affect the deformation object, even though the object and curve are not in a hierarchy of any kind. This link between the two is shown visually in the Schematic view when you toggle on the Model mode from the Mode drop-down menu in the Schematic title bar.

ANIMATING CURVE DEFORMATIONS

All the transformations of the object along the curve are animatable, but not with the SaveKey→Object→Transformations command as you might expect. Instead, there are new SaveKey cells explicitly for saving these new curve-based transformations (see Figure 14.7). If the object you are transforming is a single object, use the SaveKey→Object→Node Curve Deformation menu cells to record the current transformation of the object in curve space. If you are deforming an entire hierarchy of objects along the curve, you should use the SaveKey→Object→Branch Curve Deformation commands to set keyframes.

By setting keyframes with Node and Branch curve deformation, you can make the object move along the curve, wriggling like a worm or swimming like a fish.

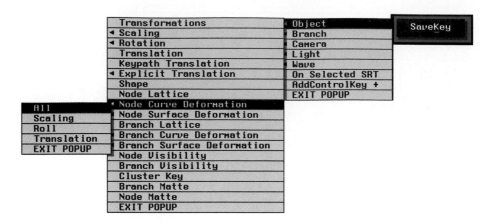

FIGURE 14.7 *The SaveKey menu cells for saving curve deformations.*

Another way to use curve deformation is to draw a curve directly inside an object so that it matches the scale of the object to be deformed. When the object is attached to the curve, the curve becomes a kind of very flexible spinal column within the object. As the curve bends, so does the object that is deformed by the curve. You can set shape keyframes on the curve at different points in time to make the deformed object change shape as well.

You can think of this method as a more sophisticated relational modeling, where you apply animation to a simple curve, and a more complex model is animated automatically.

If you change your mind about the curve deformation and decide you want the deformed object removed from the spline and returned to its original shape, select the object and use the Deformation→Node Curve Deformation→Remove command.

TUTORIAL: DANCING HAIRCUT

In this first tutorial, you explore the use of Node curve deformation to add character animation to static objects. Imagine that you are given the task of creating an original animation for Bob's Barbershop and the director for the project has asked for a pair of scissors and a can of hairspray to dance together (see Figure 14.8). You will need a simple, cheap, and, above all, quick way to generate some character animation for the client. That's a perfect job for a Node curve deformation!

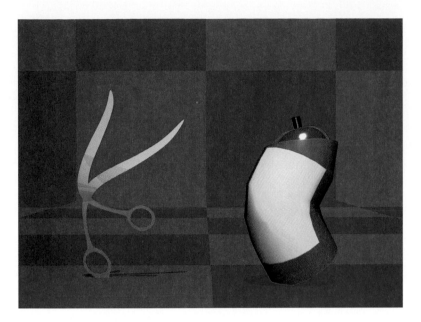

FIGURE 14.8 *The finished Dancing Haircut scene.*

1. Model the Characters.

In the Front view, draw the outline of a half pair of scissors with a B-spline, placing a few extra points along the length of the blade and the handle to assist in smooth deformation later. Close the spline at the top with the Draw→Open/Close command and then draw in another closed curve inside the handle where the thumb hole needs to be. Convert the larger closed curve to a face with the Draw→Convert to Face command and attach the hole to the face with the Draw→Attach Hole command. Modify the shape of the scissors with the M supra key to get the shape just right, and then extrude it into the Z axis as a closed polygon object. Scale the scissors extrusion in Z to get the thickness you want (see Figure 14.9).

Make the other half of the scissors, either by drawing another face if you want the two handles to be different or with the Effect→Symmetry command to duplicate the scissor half around the YZ axis.

Position the two halves together in space and rotate them slightly so that the blades are open a bit.

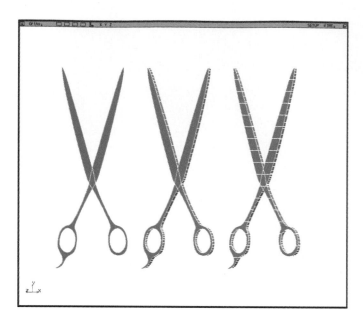

FIGURE 14.9   *The scissor face with the attached hole and the extrusions made of it.*

Combine the two halves with either a Boolean union (the better choice) or the Merge command (the easier choice). Finally, add some vertical subdivisions along the scissors with the Effect→Subdivide command to help them bend more cleanly. Set it up to add 0 subdivisions in X and Z, and 16 subdivisions in Y. Hide all the construction elements except for the finished pair of scissors.

To make the hairspray can, simply draw a revolution profile in the Front view next to the Y axis using a linear spline. Make sure to add some points in the vertical wall of the can so it can bend fluidly. Revolve it into a spline revolution with 16 steps around Y Figure 14.and hide the revolution profile (see Figure 14.10). Translate the hairspray can to the global center and verify that it is standing up in positive Y. Freeze the transformations on the can for good measure with the Effect→Freeze→Transformations→All command.

2. Draw the Deformation Curves.

The curves become the backbones of the two characters you built. They can be located anywhere in space but should probably be drawn using a B-spline (Draw→Curve→B-spline), starting with the first point at floor level and working up in positive Y. Add four more points to create a curve with five total Control points. This curve will act like a spinal column with five vertebrae.

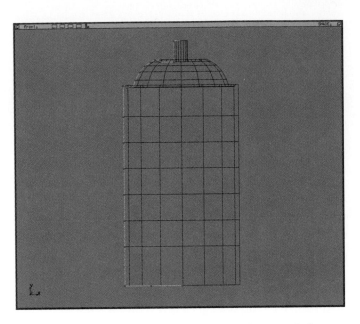

FIGURE 14.10 *The hairspray can revolution profile and the revolution made from it.*

Draw another similar curve for the other character (see Figure 14.11). Next, create a null object with the Get→Primitive→Null command and make the null the parent of both curves. This null makes animating both the characters simpler because you can grab the null as a branch to translate and rotate both characters together, or select just one curve to move the characters relative to each other.

3. **Deform the Characters.**

Select the scissors character and attach it to the curve as a Node curve deformation by choosing the Deformation→by Curve→Node→Create command. Then complete the command by picking the curve. The scissors jump to the location of the curve and squash down. Reset the scale of the scissors by selecting the triangular tab in the Scale menu cells and clicking the Set button to return the scissors to a scale of 1,1,1. If the scissors aren't positioned at the ground level, you may use the TransY menu cell to slide the scissors up the curve into a good starting position.

Select the hairspray can and repeat the process, attaching it to the other curve with the Deformation→by Curve→Node→Create command. Then reset the scale and translation to get it ready to animate.

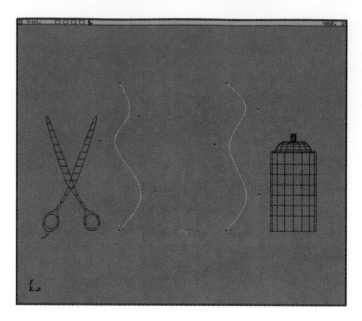

FIGURE 14.11   *The dancers next to their deformation splines.*

4. **Animate the Curves.**

On the first curve, use the M supra key to move a few points around in the Front view. Notice how the scissors deform to follow the shape of the curve (see Figure 14.12). We can animate the scissors bending and dipping by moving points on the curve, and saving the shape of the curve with the SaveKey→Object→Shape command at frame 1. Then move the Time Slider to a new location in time about five frames later, change the shape of the curve, and set a new keyframe. Repeat to animate a series of shapes for the scissors, as if they were wriggling to a beat every five frames.

Select the curve that is deforming the hairspray can and set some keys for it as well. If the curve for the hairspray can bends toward the curve for the scissors as they bend away, the two characters look more like they are interacting on the dance floor.

5. **Translate and Rotate the Dancers.**

Select the top null as a branch (middle mouse button and Spacebar) and save an explicit translation keyframe at frame 1 to start the dance. Move the Time Slider to a frame 25 and translate the null to a new location in the Top view. Note that the curves follow the null because they are its children, and that the characters follow the curves because they are deformed by the curves. Save a new keyframe for the explicit translation of the top null.

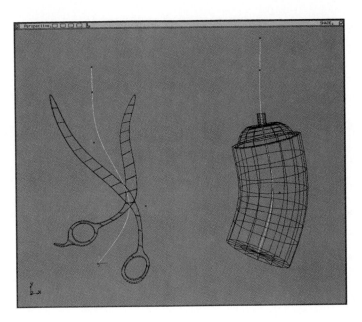

FIGURE 14.12 *The dancers deforming along with the curves.*

Move to frame 50 and set a keyframe for a different position. Repeat until frame 100.

Now go back and add some rotation around Y to the top null. Save a key at frame 1 with no rotation in Y, then at frame 33, rotate the null 180 degrees in Y, and set a keyframe. Repeat at frames 66 and 99 to create a swirling motion for the character.

6. **Test, Tweak, and Render.**

Examine your animation by playing it back and make edits as needed to create the dance you want. When you like the results, add materials to the objects and a floor plane. Then render a preview at 300 × 200 pixels and play it back in the FlipBook.

> **NOTE**
>
> Because each character is a single object, we were able to use the Node curve deformation, which affects only a single object. When you need to deform multiple objects in a hierarchy, use the Branch curve deformation tool.

As you can see, animating the shape of the curves is a fast and easy way to make changes to the entire shape of the characters, adding appeal to their movements.

TUTORIAL: SNAKE EYES

Another use for curve deformation is to leave the curve alone and translate the deformed object along the curve. This tutorial explores how a Branch curve deformation is used to bend and twist a snake along a curve path (see Figure 14.13).

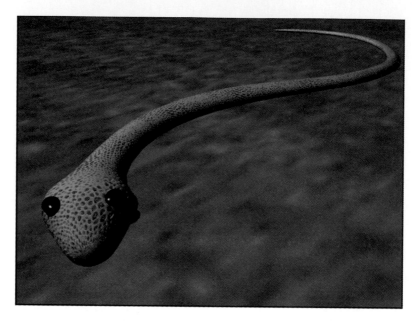

FIGURE 14.13 *The completed snake scene.*

1. **Model the Snake.**

   Create the snake by drawing a profile for the snake next to the Y axis. Be sure to include points along the length of the snake body so it can bend smoothly. Revolve the profile around Y as a B-spline patch object.

   Tag the points of the head and, in TAG mode, flatten the head by scaling the Z axis. Tag just the row of points in the mouth and translate them into the snake to pull in a mouth, if you wish (see Figure 14.14).

   Get primitive nulls to serve as the eyes and place them correctly on either side of the snake head. Then make them both children of the snake body. We'll have to use a Branch curve deformation because the snake is now a hierarchy of objects.

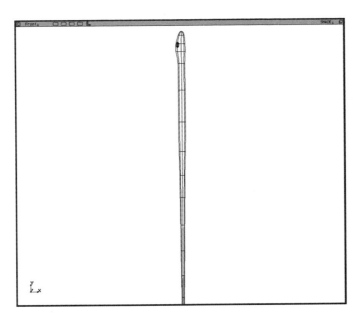

FIGURE 14.14   *Modeling the snake in a Y up position.*

2. **Draw the Curve.**

   In the Top view, draw a B-spline curve that meanders around the scene. This will become the path that the snake follows.

3. **Deform the Snake to the Curve.**

   Select the snake hierarchy as a tree and choose the Deformation→by Curve→Branch→Create command; then complete it by picking the curve. The snake deforms to the curve and, because he was built with his nose pointed in positive Y, he should be correctly oriented along it.

   You can scale the snake to make him relatively small in relation to the curve, so he has a long path to travel (see Figure 14.15).

4. **Animate the Snake.**

   With the whole snake hierarchy selected, use the TransY menu cell to move him to a good position at the start of the curve. Save this position at frame 1 with the SaveKey→Object→Branch Curve Deformation→All. Please note that this is not a regular object explicit translation keyframe as you might expect, but rather a special keyframe for the transformation of the object in the curve parameter space.

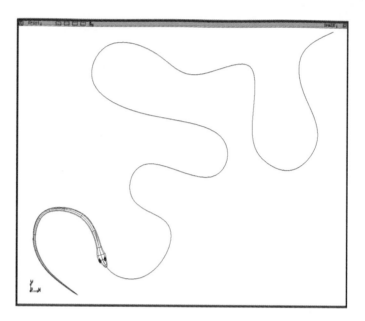

FIGURE 14.15 *The snake on the meandering spline.*

At frame 100, use the TransY cell again to drag the snake along the path to the end. If the snake moves really slowly, drag with the right mouse button to make the value of TransY change faster. Again set a keyframe for the Branch curve deformation. When you drag in the Time Slider, Softimage interpolates the change in the Y curve translation and moves all the snake points along the curve (see Figure 14.16).

Translating an object or a hierarchy of objects along a path using curve deformation is a fabulous way to slither snakes, swim fish, and crawl worms. The curve deformation method differs most noticeably from the regular method of path animation (Path→Pick Path) in that the objects don't just move along the path, they twist, turn, bend, and wriggle along it as well. The active, dynamically changing objects created this way have much more life in them than standard, stiff, static path animation.

CURVE DEFORMATION MODELING USES: NODE AND BRANCH

You can use Node and Branch curve deformation as a modeling tool as well. After attaching an object to a curve and deforming it by changing the curve's shape, you can freeze the object in that shape permanently with the Deformation→Node Curve

Deformation→Freeze command. The newly frozen object is free of the curve and can be animated separately, but its vertices remain locked in their last position before the deformation was frozen. You could use this type of method to create a pretzel model by deforming an extruded cylinder along a curve and then freezing the deformation when you have it knotted the way you want it.

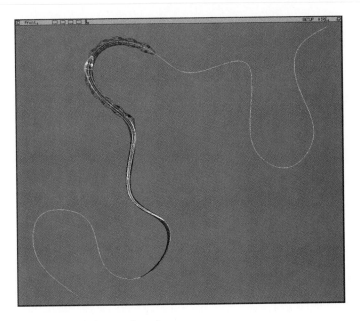

FIGURE 14.16   *The snake slithering along the curve.*

DEFORMATION BY SURFACE

Deformation by Surface (see Figure 14.17) works much the same as deformation along a curve, but because the patch has both a U and a V parameter, the object can now be deformed into the U and V space of the patch. Therefore, it moves around on the patch as if is glued to the surface.

The X axis of the object becomes mapped to the U parameter of the deforming mesh, and the Z axis of the object becomes mapped to the V parameter of the deforming mesh (see Figure 14.18). The Y axis of the object becomes mapped to the normal orientation of the surface, so that what was positive Y on your deformed object always points out, perpendicular to the deforming surface. The easiest way to visualize this is to examine it in action, in a simple case.

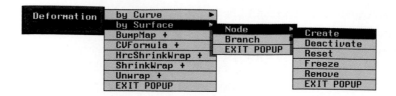

FIGURE 14.17   *The Deformation menu cells for deforming objects on a patch.*

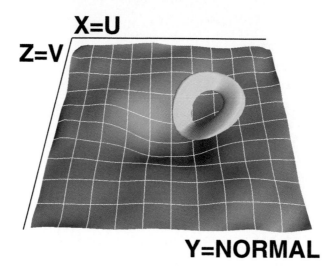

FIGURE 14.18   *In a patch deformation, the X and Z axes map to the U and V parameters.*

1. Get a NURBS grid.

    Get a 10-by-10 NURBS primitive grid to act as the deforming patch and tag a rough square of points in the middle section of the grid. Then translate only those tagged points (in TAG mode) down a bit to create a grid with a trough in it. You can also rough up the grid if you wish by changing back to OBJ mode and running the Effect→Randomize command on the patch with a Y value of 0.15.

2. Get a NURBS torus.

    Get a primitive torus made of a NURBS surface and scale it down to be fairly small relative to the grid. The torus happens by default to be correctly aligned, facing up in positive Y, so it fits onto the patch correctly. Freeze the scaling you performed on the torus with Effect→Freeze→Transformations. This command is always a good idea before a patch deformation.

3. Deform the torus.

With the torus selected, choose the command Deformation→by Surface→Node→Create and pick the grid. The torus will be stretched onto the grid.

All transformations to the torus now apply relative to the UV parameter space of the grid. If you scale the torus in X and Z, the torus gets bigger or smaller along the U and V directions of the grid. If you scale in Y, the torus shrinks or grows in the direction that is normal to the surface.

If you translate the torus in X or Z, the torus slides along the grid, deforming as it goes. Make sure you use the LCL translation mode and translate only one axis at a time for easy manipulation of the surface. If you translate the torus in Y, it moves relative to the normal direction, either moving above or below the grid (see Figure 14.19).

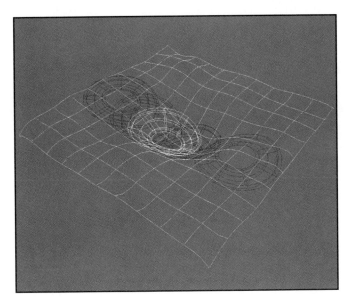

FIGURE 14.19 *The torus translates along UV space, following the contours of the patch.*

Remember that you must correctly align the object to be deformed before you can execute the deformation and finally transform the object along the patch. The axis of the model that you want to face out of the surface must be oriented toward positive Y before you execute the deformation, or the model will be mangled beyond comprehension.

The starting location of the object before deformation determines where the object starts out on the deforming patch. If the object is translated above the ground plane in positive Y, it starts as a deformed object by hovering that much above the surface that deforms it. Similarly, the object's X and Z positions determine where it starts in the UV space of the patch. The safest bet is to translate the object to the global center before executing the Deformation by Surface. Finally, the local transformations of the object don't count, so make sure you make them consistent with the global axes by executing the Effect→Freeze→Transformations command.

TRANSFORMATIONS ON THE PATCH-DEFORMED OBJECT

Because the Transformation controls switch from the familiar X,Y,Z three-dimensional coordinate system to a new U,V,Normal coordinate system, it's easy to get confused. Just remember that X and Z are now U and V, and try to manipulate one at a time so you don't get too confused.

Also remember that the Y axis now controls the height above the surface of the deforming grid.

ANIMATION WITH DEFORMATION BY SURFACE

Just as Deformation by Curve, there are three ways to animate models with the Deformation by Surface tools. You can transform the patch by scaling, rotating, or translating it, and the deformed objects behave accordingly. When you set regular transformation keyframes for the patch, the deformed object is animated. You can modify the shape of the patch with the M key, clusters, tagging, or another deformation and set keyframes for that change in shape with the SaveKey→Object→Shape command.

You can also transform the deformed object in the UV parameter space of the patch as keyframes for that relative transformation with the SaveKey→Object→Branch Surface Deformation→Translation.

TUTORIAL: ALL AROUND THE WORLD

A very common effect in logo animation requires that text characters, such as a company name, be deformed to wrap around a globe. With the Deformation by Surface command, we can do an excellent job of this (see Figure 14.20).

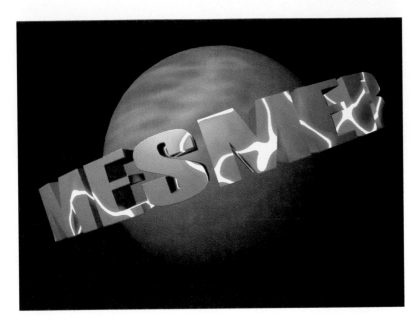

FIGURE 14.20 *The completed patch deformation.*

1. **Create the World.**

   A simple NURBS sphere will suffice for the world, so get a primitive sphere made of a NURBS surface.

2. **Create the Text.**

   Use the Get→Text tool to create a text element of your name or your company's. Specify to make the text out of faces to save us a step later.

   These faces now need to be extruded, so with the entire hierarchy selected, extrude them in Z 1 unit as closed polygon objects with the Surface→Extrude command. Open the Schematic view and hide the hierarchy of faces created by the Text tool. Note that the new extrusions are all separate elements. For maximum flexibility, we need to parent them all to a null object, so get a null and make it the parent of all the text objects.

   The axis of the text object that faces in positive Y will face out of the sphere after we deform it, so we need to rotate the text around Z by 90 degrees to make the faces of the letters point in the right direction, which is straight up in Y (see Figure 14.21). We can also scale the text hierarchy down quite a bit to be smaller than the sphere and finish off by freezing the transformations for the whole text hierarchy with the Effect→Freeze→Transformations command.

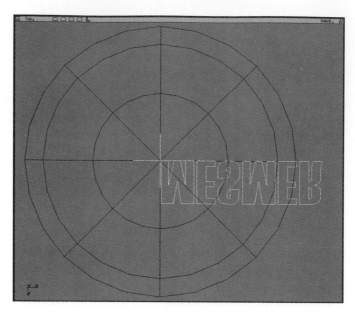

FIGURE 14.21 *The extruded text oriented Y up so that the front faces of the letters face along the patch normals.*

3. Deform the Text.

With the text hierarchy selected, choose the Deformation→by Surface→ Branch→Create command and then pick the sphere. The text jumps to the surface of the sphere. We now need to reset the relative scale and translation of the text to be around the equator of the sphere, several units out from the surface. The keys to this operation are to make sure that the Translation mode is LCL, to start by scaling only the Z axis so you get a feel for what is the U direction of the sphere, and to make the text smaller relative to the sphere so it doesn't look so distorted. Next, translate the text in Z to a position on the equator of the sphere.

After the text is properly positioned and scaled in Z, position and scale in X (the V direction). Finally, translate the text in the Y axis to move it in the direction of the surface's normal and move it a few units out in front of the sphere (see Figure 14.22).

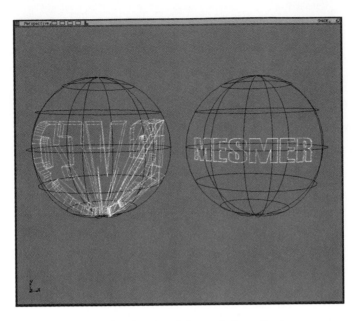

FIGURE 14.22   *The text deformed to the sphere before and after scaling it to correct proportions.*

4. Layer on the Animation.

First, use the TransX menu cell to move the text to a starting position on the sphere and save a keyframe at frame 1 with SaveKey→Object→Branch Surface Deformation→All. Then at frame 100, use TransX to move the text all the way around the sphere and set another keyframe with the middle mouse button on the SaveKey menu cell. Play the animation to see the text revolve around the world (see Figure 14.23).

Next, select the sphere and save a keyframe at frame 1 for all its transformations with SaveKey→Object→Transformations→All. At frame 20, scale the sphere to be half the size and set another keyframe. At other frames, change the size and rotation of the sphere, and set transformation keyframes. Play back the animation to see how that animation also affects the text.

Finally, move to frame 1 and save a key for its shape with the SaveKey→Object→Shape command and the sphere selected. At frame 50, tag four points on the equator of the sphere. In TAG mode, scale them out so the sphere has long bumps extending outwards. Save another key for the sphere shape and play back the animation to see that the shape of the sphere changes the deformation of the text as well.

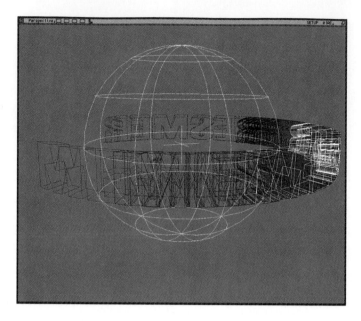

FIGURE 14.23   *The text revolves around the patch as you translate it in the U parameter with the TransX menu cell.*

That's all! Deformation by Patch works well with all objects except Meta-Clay systems. Once you get the hang of transforming objects in U,V,Normal space instead of X,Y,Z space, deforming by surface becomes a valued part of your animation bag of tricks.

PATCH DEFORMATION MODELING USES

Deformation by Surface is a fantastic tool for achieving psychedelic deformations of previously rigid objects and hierarchies of objects. Characters can be easily flattened against a curved wall and smeared around; text can be deformed around any patch you can model; and faces can be animated coming out of walls by deforming them to a surface and then animating the scale in Y to change them from flat to patch to three-dimensional.

DEFORMATION BY LATTICE

Deformation by Lattice is another Softimage original tool so useful that it is finally showing up in other high-end animation tools. Even though other software now has similar technology, Softimage's implementation is still the most powerful and functional because it allows for nested hierarchies of node and branch lattice deformations (see Figure 14.24).

FIGURE 14.24   *Examples of deforming objects using lattices.*

A lattice is a simplified wrapper or bounding cube that you can make around any object, hierarchy of objects, or portion of a single object. The lattice then takes over transforming the vertices of the object contained within it. You can make broad changes by moving a few lattice Control points, which in turn deform lots of surface vertices in a smooth, easy to understand fashion. A lattice is an easy way to deform lots of geometry.

Lattices also make possible many cool deformations that can be used in animations, such as twist, taper, bend, and the like. Deformation by Lattice is also a potent character animation tool and works particularly well for 1920s-style rubber hose animation and 1990s-style squash-and-stretch cartoon animation.

Deformation by Lattice is so important in Softimage that it rates its own menu, the Lattice menu in the Model module (see Figure 14.25).

LATTICE TYPES

Softimage offers three types of lattices:

- Node
- Branch
- Local

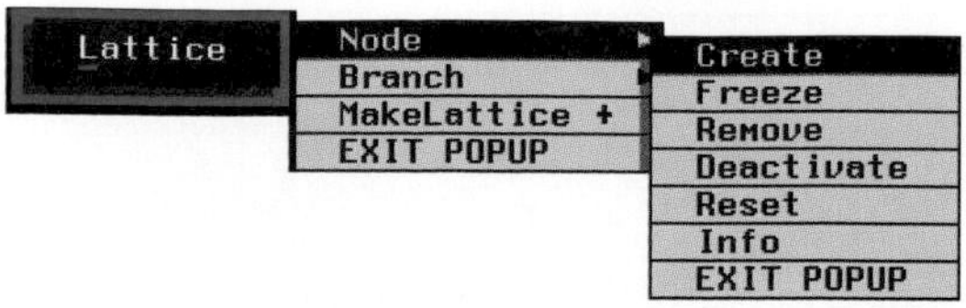

Lattice	Node ▶	Create
	Branch	Freeze
	MakeLattice +	Remove
	EXIT POPUP	Deactivate
		Reset
		Info
		EXIT POPUP

FIGURE 14.25 *The Deformation by Lattice menu cells.*

Node lattices can be applied to single objects, branch lattices may be applied to hierarchies of objects, and local lattices can be applied to only selected portions of a single model. Lattices themselves can exist in a hierarchy with branch lattices containing many smaller node lattices.

When you apply a lattice around an object, you get to specify the resolution of the lattice mesh that deforms the object. If you choose low detail on the lattice, you have a simple way to make broad changes to the object geometry. If you choose a lot of detail, you can make finer adjustments to localized areas of the object mesh.

NODE LATTICES

To apply a lattice to a single object, use the Lattice→Node→Create command (see Figure 14.26). When you execute the command, the Create Lattice dialog box pops up, allowing you to specify the resolution of the lattice that surrounds the selected object (see Figure 14.27).

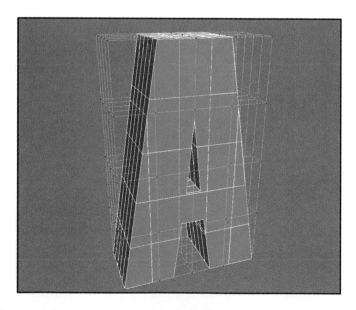

FIGURE 14.26 *A node lattice is a lattice around a single object.*

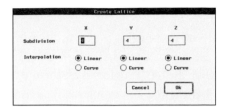

FIGURE 14.27 *The Create Lattice dialog box.*

Generally it is a good idea to put the minimum detail possible into a lattice, which makes it easier to choose all the Control points and animate them. The Linear interpolation method is generally inferior to the Curve interpolation method, which gives smoother deformations. Setting two subdivisions in X, Y, and Z is generally sufficient for smooth deformation yet still results in a simple lattice that is easy to manipulate.

You deform the lattice, and therefore the geometry inside it, by moving lattice Control points with the M supra key, or by tagging groups of lattice points and transforming them in TAG mode with the regular transformation menu cells (see Figure 14.28). Often, models that don't lend themselves to IK can be animated in this way, by tagging groups of lattice vertices where the extremities of the model are and translating them to deform as if there was actually a skeleton inside. Dancing cereal boxes, toasters, and gas pumps have all been animated this way.

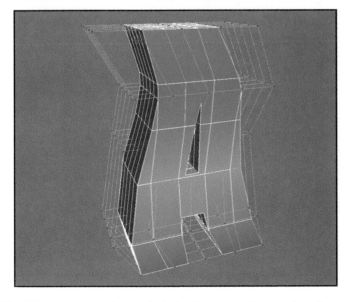

FIGURE 14.28 *When you move points on the lattice, the shape within is deformed.*

BRANCH LATTICES

Other cool animation effects are possible when using a branch lattice. When you apply a branch lattice to the top of a hierarchy (using the Lattice→Branch→Create command and Create Lattice dialog), it deforms all the models in that hierarchy (see Figure 14.29). The model at the top of the hierarchy becomes the bounding model for the entire lattice effect.

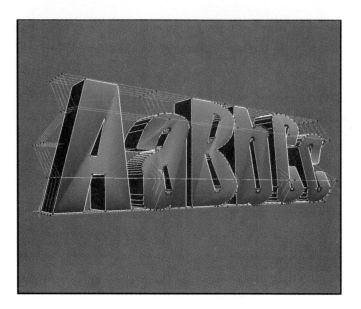

FIGURE 14.29 *A branch lattice deforms a hierarchy of multiple objects.*

Although the lattice stays wrapped around the model at the top of the hierarchy and moves along with that model, children of the hierarchy are free to move around within the lattice. When the children move within the lattice, they are deformed by the shape of the lattice at that point in space (see Figure 14.30). As a result, the branch lattice can be put on a larger bounding cube at the top of the hierarchy, and then the lattice can be edited to scale, stretch, and twist as you wish. When the child objects are translated through the bounding cube, they will scale, stretch, and twist as well. This effect works tremendously well for pouring large objects into and out of bottles, through keyholes, and down drains of various types.

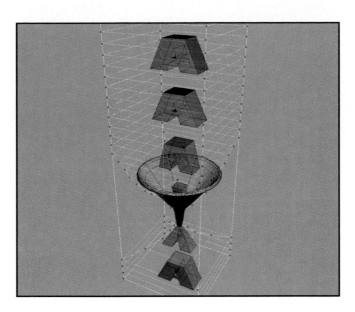

FIGURE 14.30 *Moving a child through the branch lattice of a parent animates the deformation of the child.*

LOCAL LATTICES

A local lattice is simply a small lattice that affects only certain parts of a model, not the whole thing. A local lattice can be placed anywhere on an object to deform the points in complex ways and can be animated in size and translation to create moving deformations, such as the bulge of a character traveling through a garden hose. Local lattices are based on a primitive object that you create.

This starting model provides the bounding shape for the local lattice. Select a primitive cube and execute the Lattice→MakeLattice command to generate the local lattice icon. Then attach the new local lattice to a specific model that you want to deform with the Effects→Local Lattice command in the Motion module and edit the local lattice points in the same manner as you would for a regular node or branch lattice.

ANIMATION WITH DEFORMATION BY LATTICE

You can animate a lattice's Control points using a method similar to shape animation. Each lattice keyframe saves the shape of the lattice Control points, which in turn deforms the object geometry beneath them.

After you have changed the shape of a lattice, save that shape at the current frame with the SaveKey→Object→Node Lattice or SaveKey→Object→Branch Lattice command. As the lattice vertices interpolate over time, the deformation of the object also changes, producing smooth animated shape interpolation.

After you have changed the shape of the lattice and deformed the object, you can use some of the other Lattice commands:

- Lattice→Remove
- Lattice→Reset
- Lattice→Deactivate
- Lattice→Info
- Lattice→Freeze

The Lattice→Remove command detaches the lattice and throws it away, so that the object that was deformed is no longer affected by the lattice and regains its former shape. If you don't like the lattice animation you made, or if you want to make a new lattice with different subdivision detail, you can always remove the lattice with this command and start over.

The Lattice→Reset command is similar to Remove in that it returns the object to its original shape by returning all the changed lattice edit points to the default original position for that lattice. The lattice remains attached to the object, however, so you can re-edit it. This command is very useful when animating shapes because you will often want the model to return to a standard shape before you transform the lattice into a new shape.

The Lattice→Deactivate command is critical for combining local and branch lattices on one hierarchy of models because it temporarily turns the lattice off while retaining all the previously set animation. When you have two active lattices on a hierarchy, one as a local lattice and one as a branch, only the top lattice can be edited. If you need to re-edit the lattice lower down in the hierarchy, you can deactivate the top branch lattice to make the lower lattices accessible. Once deactivated, you can use the Lattice→Info command to reactivate the lattice.

The Lattice→Freeze command cooks the vertices of the deformed object into the current shape and discards the lattice that is attached. It's not possible to return to the original shape of the model after this command unless you have previously set a shape keyframe for it.

One simple but gratifying use of node and branch lattice modeling and animation is in the creation of a simple, rubber hose-style cartoon street (see Figure 14.31). You can use a node lattice to model the houses into funky, deformed cartoon shapes, and you can use a branch lattice to make the houses on either side of the street dance by stretching up and down in time to music. If you are really ambitious, you can even use a local lattice to deform the chimney on one house as it huffs and puffs, blowing smoke rings.

FIGURE 14.31   *The completed happy street.*

1. **Make Some Houses.**

    There should be at least two different styles of houses, built by drawing a linear spline in the Front view with Grid Lock on to ensure accurate lines. Simply draw the outline of the front of a house; then close the curve and convert it to a face before you extrude the house in the Z direction, as a polygonal object, to give the house some depth.

    We need the house to have some doors and windows, and we also need the house to have enough subdivision to deform smoothly. Both can be accomplished at the same time by executing the Effect→Subdivision command in the Model module (see Figure 14.32). We primarily need detail added in X and Y, so add eight subdivisions in each of them, and none in Z.

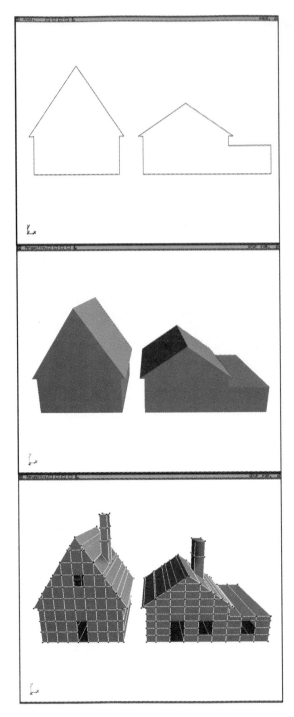

FIGURE 14.32 *The linear house outline, the extruded house, and the subdivided house.*

Now with the added polygonal detail, select some polygons in the shape of doors and windows, and delete them (with Delete→Selection in the POL mode in the Model module).

To add the chimney, select a roof polygon and duplicate it in the POL mode, then scale it to a square shape, and duplicate again to form the first row of bricks in the chimney. Translate the new brick layer in global Y, and then duplicate and repeat the translation eight times to build up the chimney. You may add in more detail around the doors, windows, and roof line using polygonal modeling techniques.

Finish off two different houses.

2. **Make Eight Different Houses.**

We need a row of houses for this shot, all slightly different. They will be grouped in two sets of four houses so that the two groups can be animated differently to counterpoint the music.

Duplicate each original house three more times and arrange all the houses next to one another (see Figure 14.33). If you wish, add a polygonal street and sidewalk in front of them with an extrusion.

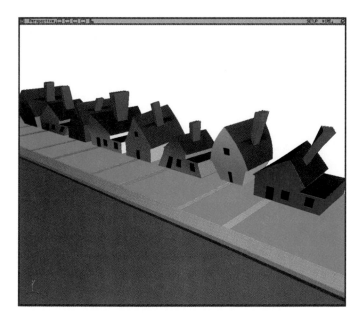

Figure 14.33 *Arrange the houses on the street.*

Select the first house and apply a node lattice to it with the Lattice→Node→Create command. In the Create Lattice dialog box, change Subdivision to 2,2,2 for X,Y,Z and change the Interpolation to Curve for each axis. When you click Ok, a lattice is formed around the house. Tag the top row of points and rotate them slightly to give the house a funky, ramshackle cartoon appearance. Tag different groups of points to change the shape of the lattice, and therefore the house. When you are done, freeze the house into this new shape with the Lattice→Node→Freeze command. Move on to the next house, making them all slightly different by adding a lattice and modeling the house with it. When you like them, freeze them all to remove the node lattices.

3. **Make the Groups.**

Create a primitive cube and scale it to a size that encloses all the houses. This object needs to become the parent of the first group of houses, houses 1, 3, 6, and 8. Name the cube outer_houses, then duplicate it, and name the new cube inner_houses. Make the inner_houses cube the parent of houses 2, 4, 5, and 7. Select the outer_houses cube as a branch and use the Lattice→Branch→Create command to make a new lattice with curve interpolation and three subdivisions in X, Y, and Z (see Figure 14.34). Repeat with the inner_houses object, so you have two branch lattices.

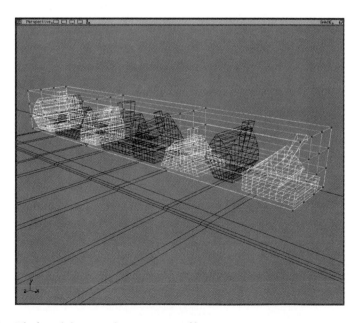

FIGURE 14.34   *The branch lattice encloses one group of houses.*

4. **Animate the Houses.**

The houses squash and stretch to a beat that happens twice a second, or every 15 frames. By simply tagging groups of points on the lattice and scaling them in X, Y, and Z, or rotating them slightly around Z, you can make the houses all lean inwards, outwards, rotate side to side, and stretch up and down. Experiment on the outer_houses to get a feel for what you can do; then return the lattice to the starting position with the Lattice→Branch→Reset command.

The inner and outer houses will have a different animation pattern to add to the effect of a chorus line. The pattern will have main beats every 15 frames and static beats every seven frames where the houses return to normal shape. The outer houses start on frame 1, and the inner houses start on frame 8.

Because we want the houses to return to the default pose between beats, we need to save lattice keyframes in advance. Select the outer houses and save a keyframe with the SaveKey→Object→Branch Lattice command at frames 8, 22, 37, 52, 67, 82, and 97. Remember to use the middle mouse button on the SaveKey menu cell to save time and enhance workflow.

Repeat the process with the inner houses to prepare them to animate. Set default keyframes on the branch lattice at frames 1, 15, 30, 45, 60, 75, and 90, so that the inner houses are syncopated with the outer houses.

Now it's time to animate the outer houses branch lattice. Edit the lattice shape to stretch up and scale inwards a bit, and then save a keyframe with SaveKey→Object→Branch Lattice at frame 15. Move forward 15 frames, changing the shape of the branch lattice to deform the houses up and down and in and out, saving keyframes at 30, 45, 60, 75, and 90.

At last, animate the inner houses. These inner houses predominately twist and rotate side to side in counterpoint to the outer houses up and down motion. Set branch lattice keyframes for the inner_house lattice at frames 8, 22, 37, 52, 67, 82, and 97.

5. **Play the Animation and Tweak.**

Play the animation to get a sense of the timing and make any changes you want to on the branch lattices.

If you are feeling tricky, create a local lattice out of a small cube with the Lattice→MakeLattice command, edit the points on the resulting lattice object to bulge it out in the middle, and translate it to sit around the chimney of one of your houses. Connect that house to the local lattice with the Effect→LocalLattice command in the Motion module; then animate the shape of the local lattice to look as if the chimney is huffing and puffing.

6. **Add Color and Render.**

Add some primary colors to the happy houses with local materials. Render the finished work at 300 × 200 and view it in the FlipBook to get a good sense of your animation and timing.

That's all there is to it! The animated lattice deformations are a tremendously simple and effective way to create sophisticated animation effects without a lot of tedious animation drudgery.

CONCLUSION

When you animate with static surfaces, your characters are almost certain to be stiff and lifeless. Softimage 3D's great deformation tools finally make it possible to truly bring characters to life quickly and easily. The animated deformations that Softimage 3D pioneered are a huge reason for the overwhelming success of Softimage 3D in the character animation business. Judicious use of these powerful tools will set your work apart and bring you into new realms of imagineering!

In this chapter, you learned how to:

- Deform static geometry with simple curves.
- Animate those Curve deformations, making possible effects like dancing scissors and slithering snakes.
- Wrap objects onto other patch objects for clever text effects and a lot more.
- Animate with lattices for quick and easy squash and stretch cartoon style work.

© *Bryan Ballinger 1997.*

CHAPTER 15

THE ACTOR MODULE WITH INVERSE KINEMATICS

Inverse Kinematics (IK) is probably the most popular topic in 3D animation today. Softimage 3D was one of the first 3D animation programs to implement a production IK package, and now Softimage has one of the most complex and flexible models in the animation business. The Softimage IK system is a primary reason for the dominance of the Softimage Creative Environment in movie creature effects, and it is a large part of why Softimage 3D is considered the greatest character animation tool in the world.

Despite the fact that IK is rarely used in production, that very few software packages support IK with sufficient complexity to animate a carrot, and that it is just plain tough to understand, everybody wants it. But what is it? In this chapter we'll answer that question and lead you through practical examples, starting simply and working up to complex IK systems.

In this chapter you will learn:

- All the terminology, such as IK, joint, chain, and effector
- How to build a single IK chain
- How to operate your chain with an effector
- How to group many chains together for complex skeletons
- How to animate your IK systems
- How to build IK skeletons with constraints and clusters

INVERSE KINEMATICS BASICS

At its most basic, IK, like the simpler Forward Kinematics, is a method of animating a hierarchy of objects—such as a skeleton (see Figure 15.1).

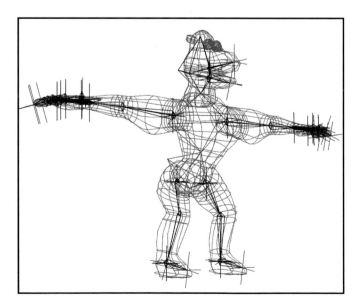

FIGURE 15.1 *Julian showing off his skeleton.*

To understand Inverse Kinematics, first consider Forward Kinematic systems. If you make an arm by building the upper arm, attach a parent forearm object to it, then a palm to the forearm, then a first finger joint to the palm, and then each other finger joint to the previous, you are constructing a Forward Kinematic system. If the local center of each child object is located at the joint position between the child and the parent object, as you rotate the parent all the children move as well. By a painstaking process of saving rotational keyframes for each joint in the bone structure, you can animate the arm moving while opening and closing the fingers (see Figure 15.2).

In the early days of computer graphics, all motion was performed this way, with a hierarchy of transformations on each object. The major problem with this approach was that, although accurate, it was a very slow way to generate animation. Each and every joint was keyframed at each and every transition frame, and when changes were necessary, each and every joint was re-keyframed. Forward Kinematics lacks the ease, speed, and flexibility of Inverse Kinematics as an animation system.

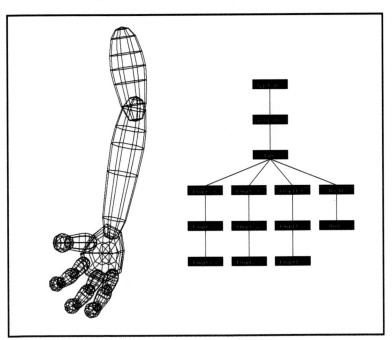

FIGURE 15.2   *A Forward Kinematic hierarchy.*

Inverse Kinematics is the simple theory that if you build an articulated model, such as an arm, you should be able to move the arm by pulling on the finger, not just by rotating the shoulder joint, the elbow joint, the wrist, and then each joint in the finger (see Figure 15.3). The software should understand the relationship between each bone in the system and how they are connected by joints that can rotate. When you translate the end of the bone structure (the finger), each joint in order from the finger to the wrist to the elbow to the shoulder should flex and rotate to allow the arm to move. That is, after all, the way it seems to work in real life.

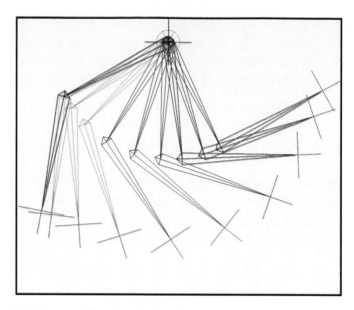

FIGURE 15.3   *With IK, you pull on the end of the chain to rotate the joints.*

NOTE

Actually, in real life if you grab your friend's arm and pull it, that is Inverse Kinematics. But if you wave your own arm, that's Forward Kinematics, because you have muscles that rotate each joint independently, while your brain calculates how much of each is required to get the finger where it needs to go.

In an Inverse Kinematic system, you need to save a keyframe for only the position of the end of each bone structure at different points in time. The IK system interpolates the rotation of each joint in that bone structure to get the end where you want it, when you want it.

IK systems are flexible and easy to edit in Softimage. When changes are necessary, only the end of the bone structure needs to be re-keyframed or edited in the F-curve window.

What's more, in a software IK system, a number of smaller bone structures can be linked together to form a more complex skeletal structure (see Figure 15.4). Then each bone structure can move, either dependent on its parent or on its own. The positions of the end of each IK bone structure can be keyframed, so that as one part of the skeleton moves, all those bone structures attached to it also move.

Finally, a skin can be wrapped around the skeleton so that just like a skeleton the IK system provides support for the skin and bends it as the skeleton moves around (see Figure 15.5).

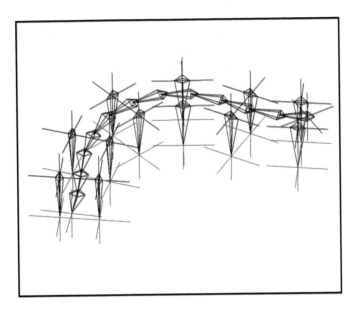

FIGURE 15.4   *Several IK structures parented together.*

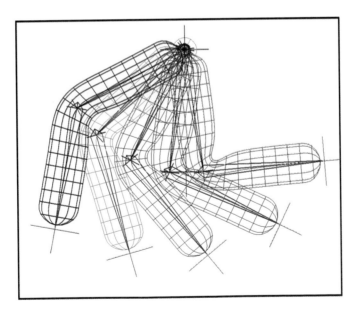

FIGURE 15.5   *A polygonal skin wrapper around the IK system.*

But IK isn't all smiles and roses. Unlike Forward Kinematics systems, in which each joint rotation is specified explicitly, the rotation in IK systems is specified implicitly by the position of the end of the bone structure. This means that there could be more than one way to get the bone structure to its end position (called an *IK solution*). When there is more than one IK solution, the bone structure may behave erratically. The capability to precisely control the behaviors of the bone structures and the skins over them is what makes using IK so tough.

TERMINOLOGY

In Softimage, all the Inverse Kinematics controls, along with the other controls necessary for adding dynamic forces and applying skins to your characters, are located in the Actor module. Click the Actor module at the top of the screen, or press the F3 button to go there.

In Softimage, each bone structure is called an *IK chain*. In the arm analogy, the arm itself is a chain, while each finger is a separate chain.

On a single chain, the top of the hierarchy is called the *root* of the chain. The root is a null object that anchors the chain in space. After the root comes a *joint*. The joint is also a *bone segment*, with the rotational joint at the top, at the thick end of the bone, near the root. The joint can rotate, and scaling the joint segment can make the joint bigger or smaller (see Figure 15.6).

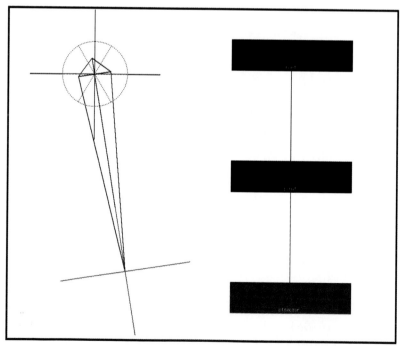

FIGURE 15.6 *IK terminology.*

That joint can also be followed by one or more additional joints, each with the capability of rotating around the end of the joint above it in the chain. There can be any number of joints in your chain in addition to the first one.

Finally, at the end of the last joint is the *effector*, the most important part of the chain. Colored in red by default, the effector is a null object that acts as the handle for the IK chain. When you select the effector and translate it, the Softimage IK system rotates each joint in the chain to try to get the effector where you are dragging it. If you try to translate the effector away from the chain, the chain just rotates to its maximum length and points towards the direction you are trying to move it. IK chains are not elastic.

When you create an IK chain, you will notice a pair of dotted cones protruding from the top of the first joint (see Figure 15.7). Also known as the cones of death, these cones are the visual indicators of the *critical zone*. When the effector is translated into the area of the critical zone, unexpected flipping may occur as the IK chain changes orientation rapidly. It's a good idea to keep your effector away from the critical zones.

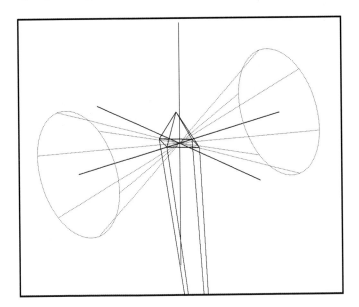

FIGURE 15.7 *These cones are the critical zones.*

TUTORIAL: DRAWING YOUR FIRST CHAIN

It's time to put all this theory into practice and forge an IK chain.

1. **Enter the Actor Module.**

   Click the Actor module at the top right of the screen, or press the F3 key on your keyboard. The Actor module is where all the commands that control Inverse Kinematic systems are located.

2. **Draw the Chain.**

   Choose the command Skeleton→Draw 2D Chain (see Figure 15.8). Click with your left mouse button in the Front window to drop the root. Then move your mouse and click and hold the left mouse button to place the first joint. While your mouse button is down, you can drag the end of the joint to a favored position. Click again to place a second joint, a third, and so on until you have all the joints you need (see Figure 15.9).

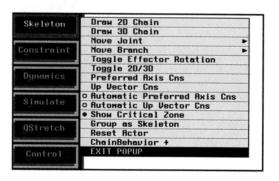

FIGURE 15.8   *The Skeleton menu cells.*

3. **Move the Chain.**

   Convert one of your View windows (the lower right one is traditional) to the Schematic view, and examine the schematic representation of the IK chain. Observe the root at the top, a series of joints in the middle, and the effector at the bottom (see Figure 15.10).

   Select the effector, either in an Orthographic view or in the Schematic view. Activate all the Translate menu cells, and check the Mode box to ensure that you are in DRG mode, the easiest way of translating things around. Drag in the window you drew the chain in to move the effector, which causes the joints to rotate to keep the effector moving where you want it!

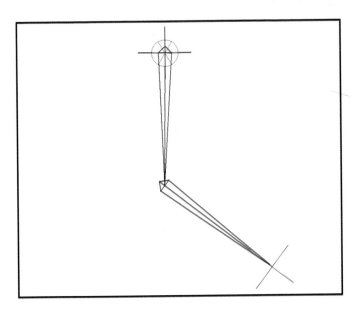

FIGURE 15.9   *Your first IK chain.*

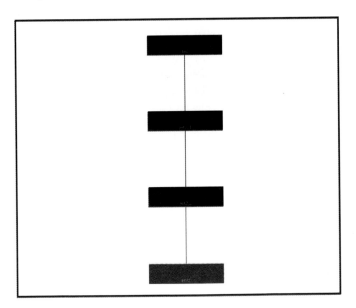

FIGURE 15.10   *A Schematic view of your IK chain.*

4. Animate the Chain.

At frame 1, place the effector somewhere in space, and save a keyframe for the explicit translation of the effector. At frame 10, move the effector and save another keyframe. Play the animation to see the IK system interpolate the joint rotations to get the effector where it needs to go.

That's it! Creating and animating a basic IK chain is that easy! Of course, it just becomes more complicated and difficult from here.

TYPES OF CHAINS

Softimage offers two major categories of IK chains: 2D chains and 3D chains. The difference revolves around the kinds of joints found in the chain. Before we discuss the differences, however, you must understand a couple of hard and fast rules.

First, a chain's root is always a 3D joint, which is to say that it can rotate around any axis freely. The reason that the root is always free to rotate in 3D is that it is just a null object.

The first joint is also always a 3D joint, meaning that it can rotate freely around its local X, Y, and Z axes. You may think of this first joint as a ball joint. The reason that the first joint is always a ball joint is that most creatures start each articulated skeletal segment with a ball joint, and then move on to 2D hinge joints for each subsequent joint. Think about it—your arm starts with a ball joint (the shoulder) and then has a hinge (the elbow). Same with your legs (hip to knee). Your fingers each work the same way, connected to the palm with a ball joint (a 3D knuckle) and then a series of hinges (2D knuckles) (see Figure 15.11).

The rotation of the effector at the end of the chain is another special case and is very important to understand, because the effector is often used for parenting other objects into the chain. The effector by default is rotated by the last joint in the chain, so the effector always has the same orientation as the last joint. In some cases, that is not desirable, so the effector rotation can be toggled on and off at will with the Skeleton→Toggle Effector Rotation command (see Figure 15.12). When Effector Rotation is off, you can rotate and keyframe the effector according to the global axes, not the local axes of the joint above it. You would turn Effector Rotation off, for instance, to keep a character's feet parallel to the floor, no matter what the character's shin is doing.

2D CHAINS

In a 2D IK chain, all joints except the root and the first joint rotate in a 2D plane, meaning that they rotate on only one axis, the local Z axis. When you draw a chain, the joints are created with the X and Y local axes in the plane you drew the chain in, and the Z axis extending perpendicular to the drawing plane. The second and subsequent joints in a 2D chain, therefore, rotate around their Z axes (see Figure 15.13).

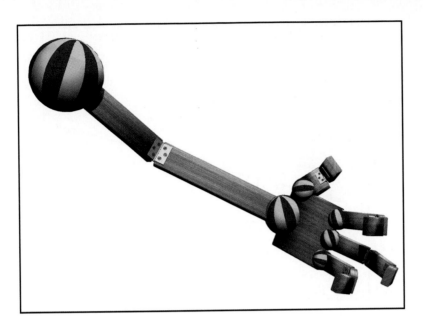

FIGURE 15.11 *2D means a hinge joint; 3D means a ball joint.*

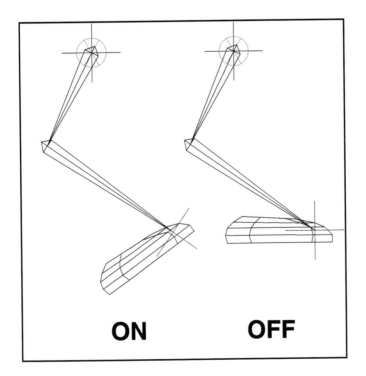

FIGURE 15.12 *Effector Rotation on and off.*

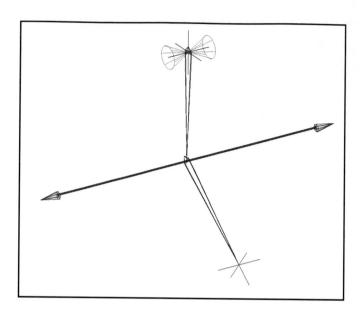

FIGURE 15.13   *IK chains always have the Z axis perpendicular to the draw plane.*

NOTE

Knowing which axis a 2D chain rotates around is vital when you try to animate and constrain the chain. Repeat to yourself right now "It's always the Z axis. It's always the Z axis. It's always the Z axis—at least on 2D chains after the first joint."

The position that you draw the chain in, therefore, has a great deal to do with how it functions. The chain also has an inside and an outside for each hinge joint, which will determine which way the hinge will bend when you move the effector. The inside of the joint is the side where the joint segments form an acute angle (less than 180 degrees), while the outside is the side where the joint segments connect at an obtuse angle (more than 180 degrees). Look at your own leg to find the inside and outside of your knee. The IK joint behaves as if it doesn't like to rotate past the full extension, the 180 degree rotation where the upper and lower joints are aligned. On your own body, the preferred angle keeps your knee bent in the right direction, and going past 180 would break your knee. (Ouch!) The moral of this story is that it's a great idea to draw your chains in the View window that is in a plane with the movement you want from the chain, and to draw the chain with a slight bend to indicate which side of the hinge is inside and which is outside. Imagine that you will build a character with a slightly loose pose, as if he is standing with arms and legs slightly bent. The angle that you draw the chain in is called the *preferred angle* (see Figure 15.14).

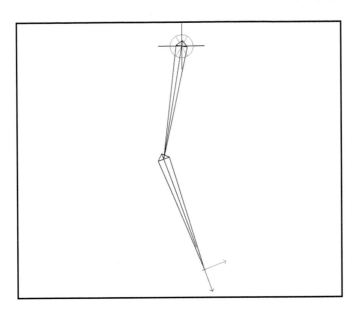

FIGURE 15.14 *An IK chain showing the preferred angle and the inside and outside of the joint.*

Because they come complete with one ball joint and a number of hinges, 2D chains are the most useful for performing the majority of animations, particularly animations of humans.

3D CHAINS

These chains are built so that each joint can rotate completely in all three axes (see Figure 15.15). These joints are much harder to control than the 2D hinge joints, but some types of bone structures, such as spines and tails, have joints that rotate in all directions. 3D chains can be used for these occasions when you want the IK chain to have a full range of motion. 3D chains still have a preferred angle, however, so it's still a good idea to draw them with a slight bend at each joint.

> **NOTE**
>
> The IK system doesn't like to hyperextend hinge joints when you move the effector, but if you forget to draw the chain facing in the right direction, you can rotate the joint in the Z axis manually with the Rotate menu cells until the joint bends in the right direction, and then resume using the effector to move the chain.

You can convert chains between the 2D and 3D chain types easily with the Skeleton→Toggle 2D/3D command.

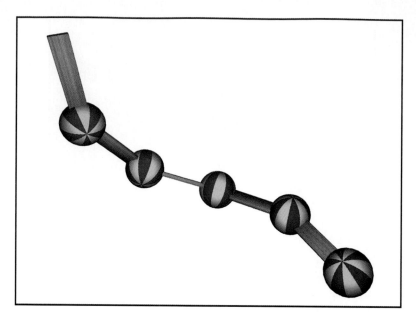

FIGURE 15.15 *3D IK chains.*

THE RESOLUTION PLANE

In a 2D chain, the hinge joints enable the segments to rotate in a 2D plane, but the ball joint at the top of the chain controls what exactly that 2D plane of rotation is. For accurate animation, you must be able to specify the 2D plane in which the 2D chain's hinges rotate. This 2D plane is called the *resolution plane* of the chain, because it is in the space of this plane that the IK system resolves the rotations of the joints necessary to get the effector where you want it (see Figure 15.16).

To get the real idea, stand up and perform this exercise. First, make a fist and extend it in front of your face and then flex your bicep like you are lifting weights, doing a bicep curl. As your arm bends, it forms an angle at the elbow. That bend occurs in a 2D plane extending in front of your face. When doing a bicep curl, that plane (your arm's resolution plane) remains static. Unless you change the resolution plane, all you (or your character) can do is bicep curls.

Now pretend that you are playing tennis, and swing your racket underhand as if returning a lobbed tennis ball lazily floating over the net. Do that a few times, examining how your elbow is bending.

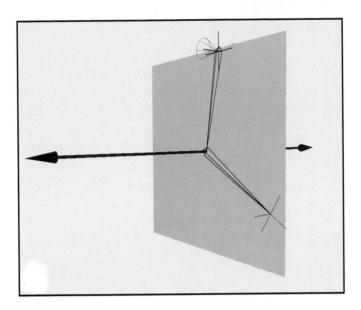

FIGURE 15.16 *The resolution plane is the plane the IK chain wants to move in.*

Your elbow joint is bending the same as it was, but the motion is obviously much more complex. That's because the resolution plane of the elbow doesn't remain static during your tennis return; it animates as your shoulder changes the angle between your arm and your body. If you couldn't control the resolution plane of your own arm you would move very stiffly, bending only at the waist to get your arm in position to bend. That's what badly animated IK characters look like, stiff. If you stop to examine the motion of your own arm as you make routine motions, you'll find that you change the resolution plane of your elbow constantly. Your characters should as well.

The resolution plane of a 2D chain is always perpendicular to the Z axis, because that's the one axis that the hinge rotates in. So you can control the resolution plane of your chain by rotating the top (ball) joint in Y and X. There is fortunately a pair of easier ways to animate the resolution plane: You can constrain the axes of the first joint with a preferred axis constraint or an automatic up vector. Each of these constraints gives you a simple null object that controls the resolution plane, so you can set simple explicit translation keys to animate the motion of the plane.

PREFERRED AXIS CONSTRAINT

The preferred axis of rotation in an IK chain is by default the Z axis. The second and subsequent joints in the chain then rotate like a hinge to change positions in the plane perpendicular to the Z axis, the XY plane. If you visualize the hinge of the joints, the hinge pin on which they rotate is pointed directly at the local Z axis.

An easy way to change the orientation of this hinge (in reality, it is the preferred axis) is to constrain it to a null floating in space so that the Z axis always is oriented towards that null. This null is call the *preferred axis constraint* (see Figure 15.17). On your own arm, imagine a hinge in your elbow pointing directly to the side of your body. If you welded a bar to the hinge and then welded a ball at the end of the bar, the ball would be the preferred axis null. When you grab the ball and pull it to a different position, it changes the orientation of the hinge in your elbow and the resolution plane of your entire arm changes.

FIGURE 15.17   *The preferred axis constraint shows the Z axis.*

You can manually add a preferred axis constraint to any chain by creating a null object and positioning it to the side of the chain in the local Z axis of the first joint (more or less is fine). Then select the first joint, choose the Skeleton→Preferred Axis Cns command, and pick the null object you made as the constraint. Now select the null object and translate it around to see the effect on the resolution plane of the chain.

The easiest way to get a preferred axis constraint on each and every chain is to toggle on the Automatic Preferred Axis Cns in the Skeleton menu cells. Now all the new chains that you draw are automatically assigned a null object placed perpendicular to the resolution plane as a preferred axis constraint.

AUTOMATIC UP VECTOR

The *up vector constraint* is another way of controlling the resolution plane of each chain in your IK system. The up vector precisely constrains the Y axis of the first joint to point at a null object that is the constraint object. The location of the effector determines the X axis of the resolution plane (see Figure 15.18).

FIGURE 15.18   *The up vector also shows the resolution plane, by defining a third point in the plane.*

Therefore, between the two objects (the null and the effector) you can control the Y and X axes, and the Z axis must always be perpendicular to that plane. In that slightly roundabout way, you control the resolution plane of the chain. When I began working with IK systems, I found the preferred axis constraint simpler to visualize and use than the up vector constraint, but in some ways the up vector constraint is more useful in IK systems with symmetry, like bipedal humans.

Unlike the preferred axis constraint, the up vector constraint is usually placed above the first joint in the Y axis. Visualize a rod strapped onto your bicep, protruding above your head with a null at the end of it. As you move the null at the end of the rod, your arm is forced to rotate around the shoulder in a predictable way, changing the resolution plane of your elbow.

To add an up vector constraint to an existing chain, create a null object and translate it above the root of the chain. Then select the first joint, choose the command Skeleton→Up Vector Cns, and pick the null object to complete the command. Translate the null to see the effect on the chain.

You can choose to have an up vector constraint added automatically to each new chain you draw by toggling on the Automatic Up Vector Cns control in the Skeleton menu. The up vector constraint and the preferred axis constraint accomplish the same task, so it's not possible to have both added automatically, although you can add both manually. If you do add both, the up vector takes precedence over the preferred axis.

CONSTRAINING ROTATIONS

When you build a complex character with many different IK chains, you'll quickly find that it becomes difficult to keep all the chains behaving in a realistic manner. Like unruly children, they habitually wander all over the place. As you chase one down and put it where it needs to go, others may take off and do something weird.

Another related problem is that unlike real creatures, IK chains are perfectly limber. They can put their legs behind their ears with no problem, or break an elbow and spin the arm freely around and around. Besides being disturbing to watch, this spaghetti joint capability makes IK difficult to animate convincingly.

The solution to both problems is to set some rules for each joint, determining where and how much it can rotate (see Figure 15.19). For instance, the hip joint should be able to revolve freely with about 30 degrees of freedom. But the knee should bend only one way, and then only about 120 degrees. Otherwise your character could plant his own foot in his butt.

In Softimage, you establish these rules for each joint by setting *rotation limits* on each axis of each joint. This is accomplished by selecting a joint and then choosing the Constraint→Rotation Limits command in the Actor module (see Figure 15.20).

Once an IK chain rotates a joint to the limit you set, that joint just won't rotate any further. If other joints still rotate in a way that gets the effector closer to the goal, they continue to rotate until they hit their limits and stop. Each joint can have a minimum and a maximum rotation limit for each axis, so you can set a range of motion.

Softimage can even set damping principles to the ends of the limit range, so that the joints don't snap into the final position but instead ease into them as if the resistance in that joint is increasing as it approaches its limit. Unfortunately, this damping doesn't occur automatically in regular IK and can only be activated when the IK is driven by a constraint or dynamics. (We'll discuss this in Chapter 16, "Animating with Dynamics.")

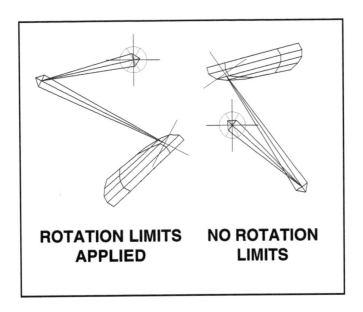

ROTATION LIMITS APPLIED   **NO ROTATION LIMITS**

FIGURE 15.19   *An example of joint rotation limits.*

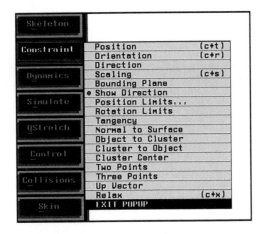

FIGURE 15.20   *The Actor module Constraint menus.*

When you invoke the Constraint→Rotation Limits command, a dialog pops up, allowing you to set the limits you want (see Figure 15.21). There is a check box next to the Min and Max Rotation for each axis, so you can specify rotation limits in only certain axes if you wish.

Thomas Schelesny

Animation Supervisor

Tippett Studio

Tippett Studio is a unique company in the visual effects world. Established in 1983, in Berkeley, California, Tippett focuses exclusively on character animation and visual effects for major motion pictures. Under the guidance of its founder, internationally acclaimed animator and visual effects master Phil Tippett, the studio consistently ranks in the top tier of the world's animation and visual effects studios.

Anthony: So Thomas, what are you working on now?

Thomas: We are currently wrapping up *My Favorite Martian*. As the animation supervisor, I work with 15 animators in our department. My job is to take the requests from the director and break these down into specific animation-related directions, so that all the animators know exactly what the performance elements are, and what we need to deliver. Before

Martian, I served as the animation supervisor on a film called *Virus*, and before that, as an animator on *Starship Troopers*. Prior to arriving at Tippett I worked for a small effects house in Vancouver, creating visual effects for TV shows and TV movies and commercials. In total, I've been using Softimage for about five years.

Anthony: Do you prefer working as the animator, hands on, or directing other animators?

Thomas: Both jobs have their own rewards. Being an animator gives you a real sense of ownership and pride on an individual shot. On the other hand, as an animation aupervisor, the rewards come from helping to bring an entire sequence of shots together. I now have the opportunity to review the animations from the many talented people in our department and learn from the work that they have done.

Step 1: The background plate, shot on film. The actors are imagining deadly foes.
Property of TriStar Pictures © 1997. Courtesy of Tippett Studio.

Step 2: The background plate rotoscoped into Softimage 3D to aid in positioning the bugs for the shot. Property of TriStar Pictures © 1997. Courtesy of Tippett Studio.

Anthony: Where are the animators at Tippett coming from, and what kinds of skill sets do they have?

Thomas: Phil Tippett has always made it clear that he wants talented artists working here, to whom we can teach the modern digital tools. That philosophy resonates from one end of the company to the other. Phil hires people who bring with them experience from other fields, like stop motion animation or sculpting. There are animators here who had never previously used computers, and we literally taught them on the job.

We look for animators who already understand motion, posing, and timing, and those skills can also be found in stop motion and 2D animators, as well.

In looking in several related fields, there is a wider talent pool for us to draw from. Let's face it, it's difficult to go out and find computer experts who also happen to be amazing artists. It's much easier to find talented artists to whom you can teach the necessary computer skills.

Anthony: What other skills did you have that you brought to animation?

Thomas: Animation is the observation of reality and the interpretation of that reality into a performance. It's impossible to create an interpretation without first observing, studying, and then interpreting. I have always felt pretty comfortable in getting up and physically acting out my ideas in order to better understand the mechanics of a particular movement or gesture.

Basically, not being afraid to pantomime or experience the movements for myself.

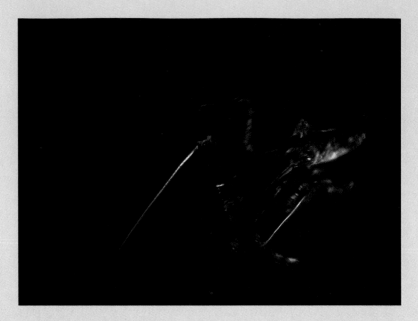

Step 3: The fully rendered bug. Note the motion blur. Courtesy of Tippett Studio.

Getting up and performing something with a stopwatch and shooting reference videos, these are things that I enjoy doing and try to help other animators find value in doing. After a while, everyone stops feeling self conscious, and pantomime becomes a natural extension of how we discuss animation issues. Now, it's almost impossible for me to discuss a performance with an animator without us actually acting it out. So much clarity would be lost in attempting the same conversation with only words.

Anthony: What's the part of the process that most interrupts your creative flow?

Thomas: Hardware and software issues are my stumbling blocks. I always likened using Wavefront to be like driving a stick shift, where you have to do everything yourself. Then I learned 3D Studio, which was like driving an automatic where you give up control for its ease of use. Softimage is like driving a Hondamatic, where I still have the control I need, but the software deals with much of the background rocket science that I don't care that much for. In general though, with all these programs, the interface between the artist and the computer is the main limitation.

I wonder whether the current type of computer monitor and mouse combination is the best way for animators to view and manipulate their scenes. A 2D representation of a 3D computer environment, and the manipulation of such an environment by sliding a mouse on a flat table top seems somewhat counter productive. Tools like our studio's direct input devices, which translate the poses of an encoded armature directly into the Softimage scene, seem like steps in the right direction. I guess 3D glasses are next on my wish list.

*Step 4: The fully composited frame with both live action and CG elements. Property of TriStar Pictures ©
1997. Courtesy of Tippett Studio.*

Courtesy of Tippett Studio.

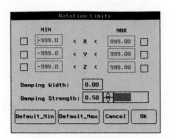

FIGURE 15.21   *The Rotation Limits dialog box.*

SETTING ROTATION LIMITS: THE WORKFLOW

You can type values directly into the Rotation Limits dialog box's limit text boxes if you wish, but that's a slow method for setting limits. The preferred workflow is a lot easier, but like so many things in Softimage 3D|Extreme, it's not exactly plainly evident.

1. Constrain the first ball joint.

   Remember the first joint is always a ball joint, so we need to consider all three axes. Select the joint, and then use the Constrain→Rotation Limits command to bring up the Joint Rotation Limits dialog. Click the Default_Min and the Default_Max buttons. These buttons load the current rotation of the selected joint into the limit boxes. Now you know exactly the current rotation of the joint without having to figure it out! Give the ball joint a little freedom to revolve by subtracting 20 degrees from each of the MIN limits and adding 20 degrees to the MAX limits. Click Ok to complete the command (see Figure 15.22).

2. Constrain the second joint.

   Select the second joint and click the RotZ menu cell. We know that the hinge axis for that joint is Z, so revolving only Z keeps the joint properly in the resolution plane.

   Drag the mouse in the View window to rotate the joint back and forth a bit to get a feel for the action. Then rotate the joint to its minimum position, the point at which you want it to go no further. Click the Constraint menu cell with the middle mouse button to recall the Limits dialog. Click the Default_Min button and click Ok. Because we are primarily concerned with the hinge axis, the Z axis, you don't have to set any constrained limits for rotation in X and Y, as long as you plan to use one of the resolution plane constraints to keep the chain from misbehaving in those axes.

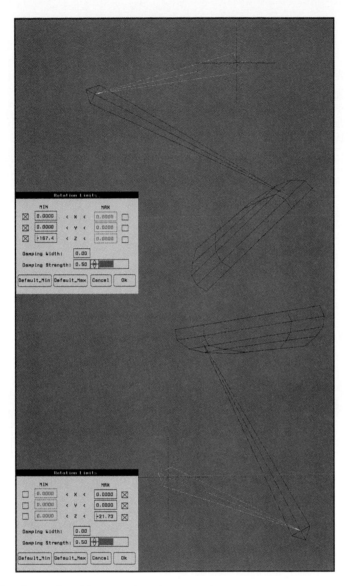

FIGURE 15.22 *Setting the minimum and maximum rotations.*

Now rotate the joint to the maximum position, the point at which the joint is totally extended and going further would break something. Again click the Constrain menu with the middle mouse button and use the Default_Max button to enter the current rotation limits. If you want the joint to have some looseness in the hinge, you can add a little to the default max values for X and Y to give the joint a little play.

3. Lather, rinse, repeat.

Repeat the process outlined in step 2 for each joint in the chain.

When you are done, the chain moves only where you want it and is much easier to animate realistically.

PARENTING IK CHAINS TOGETHER

So far we have dealt only with single IK chains, the simplest case. But except for worms, snakes, and other creatures that slither on their bellies, a single IK chain isn't good enough. People, for instance, have the head bone connected to the neck bone, the neck bone connected to the back bone, the back bone connected to the leg bone, the leg bone connected to the foot bone, and the foot bone connected to the toe bone.

IK chains can be parented together to form complex hierarchies of IK motion. A chain root, joint, or effector can become the parent of another entire chain or several chains in the usual manner, with the Parent menu cell. If you make the effector the parent of another IK chain, the root of the child chain will be transformed by the effector, moving and rotating in space to stay attached to the effector. Then that second child chain can become the parent of a third IK chain, and so on indefinitely (see Figure 15.23).

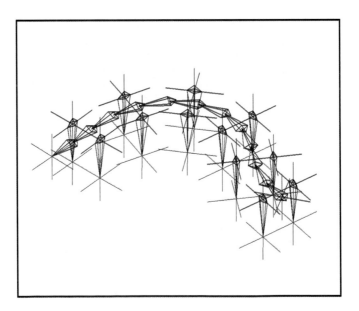

FIGURE 15.23 *One big IK chain is the parent of many small ones.*

Each joint in a chain can also be the parent of another chain, and as the effector rotates the joints, they drive the translation of their children appropriately. Try it out by building a millipede with one 20-joint IK chain as the spine and a bunch of simple, one-segment IK chains as the legs.

METHODS OF ATTACHING GEOMETRY TO IK

So far, we've built IK chains and moved them around, but we haven't attached any geometry to them. IK chains can do two things to the models you attach to them. They can:

- Transform them in space.
- Deform them by moving vertices and Control points on the object.

When an IK chain transforms an object without deforming it, the object stays rigid (see Figure 15.24). This method is best for mechanical objects and other non-organic models. The joints in the IK chain need something to cover them in a rigid model to hide the fact that there is nothing at the joint. That's why the ubiquitous robot and mechton models frequently seen stomping through bad animation invariably have shoulder pads and knee guards.

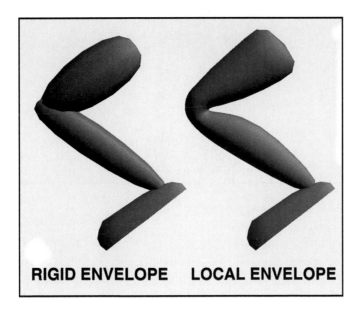

FIGURE 15.24 *Rigid IK versus bending.*

When an IK chain deforms a model, much more complex and accurate animations can be created. The IK chain can bend the model where the joint is to simulate the crease in the skin caused by bending, or the IK chain can bulge the model to indicate changes in the musculature beneath the surface of the skin. When using IK to deform a model, you can add one piece of skin over the entire IK system to avoid unsightly seams and missing joint geometry.

PARENTING

The simplest way to attach geometry to an IK system is to directly parent the pieces onto the IK chains, connecting each element of the model to the IK joint that controls it. This method transforms the geometry but does not deform it, making parenting most appropriate for very simple mechanical characters and objects (see Figure 15.25).

FIGURE 15.25 *An IK stickman using parenting.*

The process is simple—create the IK system you want and then create models for each joint. Position each segment of the model directly over the joint that will drive it, and rotate it appropriately to face in the same direction as the joint. Next make the model a child of the joint that lies under it. After all the models are connected to the IK hierarchy, you can translate the effectors of the chains to see the models translated and rotated by the chain.

ENVELOPES AND SKIN-BASED ATTACHMENT

The parenting method of attaching geometry to your IK chains makes the assumption that you have separate pieces of the model that can be attached to each joint. This works for articulated rigid models, but it has serious shortcomings for animating characters. You cannot, for instance, use the parenting method to animate a seamless mesh object, because you need discrete chunks of the model broken out separately for each IK joint. It also does very little for models composed of a hierarchy of objects, because each object is parented to one single IK joint at most.

Without the capabilities to animate seamless models and use hierarchies in IK systems, the IK system is pretty limited. Fortunately, the Softimage IK system offers three more methods of assigning geometry to IK chains that allow the user to animate just about anything with an IK chain, while retaining complete control over how the models bend and move as they are transformed and deformed by the IK system. These three methods are Rigid Envelope, Local Envelope, and Global Envelope, and they all rely on the concept of a skin.

A *skin* is any single model or hierarchy of models that composes the outer shell and visible geometry of the IK system you are animating—just like your own skin. The skin can cover just a part of an IK chain, or it can surround the entire IK system. The skin can be composed of a single spline, NURBS, or polygon mesh, or it can be composed of discrete parts connected together in a hierarchy. The skin is connected to the IK chains with the commands in the Skin menu cells (see Figure 15.26). Each of the envelope types has advantages and disadvantages. Let's look at them one by one.

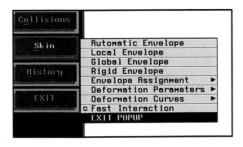

FIGURE 15.26 *The Skin menu cells.*

RIGID ENVELOPE

The Rigid Envelope method is a special case of the parenting method of assigning geometry. It is unique because it is the only skin assignment method that transforms the attached geometry without deforming the attached geometry.

You start by preparing the hierarchy of model geometry that you want moved by the IK system. The hierarchy can have any number of elements, either more or less than the joints in the IK system that you plan to use to transform it. There must be a null at the top of the hierarchy. The hierarchy may be one or more levels deep. The order in which elements are parented in the hierarchy is not important, so it's a good idea to keep all the model elements loose under the null, rather than spend time parenting them together in some complex manner (see Figure 15.27).

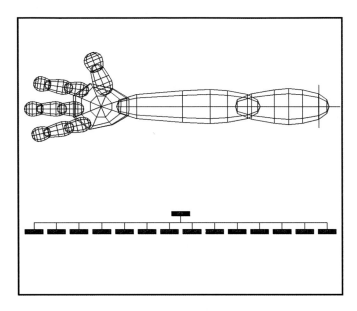

FIGURE 15.27 *A rigid envelope, made from a hierarchy of blocks.*

After the geometry is prepared, place the IK chain within the model, so that it is in a starting position that makes sense for the object you create. If you use this method to make a hand out of a hierarchy of blocks, for example, the finger chains should lie within the row of blocks for that finger. The IK chains should themselves be parented together into a hierarchy if you use more than one chain, again in a way that makes sense for the model.

Finally, select the hierarchy of the IK chains, and choose the Skin→Rigid Envelope command. Complete the command by picking the hierarchy of the models.

Each model is automatically assigned to a joint based on the proximity of that model to the joint. You can now animate the model hierarchy by translating the effectors of the IK chains.

This Rigid Envelope method is tailor made for animating a Meta-Clay system, because a Meta-Clay system is comprised of a root null at the top of a hierarchy with any number of meta elements parented into the hierarchy as children of that root null. When the IK chains in a rigid envelope transform the meta elements, they remain connected with a smooth metasurface, creating an unbroken skin at every frame.

Try this out by reloading the Meta-Clay hand you made and drawing a hierarchy of IK chains within it, one segment for the palm connected to one chain for each digit. Then use Rigid Envelope to connect the Meta-Clay hand as a skin to the IK hierarchy.

Rigid Envelope is a very simple, easy, non-modifiable way to create a quick-and-dirty IK skin with minimal effort. However, because it does not deform any geometry, it is of limited use in animating organic creatures.

LOCAL ENVELOPE

The Local Envelope method of attaching a skin to an IK system is the first step toward more complex manipulation of a skin. The rule for this method is that only one IK chain or one hierarchy of IK chains can be within the geometry that's used as the skin (see Figure 15.28). That's what makes it local. Global envelopes can have any number of IK chains within the skin, and for this reason, local envelopes are most useful when you can plan ahead. Be sure when you attach the skin that you have all the IK articulation you need built into the hierarchy of the IK chains.

Local envelopes don't just transform the geometry they control; they also deform that geometry. This means that the skin bends around the joints in the IK chain to make a realistic crease on the inside and stretch on the outside of the bending joint (see Figure 15.29).

The geometry used for the skin in a local envelope should be a single merged polygonal mesh or a single contiguous patch surface for best results. When these surfaces are attached to the IK system, they act just like a human skin does—like a bag of water hanging around a skeleton that provides structural support. As the skeleton moves, the bag of water stretches and deforms to remain around the skeleton (see Figure 15.30). You can add more complex skeletal components to suggest the movement of muscles under the skin, and you can use dynamics to make the skin hang, sag, and sway with inertia and gravity (see Chapter 16). In short, local envelopes are a wonderful thing.

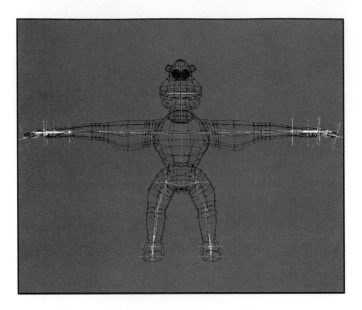

FIGURE 15.28 *Local envelope means only one IK hierarchy or chain per skin.*

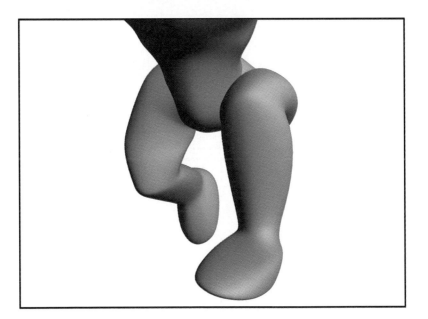

FIGURE 15.29 *Julian's skin, bent by an IK chain.*

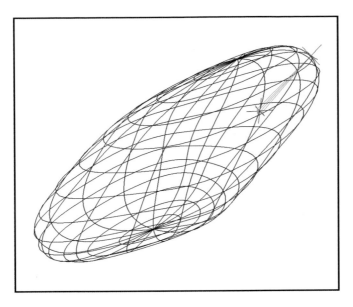

FIGURE 15.30 *A simple sphere being deformed by the IK within it.*

SKIN DEFORMATION

The way skin deformation works with local envelopes is simple to understand, but complex to control. When an IK chain is connected to the skin with the Skin→Local Envelope command, each vertex or Control point on the skin model is assigned to the joints that lie within the skin, in direct proportion to the proximity of that vertex or Control point to the joints. Points on the skin that lie one unit from one joint and three units from another will be assigned, or *weighted*, 75% to the nearer joint and only 25% to the further joint. When the further joint rotates, the Control point moves a bit to follow the location of the joint, but when the nearer joint rotates, that vertex moves a great deal. In this way, each joint in the skin modifies the shape of the skin as it rotates. As the effector of the IK chain translates through space, all the joints rotate and all the vertices on the skin move to follow them, so the skin remains wrapped around the IK chain. When the IK chain bends, the skin bends as well.

The default settings for the Local Envelope command do a good job of weighting the points on the skin to the joints in the skeleton, but if sections of the IK hierarchy get too close together, the skin may be shared between joints that shouldn't be considered. For instance, if you build the skin of a hand with the fingers close together, and then put a hierarchy of IK chains in the hand and connect the IK hierarchy to the skin with the Local Envelope command, the skin of the little finger might be shared between the joints in the little finger and the next finger over. This would make the skin stretch in a weird way when the little finger effector moved (see Figure 15.31).

FIGURE 15.31 *Bad weighting shows up in strange skin action.*

In cases like this, you can manually control the weighting of the points on the skin to determine which joints affect them. The methodology for this control is detailed in the "Weighting Skins" section a little later in this chapter. It is always a good idea to consider how the automatic weighting works when constructing the skins, to minimize the manual weighting work that must be done. Building your skins in poses with limbs apart (the natural pose) will be a big timesaver later on in the process.

LOCAL ENVELOPE WORKFLOW

The workflow for using a local envelope is straightforward:

1. Create the skin.

   Any type of mesh can be used for the skin, but make sure that there is enough detail in the skin model to allow it to deform accurately. IK chains can deform skins by moving existing vertices only, so if no existing vertices are near the joint, the model won't bend there. Thus, it is a good idea to model in extra detail around joints in the skin, such as knees and elbows, so the deformation at that point can be smooth (see Figure 15.32).

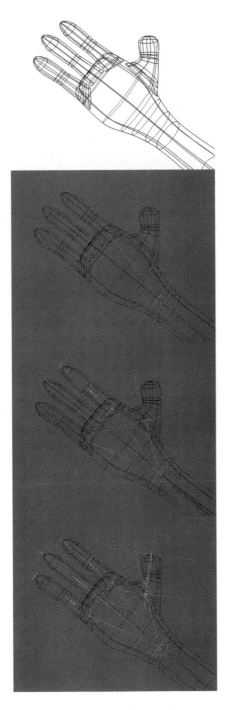

FIGURE 15.32 *Make a skin, then draw in chains and parent them together.*

2. Draw the IK chain.

    Draw the IK chain within the geometry to be used as the skin. By creating the skin first, you have a guide to draw the chain in the right scale and position. Remember to draw the chain with a slight bend in it to indicate to the chain your preferred bend angle.

3. Attach the skin to the chain.

    Select the IK chain, choose the Skin→Local Envelope command, and then pick the skin mesh. A dialog pops up, asking you to confirm the model assignment and weighting depth. Leave all the values at the defaults and finish the command with the Ok button. The skin will now be attached to the IK chain. Select the effector of the chain and translate it in space to see the results!

    The limitations of the local envelope are simply that the IK hierarchy is local to the skin model, and only one IK hierarchy can be used within that model. Although this is acceptable for simpler models, like worms or even hands, it is insufficient for robust, complex skeletal structures. That's where global envelopes take over.

GLOBAL ENVELOPE

The Global Envelope method of connecting a skin to an IK system is the most complex method offered within Softimage 3D|Extreme and fills in the rest of the gaps in the functionality of the Local Envelope method. With a global envelope, a skin model or hierarchy can have as many IK chains and systems within it as you want (see Figure 15.33).

The more the merrier is the theory behind the global envelope. The IK chains in the skin can be parented together, constrained with nulls, attached to clusters, or parented to other objects. The IK chains that deform the skin can, in fact, be any objects at all, a concept covered in depth in the "Pseudo-IK: Group As Skeleton" section. In short, anything goes. This freedom to mix and match IK chains within a skin makes it possible for you to create models of any complexity and animate them in any way. It also makes for some heart-rendingly complex Schematic views and some tough to understand kinematic animation hierarchies. Power has a price, and that price for global envelopes is complexity.

FIGURE 15.33 *Global Envelope means lots of IK chains in one skin.*

The fundamentals of Global Envelope skin deformation follow the same rules as the Local Envelope method. By default, each vertex or Control point on the skin is deformed by all the joints in all the chains in the skin. The nearer a vertex is to a given joint, the more it is influenced by the rotation of that joint. The influence of each joint on each vertex is called the *vertex weighting* and is expressed as a percentage.

GLOBAL ENVELOPE WORKFLOW

Because the skin you make can have any number of chains in it, the Skin→Global Envelope command is applied in the opposite order of the Local Envelope command. The procedure is:

1. Select the skin.

2. Invoke the Skin→Global Envelope command.

3. Pick each IK chain in turn.

If the IK chains are connected into a hierarchy, clicking any of the joints in any of the IK chains adds the entire hierarchy to the envelope. Each time you pick a chain, the small Envelopes Initial Assignment dialog box pops up, asking you to confirm the depth of the weight assignment. Unless you have a specific reason to leave some joints out, leave the values at the default and confirm the settings with the Ok button (see Figure 15.34).

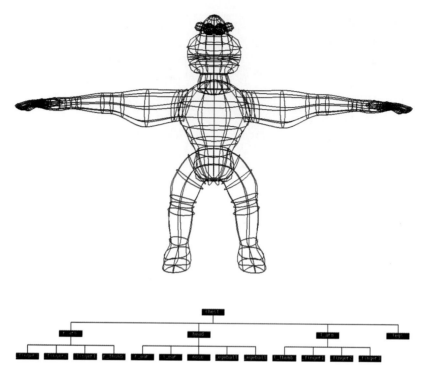

FIGURE 15.34 *Julian's skin is a global envelope.*

Although it is a good idea to add all the IK chains to the global envelope at once, it is certainly not a requirement, and you can always go back and add more later. IK chains can be removed from influencing the global envelope by simply selecting the entire chain as a branch and cutting the connection to the skin with the Cut command, just like you would separate any items in a hierarchy.

WEIGHTING SKINS

Actually, adding IK chains to an envelope is the easy part. Making the skin obey the joints and deform exactly as you have in mind is the tough part. The process of determining exactly how each area of the skin will behave in relation to each joint of each chain is called *weighting the skin.*

Because each vertex is controlled by each joint according to a percentage weight, the way that the skin deforms is determined entirely by the weighting for each joint on each and every vertex of the skin. If your skin model has a great many points, as in the case of a dense polygonal mesh, it can be very time consuming to edit the weights to your satisfaction. The easiest models to weight are those such as single piece NURBS skins that have few Control points, which are arranged so that more detail is available near the joints that bend the most.

HURRY UP AND WEIGHT

When you first assign a chain to a skin as an envelope, the weights of each vertex or Control point are calculated automatically. Inevitably, one joint in the chain or chains will be closest for each vertex, and will therefore have the greatest influence on that point on the skin. Softimage has a nifty trick that will help you immensely while weighting your skin: It colors the vertex to match the color of that joint. You can see which joints match which vertices in your model by turning on the Skin→Show Vertices toggle (see Figure 15.35).

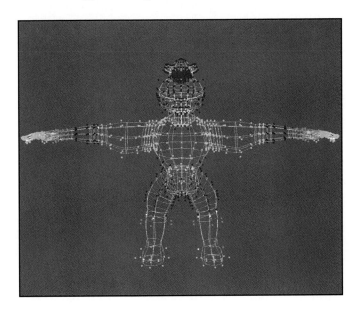

FIGURE 15.35 *Julian with his skin showing weights.*

Now when you select your skin, the vertices or Control points are colored by the joints under them. The color of the joints in the IK chains is determined automatically, and Softimage always uses the same order of colors, starting from the first joint and moving down the chain. The default colors, therefore, may not help you much in cases where IK chains of identical length are located close together, such as fingers and legs. In these cases, it would be more helpful to assign your own colors to each joint, so you can tell from the skin colors which of the two chains is influencing that area of the skin most strongly.

To change the color of a joint, select it and then use the Skin→Color Joint command. With the command active, the left mouse button lets you cycle through the available colors. Select the skin again to see the effect.

Keep in mind that the color system is not a completely accurate way to predict problems with the skin weighting, because it shows only the color of the nearest joint. Another slightly further joint could still be influencing the skin to make it stretch and tear during animation.

There are three primary ways to change the weights on the skin:

- Manual assignment
- Bounding model assignment
- Weight assignment

The most basic method is to reassign the weight of points manually.

REASSIGN MANUALLY

Manual reassignment is useful for assigning points entirely to one joint, or for removing vertices from the envelope all together. For instance, say you create a human skull and place a simple single joint chain in the jaw to move the mouth region. When you test the motion by translating the effector, you will find that the entire head flips and deforms when you drag the effector in the mouth region (see Figure 15.36).

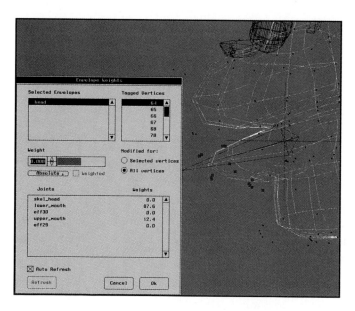

FIGURE 15.36 *Julian's jaw tagged for weight reassignment.*

With only one joint in the envelope, *all* the points must be assigned to that joint because no others are available. The solution is to remove all the points outside the joint area (the lower jaw) from the influence of the envelope. To do so, tag the jaw points, invert the tagged selection (drag a tag marquee around the entire skull with the T key and the right mouse button), and then execute the Skin→Envelope Assignment→Reassign Manually command. Finally, click with the middle mouse button to assign the tagged group to no joint (check the Status Bar for a prompt).

The other common scenario for using Reassign Manually is in weighting a tagged region of points entirely to one joint. Imagine that you are assigning a skin to a human model, and you built the skin model and the IK chains so that the legs are side by side. When you assign the IK chains to the skin with the Global Envelope command, the joints from the left leg will partially influence the skin of the right leg, and vice versa, simply because the joints are fairly close together in the model's stance. For each joint on both legs, you must ensure that the left foot joint influences only the left foot skin, the right foot joint influences only the right foot skin, and so on.

The process is to first tag the points to be reassigned, on the inside of the left thigh, for instance, and then invoke the Skin→Envelope Assignment→Reassign Manually command. With the command active, click with the left mouse button on the new joint to completely assign the tagged skin points to the new joint.

BOUNDING MODEL ASSIGNMENT

Another easy way to control which joints influence which areas of skin is to create special controls called *bounding models* for each joint. A bounding model is a primitive shape that defines the volume of space in which a joint controls the surface vertices (see Figure 15.37). A bounding model can:

- Make all points within it weighted 100% to the bounding model joint (an *inclusive limit* bounding model)

- Blend points within the bounding model (an *inclusive* bounding model)

- Exclude points from influence by the bounding model joint (an *exclusive* bounding model)

To create a bounding model for a given joint, select that joint and choose the Skin→Envelope Assignment→Bounding Model→ Inclusive command. Checking the Status Bar tells you that clicking with the right mouse button creates a bounding box, the middle mouse button creates a bounding cylinder, and the right mouse button creates a

> **NOTE**
>
> It is always a good idea to return the IK chains deforming a skin to the default position, the position they were in when first assigned as an envelope, before continuing the edit the weight points in the skin. Do this by selecting the IK hierarchy and choosing the Skeleton→Reset Actor command.

bounding sphere. You can then select the bounding model you made and transform it with the regular Transformation menu cells to fit it exactly around the skin you want assigned to the joint. It's a good idea to overlap the bounding model across the joint where the skin will deform most when the chain bends, and then repeat the operation for the next joint, also overlapping the first bounding model a bit so that they both influence the skin in the critical crease areas, such as knees and elbows.

FIGURE 15.37 *Julian with some weighted bounding models.*

You can show and hide the bounding models with the Show→Controls toggle switch.

MODIFY WEIGHTS

The Modify Weights command is the mother of all weight reassignment tools. It gives you the power to look at and change the weight assignment of each and every point on the skin, individually and in groups. You can pick a specific vertex and remove the influence of a specific joint, or you can select a group of vertices, such as the left thigh, and remove the influence on all of them from another joint, such as the right thigh bone, so only wanted joints are considered when the skin deforms.

You can manually specify the ratio of influence of each joint, changing it to an absolute value, or by adding or subtracting degrees of influence. Each vertex weight can also be blended by proximity to the affecting joint as well. Because problems in the skin weighting usually become painfully evident only during animation (you see then that moving the arm, for instance, causes the belly to stretch), you can scrub the Time Slider to see different animated poses of your creature and use this dialog to create a weighting that works for the different poses.

In short, the Modify Weights command gives you too much control, and as a result the dialog box it spawns can be confusing (see Figure 15.38).

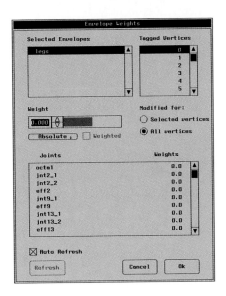

FIGURE 15.38 *The Modify Weights command calls the Envelope Weights dialog box.*

Select your skin, or skins, and tag the area of the surface that you want to work on. Call up the Envelope Weights dialog box with the Skin→Envelope Assignment→ Modify Weights command. When the dialog pops up, move it to a position onscreen where you can see your model as well (click in the dialog's title bar and drag the box). Now click the Auto Refresh toggle checkbox. Being able to see immediate feedback on the state of your model as you make changes keeps you sane while you struggle with the weights.

The name of the selected envelope appears in the upper-left portion of the dialog, and the tagged points are listed in the upper-right corner in a list box labeled Tagged Vertices. If you want to adjust the weight of a single vertex or a subset of the tagged group, select just the vertices you want in the list by Shift-clicking, and change the Modified for: radio button toggle to Selected Vertices. Otherwise, leave the toggle on All Vertices to modify the entire tagged group evenly, which is a smart move. If you leave the toggle on All Vertices, you can then select a single vertex from the list to see an accurate readout of the joint weights below. This information can help you make good decisions about what joint to re-weight and how much. In the Wireframe view, Softimage highlights the vertex you select in the Tagged Vertices list, so you can get a visual reference for that vertex's position relative to the joints that affect it.

Those joints that are influencing the tagged vertices are listed by name in the large scrolling list box at the bottom of the dialog, and the ratio of influence on the currently selected vertex is shown as a percentage.

Obviously, at this point, it is a great help to have named your joints logically so you can read meaningful names, such as leftthigh and rightfoot instead of jnt1_1. If you click a single joint in the list, that joint is highlighted in the Wireframe view, which is some help.

Reading what the ratio of joint influence is on a single point can help you spot problems in your weighting. For instance, if you are weighting a hand and you named each finger joint in each finger chain finger1_knuckle1, finger2_knuckle2, and so on, you could then tag all the points on the skin surrounding the first finger and use the Envelope Weights dialog to learn whether any of the joints from any other fingers affected those tagged points (they should not). Armed with the information about which joints are modifying the vertices you tagged, you are ready to do something about it. Select a joint in the lower joint list to begin modifying that joint's influence over the tagged and selected vertices.

The business end of this entire dialog is the small slider simply marked Weight and the inconspicuous drop box below it. First, determine the method of reassignment you want and set the drop box accordingly. Absolute lets you enter a value for each joint. Softimage precisely applies that value to each vertex you tagged and selected. This method is appropriate for changing the weight of a skin to be entirely dependent on a single chain or joint. In the example of the fingers, tagging the skin of the first fingertip, you could use Absolute assignment to directly assign all those vertices to the last joint in the first finger. This method is not a good one for blending weight values, so it is not a good idea to use it on areas of skin that bend.

If you want more careful blending than Absolute allows, you can choose from two other options: Add and Add Percent, which is confusing because the value for weight is already expressed in percent. When you choose Add, the number in the slider is added to the current number for the weight of the selected joint. If the selected vertex is already weighted 20% by the selected joint and you dial in 20 with the slider in Add mode, the new weight for that joint is 40%.

Add Percent means that the slider adds or subtracts a percentage of the current percentage weight on the selected joint. Confused? Add Percent is a more gradual method of increasing or decreasing the weight of a given joint on the selected vertices.

When you change the influence of one joint, you can change the influence of the others as well without knowing it, because all the influences added together must always stay under 100%. So if you crank up the weight on one joint, you are probably taking away weight from another joint. If you reduce weight on a joint, however, the skin just becomes less flexible there; the system doesn't give the excess weight to the other joints.

There is still something missing from our control, however, and that is control over the blending of the values. If we set values directly on areas of skin, there will be sharp changes at the boundaries of the selections we use when we animate, creating unsightly lines in our models as they move around. We need a way to make changes while retaining the blending of values that smoothly interpolates changes between joints. That control is activated only in the Add and Add Percent methods by checking the Weighted check box. (To recap in plain English, it's the Weighted box under the Weight slider in the Modify Weights dialog box.) With this option checked, when you add influence to a joint, the actual change in the value at each vertex in the selected tagged group changes depending on the proximity of that vertex to the joint being weighted.

The bottom line is this: Tag a bunch of points, and then modify them all with the Add Percent method and the Weighted check box on for best results. Don't mess around with the other settings unless you have a specific need they address.

TUTORIAL: WEIGHTING JULIAN'S SKIN

If the gorilla Julian had been created by a modeler who perhaps hadn't intended on animating him with an IK chain or didn't understand how skins are weighted, he might have been made in a pose that would not lend itself to animation, using the automatic weighting performed when a skin is set up with the Global Envelope command. The scene Julian_Skin on your courseware CD-ROM has such a pose, with the arms at his sides and the legs together, like he is riding in a VW Beetle (see Figure 15.39).

Because Julian's limbs are so close together, the proximity weighting algorithm just doesn't have enough to work with. When he's animated, Julian's skin is stretched in some very painful ways. Examine the Schematic view showing the construction of the very simple IK skeleton, and note the naming convention used to keep the different parts of the chain straight. Each chain is labeled by function and side, such as right_leg and left_leg, and each joint is named consistently by function, such as thigh and shin and foot, so that fully resolved names in the Modify Weights dialog make sense, such as right_leg.shin.

NOTE

A little bit of naming work goes a long way toward retaining sanity and gainful employment in production situations where complexity is a challenge and a productive use of time is critical. Set the name for each joint to include a reference to the name of the whole chain. Don't use the prefix for this, because the prefix doesn't show up in the Envelope Weights dialog box.

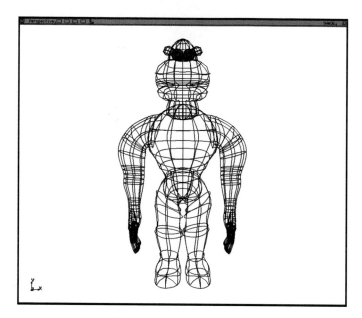

FIGURE 15.39 *Julian in an unhelpful pose for weighting.*

1. **Hook Up the Skin.**

   Select the skin geometry mesh and choose the Skin→Global Envelope command; then pick the hierarchy of IK chains. Accept the defaults in the Skin Assignment dialog that pops up.

   Show the weight assignments by turning on the vertex colors with the Skin→Envelope Assignment→Show Vertices command (see Figure 15.40).

   Because both Julian's leg IK chains are the same length and have the same number of joints, the colored vertices don't give us any information about which leg owns which points. To see this, we need to re-color all the joints on one leg. Select the thigh joint on the left leg, and assign a new color to it by choosing the Skin→Envelope Assignment→Color Joint command, and then clicking the left mouse button to rotate through the color choices. Pick one you like that is different from the thigh color of the right leg. Repeat the process for the other joints on the left leg. Now you can see which joints have the most control over each point.

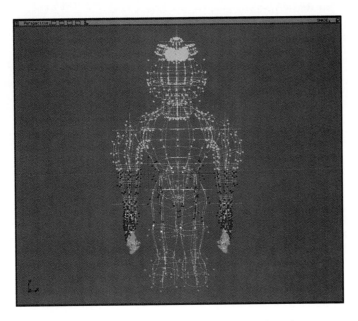

FIGURE 15.40 *The bad pose, with the IK system in as a global envelope, showing vertex weights.*

2. **Modify the Weight of the Legs.**

   Currently, when we move the right leg, some points on the left leg deform to follow the right leg, which is very bad. We need to completely remove the influence of the right leg from the skin of the left leg.

   Tag all the vertices on the left leg, extending up Julian's haunch, and following his bikini line (or where it would be if he had one).

   Enter the Envelope Weights dialog with the Skin→Envelope Assignment→Modify Weights command. Make sure the options are set for the modification of all vertices, using the Absolute method.

   In the joint list, select the right thigh joint, and look at the Skin Weight value. Because we have the skin over the left leg selected, there should be no influence from the right thigh. If there is, grab the Reassignment slider and drag it to 0 skin using the same method. Repeat the process for all the joints of the right leg.

Exit the dialog and this time tag only the skin of the right leg. Enter the Envelope Weights dialog and remove any influence of the left leg joints over the right leg skin.

3. **Modify the Weight of the Arms.**

The arms have the same problem. If the left arm effector is translated, part of the arm is partially influenced by the spinal column. Tag each arm and remove any influence from chains other than the arm chain inside the skin at that point.

When done, tag the skin on Julian's head from the top of the flexible neck on up, and make sure that no influence from the shoulder joints will wiggle Julian's ears when he swings his hairy arms.

4. **Reblend His Rump.**

So far so good, but all we've done is the simple reassignment where the skin clearly belongs to one chain. In some cases, such as his muscular buttocks, the skin will be deformed by several chains at once and must stretch convincingly as all the chains move relative to one another (see Figure 15.41).

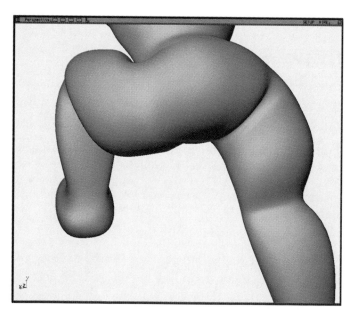

FIGURE 15.41   *A good crease under Julian's butt.*

To see the problem, rotate Julian and look at his backside in the Perspective view and, in the right view, translate his leg effector so he picks up his leg. The creasing in the butt needs work. We want the top joints in the legs to have more influence over the area predominately controlled by his spine, so that his flanks stretch smoothly, but we need the influence to diminish smoothly as the points on the skin get farther away from the legs.

Set two keyframes a few frames apart for the translation of the effector, so we can see the motion of the skin as we work on the weights.

Select the left half of the rump, from midway down his back to midway down his left thigh. Enter the Envelope Weights dialog.

Set the controls to modify all vertices, using Add Percent, with Weighted distribution. Turn on Interactive Refresh, move the dialog out of the way, and drag in the Time Slider to see the motion and deformation of the skin.

Increase the influence of the left thigh very slightly by selecting the left thigh joint from the joint list and dragging the Weight slider to just 10 percent.

Again scrub the Time Slider back and forth to detect the subtle changes in the behavior of the skin on Julian's butt. Keep making delicate adjustments up and down until his butt moves in a comic fashion while his leg pumps up and down.

Exit the dialog and swap the tagged group for the right buttock area. Animate a simple step for the right leg. Enter the Envelope Weights dialog and repeat your careful manipulations to match the behavior of the left leg.

5. **Edit the Creasing of the Knee.**

The inside of an elbow or a knee is the toughest place to correctly deform the skin in a realistic manner. On the outside of the joint, the skin has to stretch, and on the inside, it has to bunch up. Sometimes the width of the skin deformation needs to be adjusted to clamp the skin stretching and creasing to an appropriate distance from the joint, so that skin in the middle of the calf is bending in when the knee bends. We will use the Envelope Assignment dialog to modify the behavior of the inside of the knee.

Change the Perspective view so that you are examining the inside of the left leg as it bends, from the calf up the thigh. Notice how the bend is not very well localized to just the joint area. That's because the influence of the thigh is extending too far down the shin, and the shin too far up the thigh.

Tag the skin from just above the knee down to mid-shin, and enter the Envelope Assignment dialog. Set it up to modify all vertices with the Add Percent Weighted method, and turn on Auto Refresh.

Select the thigh joint and reduce the weight slightly. Then select the shin and increase the weight slightly. Scrub the Time Slider to see the changes. Continue to make small changes until the skin of the calf deforms properly, and then exit the dialog.

Tag just the thigh, from mid-thigh to just below the knee, and repeat the process for the skin of the thigh, reducing the weight of the shin and increasing the weight of the thigh. Because the Weighted check box is on, the influence of each joint falls off according to the proximity of each vertex to the joints being modified.

Repeat for the other leg, and for any other joints that need editing.

That's it! Weighting joints is a slow, arduous, painstaking process, and the best advice is to take it one step at a time and have a clear plan for what you want to accomplish.

PSEUDO-IK: GROUP AS SKELETON

I mentioned earlier that skins can be weighted and deformed by other kinds of objects than just IK chains. In fact, any object in Softimage can function in exactly the same way as an IK chain and can be weighted to influence the skin around it. The command for giving objects this power is Group As Skeleton. When an object is grouped as a skeleton, it becomes colored, just like a joint in an IK chain, and it can be hooked up to a skin using the Local and Global Envelope commands, just like an IK chain. This means that a small null, a cube, a sphere, or even a more complex hierarchy of models can be defined as a skeleton and used to model or animate deformations of a skin.

One way to use this feature is to add objects within the skin that deform it in addition to a pre-existing skeletal structure to show effects such as musculature moving under skin, muscles stretching the skin over them, and heavy swaying girth, like a fat man's stomach.

Group As Skeleton is easy to use. Simply activate the Skeleton→Group As Skeleton command, and pick one or more objects to define them as the new skeleton objects. Then you can position them as needed within the skin. They can be either parented to the existing hierarchy of IK chains or added fresh by selecting the skin and using the Skin→Global Envelope command.

Once added to the skeleton, the points around the new objects are automatically reweighted to be influenced by proximity to the new skeleton objects. When you translate, scale, or rotate the object, you use a new skeleton object and the skin deforms over the top of it. After animating the effects you need, it is often a good idea to hide the skeleton object so it doesn't ever show up in the render.

Because the actual geometry is never a part of the skeleton calculations and therefore does not have any effect on the motion of the skin, it is a good idea to choose relatively simple polygon objects or nulls for Group As Skeleton.

One fantastic use for this technique is in creating muscle bulges with Group As Skeleton and expressions (the more powerful relatives of constraints) to link them to the rotation of specific joints.

TUTORIAL: GROUP AS SKELETON COWBOY HAT

In this tutorial, we'll create a simple revolution-style cowboy hat, and then make it a little more special with controls added by Group As Skeleton (see Figure 15.42).

FIGURE 15.42   *The completed sombrero.*

1. **Make the Hat.**

   Draw a B-spline curve in the Front window, around the Y axis, showing the inside and outside of a cowboy hat. Revolve it 360 degrees into a closed B-spline patch surface with 12 subdivisions (see Figure 15.43).

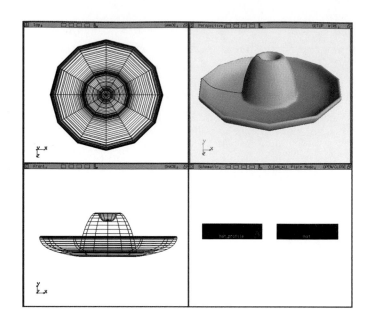

FIGURE 15.43   *The B-spline hat.*

2. **Build the Controls.**

   Any object can become a Group As Skeleton control. Start by getting a primitive cube and scaling it to be quite small, and placing it near the edge of the hat in the middle of the brim. Duplicate the cube to make four cubes, placed evenly at 90 degree intervals around the brim of the hat.

   Get a primitive sphere and place it inside the hat band in the middle of the hat. Get a null and place it slightly above the top of the hat.

   Make them all skeleton controls by choosing the Skeleton→Group As Skeleton command, and then picking each one in turn. Use the Schematic view so you don't accidentally get the hat. They change color in the schematic to indicate their new status (see Figure 15.44).

3. **Use Global Envelope to Hook Them to the Hat.**

   Select the hat and choose the Skin→Global Envelope command, and then pick each skeleton control in turn, approving the Default Assignment dialog that pops up (see Figure 15.45).

transformed. The only downsides of hierarchies are that the child gets all the transformations from the parent, not just ones we might want, and that the child can never have more than one parent.

USING CLUSTERS WITH IK

Another powerful way of connecting objects together is with constraints. Constraint→Position hooks objects together in space, Constraint→Orientation keeps an object's rotation the same at all times, and Constrain→Direction makes one object point at another at all times. Constraints allow us to pick and choose which transformation data we want from one object to drive another object. Expressions can take this farther and automate simple actions and relationships in the IK system. There is pretty much no downside to constraints.

A variation on the constraint connection method is to use cluster constraints. Using this technique, you can hook objects together with physically rigid objects, such as cubes and octahedrons (or any model). The idea is to built an internal structure for your creature with solid geometry, and then attach the IK chains as appropriate.

For example, in Julian we have used an octahedron for his pelvis and another octahedron for his collar bone, connected together with a simple IK chain to provide him with a flexible spine (see Figure 15.48). The octahedral pelvis becomes the center of gravity for the model, and most motion originates here. The pelvis drives and anchors the two leg IK chains, keeping them connected, but also separate. As the hip rotates, one leg is driven forward and the other back. As the pelvis raises and lowers, Julian bends his legs at the knee. The octahedron become very useful as puppet controls, like part of the marionette rack.

There are two parts to a cluster constraint: the clusters on the octahedron and the constraint of the IK chain. To add clusters to any object, just tag the vertex or vertices that you want and use the Shape→Set Cluster command to get the Set Cluster dialog box (see Figure 15.49). In the Set Cluster dialog, add a name for the cluster that makes sense, make sure that the Create Center check box is off (for this particular use), and click the New button to create the cluster. You can set as many clusters on an object as you wish.

To constrain any object, including an IK chain, to the clustered set of points, first select the object and call up the Cluster List dialog with the Shape→Cluster List command to see the list of current clusters for that object (see Figure 15.50). Select the named cluster that you want from the list to activate it, and then close the list.

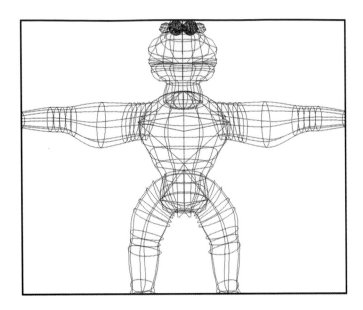

FIGURE 15.48 *Julian with a new set of shoulders and hips.*

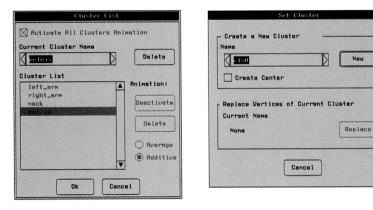

FIGURE 15.49 *The Set Cluster and Cluster List dialog boxes.*

Next, select the object that you want to constrain to that cluster, execute the Constraint→Object to Cluster command, and pick the object that has the active cluster you want to constrain to. The selected object instantly hops through space to align its center precisely with the cluster of points active on the master object. When you translate the master object, the constrained object follows it at all times, even though they are not actually parented into the same hierarchy. If you want to release the constrained object from the master, select the constrained object, use the Constraint→Relax command, and click the master object to complete the command.

TUTORIAL: MR. PELVIS

In this simple tutorial, you will create a pelvis and hook up a pair of IK legs to it for purposes of experimentation.

1. **Build a Pelvis.**

   A primitive octahedron makes a great pelvis. Get one and then scale it in X so that it is wider than it is tall. Scale it down in Z so that it is relatively thinner in Z than in Y or X. Name it mr_pelvis. Tag the points on the right side of the pelvis (positive X) and use the Shape→Set Cluster command to create a cluster (called r_hip) from the tagged points. Untag that cluster, tag the point on the left of the pelvis, and make it into a cluster named l_hip (see Figure 15.50).

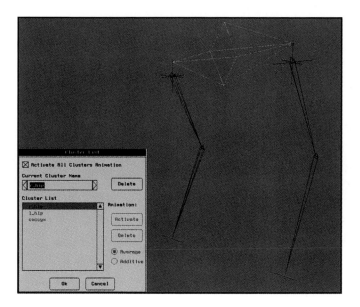

FIGURE 15.50 *An octahedral pelvis with unattached legs.*

   For good measure, create a cluster (called coccyx) for the spine to attach to the top of the pelvis and another cluster in the back of the pelvis in case you feel like adding a prehensile tail at a later date. It's always a good idea to plan ahead.

2. **Make Some Legs.**

   In the Right view, drag out a two-segment 2D chain (Skeleton→2D) with its root more or less at the middle of the pelvis and its effector below about 8 units, with the knee slightly bent forward. Duplicate the IK chain, name one r_leg and the other l_leg, and then translate them in the Top view to the left and right sides of the pelvis. Because we are going to constrain the positions of the IK chains later, you don't have to be all that precise. Set up the rotational constraints for each joint (Constraint→Rotation Limits) so that the leg can move only in a natural manner.

3. Hook Up the Legs.

Select the pelvis and activate the r_hip cluster in the cluster list with Shape→Cluster List. Now select the corresponding leg, choose the Constraint→Object to Cluster command, and pick the pelvis to snap the root of the r_leg to the r_hip cluster.

Select the pelvis again and in the Cluster List activate the l_hip cluster. Constrain the position of the other leg to it in the same manner.

4. Try It.

Select the two effectors and save an explicit translation keyframe for each one on all axes to pin them to the floor where they stand.

Now select the pelvis and translate it up and down to see the legs bend. Try rotating the pelvis around the Y axis to see how the pelvis rotation drives one hip forward and the other back. Experiment to get the full idea, and if you want, set explicit translation keys for first one foot moving forward, then the pelvis, and then the other foot, about every five frames. Remember to set a keyframe for each effector and the pelvis at each new point to keep the back foot planted while the front foot travels.

For extra credit, pace up and down the nearest hallway and pay attention to the position of your pelvis relative to your feet at each point in your stride, and also how your hip swings forward as you step forward. Generally, your pelvis remains centered between your feet at all times and rotates slightly around Y as each foot steps forward. Because your legs are a fixed length, at your most extended point in each stride, your legs form a triangle with the floor, and your hips are lower (closer to the floor) at that point than at any other time in your stride. All these behaviors of the pelvis are easily set up with an expression, so they happen automatically as you move the feet of your creature.

YOU CAN'T BEAT A GOOD NULL

No part of the IK construction process is as critical as a firm understanding of the benefits of a null hierarchy. Basically, in a properly constructed IK system, you will never actually move any of the IK chain effectors themselves; you will always move nulls that drive the effectors.

Setting explicit translations on the effectors themselves is a very bad idea. When you set an explicit translation keyframe on an effector, you are specifying a precise translation in space relative to the global axes at that point in the timeline. If you ever move the whole skeleton or the vehicle the creature was riding in, or make any other change to the model, such as rotating it in space to face a new direction, your effectors will still want to be in the same old place as they were. The creature's limbs will suddenly shoot out to stretch in the direction they came from (see Figure 15.51).

FIGURE 15.51 *What happens if you keyframe effectors directly.*

Try this out by setting some keyframes on the effectors of the pelvis model you just made, then selecting the pelvis, moving it to a different part of the scene, and rotating the pelvis about its axes. Imagine your art director just told you that the script changed, and that now Mr. Pelvis is aboard a ship, rolling in high seas, crossing the Atlantic. Your model won't work for that.

When you keyframe an explicit translation directly on an effector, the translation is not relative to anything but the global axes. We need the translation of the effector to be relative to the object that is driving the chain itself, such as the pelvis, so that the motion of the effectors can be added to the motion of the whole chain, the whole creature, or the whole scene. To do that, we need a parent-child hierarchy, because the rules state that all translations of a child are performed relative to the position of the parent.

The big problem is that each child can have only one parent, and the effector is already a child of the joint directly above it in the chain. What to do? Add a null hierarchy!

The null, or other primitive object, should be placed where the effector is currently located. Then select the effector and use Constraint→Position to affix the effector to the precise location of the null. Now you can activate the IK chain and drag the effector around by selecting the null, not the effector. For our example, make the null the child of the pelvis (see Figure 15.52).

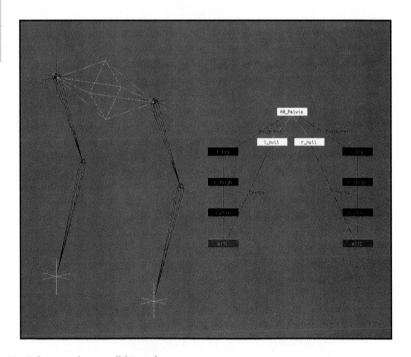

FIGURE 15.52 *Mr. Pelvis now has a null hierarchy.*

Now when you animate Mr. Pelvis, you animate the nulls, never the effectors. When the art director asks to move Mr. Pelvis to a new locale, you just select the top of the hierarchy as a tree, and move the whole thing to a new spot in space. The animation you created moves as well and still plays back appropriately. You can rotate Mr. Pelvis, parent him to another object, or whatever, and the animation stays correct.

It helps to think about the null hierarchy as the strings operating the marionette. The effectors of the marionette are nailed onto tiny nulls that are parented by strings onto the control rack. Above the nulls that control the effectors are more nulls in a hierarchy to make up that rack. That's a null hierarchy, and it works the same way in Softimage 3D|Extreme as it does for a marionette.

Null hierarchies have another important function. They abstract one layer of movement from another, because each level of the hierarchy can have its own animation or not, depending on the needs. Thus, each new null level in the hierarchy gives you more flexibility and control over your model. You can group the effectors in a hierarchy by your possible needs to illustrate this. The effectors of the feet are controlled by foot nulls. The foot nulls are controlled by a pelvis null. The pelvis null and the collarbone null are controlled by a higher null at the top of the stack. Each has power over those under it, so that if you want to move one foot, you use a foot null. For both feet, you use the pelvis null. For the whole body, you use the top null. Take a look at the Schematic view for a fully flexible IK system placed in Julian (see Figure 15.53).

TUTORIAL: DON'T JUST WALK, CLIMB

Walk cycles have gotten out of hand. In the 2D days, a traditional cel animator did a walk cycle as part of a job interview, to prove that he could draw and animate with some skill under pressure. Now in the 3D world, beginning animators seem to think that walk cycles have some intrinsic value in and of themselves.

Let me fill you in on a secret: Walk cycles are way played out. If you clutter your demo reel with a walk cycle in which a character just walks down the street with no goal, no plot, no story, no conflict, no resolution, you will be advertising that you have no creative skill and are willing to work very hard on pointless, derivative material that everyone has seen a million times.

Put a little thought into your character, and make sure you have a reason for him to exist before you start animating him. Good reasons for a character to be in a walk or run cycle include runway fashion modeling, health club aerobic exercise, bank robbery, and the best (but hardest) of all, dance contests. A gorilla's natural goal is to walk to something he can climb, which brings us to the next tutorial.

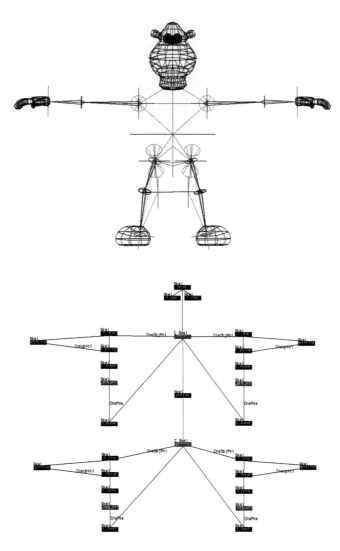

FIGURE 15.53 *Julian with the complete skeleton in him.*

To practice animating a complex IK system, you will help Julian walk to the Empire State Building and climb it. Load the Julian_IK_Climb scene from the courseware CD-ROM to use the prebuilt Julian model, or create your own using cluster constraints and a null hierarchy like the one printed here. In the tutorial, we'll take the completed Julian IK system, hide the skin, and use explicit translation to animate a complex IK motion—climbing! (See Figure 15.54.)

FIGURE 15.54 *Julian hanging off the building, looking for biplanes.*

1. Learn How to Puppet the Skeleton.

A properly constructed IK system is much like a puppet, in that you control the motions of the hands and feet indirectly with handles. How well or poorly built those handles are determines how easy or difficult it is to animate. A well-built IK puppet has a full range of motion appropriate for the character and can be moved with a hierarchy of controls that provide different levels of control, so you can get the action you want, fast.

Take a look at the Julian_IK_Climb scene while you read the following descriptions of his various components (refer to Figure 15.53). Remember this is just one way to build an IK system; there are as many good ways to build an IK skeleton as there are good artists (and an infinite number of bad ways).

top_handle   There should be a null control at the top of the hierarchy that is the parent, either directly, indirectly, or through constraints, of all the other items in the IK system. This control is used to position and rotate the character into position in the scene, to attach the character to other objects that the character might ride, and in general provides the greatest degree of control with the least degree of specialty in the whole system. When you move this null, called top_handle in the scene, the entire IK system goes with it. The top_handle is the direct parent of the torso_handle and the arms_n_legs_ handle. Select the top_handle as a tree (spacebar and right mouse button) and move the whole IK system around.

torso_handle   The torso_handle, one level down from the top_handle, controls the movement of the whole torso, including the shoulders, the pelvis, the spine, and the tops of the arms and the legs. When you grab the torso_handle and move it, the body gyrates while the hands and legs stay put. The torso_handle is critical for pulling the body up the building. The torso_handle is the direct parent of the shoulders' octahedron and the pelvis' octahedron. Select the torso_handle as a branch (Spacebar and middle mouse button) and then translate it to see the effect.

arms_n_legs_handle   The arms_n_legs_handle controls all the ends of the arms and legs at the same time. Because the character rarely moves its arms and legs at the same time in the same way, this handle exists mainly to help keep the hierarchy together and well organized. The arms_n_legs_handle is the direct parent of the left_arm_handle, the right_arm_handle, the left_leg_handle, and the right_leg_handle. Each of the arm and leg handles is a final actual control, the one that you will animate most often. Each one controls the effector of an IK chain, because that effector has a positional constraint to the control. The use of positional constraints and parenting is the secret to this IK system. Because we want mainly to animate these nulls, I've made all the other IK chains unselectable with the Select→Selectability→Toggle Selection command, so that when we select with the Spacebar, they are easy to get. If you want to select an IK chain for some reason, you must do it in the Schematic view.

Try the arm and leg handles out by selecting them in the Orthographic view and moving them around to see the IK chains follow.

shoulders   The shoulders object is an octahedron with named clusters at each end. Select the shoulder and use the Shape→Cluster List command to examine the clusters. The left arm IK chain is constrained to the l_shoulder cluster, and the right arm IK chain is constrained to the r_shoulder cluster, using the Constraint→Object to Cluster command. Therefore, when the shoulders move, the IK chains go with it, and when the shoulders rotate, the rotation drives the IK chains as well. Remember the shoulders are a child of the torso_handle, but they can be animated separately for subtle movements on their own. Try moving and rotating the shoulders to get a feel for what they do.

pelvis   The pelvis object is an octahedron with clusters on it for the two legs and the spine. Those IK chains are attached with the same Constraint→Position tool, and the pelvis works in the same way as the shoulders.

handles   This is a special control designed to assist in the animation workflow. It is a saved selection group, made with the Select→Set Named Selection tool. When you select it twice with the Spacebar and the left mouse button, it instead selects all the arm and leg handles for which we will be saving keys. Try it out.

You should now be able to move the creature anywhere, make it mambo, polka, or check the mail.

2. **Plan the Animation.**

   You badly need a working plan before you start moving things around on the screen, or your work will not go smoothly. Ours is simple. Each limb movement happens at five-frame intervals. We will save the explicit translation of each handle at each interval.

   Julian will move his arm and leg controls and then his torso controls to walk over to the building, and then he will reach up and grab the first window, and pull himself up. When he can stand on the window sill, he'll reach for the next one and repeat the process.

   Hide Julian's skin while you work to speed redraw and your own workflow.

3. **Walk.**

   At frame 1, select the torso_handle and save a keyframe with SaveKey→Object→Explicit Translation→All. Select all the arm and leg handles by using the special handles object, and save a similar key using the middle mouse button shortcut on the SaveKey menu cell.

   Select the pelvis and the shoulders, and save a key for them, too. This process of saving a keyframe for everything you animate at frame 1 creates F-curves for each object and glues them into place relative to one another, saving hair-pulling time later.

   At frame 5, select the back_foot_handle and move it to a position up in the air in mid-stride. Move the back_arm_handle forward as well, and then save a key for all the handles, to keep those you didn't move locked in place.

Select the torso_handle and move it forward as well to a position that looks good. Save another explicit translation key for it.

At frame 10, put the handle for the foot in motion back on the ground in front of the body, and swing the back arm forward. Save an explicit key frame for all the arm and leg handles. Move the torso_handle forward and save an explicit key. See the pattern here? Move forward five frames in time, reposition all the arms and legs and the torso, and save a keyframe for everything. Repeat until Julian gets over to the wall he needs to climb (see Figure 15.55).

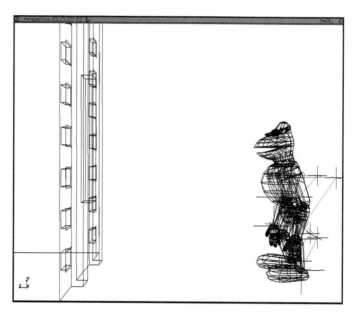

FIGURE 15.55 *Julian starting out on the ground.*

Remember that if one of his limbs looks funky, you can easily move to the nearest keyframe (always a multiple of five), move the handle for that limb to a better position, and save a key. Animation is a non-linear process of incremental improvement. As you get better at it, your initial gut decisions about where to place a handle on the first try will get better and better, and your animation will require less and less tuning.

4. **Climb.**

Julian should now be standing in front of the wall to be climbed. Move forward five frames. Translate the right_arm_handle so Julian reaches forward and grabs the top of the window sill nearest him. Save a key for *all* the handles (see Figure 15.56).

Move forward five frames and place Julian's left_foot_handle on the bottom of the window sill. Then save a key frame for all the handles at that frame (see Figure 15.57). If Julian is too close to the wall, so that his foot extends into the building, you can select his pelvis and translate it away from the wall, pulling the foot back. Make sure you save a key then for the pelvis as well.

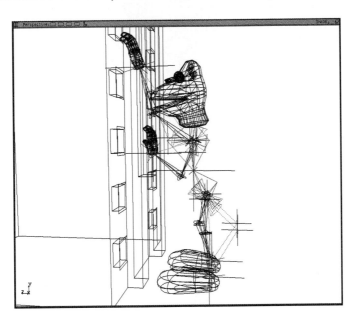

FIGURE 15.56 *Julian reaching up for a window.*

Move forward five frames. It's time for Julian to pull himself up and grab for the bottom of the next window sill in one fluid motion. Select the torso_ handle, translate the torso up until Julian is standing on the lowest window sill, and save a key for the torso. As he stands, he can move closer to the building face as well. If his arm intersects the building, select his shoulders and pull them away from the wall, and save a key. His trailing leg can join the first leg on the bottom of the window sill. Select all the handles and save a key.

Next move forward five frames and reach his trailing hand upward, as if to reach for the next window. Move the trailing foot to become the leading foot, on the top of the next sill. Move the shoulders and pelvis to look good. Save a key for everything, including the torso_handle. Remember the rule: Keyframe everything every five frames to prevent unwanted slippage between keyframes.

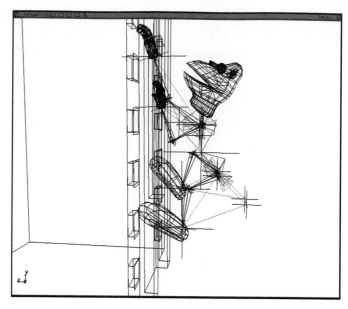

FIGURE 15.57 *Julian pulling himself up to the first window.*

Move forward five frames and select the torso_handle and translate it up the building, as if Julian is pulling himself up to the next sill.

See the pattern here? Julian moves his opposite arm and leg to a new handle and footing in one five-frame movement; he steps up and pulls himself to the next position over the next five-frame period. He then repeats the process with the other hand and foot.

Repeat this for one or two windows.

5. **Mix It Up.**

If you simply cycle the same pattern, the result looks mechanical and lacks creative vision. Try mixing up Julian's movements by thinking how else you might climb. Try moving one hand, then the other to the top of the next sill, and then the torso, leaving the legs dangling as he pulls himself up. Kick the legs quickly for realism (see Figure 15.59).

6. **Add Shoulder and Torso Movement.**

Go back to the first frame and start to add secondary animation to the pelvis and shoulders. In a real creature, when the right arm stretches upward, the right shoulder helps out by lifting up and the left shoulder pushes down. On the pelvis, when one leg raises, the pelvis raises a bit on that side as well, forcing the other side down. This phenomenon gives supermodels their sexy walks. We can add it into the mix after the initial animation is done by animating the rotation of the octahedrons that form the shoulders and the pelvis (see Figure 15.58).

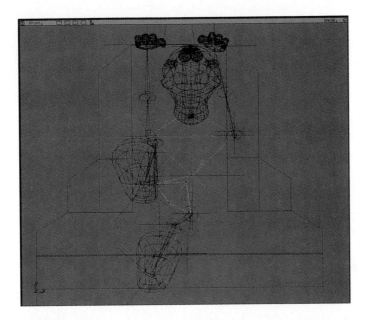

FIGURE 15.58   *Close-up of Julian's pelvis rotated to help lift a leg.*

On the first frame, select the pelvis and save a keyframe for the rotation at 0 with SaveKey→Object→Rotation→All. Move forward to five frames before he makes his first step onto the building, and save another zero-rotational keyframe to lock the pelvis in the intervening frames.

Move forward to the frame (a multiple of five) where the first foot is on the window sill. Rotate the pelvis slightly on the Z axis, which raises the root of the lifted leg a bit, and also gives a nice arch to the spine. Save a keyframe.

Five frames later, when the other leg joins the first on the sill, return the pelvis to a neutral rotation and save a keyframe.

Move forward in time, looking at the legs, and add a new rotational setting and keyframe to the pelvis where you find that one leg is lifted above the other.

Do the same with the shoulders and check your work.

You can also animate the translation of the shoulders relative to the pelvis to make the spine straighten and bend during the animation. This translation is added to the animation of the torso_handle, making it more complex and subtle.

7. **Innovate.**

   You can now control the puppet quite well. Think up the rest of the story, and execute the animation.

A functional IK system isn't exactly intuitive, but if you take the time to set it up right, it is easy to animate. Because Softimage sets keys only for specific attributes, it is easy to go back and make additions to the animation, layering on rotational animation on top of translational animation. This approach is what Softimage's developers mean by non-linear animation, and it is a Softimage specialty.

BULGING MUSCLES AND IK SYSTEMS

When you have built an IK system and properly weighted it to the skin you create, that skin moves with the IK system and bends at the joints in the system. Basically, the IK system provides the bones and joints to hang the skin on. But in humans and most other creatures, there is a layer of musculature between the skeleton and the skin that also deforms when joints move—bending, bulging, and rippling the skin.

To design believable IK systems, we need a few ways to control the action of the skin automatically, depending on the action of the joints that lie within it. Fortunately, Softimage 3D|Extreme provides a number of options, and in keeping with the software's general philosophy, you can certainly make up more of your own by combining these techniques with other tools.

BULGING MUSCLES WITH INNER/OUTER JOINTS

In real life, a muscle contracts in length, becoming wider and broader as it does. The contraction of the muscle pulls on the inner side of the next joint, causing it to rotate about its preferred axis. So, on the inside of that joint (the preferred direction of the joint), the skin in our IK system should bulge as the joint closes, and the other side should bulge a bit as the joint opens. Softimage 3D|Extreme has a very useful automatic way to connect the rotation of a single joint to the deformation of the inside and outside of the skin around this joint, called Skin Deformation Parameters (see Figure 15.59).

First, decide which joint you want to work on, and whether you want to edit the behavior of the skin on the inside of that joint (the bicep), or the outside of that joint (the tricep).

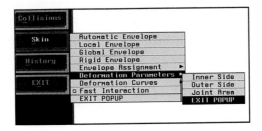

FIGURE 15.59 *The Skin Deformation Parameters menu cells.*

Next, select the joint you want to control and rotate it around Z (the preferred axis) so that the skin is in a deformed state. Choose either Skin→Deformation Parameter→Inner Side to work on the inside (bicep) of the joint or Skin→Deformation Parameter→Outer Side for the tricep side of the joint. In either case, the Flexible Envelope Parameters dialog appears (see Figure 15.60). In the Flexible Envelope dialog, you control the bulge of the muscle under the skin, how high it bulges, and how far it extends from joint to joint.

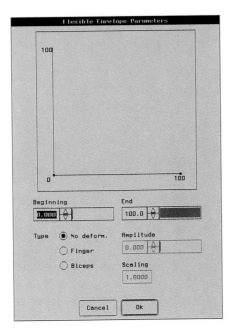

FIGURE 15.60 *The Flexible Envelope Parameters dialog.*

NOTE

To create and use a custom muscle profile, first draw two curves in the front window running from left to right, one for the top of the muscle (the inside curve) and one for the bottom of the muscle (the outside curve). The curves represent the shape of the skin at maximum muscle bulge, so draw them like an advertisement for anabolic steroids (see Figure 15.61).

The curves must not go vertical or double-back on themselves at any time, or they will not be acceptable deformation curves. For best results, the start and the end of the curves should be at the same height (the same Y value).

Next, select the joint in question, and choose the Skin→ Deformation Curves→Inner Side command, and then pick the top muscle curve. With the joint still selected, choose Skin→Deformation Curves→ Outer Side and pick the bottom muscle curve (see Figure 15.62). That's it! Now these curves will be used in the Flexible Envelope Parameters dialog.

The Beginning and End sliders determine how close the bulge is to the beginning and end of the joint segment. For example, on highly-defined body builders, the bicep forms a peak in the middle of the upper arm with a sizable gap between the inside of the elbow and the shoulder. You might set Beginning to 20 (20 percent) and End to 80 (80 percent) to create this more dramatic effect.

Type determines what the profile of the musculature at maximum deformation will look like. You can draw your own curve (highly recommended), or you can choose from predefined curves that are meant to look like biceps and fingers. Each Type option has a different curve for the inner and outer sides of the joint. The default, No Deform, has no effect on the skin, so make sure you choose one of the other options.

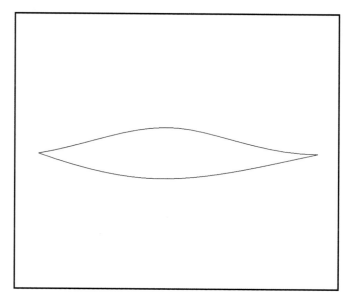

FIGURE 15.61 *Curves drawn for bicep and tricep profiles.*

Amplitude is the first way to tune up the effect. Set it to 50 (50 percent) to start with, and then turn it up and down to change the burliness of your character.

Scaling is another factor with which you can pump up your figure. The default value of 1 should be adequate unless your muscle deformation curves are too wimpy.

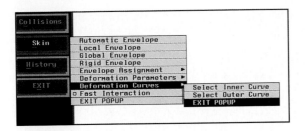

FIGURE 15.62 *The Skin→Deformation Curves menu cells.*

NOTE

You can set identical parameters for all joints in a chain by selecting the chain as a tree, and executing the Skin→Deformation Parameters→Inner and Outer commands just once on the whole tree.

Close the dialog to see the effect. Select the effector of the IK chain containing the joint you were working on, and translate the effector to see the muscle bulge as the joint closes! You can tune the parameters for the outside of the joint next with the Skin→ Deformation Parameters→Outer Area command.

TUTORIAL: PUMP JULIAN UP

In this quick tutorial, we'll load the climbing scene and by drawing a few curves and assigning them to his biceps, give Julian some muscular movement to make his climbing look more realistic.

1. **Draw Monkey Muscles.**

   Load the Julian_Arm_Muscle scene from your courseware CD-ROM.

   In the Front window, draw B-spline curves for his ape-like upper arms, including a top curve for his bicep and a bottom curve for his tricep. Name them and organize them so you remember their positions.

   Now create just an inner curve for his shins, so his calves bulge as he climbs. He doesn't need an outer curve for his shin, because there is no muscle on the outside of the shin (see Figure 15.63).

2. **Assign the Muscles.**

   Select Julian's arm joint, choose the Skin→Deformation Curves→Select Inner Curve command, and then pick the bicep curve to use that curve, instead of the default curve in the skin deformation. With the same joint selected, use the Skin→Deformation Curves→Select Outer Curve command and pick the tricep curve.

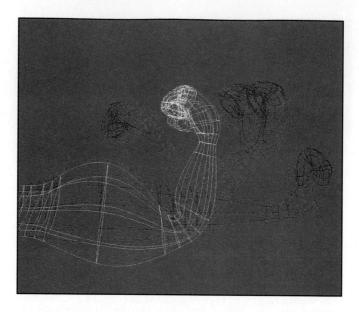

FIGURE 15.63   *Draw curves like these for the arm and leg muscles at maximum burliness.*

Select Julian's bicep joint and use the Skin→Deformation Parameters→ Inner Side command to set the parameters for the deformation. Set the Beginning slider to 10, the End slider to 90, and the Amplitude to 50. The Type selectors should be grayed out to indicate that a custom curve is assigned. Click Ok to accept the parameters and repeat for the three other joints.

3. **Test and Tune.**

Play the animation of Julian climbing to see the results. If his muscles are too wimpy, use Skin→Deformation Parameters to increase the Amplitude and Scaling of the muscle deformation. If his muscles are too freakish for you, and you prefer a more petite, lithe Julian, use Skin→Deformation Parameters to reduce the Amplitude and Scaling of the deformation. When you are completely happy with the results, save the scene as Julian_IK_Muscles so we can use it again.

With these fairly simple controls, you can assign any deformation curve that you can draw to a muscular action, and link the behavior of that muscle to the rotation of a specific joint, creating complex skin behaviors that go far beyond the simple joint bending found in other IK programs.

MUSCULATURE WITH GROUP AS SKELETON

Another way to influence the behaviors of the skin in addition to the per-joint IK deformations is to add your own deformations with the powerful Group As Skeleton concepts discussed earlier in this chapter. You can place a small object, such as a sphere, a cube, or a null, inside the skin of your character and group it to the IK system so that it also deforms the skin. Then you can animate the scale, translation, and rotation of the object to stretch and bend the skin around it in any way you can think up. You can use as many of these small controls as you need to create complex, overlapping movements under the skin of the creature to suggest the movement of muscles or bones under the skin.

To demonstrate the possibilities in a simple way, load the Julian_Breathing scene from the courseware CD-ROM, and try out the following tutorial.

TUTORIAL: JULIAN BREATHES

We want his chest to expand and contract in a cyclical manner as he climbs as if he taking great breaths to fuel his climb, but no one joint in his body seems appropriate. The solution: Add a Group As Skeleton component that expands his whole chest.

1. **Add a Primitive Element to the IK System.**

   Use the Get→Primitive→Sphere command to get a polygonal sphere, and then at the first frame of the animation, scale the sphere to fit within Julian's chest. Freeze the scale of the sphere with the Effect→Freeze→Transformations→Scale command to make it easier to scale up and down precisely. Position the sphere in Julian's chest just below his pectorals, in the position where his diaphragm would be, and name the sphere diaphragm with the Info→Selection command (see Figure 15.64).

Choose the Skeleton→Group As Skeleton command and then pick the new primitive diaphragm with the left mouse button, which designates the diaphragm as an IK element.

2. **Add the Diaphragm to the Skin.**

The diaphragm now needs to be grouped into the IK hierarchy, so that it influences the behavior of the skin. Unfortunately, this causes any manual skin weighting you have performed to be lost, as the entire IK system is reweighted automatically to include the new diaphragm.

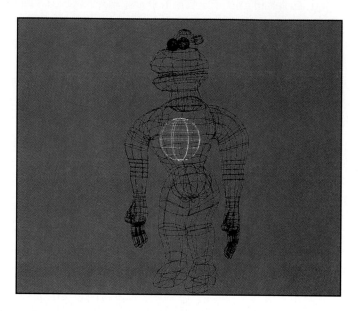

FIGURE 15.64 *Julian with a spherical diaphragm in his chest.*

Select the skin and use the Skin→Global Envelope command. Then pick the diaphragm and accept the default values in the Envelope Assignment dialog box to accept the weighting changes.

Look at the animation to see if any parts of the skin are incorrectly weighted to other joints, causing skin tearing and stretching. You can fix those problems by reassigning the envelope weights with the Skin→Envelope Assignment→Modify Weights command.

3. **Animate Some Breaths.**

To make Julian's chest heave, all we need to do is change the scale of the diaphragm sphere now linked to his skin as part of the IK system. Select the diaphragm and at frame 1 set a keyframe in the Motion module for the starting scale of the diaphragm with the SaveKey→Object→Scale→All command.

Next move forward in time about 15 frames, and change the scale of the diaphragm to make Julian's chest blow up like he is taking a great big breath.

Save a keyframe for the diaphragm by clicking the SaveKey menu cell with your middle mouse button.

Set another ending keyframe at frame 30 for the diaphragm at the same size as the initial keyframe by dragging first to frame 1 with the left mouse button. Then drag the Time Slider to frame 30 with the right mouse button, which leaves the sphere at the size it was in frame 1. Finally, click the SaveKey menu cell with the middle mouse button to save a key there at 30.

4. **Cycle the Breath.**

We want Julian to keep breathing, no matter what, but it seems like a lot of redundant work to keyframe in every breath manually. It is a lot of work and Softimage provides a better way. We can cycle the animation we just created.

With the diaphragm selected, show the Scale F-curve by choosing the F-curve Select→Object→Transformation→Scale→All command.

Now just cycle it by choosing the F-curveEdit→Extrap Mode→Cycle command. Zoom out of the timeline with the Z supra key to see that the breath repeats every 30 frames. Go ahead and change the timing or scale of the breath if you wish by moving points on the F-curve with the M supra key to see that the cycle automatically updates.

There you have it—simple breathing! Go crazy, adding in more animated IK elements if you want, and save your scene for future use.

CONCLUSION

Did you get all that? Good! You are ready to animate anything using complex IK systems, glued together with parenting, constraints, and clusters. Keep in mind that IK is usually the most complicated, and therefore the slowest, method of animating a character. Use IK only when it's really necessary, not just when you feel like it. Above all, use IK to solve creative problems, not because it looks neat.

Advanced users can take IK systems even farther in the next chapter, by using dynamics and IK at the same time!

In this chapter you learned how to:

- Build simple and complex IK chains
- Determine and animate the resolution plane of each IK chain
- Group IK skeletons together with constraints and clusters
- Constrain joint rotations so your characters don't break a leg
- Animate an IK-driven character doing more than walking
- Connect skins to IK systems and modify the weights of the envelope
- Pump up your animation with automatic muscle bulging
- Use Group As Skeleton to make any model part of an IK system

"The City of the Lost Children" copyright Claudie Ossard (production), 1995. 3D Animation and Visual Effects by BUF Compagnie, Paris. Image rendered with mental ray.

CHAPTER 16

ANIMATING WITH DYNAMICS

In the Actor module, Softimage offers a sophisticated, rigid-body dynamics system. Using the Dynamics menu cells (see Figure 16.1) and their dialogs, you can give volume, mass, and kinetic energy to every object in your scene that has a closed surface. Objects can then be affected by gravity, collide with other objects, bounce, spin, and tumble to create more natural-looking animation than is possible to create manually.

FIGURE 16.1 *The Dynamics menu cells.*

These dynamic effects can be simulated to create F-curves that you can then use in other animations. Regular F-curve animation can be mixed with simulation data within a single F-curve to create sophisticated effects, augmenting the three major effects—Gravity, Wind, and Collisions—with other user-defined behaviors.

Most incredibly, Softimage's IK system can obey dynamic physical properties, adding gravity and joint damping effects to existing IK systems. By combining IK and dynamics, you can add an accurate Gravity effect on a mass of skin to Softimage's other character animation tricks. This sort of dynamic deformation of skin is perfect for adding realistic hang and heft to such large creatures as dinosaurs and has been exploited extensively in feature films.

The limitations of Softimage 3D|Extreme's dynamics are that the system calculates only the direction, velocity, acceleration, rotational velocity, and rotational acceleration data for an object in a dynamic simulation. It does not calculate the rigidity, strength, or deformation of an object under stress. This means that using dynamics to drop a 10,000 pound anvil on a 12-ounce aluminum can does not flatten the can. By combining the dynamics system with QuickStretch controls, however, you can achieve a measure of this more complex soft body dynamics.

In this chapter you will learn how to:

- Set Dynamic properties on objects
- Run the dynamic simulation
- Set up collision objects
- Use dynamics with IK systems
- Use Special Controls with IK and dynamics
- Use QuickStretch to automate squash and stretch

SETTING DYNAMIC PROPERTIES

The multistep process for correctly using dynamic simulation in Softimage 3D starts with defining the physical properties on a single object. To examine these physical properties, get a sphere and execute the Dynamics→Physical Properties command to call up the Model Physical Properties dialog box (see Figure 16.2).

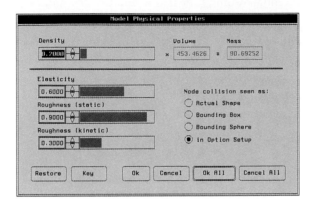

FIGURE 16.2 *The Model Physical Properties dialog box.*

You can assign physical properties to any model, hierarchy of models, or IK chain, but you cannot assign them to objects with zero volume, such as splines. Each object in a dynamic simulation can be accelerated by Gravity and Wind and can affect other dynamic objects in a collision.

DENSITY AND MASS

Softimage uses the *mass* of the object to determine how the object is affected by Wind and how a collision between two dynamic objects changes the inertia of each. With the Density slider in the Model Physical Properties dialog, you can change the object's density. Softimage then uses this value to automatically calculate the object's total mass, using the formula Mass = Density × Volume. No units are given, so the values for mass are relative to one another only.

ELASTICITY

The elasticity of an object is how much kinetic energy is lost in a collision. A value of 1 means that no energy is lost, and the object will likely bounce like a superball. An elasticity of 0 means that all energy is lost and the object will not bounce at all.

STATIC ROUGHNESS

The Roughness (Static) control determines how much energy is converted from inertia to rotational velocity at the contact patch between the two objects due to lateral motion. In a system where a ball falls straight down and bounces vertically back up, no static roughness is needed. But if the ball was also traveling forward as it fell, some of the forward momentum of the ball would be converted, as it stuck the floor, into rotational velocity. If the ball was very smooth and the floor waxed to a slippery sheen, the ball would spin very little. Setting a static roughness of 0 on the ball would simulate this kind of collision.

If the ball was rough like a rubber superball and the floor was rough like a wood floor, the ball would slip very little as it traveled forward on the floor at the moment of impact, so the difference between the inertia of the top of the ball and the inertia of the bottom of the ball in contact with the floor would rotate the ball around the center point, causing the ball to spin. A Roughness (Static) setting of 1 would keep the ball from slipping and it would therefore spin a lot after bouncing.

KINETIC ROUGHNESS

Roughness (Kinetic) controls the friction between the two objects at the same contact patch as Roughness (Static), but instead of converting to rotational velocity, it simply controls the loss of momentum. When Roughness (Kinetic) is set at 0, the objects are very slick and slide along each other laterally with no loss of energy, continuing to slide forever. A setting of 1 means the objects are very rough, and they quickly grind to a halt as they slide along each other.

NODE COLLISIONS SEEN AS

When Softimage 3D|Extreme runs the dynamics simulation and looks for a collision between objects, it needs to know how accurately to check for that collision. Your setting for Node Collisions Seen As tells Softimage how picky to be. Checking more accurately means longer computation times; checking less accurately means less precise collisions. The slowest, most accurate way to check is to examine each and every Control point or vertex of the moving object against the collision objects at every frame. This works well but may become slow. If this is your choice, set the Node Collisions Seen As to Actual Shape by clicking on that radio button.

A faster way is to create a bounding model around the moving object and just check the extent of that bounding area against the collision objects. This is less accurate for models with fine detail but is a lot faster. A roundish model is best served by the

Bounding Sphere radio button, which more closely approximates the model's surface; rectangular objects collide more naturally using the Bounding Box radio button. The In Option Setup button allows you to defer the choice to a later date, and even change your mind easily, by changing the method in another dialog, the Dynamics→Option Setup dialog.

APPLYING THE PROPERTIES

Softimage lets you be flexible about applying the properties you set. You can keyframe the dialog's values with the Key button, and you can apply dynamics to a single object in a hierarchy with the Ok button or to all objects in the selected hierarchy with the Ok All button. If the effect doesn't work out as planned, you can always go back to the Model Physical Properties dialog to change the parameters you set on an object, change the outcome of a simulation, or try something different.

OPTION SETUP

After you have added physical properties to your model for the first time, you can fine-tune your simulation. To do so, choose the Dynamics→Option Setup command to call the Option Simulation Setup dialog (see Figure 16.3).

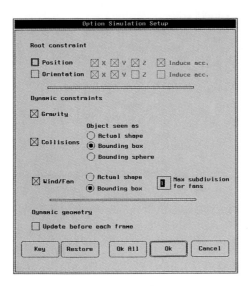

FIGURE 16.3 *The Option Simulation Setup dialog.*

The Root Constraint option, on by default for IK chains, means that the root of the dynamic chain is not itself affected by dynamics. Imagine animating a dancing ball and chain. If its root is affected by gravity, for example, the whole chain would just fall into a pile on the floor (or fall forever if there was no floor) instead of writhing in the air as planned.

Also on by default for IK chains is the Induce Acceleration check box. This setting is incredibly useful for dynamics and IK because it transfers the momentum of the parent model to the root of the IK chain only, leaving the rest of the chain to hang free. We will explore this incredible effect a little later in this chapter.

Root Constraint Orientation determines, in a similar fashion to Induce Acceleration, how the rotational velocity of the parent model is transferred to the IK root.

The Dynamic Constraints portion of the dialog is where you can turn off Gravity, Collisions, and Wind effects if you don't plan to use them. Turning them off saves processing time and speeds up your simulations. Here is also where you can change the way in which Softimage 3D|Extreme looks for collisions between the selected object and the assigned collision objects. The Actual Shape option is slower but more accurate, while Bounding Box is quick and dirty.

If the shape of the object is changing over the duration of the simulation, either due to shape animation or dynamic QuickStretch animation, checking the Dynamic Geometry box tells Softimage to check the shape of the object before each frame to make sure collisions are accurate.

As you can see in the Model Physical Properties dialog, in Options Setup, you can change the settings for a single selected item with the Ok button. You can also change the settings for all items in the hierarchy with the Ok All button, and the values can be keyed.

GRAVITY

NOTE

The length of the Gravity vector, 910 units, is close to 9.8 meters per second squared, the acceleration due to gravity in the real world.

The instant that you click the Ok button in the Model Physical Properties dialog, gravity is added to your world. The only way to get rid of it is to turn it off in the Options Setup dialog. Gravity is a vector icon, located in your scene at the origin and pointed down in the negative Y direction. The scale of the vector determines the strength of the force of gravity and is set by default to 910 units.

You can directly set the Gravity strength by scaling the vector in Y. You can also rotate the vector, which directs the force of gravity along the new local Y direction of the vector. Of course, special effects can also be created by animating the transformations of the Gravity vector.

To run the simulation for an object, you must first specify start and stop frames for the simulation by dragging the Time Slider to a start frame and, with the dynamic object selected, clicking the Simulate→Save Start/End command.

If you save a start, Softimage automatically sets the end to the last frame in the timeline. You can, however, set an end frame manually if you want.

Finally, just choose the Simulate→Automatic command to run the simulation and generate data for the translation and rotation of the selected objects.

TUTORIAL: DROPPING THE BALL

In this simple tutorial, we'll practice setting up a simple dynamic situation and run the simulation to generate F-curves.

1. **Make the Chain and Balls.**

   In the Front view, draw a 2D IK chain with the Skeleton→Draw 2D Chain command so that the segments go back and forth and look bunched up as in Figure 16.4.

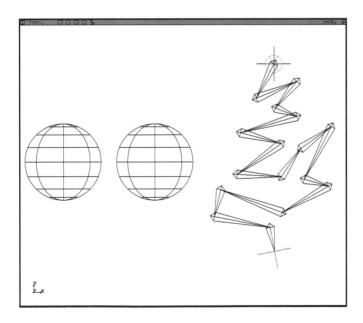

FIGURE 16.4 *The IK chain and two balls.*

   Also get a primitive sphere and duplicate it so you have two copies. We'll apply dynamics to both a model and an IK chain to see the similarities and differences.

2. **Set Properties.**

Select the first ball and choose Dynamics→Physical Properties. The settings are unimportant to us, so just click the Ok button.

A Gravity vector is created in the global center. Select it and reset the Gravity force to 400 by scaling it in Y to that value. Also rotate the Gravity vector slightly around the Z axis, so Gravity doesn't pull straight down, just for kicks.

Select the entire IK chain, choose the Dynamics→Physical Properties command, and click the Ok to All button to accept the settings for all joints in the chain. Watch your Wireframe display as the joints all flash, taking the dynamic information. This now means that each joint has some mass and will, therefore, be affected by gravity, as well as by the fact that it is connected to the rest of the chain.

Select the second ball (the one without dynamics) and use the Constraint→Position command to constrain it to the effector of the IK chain. The ball should hop to the location of the effector.

3. **Save a Start and Simulate.**

Select the first dynamic ball and save a start with Simulate→Save Start/End.

Select the IK chain and save a start for it as well.

Select both the first ball and the chain in Multi mode and run the simulation with the Simulate→Simulate (automatic) command. The ball drops away as gravity takes it, while the chain unfolds and flaps back and forth.

After the simulation is over, select the first ball and examine the F-curve for translation with the F-curve Select→Object→Explicit Translation→All command. Note how the simulation saves a value for the ball at each frame. This is called *cooking the simulation* or *baking the F-curve*. It means that you can play the animation without the time and computation required by the dynamics.

4. **Change Some Values.**

Select the Gravity vector, make it longer, and rotate it to head straight up.

Play the animation. The ball and chain behave exactly as before, because we haven't resimulated the dynamics with the new data for the Gravity vector.

Fix this omission by selecting the IK chain and running the simulation again with the Simulate→Simulate command. Now the changes are made and the new F-curve data is cooked. Save the scene for later use as Ball_drop.

So much for the simple stuff. It's time to move on and introduce collisions into the dynamic simulation.

COLLISIONS

A collision is the occurrence when two models try to share a physical point in space at the same instant. Another way to describe a collision is the point in time where the volumes of two objects overlap in space.

Most objects in the real world have an impermeable boundary layer and so cannot share a volume of space with another object. So when the two objects moving together collide, their momentum presses them together until the elasticity of the object converts that momentum into a displacement of matter perpendicular to the direction of motion. If the objects retain their cohesion, they convert that displacement back into momentum in the opposite direction. The actual behavior of each object depends upon the mass of each object relative to the other and the angle at which they strike, as anyone who has been in a car wreck or played pool can tell you.

In Softimage 3D, we've already set up the density, and therefore the mass, of each object for which we plan to calculate dynamics. What remains is to tell the dynamic object what to collide with using the Collisions menu cells (see Figure 16.5). Then during the simulation, Softimage can move the dynamic object and check to see if its volume ever intersects with the volume of another object. When the objects intersect, Softimage's dynamics simulator uses the mass and velocity of the dynamic object, the angle of incidence to the collision plane, and your settings for the static and kinetic roughness to assign new velocity, acceleration, and rotation data to the dynamic object at each frame.

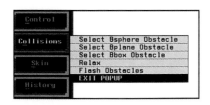

FIGURE 16.5   *The Collisions menu cells.*

In Softimage 3D, a dynamic object can use its own shape to detect collisions, but not the shape of the collision obstacles. The obstacles may be only a bounding plane that extends infinitely, regardless of the dimensions of the bounding model, a bounding box, or a bounding sphere. More complex boundaries for collisions can be constructed easily by combining many smaller bounding models into a hierarchy.

NOTE

You cannot assign a hierarchy of models to be its own collision obstacles, creating self-collisions. The same effect can be created with more work by setting each of 10 bowling pins, for instance, to collide with the bowling ball, the lane, and nine neighboring pins, but not itself.

It helps to think through the effect you want before you jump in, just to decide which objects in the relationship are dynamic objects, which are collision objects, and which are both.

To actually assign a single object or a hierarchy of objects as a collision object to another object that already has dynamics applied, select the collision object and, in the Actor module, select the Collisions menu cell that best applies to the shape of the objects. Floors are best created with Collisions→Select B-plane Obstacle, but Collisions→Select B-sphere Obstacle and Collisions→Select B-box Obstacle work well for hierarchies of smaller collision objects.

TUTORIAL: KNOCK YOUR BLOCK OFF

In this tutorial, we will build on the previous tutorial, "Dropping the Ball," by adding some dynamic collisions.

1. **Build a Wall of Blocks.**

   We want to build a wall of cubic blocks in a position where the arc of the ball on the chain plows through them, knocking them for miles in a gratifying smashup. If you select the effector and drag it now, it won't follow your mouse because the dynamic forces on it act as a constraint to its position. You will need to remove the previous dynamic data before you can translate the effector to a new spot and resimulate. Use the Simulate→Delete Transition Curves command on the entire chain to remove the dynamic data. Grab the effector, pull it to the left in the Front view, and save a key for the explicit translation at frame 1.

   Set the Gravity vector to point straight down again by changing its rotation and scale.

   Run the simulation and edit the location of the effector, remembering to save a key each time. Rerun the simulation until you like the arc of the ball swinging through space. The intention here is to set the chain up in such a way that as it unfolds it swings violently to the right side. Imagine the blocks in its path.

   Now get a primitive polygon grid and transform it to be the ground plane, just under the lowest point of the wrecking ball arc.

   Get a primitive cube, and scale and duplicate it nine times, arranging the blocks artfully into a wall directly in the path of the wrecking ball (see Figure 16.6).

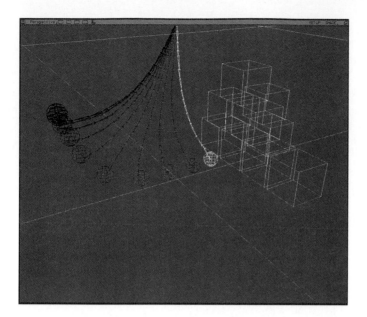

FIGURE 16.6 *The wrecking ball swinging towards our blocks.*

2. **Assign Dynamics.**

   Select the blocks all at once in Multi mode and use the Dynamics→Physical Properties command to assign some properties to them all. In the dialog, pick a Density, Roughness (Static), and Roughness (Kinetic) of your choice, and set the Node Collisions selector to In Option Setup, so we can set some parameters there as well.

   Again with all the blocks selected, use the Dynamics→Option Setup command, and in the Options Simulation Setup dialog, make a few changes.

   Turn off the dynamics for Wind/Fan because we won't be using them. Set the Collision Object Seen to be a bounding box because that best matches the shape of the individual blocks.

3. **Assign Collisions.**

   Again with all the blocks selected, choose the Collisions→Select B-sphere Obstacle and then pick the wrecking ball to complete the command. The wrecking ball flashes briefly to show that it has accepted the connection.

   Assign the ground plane as a collision object to the hierarchy of blocks, this time as a bounding plane. The bounding plane extends forever in the plane of the grid, so the blocks won't fall when they reach the edges of the grid. If you want that effect, choose the ground plane as a bounding box obstacle.

4. Set the Start and Simulate.

We still need to set the starting frame for the dynamic simulation of the blocks. We don't want the blocks to fall until they have been hit by the wrecking ball, so we won't turn on the dynamic simulation until just before the ball strikes the blocks. Drag the Time Slider forward to the frame just before the wrecking ball impacts the blocks, and use the Simulate→Save Start/End command to turn on the simulation at that frame. Gravity and Collision will stay on for the remainder of the simulation.

Now run the simulation and cook the data into F-curves for each block by selecting the hierarchy of blocks and executing the Simulate→Simulate (automatic) command (see Figure 16.7). Watch the blocks scatter! (See Figure 16.8.)

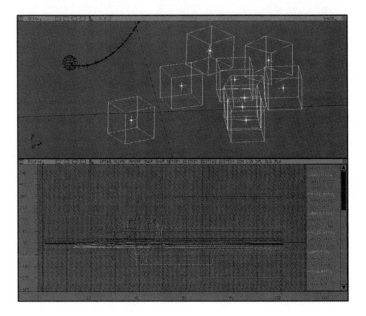

FIGURE 16.7   *The explicit translation F-curve data for all the blocks together*

You can adjust the behavior of the blocks by playing with their elasticity and roughness in the Dynamics→Physical Properties command and by scaling the Gravity vector in the scene. Remember to run the simulation again to see the changes you made.

That's all there is to it. The pattern of setting up dynamics is always the same: Add physical properties to an object, add collisions to the object, set a start, and simulate.

FIGURE 16.8 *The wrecking ball scattering the blocks.*

COMBINING IK AND DYNAMICS

As you saw in the previous tutorial, dynamic effects can be applied to IK chains as well as geometry objects. In fact, an entire suite of more complex tools is enabled in IK systems when dynamics are also used.

The most simple effect is to apply gravity to an IK chain. Each joint segment gains a certain amount of mass when dynamic properties are applied to the chain, depending on the volume of the skin influenced by that joint (if a skin is attached already) or on a default value (if no skin is presently attached). Because each joint also has a pivot point at one end, the gravity accelerates the mass of the joint and rotates the joint around the pivot. Because the root of an IK chain is exempt from the laws of physics by default, it remains fixed in place and anchors the chain as it falls.

When each segment in the chain behaves identically, the effect is like a falling rope tied to a tree limb.

WARNING

One big drawback in the current IK/dynamics system is that when dynamics are applied to a chain, the rotational limits set on each joint are overridden. They simply don't work any more and the joint rotates freely as the dynamics system dictates.

You can cleverly work around this in some cases by applying the dynamic forces to a dummy object, such as a cube (a null won't work because dynamics requires volume to calculate mass), and then constraining the effector to the dummy object with a positional constraint.

ROOT CONSTRAINT

Root constraint is the fancy name for the fact that the root of the chain is not affected by dynamics. It remains a normal null and can, of course, be attached in a hierarchy as a child of other objects.

However, it has a few more special capabilities. When it is attached to another object, either in a hierarchy or with a constraint, it inherits the momentum and rotational momentum of the object that drives it. That momentum is passed down through the joints in the chain one by one. As each joint reacts to the changes, they rotate about their axes. This makes the IK chain behave in a very different manner than normal.

Therefore, the IK chain reacts to the motion of the parent, lagging behind as if it were slightly elastic. With gravity, it creates an effect of weight and momentum; without gravity, it can be used to create antennae, ears, and other elastic body parts that sway as the body moves.

To see this in action, try the following two simple tests.

TUTORIAL: HANGING WITH GRAVITY

In this first test, we will show how an IK chain on a path inherits momentum (see Figure 16.9).

FIGURE 16.9   *An IK chain on a path inherits momentum with dynamics.*

1. **Draw a Path and an IK Chain.**

   Draw a B-spline curve for a path in the Top view, with some curves in it, such as a simple race track. In the Front view, draw a 3D IK chain with eight segments hanging straight down.

2. **Attach the Chain to the Path.**

   Attach the root of the chain to the path with Path→Pick Path, so that the chain hangs below the path you drew. Play the animation and observe how rigid the chain is while it moves. Yuck.

3. **Apply Dynamics.**

   Select the IK chain and apply dynamics with the Dynamics→Physical Properties command. Set a start frame at 1 with Simulate→Save Start/End, and run the simulation with Simulate→Simulate (automatic).

See how the chain now swings wildly, following the root as it travels along the path. Each joint now has its own momentum, dragging it in the direction it was already traveling. When the root changes direction, the chain tries to keep going in the original direction until the force of gravity causes each joint to rotate back to extend the chain straight down. The results are a fabulously complex physical performance.

TUTORIAL: AN IK BUG

The antennae on the top of a bug's head are another great application for these elastic IK chains affected by dynamics. In this case, we want the antennae to perch above the bug head and stay flopped over when the bug moves, so a positive gravity is necessary to draw the antennae upwards. The floppy antennae create automatic secondary animation that makes the character more appealing (see Figure 16.10).

1. **Design the Head and Antennae.**

   Create a bug head, or just use a sphere. Draw a four-segment 3D chain stretching upwards.

   Position the chain above the bug head in a satisfactory position, and duplicate it to create the second chain. Parent the chains to the head as children, so that when you move the head the chains move as well.

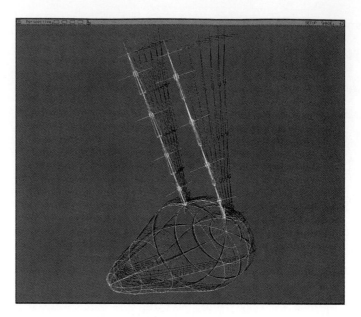

FIGURE 16.10 *A bug head with floppy antennae.*

2. **Apply Dynamics.**

   Apply dynamics to the chains, but this time also use the Option Setup dialog to turn off Gravity and Collision for the chains. Make the IK chains stiffen by selecting them and using the Dynamics→Joint Properties command to add some friction to each axis of each joint in the selected chain.

3. **Animate.**

   Set a number of quick keyframes for the bug head, moving back and forth and twisting around as if it is looking in different directions.

   Finally, set the start for the simulation and run the simulation.

Check out those bug antennae. They follow the motion of the head but also flop over as if they have inertia of their own.

JOINT DAMPING

So far, in an IK system, the joint limits act on the rotation of a joint by stopping it cold as it hits the limits, such as a door slamming shut. Similarly, when the effector of a chain is moved, the chain tries to immediately rotate to meet the new position required.

But many hinges in life don't work that simply. A door on a pneumatic closer mechanism, for instance, might swing quickly at first but then slow down and ease into the door jamb. In the same manner, you don't extend your limbs so that they hit the end of their rotational limits too hard because you would break them. If we could control how the joints approach their rotational limits, we could give an IK chain a more complex, fluid motion that would be more natural. We could also control the stiffness of the joints and, therefore, the force required to rotate one joint versus another. That way we could make the joints in a chain unfold one after the other if we wanted, instead of all at once.

In Softimage 3D, the control we want for these kinds of effects is called *joint damping*. To specify the joint damping limits for your chains, use the Constraint→ Rotation Limits command to call the Rotation Limits dialog (see Figure 16.11). A related command is Dynamics→Joint Properties, which controls the joint friction of each joint in a dynamically animated chain (see Figure 16.12).

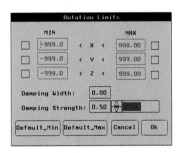

FIGURE 16.11   *The Rotation Limits dialog box.*

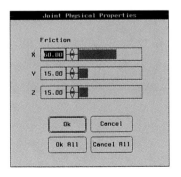

FIGURE 16.12   *The Joint Physical Properties dialog.*

NOTE

The Damping Width text entry box seems to have broken in the Softimage 3D 3.7sp1 release, and it won't hold a value after the Rotation Limits dialog is closed.

Joint damping is calculated only either when dynamics are run on an IK chain or when the effector of an IK chain is being controlled by a constraint. This means that in a simple system where the IK chains are hooked together and the effectors are directly animated, joint damping doesn't work. But when you can use dynamics in your system, it's worth the extra effort.

To set the joint damping, consider the two values you must specify for each joint, the Damping Width and the Damping Strength. The Damping Width is expressed in degrees and is a buffer to the edge of either side of the hard joint limits. For instance, if you set the Rotation Limits of the joint to –45 degrees and 45 degrees and set the Damping Width to 15 degrees, the joint would start to stiffen and rotation would start to slow down at –30 degrees and 30 degrees. The joint would constantly become stiffer until it came to a gradual halt exactly at –45 or 45 degrees. The Damping Strength value sets how evenly the resistance of the joint is spread through the Damping Width. Higher Damping Strengths will result in more dramatic results.

NAILS AND OTHER CONTROLS

FIGURE 16.13 *The Get Special Controls menu cells.*

One last feature group remains in the IK and dynamics systems: special controls. A special control is another force that can act on an IK chain that has dynamics applied to make it behave in a certain way.

Gravity is a control that is created automatically when dynamics are applied, but there are more. Force, Wind, Fan, and Nail are additional controls you may use to make the dynamic simulation even more complex.

Force, Wind, and Fan are variations on a theme, moving the objects they influence in similar ways. Nail is different, and it is powerfully useful in creating complex IK systems (see Figure 16.14).

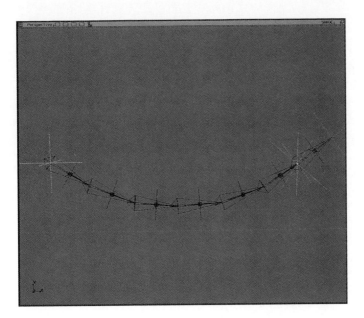

FIGURE 16.14 *A dynamic IK chain hanging from a root on one side and a nail on the other.*

Nail creates another root for an IK chain, so that a given chain can be constrained at more than one location. Imagine that you want to create the effect of a length of chain stretched loosely between two posts. The original root of the IK chain could be attached to one of the posts, but because dynamics overrides positional constraints, the effector can't be constrained to the second post. The solution is to add a nail to the IK chain, pinning the last joint in the chain to the second post. When the dynamics are run on the IK chain, it swings down from both sides, creating the effect you want.

This has an even more powerful application in deforming bags of hanging skin for creature IK animation. Imagine that you are animating a large dinosaur with a pendulous belly. An IK system with dynamics would be perfect if you could accurately simulate how the skin hangs on the creature. Placing an IK chain in the skin of the belly, constrained by the root on one side and a nail on the other, would work perfectly.

To try out a Nail special control, get one with the Control→Get Special Control→Nail command. The nail comes into the scene at the global origin, and you can then select it and place it wherever you want. Draw an IK chain hanging in a semicircle in the Front window, and place the nail just above the last joint before the effector. Add dynamics to the entire chain with the Dynamics→Physical

Properties command. Without dynamics, you cannot associate the nail to the chain. Select the last joint, choose the Control→Select command, and then pick the nail. The chain now has a new root located at the position of the nail. The nail and the root can each be parented to another object with animated translation, and when dynamics are run on the IK chain, it swings freely between the two root constraints. A chain can have as many nails as it has joints, and it tries to solve between them if they pull it in different directions.

The other controls are applied in much the same way. An object with dynamics applied is required for a control to do anything, but many different objects can be associated with the same control. Each control has an icon that determines the strength and direction of the control. You can set the power of the control directly by scaling it in different axes and direct it by changing its rotation.

Experiment with the special controls acting on simple primitive spheres without gravity to get an idea of their effects.

COMBINING QUICKSTRETCH AND DYNAMICS

The Softimage dynamics system itself is a rigid body system, which means that although objects under the influence of dynamics can translate and rotate through space, the Control points that make up the object stay rigidly in the same position as they were in when they started out.

The alternative to a rigid-body dynamic system is a soft-body dynamic system. In a soft-body system, objects can be deformed by dynamic forces. For example, in cartoon animation, the faster a character is moving, the more the character stretches out from the leading part of his body (usually the legs or belly). Or, when a rubber tire bounces down stairs, it should deform when it strikes each step, squashing down as it absorbs kinetic energy and stretching up as it releases that energy and rebounds off the stairs. When a cartoon racer peels out, his tires balloon out due to the effect of centripetal force on the elastic rubber, and when a cartoon character is flung into a wall, he flattens out on impact. You can add these soft-body effects to your scenes automatically by combining the QuickStretch and dynamics systems together.

While the dynamics system actually moves objects, the QuickStretch system looks at the movement of objects over a number of frames to generate values for the object's velocity, acceleration, rotational velocity, and rotational acceleration.

QuickStretch creates two new icons in the Schematic view for each object with QuickStretch applied: the *Linear Velocity vector* and the *Rotational Velocity vector*.

These vectors follow the object and indicate the direction and degree of velocity at that frame. Acceleration can be deduced from changes in the velocity between frames. Those new acceleration and velocity values can then be used to displace each control point in the object from the center of mass of the object, according to parameters that you set up.

The net effect is that QuickStretch lets you deform your objects to suggest the forces working on them. As objects accelerate, you can stretch them backwards to suggest conservation of momentum. When objects are moving quickly at a constant rate of speed, they can become more teardrop shaped as if deformed by air friction. As objects spin, they can stretch and wobble as if pulled apart by centripetal force.

> **NOTE**
>
> You may also plot these acceleration and velocity values to generate function curves that may be edited and used later to fine-tune the effect you need. The commands to plot them are located in the Motion module, in the Plot menu cell.

The best way to learn about QuickStretch is to try it out. If you apply QuickStretch to an object and then translate the object with your mouse in DRG mode, you can get an instant approximation of the final effect. Just turn on some Flex in the Qstretch menu cell and try it out! To apply QuickStretch to an object that already has dynamic forces applied, select that object and choose the QStretch→Setup command in the Actor module to call up the Quick Stretch Setup dialog box (see Figure 16.15).

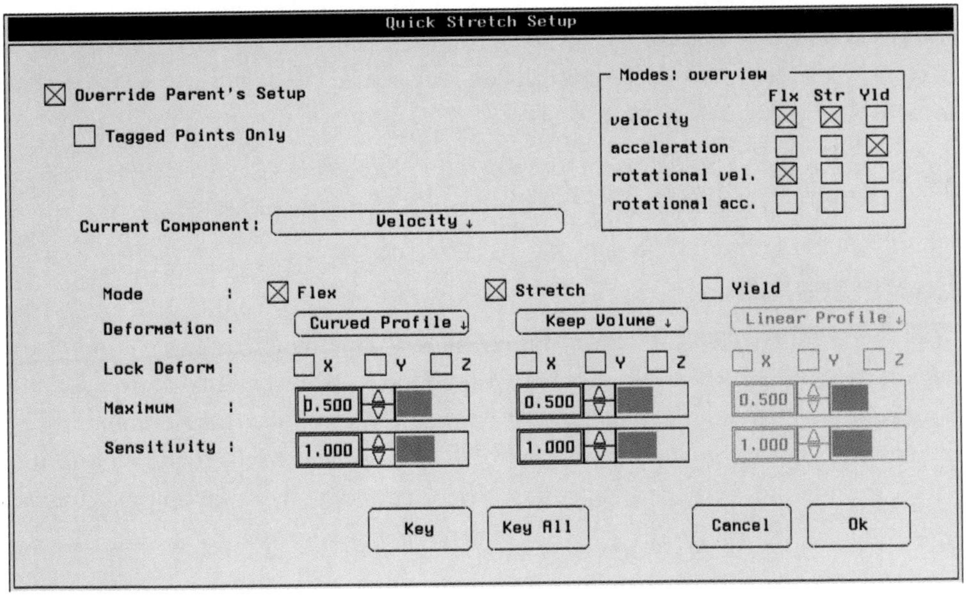

FIGURE 16.15 *The Quick Stretch Setup dialog.*

There are three ways in which an object with QuickStretch can deform, and each works better in some cases than others. Objects can Flex, Stretch, and Yield. And each Flex, Stretch, and Yield can be paired with Acceleration, Velocity, Rotational Acceleration, and Rotational Velocity.

Flex is good for adding motion effects to objects that will be traveling quickly. When an object flexes, it appears to experience wind resistance, and the faster it moves, the more it flexes. Flex is best paired with Velocity in the Quick Stretch Setup dialog.

Stretch is good for adding generic cartoon squash-and-stretch effects, in which characters seem to elongate and stretch when they start moving and then compact and flatten when they come to a stop. Stretch is best paired with Acceleration in the Quick Stretch Setup dialog.

Yield causes objects to bulge in ways that simulate the internal mass of the object shifting due to acceleration, like a bowling ball shifting around in a character's fat belly. Yield works well with both Velocity and Acceleration.

The grid of check boxes in the upper-right corner of the Quick Stretch Setup dialog helps you quickly pair the accelerations and velocities with Flex, Stretch, or Yield, while the drop box in the middle of the dialog allows you to pick one acceleration or velocity at a time and precisely adjust the degree of Stretch, Flex, or Yield.

When QuickStretch is enabled on an object with dynamic forces, QuickStretch automatically takes control and deforms the object according to the settings you choose in the Quick Stretch Setup dialog, and the velocity and acceleration that come from the Dynamics simulation.

QuickStretch is best added to a finished animation, as the last step before the render, to add a very slight variability to the motion of the characters.

CONCLUSION

Applying dynamic forces to objects probably isn't something that you will do every day, but it is there when you need it. Some effects, such as falling down stairs or bouncing a ball, would be hard to do convincingly without dynamics. Sometimes dynamics and collisions are the best alternative for special effects, such as a bowling ball scattering pins in a realistic manner: The pins are the dynamic objects and also collide with each other and the lane as they tumble.

QuickStretch, on the other hand, should be part of your regular bag of tricks because it's an automatic way to add the anticipation, secondary animation, and appeal that make your characters stand out. Just remember—keep it subtle. Don't beat your audience over the head with QuickStretch, and they will think that you spent weeks masterfully crafting small changes in the shapes of your characters to make them more believable.

In this chapter you learned:

- How to set up the mass, elasticity, and roughness of objects
- How to set the start frame and run a dynamic simulation to generate F-curves
- How to choose collision objects and set up Node Collision parameters
- How IK systems work with dynamics, with and without root constraints
- What to do with special controls and dynamics
- Why QuickStretch is the easiest animation tool in Softimage 3D

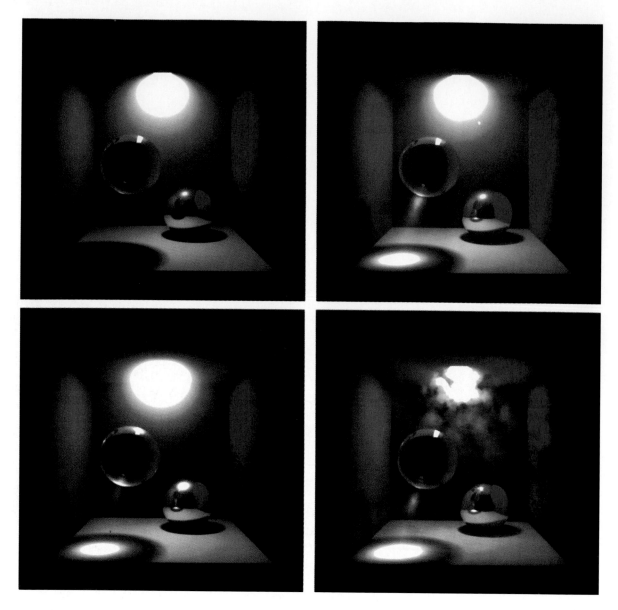

Four images rendered with mental ray 2.0, showing global illumination and caustic effects with photon maps and showing volume light scattering in homogenous and non-homogenous media. Image reprinted with from the paper "Efficient Simulation of Light Transport in Scenes with Participating Media Using Photon Maps," by Henrik Wann Jensen and PerH. Christensen. Copyright Mental Images GmbH & Co.

CHAPTER 17

THE MENTAL RAY RENDERER

The built-in Softimage renderer that ships with the standard version of Softimage has two big advantages. It is extraordinarily fast and it combines scanline and raytracing algorithms to accurately and speedily render objects even when they are reflective, transparent, and refractive.

Although the Softimage renderer is fast, it is not the most attractive renderer in the world. Subtle colors are difficult to make visible and roughness isn't always done in a believable way. Nor does the Softimage renderer produce special effects, such as glows, flares, or other optical effects. The Softimage renderer isn't particularly flexible and there is no way for programmers to extend its functionality by writing new rendering tools called shaders.

Because the fine Softimage 3D|Extreme modeling and animation tools deserve a renderer just as excellent, the Softimage engineers set about looking for a new renderer to accompany the 2.7 release. After a search, they chose the mental ray (see Figure 17.1), a program developed in Berlin by a company named Mental Images.

FIGURE 17.1   *The mental ray just makes good-looking pictures. This is the volumic lightning shader.*

In this chapter, you will:

- Find out where the mental ray comes from
- Discover how shaders work
- Learn to spot mental ray functions in the Softimage interface
- See examples of material shaders, texture shaders, and volume shaders

MENTAL RAY BASICS

The mental ray is a completely standalone rendering program, a small piece of software that runs independently of other animation software and takes care of only the rendering part of the process. The mental ray has no interface and takes as its sole input an .mi file that describes the entire scene to be rendered, including all geometry, all lights, the camera position, and all rendering settings, such as resolution and antialiasing.

Each frame to be rendered must be converted by the animation software used to the .mi format and written to disk before the mental ray can read it. When the mental ray is done rendering the file, it writes the file to disk as an image.

The mental ray is slated to become the sole rendering engine for Softimage 3D| Extreme and will be completely integrated into the upcoming Sumatra product. The mental ray also forms the rendering engine for the Twister rendering product.

The mental ray is an astoundingly sophisticated rendering engine. It was designed as a parallel rendering engine, capable of running on large supercomputers with many processors and a shared memory space oracross networks of many smaller machines. The mental ray can divide up each frame to be rendered into small tiles that are sent out to render on machines over an Ethernet network, and then be returned the same way for the mental ray to combine into the finished image.

MENTAL RAY'S STRENGTHS

The mental ray, like the Softimage internal renderer, is both a scanline and a ray-traced renderer, and can efficiently and accurately calculate reflective, refractive, and transparent surfaces. The mental ray has more internal features than the Softimage internal renderer, including:

- Displacement mapping
- Ambient lights
- Adaptive surface tessellation
- Automatic edge connection

The mental ray is a higher quality renderer, internally using 16 bits per color channel as it renders, creating 48-bit color output. The mental ray does a better job with Bump mapping and in general its results look better than those from the Softimage internal renderer.

The mental ray also does a better job with special effects. It can render sophisticated volumic and atmospheric effects, such as fog, lightning, or smoke. The mental ray supports pre- and post-process rendering to add such effects as lens flares, glows, fur (see Figure 17.2), and paint effects to rendered images. The newest version of the mental ray even supports light caustics and can render radiosity effects.

FIGURE 17.2   *The fur post shader adds hair to objects after they are rendered. Note the absence of hair in the reflections.*

AN INTRODUCTION TO SHADERS

Most importantly, the mental ray architecture is extensible and uses *shaders*, small programs for specific functions, to extend the capabilities of the renderer. Many such shaders exist now, enabling you to create cool effects, such as water, lasers, lightning, and many more. New shaders are written every day as well and are posted on the Web and on bulletin boards for you to download for free. If you are a C programmer and understand the basics of rendering, the Softimage 3D|Extreme documentation includes a book entitled *The Mental Ray Programmers Guide*, which can help you write your own shaders. A visual shader development tool called ShadeTree is also available to speed development times.

The shaders that come with Softimage 3D|Exteme are generally located in two databases, the Shader_Lib database and the Shader_Gift database (see Figure 17.4). Those shaders in the Shader_Lib are supported by Softimage and are likely to work well. Those in the Shader_Gifts database are included as a courtesy only, are not tested by Softimage, and may not function as advertised.

FIGURE 17.3 *The collection of mental ray shaders from Lume, Inc., brings extra realism to this scene. Clockwise from top left: Starting image without shaders, then with the Illumination shader for accurate light falloff, then the Translucency shader to make the glass visible, then the Glare shader to overexpose the image in the brightest areas. Images copyright and courtesy of Lume, Inc., 1997.*

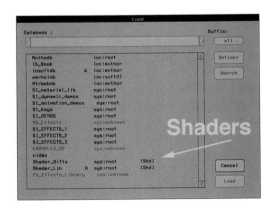

FIGURE 17.4 *The Shader_Lib and Shader_Gifts databases in the DB browser.*

A good description of many shaders, as well as instructions for use and sample renders, is located in the HTML document named Effects_Overview that ships with Softimage (see Figure 17.5).

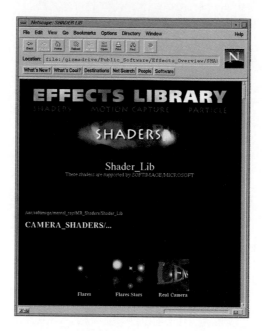

FIGURE 17.5 *Effects_Overview is HTML documentation for many mental ray shaders.*

USING SHADERS

Because the mental ray was added to Softimage well after the initial interface was designed, the mental ray and its shaders look like they were strapped into the interface wherever there was room. Although that isn't exactly true, the controls for the mental ray are not collected into one coherent place with one coherent organization. Instead, mental ray features and shaders can be found in many different spots throughout the Softimage 3D|Extreme program.

Generally, features in the mental ray that can be accessed via the regular Softimage interface controls are marked with a small (mr) to indicate that they operate only with the mental ray renderer (see Figure 17.6). When you can select a shader, there is a small box with a label indicating "mental ray shader," along with a Select button to browse the shaders on your hard disk and an Edit button to edit the shaders' parameters.

FIGURE 17.6 *Mental ray–specific features are generally marked with an (mr).*

You can think of the mental ray as a big machine with sockets at different locations where these shaders can be plugged in at render time to add new features. These sockets occur at various points in the rendering process and are found at different points in the Softimage interface. When you locate a shader socket, you can click the Select button to browse the file system to locate a shader file to connect or *link in* (see Figure 17.7).

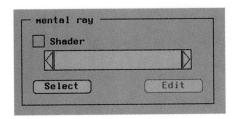

FIGURE 17.7 *Mental ray shaders can be linked in when you see this box in the Softimage interface.*

TYPES OF SHADERS

These shaders can be linked in at different points along the life of the ray, traveling along through the rendering process, starting with lens shaders.

Lens shaders can be linked to run when rays pass through the virtual camera lens. The shader selection for lens shaders is found in the Camera→Settings dialog box (see Figure 17.8).

Volumic shaders can be run as the ray passes through space on the way to hitting an object in the scene. The mental ray is the only popular renderer to allow true volumic sampling. These shaders can be selected in two places. Go to the Atmosphere→Depth Fading dialog to apply the shader to the entire scene, or open the Material Editor to apply the effect inside a volume bounded by an object.

Material shaders can be run when a ray strikes a material to determine the ambient, diffuse, specular, reflective, transparent, or refractive properties of the material. These shaders are found in the Material Editor as well.

FIGURE 17.8 *Light glows and lens flares are actually lens artifacts, and these shaders are found in the Camera→Settings dialog.*

When a ray strikes an object with a 2D texture, a shader can be called. You apply *2D texture shaders* in the 2D Texture File dialog to create infinitely large, procedural 2D textures, imitating fabrics and other materials.

A shader can come to life when a ray strikes an object with a 3D texture. These procedural *3D texture shaders*, for such surfaces as rock, lava, wood, and marble, are found in the 3D Solid Texture dialog box.

When a ray hits an object, it is then tested against the lights illuminating that object. *Light shaders* can be called at that time for lighting effects, such as gels and slide projectors. Light shaders can be linked in the Light→Edit dialog box.

When an object is found to occlude a light that shines on a surface, a shadow ray is generated and shadow rays can have shaders as well. You will find *shadow ray shaders* in the Material Editor dialog box.

Finally, after the image is completely rendered, *post shaders* can be run to add in effects, such as depth of field, fur, or paint effects. These post shaders are located in the Render Options dialog.

CHOOSING MENTAL RAY

To choose the mental ray as your renderer, simply select mental ray from the Rendering Method drop-down box in the Render dialog. You can preview with the mental ray by enabling it in the Preview→Preview Options dialog box.

MENTAL RAY RENDERING ENHANCEMENTS

When you can render with the mental ray, a number of clever new tricks become available for working with surfaces, object visibility, and Texture mapping. The mental ray supports some very sophisticated techniques for enhancing the quality of your work and reducing the time required to render these effects. The first of these techniques is adaptive surface subdivision.

ADAPTIVE SURFACE SUBDIVISION

Normally, Softimage tessellates patch-based objects into triangles before rendering the surface according to the Parametric Step setting in the Info→Selection dialog box. Using more subdivisions by setting a higher step results in smoother surfaces with more polygons. Very smooth curved objects can have a great many polygons in them, and scenes with a lot of curved objects can quickly approach or exceed a million polygons, enough to slow down any machine during the render.

So what do you do when you really need that smoothness in an object?

Let's say that you have a scene of a restaurant dining table with cut crystal goblets sparkling, and you need both closeup and long shots of the table settings. In the closeups you will need the goblets to be very smoothly rendered, with large numbers of polygonal tesselation to make them look great. In the long shots, the goblets won't be as crucial, because less detail will be visible.

You could save lots of render time by having less polygonal detail in the far off goblets than in the closeup goblets. What would be perfect is a rendering engine that decides how thoroughly a patch object should be tesselated down into triangles based on how much of the detail in that object is visible in each frame. That way, each glass could have a different level of polygonal detail depending on how well the glass can be seen.

In fact, the mental ray has just such a facility called *adaptive surface subdivision* and it's a terrific time saver. You can set Parametric Step to the minimum (1 by 1) on all your patch-based objects in the entire scene—guaranteeing faster Wireframe and Shaded views, as well as faster feedback while modeling and animating—then tell the mental ray to add parametric detail to the model at render time.

This can be set up in either of two ways. For single objects, you can set Parametric Step to the minimum and, in the Info→Selection dialog, turn on Adaptive Surface Subdivision under the Render Setup button. For a group of selected objects or all objects in the scene, use the Info→mental ray command (see Figure 17.9).

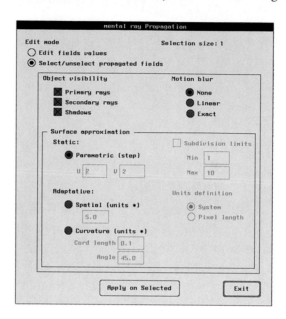

FIGURE 17.9   *The Info→mental ray command sets parameters for many objects at once.*

There are two methods of Adaptive Surface Subdivision, but only one works consistently in all cases. The idea is that the number of triangles in an object should be linked to how big that object is onscreen at each frame during the render. In this way, an object that starts far away and approaches the camera starts with few triangles and progressively grows to include more and more triangles as it approaches.

The mental ray accomplishes this multiplying-triangles feat by looking at the lengths of the spans between Control points on the model. If a span is longer onscreen than a specific number of pixels that you set, mental ray divides the span in half. It then tests each half of the span against the new smaller span's onscreen size in pixels, and if the span's onscreen size falls over the threshold you set, mental ray again divides the span in half. Each U and V parameter of the model is subdivided in this way until it is properly chopped up into small segments, and those segments are used to tessellate the surface into triangles. This method is called *Adaptive Spatial Subdivision.*

If you set the threshold to 10 pixels, no triangle in the surface is ever longer than 10 pixels onscreen. If you set the threshold to two pixels, no triangle is ever larger than two pixels wide onscreen. Practically, a setting between five and eight pixels yields great results, because we can't really see detail under eight pixels, especially when it moves and changes. This process of chopping each span in half and then testing each half is called *recursion* and can, in theory, go on way too long if you set the number too low, resulting in an enormous number of triangles, choking your machine and bringing the renderer to a screeching halt. You can put an extra failsafe stop on the process by using a *recursion limit*, setting the number of recursions possible for each span to seven or eight.

TUTORIAL: RESERVE A GOOD TABLE

To explore the productive use of the Adaptive Surface Subdivision method, build a restaurant scene (see Figure 17.10) and see how various settings affect it.

CAUTION

The mental ray supports a more complex method called *Adaptive Curvature Subdivision* that evaluates the curvature of the span, as well as the size, to further reduce the number of triangles produced by tessellation on the assumption that flatter objects need fewer triangles than more curved ones. I've played with this method, however, and I think it's way too complex for use in production. More likely than not, it will actually *increase* the triangles and render time required.

FIGURE 17.10   *The rendered restaurant floor.*

1. Build Your Scene.

To stress the capabilities of Adaptive Surface Subdivision, we need to build a scene that could have a great many polygons when tessellated for a render.

Construct a restaurant floor with a table set with NURBS plates and glasses formed of a revolution. Group the plates and glasses to the table in a hierarchy, and duplicate the table 11 more times to create a restaurant floor with 12 tables set with plates and glasses. Check the size of the entire scene with the Info→Scene command, and if it isn't above a million triangles, add more tables.

You should notice that just orbiting your Perspective view around has become slow and cumbersome as Softimage tries to keep a million triangles drawn to the screen. If you feel like testing the limits of that spiffy, new OpenGL card you just spent the rent money on (and can take a disappointment), change the Perspective view to Shaded mode and see how that moves around. Obviously, this kind of performance problem makes it tough to get your work done on time. We need to make the scene easier to work with, while retaining the smoothness of the rendered image.

Position the camera at one end of the restaurant, looking along the tables with one place setting quite close and the rest diminishing into the distance. Try a preview render with the mental ray and time the render for comparison later.

2. Set the Patch Step to the Minimum.

Select a patch object and examine the step used for the U and V parameters in the Info→Selection dialog. Also take note of the number of triangles in the object, also listed on the left side of the same dialog. Now change the U and V Parametric Step settings to 1 and 1, and see the change in the number of triangles required to render the object.

We need to change the U and V steps to 1 for all the objects in the scene to make the scene lighter and easier to deal with. Fortunately, there is a quick and easy way to do this.

Select all the objects in the scene with the Select→All command, and then execute the Info→mental ray command. This brings up the mental ray Propagation dialog box, which allows you to set the Render options for many objects at the same time. The box offers a choice of two edit modes: Edit Selection mode and Edit Fields mode.

Enter Edit mode (click the Select/Unselect Propagated Fields radio button) and click the radio button next to the group of fields you want to edit, in this case, the Surface Approximation: Static radio button. Now you can switch to the Edit Fields mode (click the Edit Field Values radio button) and change the values you want to change. In this case, change the Parametric Step to be 1 in U and 1 in V. Then, finally, to make the changes permanent, click the Apply on Selected button and exit the dialog.

You will now note that the patch objects are reduced to their simplest form and appear faceted, but your scene orbits and renders much more rapidly. Check the Info→Scene dialog to find out how many triangles you just saved (see Figure 17.11). We are halfway there; the scene is manageable again but renders badly.

FIGURE 17.11   *The restaurant with 997,340 triangles and 22,300 triangles.*

3. Turn on Adaptive Surface Subdivision.

Now we need to turn on Adaptive Surface Subdivision and set the span length and recursion limits (see Figure 17.12). Again with everything in the scene selected, call up the Info→mental ray dialog.

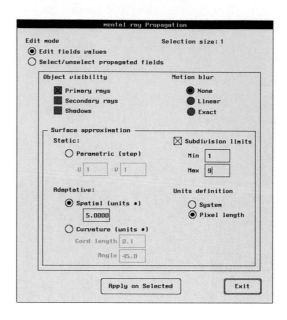

FIGURE 17.12   *The settings for Adaptive Surface Subdivision.*

Choose the Edit mode and click the Surface Approximation Adaptive radio button. Switch to the Edit Fields mode and set up your choices in the Adaptive Subdivision controls. First change the Units definition to be Pixel Length, which tests each span against its own length onscreen in pixels. Otherwise, you would have to know in Softimage units how big the span is, which will never happen. Next change the Subdivision Limits to 1 for Minimum and 8 for Maximum to prevent runaway recursion that might clog the renderer and take forever to render.

Then change the Spatial (units) setting to the number of pixels wide that a span must be greater than before it is chopped in half. A good setting to start with is 8 pixels, which results in reasonably smooth surfaces without a huge number of triangles.

Finally, press the Apply on Selected button and exit the dialog. Your scene remains faceted in Wireframe and Shaded modes, but when you render a preview with the mental ray, you get smoothly rendered surfaces! What's more, the nearer glasses and plates are tessellated with more detail than the further glasses and plates, putting the polygonal detail where it does the most good—up close. Render another preview and time it to compare the speed of the render. Adaptive Surface Subdivision takes longer to get started on the render, because it has to tessellate each object individually while testing it against its size onscreen. But after tessellation is completed, the resulting render should be faster, particularly when shadows, reflections, and refractions are calculated.

Adaptive Surface Subdivision is a powerful tool and a huge advantage of the mental ray when rendering large scenes with many patch-based surfaces.

> **NOTE**
>
> You can see the amount of detail added in by the Adaptive Surface Subdivision process by going to the Render dialog, clicking the Options button, and enabling Contour rendering. Contour rendering writes a .lin file containing the lines that describe the tessellation of the surface. This process is not visible during the render, so you must wait until it is done and then view the image with the Picture command in the Tools module.

PRIMARY, SECONDARY, AND SHADOW RAYS

The mental ray also gives you complete control over whether objects are visible to primary, secondary, or shadow rays in the render. *Primary rays* are rays that have just shot out of the virtual camera lens and haven't hit anything yet. *Secondary rays* are rays that have already hit an object and are the result of reflection, transparency, or refraction. *Shadow rays* are those rays shot from an object to a shadow casting light to determine if any other objects are in the way of the light and would therefore cast a shadow (see Figure 17.13). The mental ray's level of control allows for some neat render tricks, and more importantly, enables you to highly optimize your renders and save huge amounts of valuable render time for more important machine tasks.

If you select an object and turn off secondary rays and shadow rays, that object will be visible only to the scanline portion of the mental ray renderer and will never be seen in reflections, refractions, or through transparent objects. The object will, however, render very fast.

If you select an object and turn off primary rays and shadows, the object will be invisible to direct rays but will appear in front of mirrors and through transparent glass.

If you turn off primary and secondary rays while leaving shadow rays on, the object casts shadows but otherwise is completely invisible.

FIGURE 17.13   *Primary, secondary, and shadow rays show different parts of the image.*

A very large part of the performance hit associated with rendering reflection and refraction is caused by indiscriminate inclusion of objects in the secondary ray database. If fewer objects are visible to secondary rays, then all reflection and refraction calculations are dramatically sped up. In large scenes, it is a fantastic idea to decide what needs to be visible in reflections, such as walls, and what does not, such as small objects in the scene. Then, using the Info→mental ray command, you can first turn off secondary rays for every object in the scene and then turn secondary rays back on for only those few objects you need to be visible in reflections.

Similarly, not everything needs to be visible to shadow rays. Examine your scene and determine what must actually cast shadows. Use the Info→mental ray command to turn off shadow rays for everything and then turn shadow rays back on for only those objects that you want to cast shadows. The impact this can make on rendering times is enormous.

DISPLACEMENT MAPPING

In traditional Bump mapping techniques, the rendered image relies on an optical illusion to imply roughness of the surface (see Figure 17.14). Although the mental ray Bump mapping is certainly much more convincing than the standard Softimage renderers Bump mapping, the illusion still breaks down in many cases, particularly where a rough surface is intersected by another smooth edge. Despite the roughness of the surface, the line where the two objects meet is perfectly smooth and clean, showing that there is no actual roughness to the surface there.

The mental ray has another method that is a great deal more sophisticated, called *Displacement mapping.* In Displacement mapping, a Texture map is used to deform the surface of the object during the tessellation phase prior to the render (see Figure 17.15). When the image returns, the surface really is roughed up and the rough spots can cast shadows and intersect other objects properly.

For this effect to work, the object must have sufficient detail to deform so that the features on the Texture map can be accurately resolved into the geometry during tessellation. The easiest way to ensure that you put the right amount of detail into the object is to combine Displacement mapping and Adaptive Surface Subdivision. The mental ray then puts as much detail into the surface as is necessary to resolve the detail in the displacement map.

To turn on Displacement mapping and use it instead of Bump mapping, toggle on the Displacement (mr) check box above the Roughness slider in the 2D Texture File dialog box. The displacement effect is very sensitive, so Roughness values of less than 1 deform the surface quite nicely.

FIGURE 17.14 *A Bump map doesn't really make bumps; it's just an optical illusion.*

FIGURE 17.15 *A Displacement map moves geometry before the rendering process.*

MENTAL RAY SHADERS IN THE MATERIAL EDITOR

The mental ray includes the capability to render materials using shaders. To do so, the Material Editor supports three types of mental ray shaders:

- Material shaders
- Volume shaders
- Shadow shaders

Shaders are set up in the Material Editor by checking the appropriate shader box and then browsing the mental ray Shader_Lib and Shader_Gift databases to find the shader you need (see Figure 17.16). When you choose a shader, you can then load it into the Material Editor and edit the Shader parameters to make the changes you wish. In each shader, there is generally a control labeled "help," "Info," or "?" that details the parameters you can edit in the shader. It is a good idea to read these through. There is also often a button that calls up the ShaderBall, which is a very small interactive rendering of a default ball with that shader on it. Using this automatic ShaderBall can save you a lot of time by giving you a quick look at the shader before you test render on your own scene.

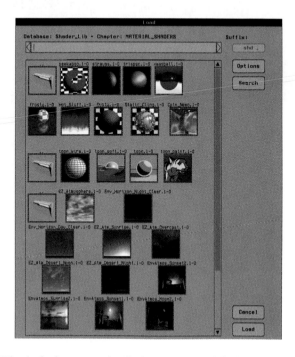

FIGURE 17.16 *The shader browser in the Shader_Lib Material shader directory.*

MATERIAL SHADERS

Material shaders are called when a ray hits the surface of an object. Although Material shaders may be as simple as a better implementation of the Phong algorithm, they can also be as complex as the Env_Atmosphere shader, which simulates an entire planet with sky, clouds, sun, moon, and stars (see Figure 17.17). Click in the Select button to enter the file browser and then traverse your file system to the Shader_Lib database.

FIGURE 17.17   *The Env_Atmosphere shader in an inverted sphere.*

The Shader_Lib database has six subdirectories for Material shaders:

- Environments
- Example_Src
- Fabric
- Matter
- RenderPass
- Toon

The Environments folder contains a series of fantastic planet shaders that can be applied to a primitive object. When that primitive object is scaled up to be very large, surrounding the camera and the entire scene, and then inverted so the normals face inwards, the renderer reveals a complete view from the surface of a planet, with fully animateable controls for the position of the sun, the moon, the stars, and the clouds.

The Example_Src folder contains some very useful general purpose shaders. Glossy randomly resamples reflection and transparency rays for better blurry reflections and transparency, which is critical for making your materials look less computery. Glass accurately renders directional and specular opacity in glass, making the glass change transparency dependent on your viewing angle to it, just like real glass (see Figure 17.18). Ghost and Alpha are useful for using objects to define areas in the alpha channel of the output image.

The Fabric folder contains the Velvet shader, which adds dramatic color shifts between the specular and diffuse colors of the material depending on the bend in the surface, just like velvet (see Figure 17.19).

The Matter folder contains some new supported shaders and some that were previously gifts. Peekaboo makes objects more transparent when a light hits them, so you can cut away an object with a beam from a spotlight or simulate an x-ray machine. Strauss implements a completely different, more intuitive rendering algorithm that generates nicer metallic surfaces than the standard algorithm. Trispec and Xmas_ball also affect the light angle and reflection of the material, to create more sophisticated looking material surfaces. Refer to Figure 17.18 for examples of all of these.

The Frosty shader melts reflections and refractions together so that the resulting images don't look as clean as traditional raytraced images. It can be very compute intensive, however, and Glossy provides similar effects with less render time. Cptn_Nemo attempts to simulate underwater caustics, Dusty deposits a layer of grime on the flatter portions of an object, Hot_Stuff is a flame shader, and Static_Cling uses the specular and diffuse colors to create pattern-like electrical bolts moving around the surface (see Figure 17.18).

In the RenderPass directory, you will find the ShadowPass shader, which, like Peekaboo, affects the visibility of objects by creating a shadow matte and storing it in the alpha channel. Other images can later be composited into this shadow layer.

FIGURE 17.18 *Samples of Strauss, Xmas_ball, and Glass shaders.*

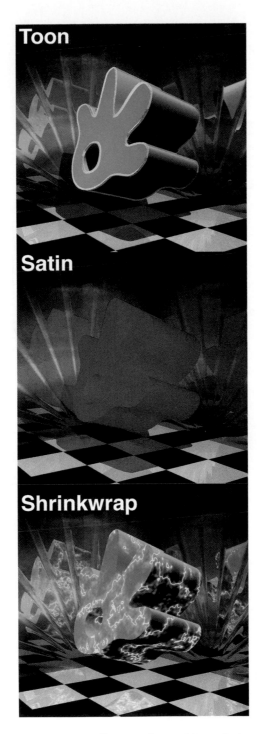

FIGURE 17.19 *Samples of Velvet, Hot_Stuff, Static_Cling, and Dusty shaders.*

The Toon directory contains three shaders: toon, toon_soft, and toon_wire. Each of these interacts with the toon lens shader to render cartoon-like versions of your scene by replacing the smooth-shaded surface with a flat-shaded surface, and drawing in detail with ink lines. By using these cartoon shaders, you can render very flat-looking 2D cutout objects in a very 3D-looking scene. The toon_wire shader is also great for rendering an object in a colored Wireframe mode, a trick very popular in TV commercials.

VOLUME SHADERS

A special kind of shader calculated only by the mental ray, Volume shaders sample the path of the ray as it travels through the volume of space bounded by the object to which the shader is applied. In a Volume shader, the object itself must be 100% transparent and won't show up at all. The object is used only to define the region of space in which the volume effect occurs.

As the ray travels through the volume, it stops to sample the area around it and pick up color information. The volume it travels in might be uniformly distributed like a gas, or it could be patchy, like fog or mist. Because each ray must be sampled many times as it travels through space, Volume shaders are generally very time consuming to render. But, by applying a Volume shader to an object in the material box, you can limit the rendering time needed by constricting the volume effect to just one area in your scene. The object on which you apply the shader becomes a bounding model that defines the volume for the effect.

The rules for applying a Volume shader to an object in the Material Editor are that the material must have a transparency set to 1.0, which is fully transparent, or the Volume shader does not work. After you set the Material Transparency to 1.0, click to check on the Volume Shader check box and browse the filesystem (see Figure 17.20). The Volume shaders available include:

- Volumic_Lights (the original volumic lights shader)
- Clouds, Bionic_Volume (the new volumic lights shader)
- Dense (simulates density of material like glass)
- March_Fractal (the father of many volumic shaders, a fractal gas volume simulator)
- Gitane
- Smoky_Room
- Sunbeams

- MF_Spot lights (the best volumic lights shader)
- Neon
- Fly_Thru
- Fog
- Mist
- Bang
- Lightning
- Smoke

Each of these shaders has sophisticated controls and would require its own chapter to accurately and completely describe. The best way to find out what each does is to apply it with a linked Spot light to illuminate it and start experimenting.

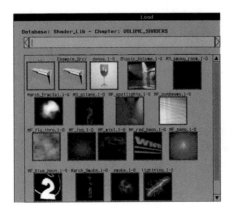

FIGURE 17.20   *The browser showing Volume shaders.*

SHADOW SHADERS

Shadow shaders are called by the mental ray when one object gets between a light that casts shadows and the rendered object. Shaders such as the Shadow Separator can use the shadow to create interesting shadow effects.

MENTAL RAY 2D TEXTURE SHADERS

The mental ray comes with quite a good selection of 2D procedural Texture shaders for creating fabrics, ground, water, and a lot more (see Figure 17.21). You link in these shaders by selecting an object to apply them to and then enter the 2D Texture

File dialog box. You must first select a regular 2D image as a texture by clicking the Select button in the Picture Filename area at the top of the box. Even though the mental ray shader overwrites the 2D image file, the dialog box requires you to have it there. Because the mental ray shader obeys the Mapping method and the Color, Roughness, Transparency, and Reflectivity values you set, you can use this 2D image to verify your settings before you link in the shader.

Next check the box in the lower-left marked "mental ray shader" and browse to the Shader_Lib database to see your options (see Figure 17.22). Each of the shaders listed does something entirely different. Try out the Fabric shaders for great surface patterns, the Ground shaders for displacement of geometry to make terrain, the Textures/Gradient tool to build ramps, such as those found in other 3D rendering tools, and Water for animating the surface of water in a pond.

DISPLACEMENT WITH 2D TEXTURE SHADERS

One very important implication of how the mental ray shaders work in the 2D Texture File dialog is that the shader values are passed back to this dialog for mixing with other materials, and the values are used by the rest of the shading algorithm you've chosen. That means that a mental ray Texture shader can be used not only to apply a color to the surface of the object but also to apply transparency, reflectivity and roughness, either through the RGB intensity of the shader or the alpha value calculated by the shader over the surface being rendered. You can even use any shader to displace the geometry of the surface at render time (see Figure 17.23). The advantages of using a procedural texture to displace the surface are that the pattern generated never repeats, always looks as if it is the perfect resolution for the size of the object displaced, and can be infinitely modified to achieve different effects with very little effort.

To displace the geometry of a surface at render time, the surface should be a patch object with enough subdivisions to accurately displace, or you should enable adaptive surface subdivision on the displaced object to allow the mental ray to add in the subdivision detail that it needs. Polygon objects cannot be displaced.

Try out 2D shader displacement with this simple exercise:

1. Set up the scene.

    Get a Cardinal grid with 30 cells in X and Y. Then apply a 2D texture to it with the Texture menu cell in the Matter mode.

FIGURE 17.21 *A few sample 2D Texture shaders.*

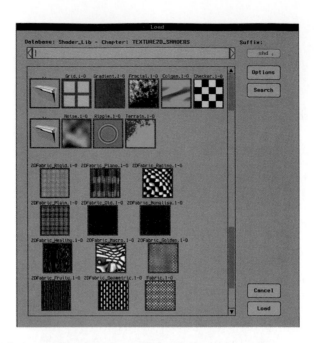

FIGURE 17.22   *The browser showing some 2D Texture shaders.*

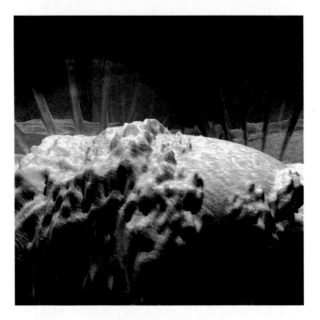

FIGURE 17.23   *A procedurally displaced sphere.*

Add two work lights, each a different color and 45 degrees off of the camera direction in opposite directions. These lights will help you see bumps in the surface. Choose a picture from the SI_Material_Lib database as a placeholder and set the projection method. The picture file itself is not used, so which one you pick is irrelevant. Adjust the Mapping method to be UV and turn the Roughness up to 1.

2. Choose a shader.

   Next click the mental ray Select button in the lower-left corner and find the Fabric subdirectory of the Shader_Lib directory. Load the 2D_Fabric_Wet shader. Click the Edit button to see the editable parameters for this shader. Note that for each Color Picker, there is an associated Alpha Value slider as well. Choose some alpha values for each color. For a complete explanation of all the controls, click the About button. When done, click the Ok button to exit the shader and return to the 2D Texture File dialog.

3. Test the Displacement effect.

   Now it is time to test the effect several different ways. Start with a preview, using a Roughness but without Displacement checked on. This is traditional Bump mapping and is not terribly effective here.

   Next toggle on Displacement and check to see that the Map Component is set to RGB Intensity, which uses the RGB color returned by the shader to displace the surface. Preview the object again to see the new detail modeled into the surface at render time. Obviously, the more detail you add to your grid, the more accurately the mental ray is able to build a surface from it that matches the effects of the shader.

   Finally change the Map Component from RGB Intensity to Alpha Channel. If the Alpha Channel option is grayed out, that indicates that the picture file you used as a placeholder doesn't have an alpha channel (which of course shouldn't matter because we aren't rendering with that picture anyway). The workaround is to enter Softimage's paint system and paint on the picture's alpha channel to add one, or to pick an image, such as a rendered frame, that is guaranteed to have an alpha channel. Preview the surface again with the alpha channel providing the displacement information instead of the color to see the differences.

Each shader you use to displace the surface has a completely different look to the results. Experiment to find ones you like, or check out the shaders made just for this purpose, such as Water, Fractal1, Terrain, Ripple, and Noise. Many, such as Ripple, can be easily animated to produce fantastic procedural animation special effects.

MENTAL RAY 3D TEXTURE SHADERS

As Softimage supports 2D and 3D textures, the mental ray includes 3D procedural shaders as well as 2D. 3D procedural shaders also affect the diffuse, ambient, specular, roughness, transparency, and reflectivity of the objects to which they are applied. The difference is that where 2D shaders map onto the surface of an object, 3D shaders extend infinitely through space, even inside of the object. The surface of the object simply intersects the texture, so that the texture changes as the surface changes, like carving away wood to reveal different patterns of rings inside a log.

You can add 3D procedural mental ray shaders to objects by clicking the Texture→3D Global menu cell and adding a shader in the mental ray shader box found in the lower-left corner.

Because solid textures aren't supported by a particular mapping projection method, the 3D Solid Texture dialog provides a transformation for the entire texture in object space. Because you can set keyframes for this transformation, you can animate the shader moving through object space, creating animated patterns on the surface of the object. When you select a mental ray shader, the controls for determining the procedural algorithm (in the top half of the 3D Solid Texture dialog) are superseded by the mental ray shader, but the Blending, Effect Value, Reflectivity, Transparency, and Roughness value sliders remain active.

The 3D shaders provided in the Shader_Lib database include 3D Clouds, the general purpose 3D Fractal shader, the Env_Atmosphere planet shader, Brick, Noise, and a huge selection of rock, lava, marble, and wood shaders found in the Matter subdirectory (see Figure 17.24). These Matter shaders in particular are well worth exploring.

ATMOSPHERE SHADERS

TIP

Many of the atmosphere shader effects interact with lights, especially Spot lights (see Figure 17.25). Before trying any out, place two Spot lights in your scene, shining on the ground in the global center.

The final class of mental ray shaders, Atmosphere shaders, contains the same set of Volume shaders that you were able to apply in the Material Editor by using a model as a bounding volume.

Another (slower) way to use these is to apply a Volume shader throughout the entire volume of space in your scene with the Shader controls in the Atmosphere→Depth Fading dialog box.

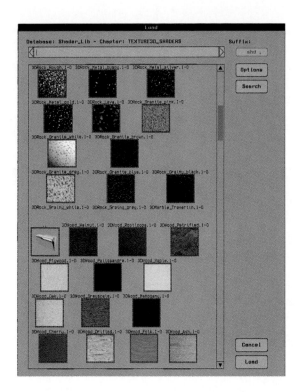

FIGURE 17.24   *Browser showing some 3D Texture shaders.*

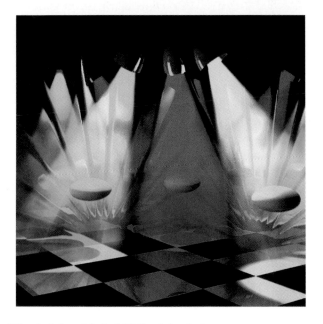

FIGURE 17.25   *Volumic lights with the MF_Spotlights shader.*

In the Atmosphere→Depth Fading dialog, Depth Fading must be turned on with the check box at the top of the screen or nothing happens. The Depth Fading controls should be set so they don't affect the scene; specify the Starting and Ending Distances as 10,000 units. Finally click the Mental Ray Shader toggle to browse the Volume shaders. Select the March_Smoke shader, which demonstrates some common Atmosphere Shader controls (see Figure 17.26). The large Fractal Ray Marcher dialog has quite a few controls, but only a couple do most of the important work.

FIGURE 17.26   *The March_Smoke shader.*

Consider the bounding box in the lower-right corner. Because it would be very expensive computationally to calculate the Volume shader for each ray as it passes through the entire scene, you can edit the bounding area of the effect in the dialog's bounding box. Sometimes when the effect is bounded too small, your camera isn't looking in the right place and no effect is visible. Always check the bounding area to see where the effect will take place, and edit it if you want it somewhere else.

The Marching controls are located at the top of the dialog. Step Size determines how many initial samples are taken by the ray. Increasing the number speeds up the render but costs in quality. The Maximum Difference specifies a form of spatial antialiasing. If the difference between two samples is more than the Maximum Difference, the section of the ray path is further subdivided and sampled again recursively until the limit set by the Maximum Subdivisions is reached. Increasing the Maximum Difference and decreasing the Maximum Subdivisions increase render speed and compromise quality.

It is always a good idea to assign at least one scattered light with the Light Scattering controls, so you can see your effect. Using Shadowed lights, however, is really computer intensive, because it allows the volume of gas to actually block lights and create shadow rays (see Figure 17.27). That's really cool but really slow.

FIGURE 17.27   *The Gitane shader with shadowed lights enabled so the column of smoke casts a shadow on the floor. Rendering time for this shot was over an hour on four CPUs.*

The final step in the dialog is to set the colors. Ambiance Color, the color of all the gas in the volume, should be set to a gray or a black. The Absorption Color setting acts as a filter, removing that color from objects that are seen through the gas. The Color setting determines the actual color of the column of smoke. Set these and try out the effect yourself.

The March_Smoke shader and the others similarly based on the March Fractal Shader Engine are the best ways to create volumic Spot lights, clouds of gas, cigarette smoke, and lightning effects that are simply impossible to achieve in any other rendering engine.

CONCLUSION

This chapter is just the merest glance at the tremendous functionality found within the mental ray. As new people write shaders, the power of the mental ray will just keep growing. New versions of Softimage 3D products will rely entirely on mental ray, and as CPU performance grows, so will the beauty of the effects that the mental ray generates. Already the next version of the mental ray incorporates groundbreaking capabilities, such as global illumination and light caustics. The mental ray produces such beautiful renders that I predict it will soon replace RenderMan as the rendering engine of choice for Hollywood film work.

Working with the mental ray has never been simple, but if you can master its charms you will be richly rewarded.

In this chapter, you discovered:

- How the mental ray looks at a scene
- Where shaders are located in the Soft databases
- How to make more attractive materials with shaders
- When to use Primary, Secondary, and Shadow rays
- How to set up visible lighting effects
- How the mental ray calculate volumic effects
- How to use mental ray displacement to reduce render times

INDEX

Q

R

S